MW01068694

THE FIRST SERIOUS OPTIMIST

The First Serious Optimist

A. C. PIGOU AND THE BIRTH
OF WELFARE ECONOMICS

Ian Kumekawa

PRINCETON UNIVERSITY PRESS

PRINCETON & OXFORD

Published by Princeton University Press,
41 William Street, Princeton, New Jersey 08540

In the United Kingdom: Princeton University Press,
6 Oxford Street, Woodstock, Oxfordshire OX20 1TR

press.princeton.edu

Jacket photograph courtesy of the Cambridgeshire Collection, Cambridge Central Library

Library of Congress Cataloging-in-Publication Data

Names: Kumekawa, Ian, author.
Title: The first serious optimist : A.C. Pigou and the birth of welfare economics / Ian
    Kumekawa.
Description: Princeton : Princeton University Press, [2017] | Includes bibliographical
    references and index.
Identifiers: LCCN 2016046573 | ISBN 9780691163482 (hardcover : alk. paper)
Subjects: LCSH: Pigou, A. C. (Arthur Cecil), 1877–1959. | Economist—Great Britain. |
    Welfare economics. | Economics—History.
Classification: LCC HB103.P54 K86 2017 | DDC 330.15/56092—dc23
    LC record available at https://lccn.loc.gov/2016046573

British Library Cataloging-in-Publication Data is available

This book has been composed in Miller

Printed on acid-free paper. ∞

Printed in the United States of America

10 9 8 7 6 5 4 3 2 1

To my parents

CONTENTS

ACKNOWLEDGMENTS

A GREAT MANY PEOPLE have had a hand in the creation of this book. It has been six years in the making, and I am deeply indebted to the many colleagues, friends, and family members who helped both the book and me along.

More than anyone, I must thank Emma Rothschild, whose steady guidance, clear insight, and great patience were essential to the creation of this book. The advice of David Cannadine, Niall Ferguson, Robert Neild, and William O'Reilly, who read significant portions or versions of the manuscript, was invaluable as well. The manuscript—and I—owe a debt of gratitude to other readers, including Aditya Balasubramanian, Tim Barker, Aaron Bekemeyer, Christopher Evans, Benjamin Hand, Patsy and Michael Kumekawa, Sabrina Lee, Dylan Matthews, Madeleine Schwartz, Chenzi Xu, and the three anonymous readers chosen by Princeton University Press. Conversations and lessons at Harvard also proved essential in shaping my thoughts about Pigou and his worlds. Great thanks to Amartya Sen, whose recollections and advice were especially important. Thanks also to Maya Jasanoff, James Kloppenberg, Ella Antell, Jon Booth, Ben Goossen, and Gili Kliger.

The Institute for New Economic Thinking offered both immense support and an ideal setting to write a good deal of the manuscript. Conversations with Pier-André Bouchard St-Amant, Rob Johnson, Perry Mehrling, Jay Pocklington, and Elham Saiedinizhad were profoundly helpful. Special recognition goes to Guy Numa and Enno Schröder, who both read parts of the manuscript and offered generous comments.

Research for this book was also partially funded by grants from the Center for European Studies and the Weatherhead Center for International Affairs, both at Harvard University. In addition, I have been lucky enough to have been affiliated with the Joint Center for History and Economics throughout the time I wrote this book. The Center's support was instrumental, its workshops and teas have been sources of inspiration, and its staff—especially Emily

Gauthier, Inga Huld Markan, and Jennifer Nickerson—have been lifesavers. Thanks also go to Travers Rhodes and Adrien Veres, whose modern-day salon proved vital at the project's beginning.

This book was researched and written in a host of archives and libraries, and I am greatly appreciative of the help I received from staff in both Cambridges, and in archives across Britain. Thanks to the Archives of the London School of Economics, the British Library, the Cambridge University Library, the Churchill College Archives, The Cumbria Archive Centre, the Harrow School Archives, the Harvard University Library, the Hoover Institution Archives, the King's College Archives, the Marshall Library, the National Archives, the St. John's College Archives, and the Trinity College Archives. In particular, I thank the Harrow School archives for granting me digital access to the *Harrovian*, and the kind assistance and advice of Patricia McGuire at King's College Archive and Rowland Thomas, Clemens Gresser, and Simon Frost at the Marshall Library of Economics at Cambridge. Thanks to Tony Nicholls of the Pembury Historical Society for helping me chase down the story of the Pigous' old house and to Joe and Jane Crowther for help understanding Pigou's life in the Lake District. Thanks also to Roger Hiley for permitting me to use his wonderful photograph of Lower Gatesgarth.

My debt to Princeton University Press is immense, not only for giving me a chance to see this book in print, but also for attentively guiding me through its production. Many, many thanks to Brigitta van Rheinberg, Claudia Acevedo, Natalie Baan, Lyndsey Claro, Quinn Fusting, Amanda Peery, other staff at the press, and Cyd Westmoreland.

THE FIRST SERIOUS OPTIMIST

History and Economics

BY 1964, SIR AUSTIN ROBINSON had achieved all the hallmarks of success as an economist. A professor at Cambridge, he was the editor of the *Economic Journal* and an active advisor to the British government. But for several months in 1964, Robinson behaved more like a historian. When handed a historical research project, Robinson became entirely engrossed, transforming himself into a fastidious researcher who kept not only reams of notes but also the receipts of his document requests from archival visits.

It helped that the topic he was researching was one of great personal interest. Commissioned by the *Oxford Dictionary of National Biography* to write an entry on his late friend and colleague, the Cambridge professor and founder of welfare economics A. C. Pigou, Robinson began by rereading a few of Pigou's books.[1] Robinson was soon sifting through student newspapers from Pigou's days as a Cambridge undergraduate in the waning years of the nineteenth century. Robinson kept digging. He read back issues of Pigou's high school's newspaper. By coincidence, he had grown up in the town of Pigou's birth on the Isle of Wight off England's south coast, and he wrote to family contacts to investigate his friend's early childhood.[2] In a matter of months, he was compiling elaborate genealogies, tracing Pigou's family back several centuries, the precise handwriting of his notes spilling over dozens of pages.[3]

One question in particular motivated Robinson's searches and inquiries. In a letter to another aging friend of Pigou's, he noted: "What puzzles me so greatly is how the vigorous extrovert pro-establishment Pigou of his undergraduate days . . . became the hermit unwilling to engage in serious argument about economic things with his colleagues, and increasingly removed from the real world of affairs."[4] For even though Robinson had known Pigou for decades, in his research, he had discovered an entirely new Pigou: a Pigou who bore little resemblance to the serious recluse Robinson had come to know.

Robinson was intrigued by Pigou both as an economic thinker and as a person in history. These are also concerns of this book. But whereas Robinson's ardor in chasing down Pigou's story stemmed in part from a desire to better understand a departed friend and teacher, this book is motivated by broader intellectual goals. For one, it seeks to understand Pigou because of his great and under-appreciated influence as a thinker. In the years after Robinson's research, Pigou slipped into the shadows of history. Caught tempo-rally between the well-remembered Alfred Marshall and John May-nard Keynes, Pigou has remained a comparatively ancillary figure in the historical imagination, seen either as Marshall's loyal student or as Keynes's rival: the economist Keynes was most concerned to address in formulating his own, now famous, theories.

Yet Pigou himself is a figure of great importance in the history of economics and of economic thought. When he died in 1959, Robinson described him in the *Times* as "the outstanding econo-mist of his generation."[5] In addition to his involvement with the formation of welfare economics, Pigou was the originator of ex-ternality theory, the idea that there are costs—like those arising from pollution—that are not explicitly accounted for by the mar-ket. His contributions made him a monumental figure in the his-tory of environmental economics, and today his legacy is both pal-pable and visible. "Cap-and-trade" policies and carbon taxes both rely firmly on Pigovian ideas and, indeed, carbon taxes are per-haps the most famous form of what are now known as "Pigovian taxes" enacted on socially harmful activities. Given his influence, understanding Pigou in his own world is a worthy project in and of itself. But Pigou's life also offers an entrée into an even larger historical topic, a lens through which to survey the pressures and triumphs of being an economist during a formative period of the discipline's history.

In particular, it offers a window on how economists—as scientific and political actors—theorized and mediated the relationship between the state and what would come to be called the market. Pigou started his career as a reform-minded Liberal. Though committed to free trade and sympathetic to laissez-faire ideas, he also saw the government as an instrument that could improve societal welfare. In his early work, he sought to provide scientific justifications for progressive government policies. But this was to change by the end of the 1920s. Like many of his generation, Pigou was left profoundly disillusioned in the wake of World War I. His comfortable Liberal worldview was shattered, and the old party of William Gladstone, free trade, and progressive reform was crumbling. Until he died in 1959, Pigou, like other Liberals of his age, would struggle to come to terms with the new political and social reality that emerged out of the war.[6] Though he served on several government committees, during the 1920s, Pigou gradually retreated from public life to academic theory in an effort to provide an "arsenal of knowledge" that could be harnessed by policymakers. But as he grappled with the rise of the Soviet Union, the Depression, World War II, and the success of the British Labour Party, he moved toward a new conception of welfare: one that had noticeably different implications for how the individual was to be reconciled with the social and how the state ought to engage with the market. Much more than his contemporary, John Maynard Keynes, through the 1930s and 1940s, Pigou drifted toward positions closely associated with the Labour Party. In this way, his story exposes the connections between late nineteenth century reformist liberalism and the agenda of the Labour Party in the middle of the twentieth century. By the time the postwar Labour government lost power in 1951, Pigou had fully—and very publicly—endorsed the welfare state.

Changes internal to the economics discipline also played a substantial role in shaping Pigou's work and thought. Pigou lived through at least two periods of radical transition in the discipline. During the first, in the early 1900s, he was a pioneer, a new breed of economist who helped usher out the age of political economy and usher in that of economic science. As this new discipline spread throughout Britain, Europe, and the United States, Pigou's work was adopted as part of the new orthodoxy of economic thought that increasingly was leveraged by national governments.[7] In those heady days, he worked as a vigorous advocate, imbued with the certitude of the convert and the optimism of youth. But in the subsequent period of transformation in the 1930s, Pigou found himself in an entirely different position. During this time, though he was an established "giant" of his field, the contours of his discipline were swiftly becoming unfamiliar to him. As mathematical and statistical modeling, Keynesianism, and Austrian influences revolutionized the practice of economic science, Pigou found himself on the wrong side of major shifts within the discipline. He not only represented, but also was partly responsible for, an "old" mode of thought and only begrudgingly accepted the developments that were leaving many of his own contributions behind. As Pigou ceased to operate on the cutting edge of the academy, he slowly turned his attention to a new audience, the public, which ironically, would offer him great consolation by the end of his life.

This book is a study of Pigou and his times—in economics, in Britain, and in the world. It is concerned both with situating Pigou in the many contexts in which he lived and worked, and with relating those contexts to one another. In this specific hybrid mission, the book is unusual. But it exists nonetheless in a long and increasingly rich tradition of scholarship on Pigou. After all, Robinson was hardly the only person to have developed curiosity about Pigou. Pigou's life has, over the years, inspired some mystery, no doubt partially fomented by his decision to burn the better part of his papers just before he died. Even the books of his library were scattered, donated in a cascading series of gifts to King's College, Cambridge; the Marshall Library of Economics at Cambridge; and the University of Nottingham.[8] Such concern for privacy bred suspicion, and for a brief moment in the 1980s, there were rumors that he had been a Soviet agent; his twin passions were, in one fanciful account, socialist economics and mountain climbing.[9]

Pigou's work has also provoked considerable scholarship. And with rising awareness and fear of climate change, many of his ideas are experiencing a renaissance. Over the past decade, his work has garnered an increasing amount of attention, both among economists and in the popular press. In 2006, N. Gregory Mankiw, the

Harvard economist and former advisor to President George W. Bush, announced in the *Wall Street Journal* the formation of what he called the "Pigou Club," a list of individuals who had publicly endorsed higher Pigovian taxes. Over the next few years, Mankiw identified a host of "members" spanning the political spectrum from Al Gore to Republican Senator Lindsay Graham. The past Chair of the Federal Reserve, Paul Volcker, has been claimed as a "member," as have Nobel laureates Paul Krugman and Gary Becker.[10] Over the past few years, Pigou's name has repeatedly graced the pages of the *Economist*, the *New York Times*, the *Financial Times*, and the *New Yorker*. Figured as a thinker who sought to correct social problems like pollution or inequality through the remedy "least invasive" to the market, Pigou has acquired significant nonpartisan appeal, a rarity for an economist in an increasingly polarized world.

Pigou's current status as politically moderate is striking in light of the long history of politicization to which his work has been subjected. Starting in the 1930s, he served as a lightning rod for Keynes and subsequent Keynesians. Despite Pigou's relatively greater emphasis on labor and unemployment, for Keynes and his followers, he was a straw man that represented the most extreme form of the so-called classical tradition of economics, which stressed the self-corrective nature of the market.[11] By 1960, the year after his death, Pigou was under attack from the right. The most notable of his opponents was Ronald Coase, who, more skeptical of government action, made the opposite of the Keynesian claim—that Pigou's theories actually painted the market as deeply flawed.[12] Only a few years later, Pigou was lauded by right-leaning economists for a minor theoretical point he made—subsequently dubbed the Pigou Effect—that was understood to vindicate laissez-faire policies and offer a way out of Keynesian conclusions.[13]

This litany of invocation and opposition from across the ideological spectrum in part speaks to the fluid way liberal thought of the late nineteenth and early twentieth century has been interpreted up to the present. Pigou's work in particular often carried strong implications about the proper relationship between the state and the market, a notoriously contentious subject. But the reception and varied use of Pigovian ideas also speak to the complicated and multifaceted nature of Pigou's oeuvre. One of this book's contentions is that, in important ways, Pigou was more sympathetic to commitments associated with the British Labour Party than were many of his Liberal contemporaries, including Keynes. In this way, it challenges the old Keynesian understanding of Pigou as conservative. But political judgments such as this one need to be advanced cautiously and tempered with nuance. Over the course of his adult life, Pigou wrote constantly, on subjects ranging from Nietzsche's moral philosophy to the price elasticity of milk. The result is that simple characterizations of Pigou or his work as "laissez-faire" or "statist," or even "left" or "right," cannot do justice either to the man or to his ideas.

Recent scholarship on Pigou's life and work has recognized this complexity. Over the past two decades, there has been a surge of interest in Pigou among historians of economic thought, and this book draws liberally from the long and blossoming tradition of analysis and contextualization of Pigou's economics.[14] More than much of that literature, however, this book seeks to answer general historical, rather than economic, questions. Drawing inspiration from a growing attention to economic thinking in historical scholarship, the book advances arguments with reference more to history than to economics.[15] For unlike Robinson, the author is an economist neither by training nor profession. And though *The First Serious Optimist* addresses the full range of Pigou's voluminous intellectual output—he wrote twenty-six books—it does not pretend to offer the rich economic analysis that Pigou's extensive body of work deserves. Its goal is instead to offer a portrait of an economist in his wider contexts.

What follows is the story of the three-way interaction between an economist, his world, and his ideas. It is a personal story of major shifts in economic thinking, told both from the perspective of the innovator as well as from that of the aging thinker of a fading era. It investigates how politics, deeply held values, and personal connections came to shape the development of economic thought. By chronicling and explaining Pigou's reactions to changes around him, this book aspires to develop richer understandings of A. C. Pigou as a person and of his own seminal work. And in the process of situating Pigou in context, parts of that very context may be defined and elucidated. Hopefully, then, this book offers a glimpse not only of a major intellectual figure but also of what it was like to be an economist in the first half of the twentieth century, a time when economists were increasingly mediating the state's relationship with the market and the economy as a whole.

CHAPTER ONE

Beginnings

IN NOVEMBER 1876, the parents of Arthur Cecil Pigou emerged from the Holy Trinity Church in Ryde, on the Isle of Wight, to the strains of Mendelssohn's *Wedding March*. Accompanied by a forty-five member wedding party, the couple advanced "over a flower bestrewn pathway" lined by a crowd of more than 3,000.[1] The bride, Pigou's mother Nora Lees, was of the minor Anglo-Irish nobility, the second daughter of Sir John Lees, third baronet of Blackrock, who had moved to the Isle of Wight in the mid-1860s.[2] Pigou's father, Clarence, was a recently decommissioned lieutenant of the Fifteenth Regiment of Foot.[3] Their marriage was as lavish as any ever held in Ryde; the presents, of which there were about 200, were "costly and almost of endless variety, forming a glittering show . . . [of] unique articles, rare specimens, curiosities, and things useful as well as valuable."[4] Among them were diamonds and rubies, pearls, and "Indian embossed" jewelry. These were gifts from families accustomed to comfort and intimately connected to empire. Nora Lees's maternal uncle, from whom the embossed jewelry came, was a well-known Orientalist, and the international connections of the Pigou family were even stronger.[5] Huguenots who had immigrated to England in the late seventeenth century, the early Pigous had made their wealth as traders and officials in China, India, and North America as well as in the manufacture of gunpowder.[6]

Pigou's father, Clarence, was born in Bombay in 1850 to a civil servant, but he grew up in England, outside London. Clarence

Pigou was comfortably rooted in the upper-middle tiers of the Victorian establishment. Though his eldest uncle was disinherited for marrying without permission and became a stationmaster for the London and Birmingham Railroad, another of his uncles was a solidly respectable Anglican priest.[7] His brother-in-law, Sir Henry Oldham, became a Knight Commander of the Royal Victorian Order for military service in China and India.[8] His first cousins, with whom he grew up while his parents were in India, managed the successful family gunpowder business located outside Dartford.[9] After finishing at Harrow, the distinguished boarding school, Clarence secured a commission in the army, but with a substantial legacy from his father, he left the service in 1876 and moved to the Isle of Wight. His wedding gifts to Nora Lees—among them "a diamond ring," a "white gold bracelet," and a "black laced parasol with [a] carved ivory handle"—reflected a life of ease.[10]

It was into this life that Arthur Cecil Pigou was born in 1877, about a year after his parents were married. Cecil, as A. C. Pigou was likely called in his youth, spent the first year of his life at Beachlands, the home of his maternal grandfather.[11] The eighteen-bedroom house sat on the seaside Esplanade in Ryde, the vistas from its large windows sweeping over the Solent toward Portsmouth.[12] It was a prestigious address, five miles from Queen Victoria's residence at Osborne House. It was, however, his grandfather's house, and his parents acted quickly to find a roof of their own. A year after Pigou's birth, the young family moved to the village of Pembury in Kent, where it grew to include a second son, Gerald, in 1878 and a daughter, Kathleen. In 1881, the year of Kathleen's birth, the Pigous lived in a large house called Stone Court with Nora's sister and a domestic staff of six.[13] By the time Pigou left for boarding school, the family had moved into The Larches, a different house in Pembury, and had taken on a seventh servant.[14]

Pembury was a small village just outside Tunbridge Wells, a prosperous resort town in southeast England that had grown in both population and wealth after visits from Victoria and Albert. Pembury itself was still largely rural: a small collection of houses surrounding a green, with orchards and fields stretching out behind. But as Tunbridge Wells gained popularity in the mid-nineteenth century, Pembury had begun to attract well-to-do Victorians, who

FIGURE 1. The Larches, now Sunhill Court, Pembury, Kent. Courtesy of Tony Nicholls.

erected houses along the road into town.[15] The Larches was one of these, substantial and stuccoed, its entrance portico sheltered by a stand of trees and its back windows surveying an expanse of meadow. This was Pigou's childhood home, the place where, according to a playful college profile, he gained "the record for the number of questions asked of a much-enduring parent per week."[16]

School drained some of the precociousness out of Pigou and when—like his father, uncles, and cousins before him—he arrived at Harrow, ten miles northwest of central London, at the age of thirteen, he had become a self-described "shy and timid boy."[17] One of the most prestigious of the English public schools, Harrow was steeped in tradition, with pupils often donning a morning coat as part of their dress. Yet it was also a place that was rapidly and self-consciously modernizing. Its setting, Harrow-on-the-Hill, was a village in the throes of maturation into a suburb. The Metropolitan Line of the London Underground arrived in 1880 and with it, a type of worldly middle-class Londoner who fit uncomfortably into the old town-gown dichotomy between Harrovian and villager.[18]

Other changes came from central London as well. The passage of the 1868 Public Schools Act obliged Harrow and six other public schools to change their administration and update their teaching in an effort to "make further Provision for the[ir] good Government and Extension."[19] Arising from a perceived need to curb abuses and to update outdated curricula, the act pushed Harrow and peer institutions to broaden their offerings beyond classical material taught mostly by members of the clergy to include modern history, modern languages, and natural sciences. Response to legislative reform had taken a stately pace, lasting well into the 1890s. Before Pigou himself became head boy in his final year, all of Harrow's head boys had received an education based on a classical, rather than modern, curriculum.

Nevertheless, Pigou would have experienced Harrow's modernization in the very wiring of his schooltime home. The Harrow house in which he lived, Newlands, was just three years old on his arrival. At its opening in 1889, the school newspaper, *The Harrovian*, had noted "two striking features in connection with it. The colours of the football shirts is a bright canary yellow, and the house is illuminated throughout with electric light."[20] The people of Harrow were also changing. Though the boys and their families had been solidly Conservative for more than three decades, throughout the Gladstone governments, the masters and governors had been predominantly Whigs and Liberals.[21] By the time Pigou arrived, however, the educators had themselves shifted to the right. Political unity between the boys and their teachers ushered in an age of self-satisfaction and breezy, often ignorant, indifference. The future historian G. M. Trevelyan, Pigou's contemporary at Harrow, fumed in 1892 at the age of 16 that "in a school of 600 boys I have found just two people capable of talking sensibly about politics . . . I might just as well talk Greek politics to the rest."[22] Harrow was, in the words of its historian, "a nursery of upper class Englishness."[23]

Harrow's fees were among the highest of any public school, between £150 and £200 per year, but for families seeking a social marker recognized by the English establishment, this was a small price to pay.[24] A high proportion—upward of 30 percent—of Pigou's classmates came from outside England or Wales, with many hailing from the four corners of the Empire. Yet the diversity at Harrow belied the powerful conformist forces at work at the school. It was, after all, a training ground for the ideal type of gentleman, a place with a very clear and quite traditional vision of what it sought to instill in its students.

Pigou grew up not with his family but at Harrow. He became involved in sports, taking up cricket and fives, a sport much like handball. He was by no means a natural athlete, but as his friend J. W. Jenkins was to later recall, "in a modest way, he was quite a useful cricketer."[25] Off the practice fields, Harrow, blanketed and insulated, offered a deeply sheltered environment, but it served as the backdrop against which serious life lessons played out, as any place might. Two of Pigou's housemates died during his time at the school, and the boys were largely left to their own devices in sorting out the "minor politics" of living and working together.[26] And there was plenty of work. "There is no spot in the three kingdoms," a doleful contributor to the *Harrovian* complained in 1893, "where a 'long lie' a lie of indefinite length, unbroken even by a nine o'clock bell, is so appreciably luxurious as at Harrow. Freedom tastes sweetest in sight of the prison gates."[27]

But for Pigou, school was likely not a jail, especially given the respect he held for his house master, Frank Marshall. "What was the first impression he made?" Pigou mused shortly after Marshall died. "Friendliness, I think, and openness and sympathy—anything but the clouded terrors of authority."[28] Marshall had studied mathematics at Trinity College, Cambridge, and was at once a mature educator, having moved to Harrow in 1871, and a steadfast Liberal modernizer.[29] As such, he was also, in the words of Head Master Henry Montagu Butler, a "faithful servant not only to the school, but to every good cause in Harrow."[30]

But just as the paucity of archival material makes it hard to parse Pigou's feelings about his early childhood, it is similarly difficult to guess how he might have reflected on his time at school. Harrow was, after all, an immensely difficult social environment, propagating a rigorous hierarchy characterized by snobbishness and entitlement, and laced with sex, bullying, violence, and conformism.[31] And, indeed, Pigou would wryly remark about the "Bacchic orgies"

to which he had given a miss.[32] Jenkins, writing in 1964, remembered Pigou as being "perhaps a bit too unconventional and eccentric to be widely popular, but his few intimates including myself
were really fond of him."[33] It was these friends with whom he would
return to Kent during holidays and organize cricket matches, pit-
ting Harrovians against "the villagers" from Pembury. Jenkins, who
traveled home to The Larches with Pigou several times, recalled
a clouded atmosphere despite the bright athleticism. Pigou "lived
with a bluff old (or who then seemed to me to be old!) father, with
whom I think he had little in common."[34]

Back at Harrow, Pigou excelled in academic pursuits. He won
three separate entrance scholarships, partly as a result of his early
study of mathematics in preparatory school, and went on to take
home nearly every major academic prize the school offered.[35] This
was no mean feat. Harrow maintained a rigorous academic program;
Trevelyan, three years his senior, claimed that he himself "was better taught in history than any other schoolboy then in England," and
Pigou was subjected to the same rigorous instruction.[36] Pigou gained
authority as well, becoming a monitor in early 1894, but sports soon
took on secondary importance.[37] He badly lost the one boxing tour-
nament he entered and though in time he came to be the captain of
Newlands House cricket team, by his fourth year, he was devoting
much more of his energy and time to the school's debating club.[38]

The Harrow Debating Society was plagued with the sort of problems that frequently dog school clubs. Members and outside commentators lamented the absence of a consistent schedule, the dearth
of active participants, and the sometimes lackluster performance of
interlocutors.[39] Still, it was an outlet for the young Pigou to express
his nascent beliefs and an institution he would come to dominate.
Pigou was barely fifteen, but he already had a well-articulated set of
convictions. His early debates demonstrate a keen faith in progress;
a student himself of "the moderns," he "denounced Greek as well as
Latin," arguing unsuccessfully that "Latin does not repay one for
the time bestowed upon it."[40] He also evinced a developed political
outlook, an awareness reflective of Harrow's cultural landscape.[41]
Boys were expected to keep up to date on current events, and
though some of the many guest lecturers spoke of sport and alpine
expeditions, others advised Harrovians on geopolitical topics—the

importance of Gibraltar as a military base, or the state of the Royal Navy.[42] For Pigou, the latter of these lessons would have had special resonance; his younger brother Gerard had joined the navy in 1893 and two years later would be posted as a midshipman to the HMS *Ramillies*, a battleship stationed in the Mediterranean.[43]

Over the course of 1894 and 1895, Pigou took strident stands on a host of politically sensitive issues. In a debate on "admitting" women to "all Social and Political Rights," he "devoted himself to utterly demolishing the idea."[44] Pigou was, later in life, accused of misogyny—even his schoolmate Jenkins noted that he "never seemed particularly at ease" with women—and it is easy to view this early debate as consonant with lifelong prejudices of a decidedly misogynistic tint.[45] Prejudice is especially clear in this case, as the young Pigou clearly prized the ideal of political freedom, at least when it came to men. In a later debate over whether "King Charles I did not richly deserve his fate," he argued that the monarch had indeed deserved to be executed, "dwell[ing] principally . . . on the general charge of 'treason against the people.'"[46] This position put him in a distinct minority, a fact reflective of his dissonance with the overwhelming Tory traditionalism of his peers.[47]

Though he may not have been "widely popular," Pigou was no doubt skillful in navigating Harrow's traditions and hierarchies.[48] In his final year, he became the head of the school, and as such, he was given ex officio roles on the boards of many of its organizations.[49] Thus he was an officer of the Musical Society despite being tone deaf; of the Racquet Committee, despite his penchant for cricket; and of the Harrow Mission, a charitable enterprise set up to help the disadvantaged.[50] This last appointment is notable because, in spite of his later writing on charity and social work, this ex officio position was arguably the closest Pigou would ever come to the London slums.[51] Still, though the number of his responsibilities had grown, it was to the Debating Society, of which he was now president and to which he delivered some of the "best speech[es] heard in . . . some time," that Pigou invested most of his attention and care.[52] "Owing to the energy of the Head of the School," *The Harrovian* noted, "the Debating Society is fortunately more flourishing at the present time than it has been for many years past."[53]

Although Pigou found a home at Harrow, he was not a creature of the place. Harrow was overwhelmingly clubby, and Pigou was too much a student for his heart to beat in tune with the rhythm of the school. The Debating Society, for instance, was, for him far more about debating than it was about society. "If members continue to take a purely silent and coffee-drinking interest in the society," he opined in his final year, "it can never be really successful."[54] In his last debate, he reaffirmed his resistance to popular pressure and demonstrated an increasingly mature liberalism of his own. Arguing against his friend Jenkins over the motion that "this house sympathises with Dr. Jameson," a hero of the colonial South Africans, Pigou "vainly protested against the new jingo patriotism . . . of the London Music Halls."[55] Whereas Jenkins "made an eloquent appeal to the chivalrous sentiments of the Society," the young Pigou coolly distanced himself from recourse to mass sympathies.[56]

By the time he graduated, Pigou had grown from a timid country boy into the head of one of the most prestigious schools in England, a teenager with a hat and cane. In his own way, he flourished at Harrow, and his affection for his home of the past six years was on display in a short article he wrote during his last year. Reflecting on the chapel services for a school holiday, he took careful note of the bond between Harrow and its past sons, pausing to pay respect to "the fair sprinkling of those [Old Harrovians] to whom the memory of their schooldays must be growing dim, but whose love for Harrow is still undiminished."[57] Harrow's easy grandeur, tempered somewhat by the reformist influence of Frank Marshall, had nurtured a sweeping and comfortable liberalism in Pigou, and he finished his time at the school by delivering "a fine rendering" of one of William Gladstone's addresses at the annual "Speech Day."[58] Thus, armed with a tidy collection of prizes, Pigou stepped forth an Old Harrovian with the words of Gladstone, the Liberal hero, ringing in his ears.[59]

Cambridge at the Turn of the Century

In 1896, Pigou's liberalism followed him to King's College, Cambridge, where it found a much more congenial home than it had at Harrow. Reform and progress were the words on everyone's lips in

FIGURE 2. King's College from King's Parade, Cambridge, ca. 1890.
Courtesy of the Cambridgeshire Collection, Cambridge Central Library.

Cambridge in the 1890s.[60] Of course everyone, or at least a great majority of everyone, had been to a public school like Harrow.[61] Though a good number of its students did not come from means, Cambridge, like Harrow, was overwhelmingly a preserve of the upper and upper-middle classes.[62] As a preserve, it had its own idiosyncratic system of inequalities. Age, college, program of study, and athletic success all mattered, but unlike at Harrow, there was a pluralism of overlapping hierarchies, so that an individual was evaluated not according to one master scale but to any number of them. A Cambridge contemporary of Pigou, Maurice Amos, wrote that "we were free from the social tyranny of any one set of people or of any one kind of taste."[63] This was largely a function of a much larger student body: just under 1,000 young men matriculated at Cambridge each year in the 1890s, whereas the total student population at Harrow peaked at about 600.[64]

Even more than Harrow, Cambridge was feeling the effects of modernization. Between 1870 and 1900, Triposes—the examinations that conferred honors degrees—were established in seven new subjects.[65] Laboratory after laboratory was being built in the city center, and by 1900, with the program in Natural Sciences attracting the most students, the longstanding dominance of the humanities at the university was very much in question.[66] Moreover, there was a general openness to the ever-rising wind of liberalization. From the 1870s onward, major clashes occurred over the extent to which Cambridge would remain tied to the Anglican Church; over the admission of dissidents, Catholics, and women; and over the provision of education for future teachers and those without means.[67]

It is no wonder that Pigou fitted in at Cambridge better than he had at Harrow. The new setting was, of course, in line with Pigou's own inclinations. And, as Amos suggested, the diversity of groups at Cambridge meant that Pigou was able to move in and out of the many sets at the university. Yet, Pigou also benefited from his conventionally prestigious education and his membership in a wealthy and well-established college. At the time he arrived, the University of Cambridge consisted of twenty-two colleges, independently endowed academic institutions run by a self-selecting fellowship of scholars who provided the bulk of undergraduates' education through individual tutorials, or supervisions. Thus, his college would have provided Pigou with a readymade community. More academic than most, King's was the first and, until 1889, the only Cambridge college to mandate enrollment in a Tripos exam of all its admitted students.[68] It was also a college that excelled in the study of history. A total of seventy students who sat for (took) the History Tripos between 1875 and 1895 received first-class honors, or Firsts. Of those, twenty were Kingsmen.[69]

History would be the primary focus of the eighteen-year-old Pigou who entered King's, and his studies led to his own First in the subject three years later in 1899. But during Pigou's undergraduate years, the parameters that defined "history" as a discipline were a matter of much contention. As a serious field of academic study with a rigorous independent methodology, it was only in the process of coming into its own in Britain. Very few of the men who taught the subject at Cambridge were professionally trained as historians and in the all-important Tripos examinations, students were mostly required to tackle dull feats of memorization and recapitulation.[70] But a new outlook was emerging, as a growing number of thinkers recognized the need to shape the discipline into a more modern pursuit. At Cambridge, this was to be done by making changes to the content of the Tripos. The test made for a convenient locus of reform. Though the bulk of teaching was conducted in specific colleges, the administration of the Tripos was the responsibility not of the colleges but of independent university-wide boards, so that the tests had broad influence across all twenty-two colleges of the university. Moreover, the tests demanded such rigorous preparation that they effectively determined the reading lists for every serious history student at Cambridge.

Yet it was by no means clear what Tripos reform might look like. As it happened, the reformers were divided into two camps. On one side were those who sought to make history a discipline for its own sake, while on the other were those who sought to make it serve a useful end, to turn it into a course of study that would train future civil servants. By the late 1890s, an uncomfortable synthesis of the pure and instrumental had emerged in the form of a highly fractured program of study, with outlets available for devotees of either approach. A special subject was created in the use of original sources, for instance, and the historian and economist William Cunningham slowly transformed the teaching of political economy into that of economic history.[71]

Pigou himself became attached to the circle of Oscar Browning, one of the chief historical reformers favoring the study of history as an end in itself. A fellow of King's and steadfast Victorian Liberal, Browning was, as the young physicist Ernest Rutherford noted, "very agreeable" and "in appearance . . . a good deal like the typical John Bull one so often sees in *Punch*."[72] "The O.B." was a fixture of King's—a social animal who professed "to know all the people worth knowing in Europe."[73] His parties were legendary functions at which select undergraduates could mingle not only with more senior academics but also with the lights of British and Continental high society. Browning was a larger-than-life bon vivant, a reveler who had left a Master's lodge at Eton for Cambridge after a suspect relationship with the young George Nathaniel Curzon, a student who later became Viceroy of India.[74] Yet for all his flamboyance, The O.B. was a serious historian, someone who advocated a regimented professional discipline in the face of a distinctly amateur tradition.[75] A passionate advocate for the creation of teachers' colleges at Cambridge, from 1891 to 1909, Browning was the principal of the Cambridge Day Training College, which catered to students who would otherwise be unable to afford education and to young educators eager to learn teaching methods. In many ways, this was an ideal outlet for Browning, who, however debauched, was a devoted teacher whose penchant for deeply sentimental relationships revealed heartfelt connections with those he taught.[76]

It is telling that, whereas Pigou was immediately drawn to Frank Marshall, a reserved, sensitive mathematician on arriving at Harrow, he gravitated toward the polar opposite in Oscar Browning at Cambridge. Pigou was now a self-possessed young man, one who immediately joined the Union Society, Cambridge's debating club, and spoke in the first debate of his first term.[77] As his correspondence with Browning reveals, the young scholar's early interests included poetry and literature as well as history. His letters were peppered with inquiries about books and travel, and with requests. He wondered whether Browning might find a way to publish a story written by his "great friend" Jenkins and was keen to see his own name in print.[78] Home on holiday, the undergraduate Pigou wrote: "You remember you told me I might send you any literary productions for criticism. Do you think it would be worth while for me to send the enclosed [sample] to any magazines & if so could you suggest which?"[79] After all, Pigou belonged to Browning's network, from which certain benefits were inevitably gleaned. Browning had been instrumental, for instance, in advising and advocating for Pigou in his successful bid for a scholarship to King's.[80] In the case of the magazine submission, however, Browning lightly demurred, suggesting that the timing for such a publication was premature.

Pigou's letters to Browning displayed by turns a youthful insouciance and an inexperienced brightness.[81] He reported taking "a fortnight's bicycle tour in Brittany." It was his first time abroad, and he "had a splendid time despite difficulties of language." He also mused about his relations. "I suppose you remain at Florence; if not, if you go Monte Carlo way by any chance you'll find a respected aunt of mine losing money for all she's worth; you might give her a little fatherly advice, and my . . . condolences."[82] But between the

playful lines of reflections, thanks, and requests, were also sprin-
kled references to academic work.

Pigou's education was broad and deep, and he soon gravitated
away from the rote memorization of history texts and toward political and social theory as well as toward English literature. He wrote
Browning that he "meant to be virtuous this vac[ation]; [and]
brought home books about that wretched early constitutional history, but haven't opened them." Instead, he read "Lecky's Democracy & Liberty & Sidgwick's Methods of Ethics, & a good many
of Shakespeare's plays."[83] Pigou read and studied widely, picking
up what he would later refer to as his "philosophical training."[84]
He filled his college notebooks with quotations from the French
poet Lamartine and sweeping observations about the corruption
of American officials. "Institutions," he opined, "can never attain
maturity. . . . if their roots are perpetually tampered with."[85] Pigou
encountered Darwin in a history class and took uncharacteristically immaculate notes on the first six chapters of On the Origin of
Species (1859). "Man selects for his own advantage," he remarked,
"nature for that of the being."[86]

Pigou soaked up evolutionary themes and would soon start
writing on eugenics, but the influence Darwin had on the young
historian was slight compared to that of renowned Cambridge
utilitarian ethicist Henry Sidgwick, whose lectures he attended.[87]
In his masterwork, The Methods of Ethics (1874), Sidgwick sought
to advance ethical theory by forging a synthesis of two ethical
movements: utilitarianism, which held that what was ultimately
good was the "greatest happiness of the greatest number," and in-
tuitionism, the theory that the final arbiter of morality was the intuitional "moral reasoning of ordinary men."[88] Intuitionally, Sidgwick argued, the maximization of utility—essentially happiness or
pleasure—was society's ultimate end. But furthermore, common
sense morality could serve as a rough proxy for utilitarian ethics in
day-to-day situations.[89] Sidgwick's utilitarian message of striving
to improve societal wellbeing resonated with Pigou's solidly Victorian upbringing. And by validating intuition—especially the intuition of educated moral thinkers—Sidgwick's philosophy worked
to encourage the young Pigou's ability to reason and expound with
confidence.

Then again, considering Pigou's active debating schedule, his self-confidence was never really in question. As it had at Harrow, debating at Cambridge—this time at the Cambridge Union Society—occupied a central place in Pigou's social life. In the subtle hierarchies of Cambridge life, the Union carried a special kind of prestige. "Almost everyone who comes to Cambridge hopes for some distinction beyond that afforded by academic success," *The Granta*, the university weekly, observed.

> The most obvious and popular ambition is for athletic fame. [However,] prominence in the Union does, or is supposed to, mean certain intellectual powers, and those who deliver themselves of speeches in that historical society are held, by some persons at the least, to be deeply versed in politics, literature and art, and all other subjects concerning which men disagree.[90]

Debate was Pigou's natural outlet and one in which he would gain considerable acclaim.

Before Cambridge, he had found himself somewhat more liberal than his peers. He had been, for instance, swimming distinctly out of the common current at Harrow when he denounced the jingoism of music halls. At the Union, Pigou found himself more squarely in the center of a more reform-minded group of young Englishmen from good families. After spending several days poring over the topics on which Pigou spoke, Austin Robinson came to the conclusion that his friend had been a "pro-establishment" "extrovert."[91] It is not hard to see how Robinson reached this conclusion.

In terms of extroversion, Pigou certainly was a comfortable speaker. In his first appearance, his words were variously characterized by "clearness, fluency, and earnestness" and a "dignified airiness." Throughout his time at the Union, he was usually "free from notes and his language was vigorous and terse," and more times than not, he benefited from the "sympathy of the House."[92] By the end of his time at the Union, he had become its president, and the writers of *The Granta* could not "remember any one else who so suddenly became a first rate-speaker."[93] All the while, Pigou maintained an active social life, replete with trips to France, Scotland, and the Lake District as well as fast friendships with other luminaries of the Union, particularly another president, a Scottish theology student named J.R.P. Sclater. Pigou was in many ways the picture of the young Edwardian, one who decried "the revival of Puritan influence in secular affairs" and who emphasized the "fall of all that was good" that arose from overly restrictive social mores.[94] Yet claims about Pigou's extroversion should be tempered. He existed, after all, in "the air of ineffable creeper-clad calm which is the most distinguished characteristic of the Union."[95] His was a society of Cambridge men and, indeed, *The Granta* wryly observed that he could "remain silent in the presence of the opposite sex beyond the belief of man."[96] But without a doubt, Pigou was far more popular than he had been at Harrow. His profile in *The Granta* positively glowed: "What Mr. Pigou's future is to be is at present vague; but it is sure to be one well worth having. For reasons which his friends know, he will never fail to gather the 'best things.' Uprightness and honour are before him."[97]

It is similarly easy to follow Robinson's reasoning that Pigou was pro-establishment. From 1896 to 1900, Pigou variously condemned anti-monarchists, a *"really* Democratic Government," and students who were speaking a little too freely in university-run theaters.[98] He defended Cambridge's cloistered college system from would-be reformers and supported French authorities throughout the Dreyfus Affair.[99] It was not just because Pigou had gained official positions in the Union—first the vice presidency in his third year and the presidency in early 1900—that *The Granta* cheekily referred to him as "Monsieur le Vicomte Pigou de l'Union et de Chateau du Roi" and "Graf Pigou von Königsschloss-bei-Kam."[100] The noble Pigou showed an affinity with vested institutional authority and flirted with right-leaning political forces. Compared with the Liberal Party, he observed at the Union in 1901, the Conservative party was "less likely to foster extreme sentiments of reform; and as a social force, was in some ways more trustworthy."[101]

But *le Vicomte* was by no means extreme in his commitments—his feelings about imperialism, for instance, were markedly less enthusiastic than were those of many of his peers. Early as an undergraduate, he argued against Britain's further involvement in East Asia, and later, he held forth against "the expansion of the United States of America," arguing that imperialism would breed further corruption.[102] During the Second Boer War, when patriotic fervor reached a febrile pitch and the university's volunteers were busy conducting training exercises and mock battles in the surrounding countryside, Pigou maintained a studied silence in all of the numerous debates concerning South Africa, and from his presidential seat in 1900, he even encouraged a Boer sympathizer to take the floor.[103] But none of this is to suggest that Pigou was anti-empire. In 1900, for instance, he vigorously defended the British nation's "competence" to "govern alien powers" against the charges of his friend Sclater.[104] Of course, there was no jarring tension between Pigou's respect for traditional forms of authority and his loose liberalism. The Liberals were the party of the reformist elite; Pigou's mentor Browning basked almost exclusively in such established circles.[105] In short, with his comfortable existence and his detached interest in social reform, it was not difficult for Pigou to act the mildly progressive Liberal.

There was really only one issue debated at the Union that stripped away Pigou's general political moderation and incited him to rhetorical heights at the expense of traditional interests: free trade. The question of protective tariffs had dogged British political life at least since the early nineteenth century, and especially after the repeal of the Corn Laws in 1846. Traditionally, landed Conservatives favored protection, while those affiliated with urban trading and manufacturing centers advocated unrestricted commerce. It was a dispute, in the first instance, between vested interests in sectors that materially benefited from opposing policies. Yet since at least the time of John Stuart Mill, the debate over free trade had acquired a subtle second dimension: an intellectual disagreement about the mechanics of how trade protection functioned in society. While many supporters of tariffs felt they were acting in the national interest, free traders were convinced that the euphemism of "protection" was just a veil: that tariffs actually harmed the national interest they purported to protect by making prices higher for everyone. Mill, drawing on themes from political economists going back to Adam Smith, had given advocates of free trade a theoretical framework with a powerful mix of erudition and simplicity, a compound that engendered strong devotion among those who took the time to understand it. Thus, though free trade was one of the most traditional Liberal causes with broad popular democratic support, it was of special importance for Mill's direct intellectual descendants, utilitarian political economists.[106] And slowly but surely, Pigou was slipping into their ranks.

Pigou's First Economics

The story of Pigou as the Edwardian attached to the circle of the larger-than-life Oscar Browning captures only half of Pigou's undergraduate experience. There was another, more restrained Pigou: the incipient economist. At Harrow, Pigou had already begun to read economic texts, including *The Economics of Industry* (1879) by the Cambridge economist Alfred Marshall and his wife Mary Paley Marshall. During his first year at Cambridge, Pigou delved further into the literature of political economy, reading, among other books, Marshall's more famous work, *The Principles of Economics* (1890).[107] But it was Pigou's second year—the year in which he first personally encountered Marshall, the most prominent economist in Britain—that proved to be the real turning point in his education. Only then, though still very much a self-styled historian, did Pigou begin to take an active interest in economics. Over the course of the year, Pigou attended Marshall's lectures and, while on a break, noted in a letter to Browning that he had read works by William Ashley, the Oxford economic historian, "which I ought to have read long ago" as well as pieces by Walter Bagehot and a book, likely Sidgwick's, on political economy.[108] That summer, while back at The Larches, "the fates were quite reproachful . . . and inflicted a sprained ankle" with the result of "long sojourning on a sofa and dutiful study of economics." "I've done quite a bit of work," Pigou languidly complained to Browning, "after getting up at the barbarous hour of seven to begin."[109]

Not coincidentally, it was also in his second year that Pigou began to hold forth on issues of political economy at the Union. During his first year, the Union held a debate on free trade—the proposer, E. W. Harrison, who was described as a "farmer," argued that "the depressed condition of Agriculture . . . demand[ed] an immediate return to protective duties on all foreign imports." *The Granta* commented that "many of the speakers did not know the most rudimentary principles of Political Economy, and at times the logic was that of the parlour of a village inn on market day."[110] Yet throughout the frustrating debate, Pigou remained silent. Indeed, during his first year—before he had come into contact with Marshall—Pigou avoided debates on all the issues that would later captivate his professional interest: the one on "Collectivist tendencies" in the British Empire, the one on trade unionism, and, of course, the one on free trade.[111]

The silence was broken in Pigou's second year. Harrison, a student at Trinity College, again proposed that "the present system of Free Trade is disastrous to the best interests of England and her colonies." Rising to oppose the motion, Pigou narrowly prevailed on the House to overturn the proposition, complaining "plaintively of the lack of economic argument in the Proposer's speech." And, *The Granta* noted, though he "rather over-burdened himself with statistics," he "showed a good grasp of his subject."[112] Pigou wielded a well-worn economic argument against tariffs: that in seeking to protect a national economy, they would raise domestic prices across many industries and in so doing hurt both consumers and industry. But Pigou also made use of a more sensitive political argument for free trade, one related to distribution. "Only the landlord will reap the benefits of Protection," he held. "It is better to have a prosperous populace in the towns than starvation and want in the rural districts."[113]

Although Pigou demonstrated a growing engagement with economic issues, until the end of his third year, he was still primarily a student of the humanities. As such, he acquitted himself brilliantly. Alfred Marshall wrote sarcastically that Pigou had "no memory" and "was bothered by the want of . . . [memory questions] on the History Tripos" in which he took a First at the end of his third year in June 1899.[114] The same year, Pigou was recognized for "composition in English verse," an ode to Alfred the Great, who led his "people far from the black slough/Of soulless greed, into more generous paths/Onwards and upwards following Truth's bright star."[115]

In fact, Pigou learned the better part of his economics after taking his degree.[116] In an effort to bring his economics up to speed, he subjected himself to a fortnight of summertime isolation in a remote Breton town, "an outlandish spot . . . a place of solitude to which I have come to work."[117] Over the following months, Pigou prepared for Part II of the Moral Science Tripos, the test that covered political economy, reading further works by such thinkers as Walter Bagehot, William Stanley Jevons, John Neville Keynes, and Marshall himself.[118] As the historian transformed into the economist, Pigou's character was riven with contrasts. "He revels in argument," *The Granta* noted, "and is a poet; he is an orator, and does not seek notoriety; he is an economist, and possesses a kindly heart; he has been a historian and remains truthful."[119]

It was during this period that Pigou grew close to Marshall. Unlike Browning, Marshall was not a social animal. Though he cared deeply for those attached to him, from an early age, Marshall "did not readily make friends," and throughout his life, he had trouble sustaining lasting friendships.[120] He was a more serious person than was Browning. He was also, certainly, a much more serious scholar. As John Maynard Keynes wrote, "Marshall belonged to the tribe of sages and pastors; yet . . . endowed with a double nature, he was a scientist too."[121] There was nothing slapdash or ad hoc about his work. His was a world of systems and models, of rigorously articulated, extensively footnoted assertions. Thus, Pigou's burgeoning relationship with him represented for the young scholar a transition to science and scientific modes of thought. It suggested growth: not only growth in his own work, but also growth away from the heady company of Browning. In April 1900, in Pigou's fourth year at Cambridge, Pigou and Browning had a quarrel that seriously damaged their relationship. The points of contention were trivial: a speech that Pigou had given to the Political Society and procedures at the Union, of which Pigou was vice president and Browning was treasurer.[122] Still, the dispute heralded a rupture in the friendship; their subsequent correspondence had more to do with club and society business than with personal news or sentiment.

The break represented more than just a personal parting, for as Pigou came under Marshall's influence and out from under Browning's, he conceived of himself less as a historian and increasingly as an economist, particularly a Marshallian economist. This distinction was important, for just as the parameters of history at Cambridge were a matter of some contention, so too were the parameters of economics.

There was, during this period, substantial overlap between the study of history and economics at the university. A good collection of classes on economic theory and history were included in the list of "Lectures Proposed by the Special Board for History and Archeology," the body that oversaw the History Tripos and organized the subject's university-wide lectures.[123] And several thinkers—most notably William Cunningham—were attempting to bring economics into the teaching of history in a systematic and integrated way. At first glance, this process of integration seems as if it would have provided a natural path for Pigou's transition from historian to economist, but it was exactly this middle ground that Pigou avoided.

Cunningham was one of several economic historians at Cambridge to subscribe to a style of economic thought then dominant in Germany that has come to be known as the historist or historical school of economics.[124] Such thinkers stressed attention to historical trends as part of an effort to inductively reach specific conclusions about contemporary economic questions. Unsurprisingly, proponents of history as an end in itself, like Browning, prickled at the core motivations of the historical school. Though Browning himself was a scholar of sometimes sloppy methodology—he once wrote a piece on Florentine art from a hotel in Lucerne without access to any sources—he was firmly committed to the concept of history as a science rather than as a preparatory course, as Cunningham saw it. And if Pigou's first Cambridge mentor distanced himself from Cunningham, his second actively sought to downplay Cunningham's influence.

Indeed, the challenges brought by historians against historical economics paled in comparison to those brought by other economists, particularly by Pigou's new mentor, Alfred Marshall.[125] English devotees of historical economics embraced the core premise that economic truths were not absolute, but culturally contingent. Economic developments, therefore, could only be explained in their historical setting.[126] For late nineteenth- and early twentieth-century practitioners like Arnold Toynbee at Oxford, William Ashley then at Toronto, and Cunningham and Herbert Foxwell at Cambridge, economic outcomes were determined by a complex matrix of time, place, institutional context, and the particularities of human interaction.[127]

Marshall's approach grew out of a markedly different intellectual legacy. Whereas Cunningham was in dialogue with a largely German humanistic tradition, Marshall, whose own education was in mathematics, was more firmly an intellectual inheritor of similarly analytically oriented Englishmen, notably David Ricardo and William Stanley Jevons. Marshall had himself studied contemporary German philosophy and was convinced that economics was a study of humankind in evolutionary motion.[128] But Marshallian economics looked considerably different from other German-influenced systems. Most importantly, it offered not a historical, contextual explanation, but a "science"; the results it yielded were meant to align observable reality with an abstract and universal Truth.[129] In the preface to the first edition of *Principles of Economics*, Marshall wrote: "As, in spite of the great differences in form between birds and quadrupeds, there is one Fundamental Idea running through all their frames, so the general theory of equilibrium of demand and supply is a Fundamental Idea running through the frames of all various parts of the central problem of Distribution and Exchange."[130] Marshall, in essence, set out to do for economics what Darwin had done for biology. And though he was respectful of history, in his economics, Marshall operated with an entirely different premise than did Cunningham.[131]

And, in shaping the future of economics as practiced in Britain, Marshall was meeting with substantially greater success.[132] Even as early as 1887, Marshall's colleague Herbert Foxwell had noted that "half the economic chairs in the United Kingdom are occupied by . . . [Marshall's] pupils, and the share taken by them in general economic instruction in England is even larger than this."[133] By the time Pigou reached Cambridge, Marshall had assumed the role of the codifier of British economic theory. That theory was based on marginal analysis, the evaluation of changes and rates of change.[134]

Marshall's influence was tied, in some measure, to the success of his seminal textbook, *Principles of Economics*, in which he had delineated his cohesive system of thought. Over ten years in the making, the book had been an immediate success when it was first published in 1890 and was already in its fourth (of eight) edition by 1898.[135] The *Principles* and the codifying spirit it embodied would be remarkably influential. Speaking to an assembly of economists many years later, Pigou asserted that until World War I, "Economic thought in this country was dominated to a quite extraordinary degree by one man—Marshall. He was our leader, practically unchallenged. . . . For the general body of economists in England, he was 'the master.'"[136]

Marshall's economics, though more scientifically detached and less directly concerned with reformist social goals than contemporary British schools of thought (such as the idealist-influenced Oxford School), was motivated by the same Victorian codes of ethics, according to which the privileged were expected to aid the needy.[137] Across Europe and America, economics and other social sciences arose as liberal responses to burgeoning social problems during an age of increasing democratization and industrialization.[138] It should come as no surprise, then, that Marshall was keenly interested in issues of social justice.[139] He visited London's slums and, as he aged, became increasingly involved in programs, economic and otherwise, to help the indigent.[140] His economic theory grew out of a worldview that he described as having a "tendency to socialism" in its determination that much of income inequality was remediable.[141]

Running throughout Marshall's economics was an established goal of maximizing societal welfare, specifically by growing the national dividend, that is, the yearly sum of a nation's income (essentially what is now known as the gross domestic product).[142] Thinking in terms of national economic productivity, Marshall thought that the way to maximize the national dividend involved the equalization of marginal products, meaning that a given unit of capital, labor, or any other input would be equally productive in any industry across the economy. But Marshall also was convinced that marginal analysis recommended a more egalitarian distribution of income. In its most basic sense, Marshall's worldview suggested that the poor, because they were needier, would be able to make more use of their money than would the rich. Thus, from the perspective of maximizing social wellbeing, a more equal distribution of income and wealth made intuitive sense. "Any diminution of . . . [inequalities of wealth] which can be attained by means that would not sap the springs of free initiative," Marshall wrote in his *Principles*, "would seem to be a clear social gain."[143]

It was not so surprising, then, that Pigou might easily move between the reformist world of letters and the emergent field of Marshallian economics, a discipline that understood itself to be an ethical science. And indeed, as Pigou gravitated toward Marshall, his involvement with economics continued to grow alongside—not to the exclusion of—his literary and philosophical interests. After taking a starred First (the star denoting exceptional performance) in Part II of the Moral Science Tripos in 1900, Pigou remained at Cambridge to prepare materials with an eye toward securing a fellowship at King's.[144] These were well before the days when a graduate degree was a prerequisite to become a British academic, and a good number of the fellows at Cambridge colleges were in their early twenties, having only recently finished their undergraduate studies. Still, election to fellowship was a highly competitive process. King's typically took on one or two new fellows a year, and despite his top marks on his examinations, Pigou would face stiff competition. In a decision that neatly reflected his bipartite education, Pigou set himself to revising two potential essays to support his candidacy. One was a work in the Marshallian vein, an analysis of British agricultural prices over the preceding five decades. The other was a philosophical essay on the poet, "Robert Browning as a Religious Teacher," that he had composed under Oscar Browning's tutelage just after his first Tripos examination.[145] Pigou would receive awards for both works the following year.[146]

Meanwhile, in the fall of 1900, he started giving lectures on economics to "the Extension people at Cambridge," adult students continuing their education.[147] Marshall was also considering offering Pigou a job as a lecturer, not on behalf of a college or the Moral Science Tripos board, but for Marshall himself as part of his effort to cement the dominance of his brand of economics at Cambridge. "I am now inclined," he had written to J. N. Keynes earlier that year, "to think that the ideal man [to lecture] is at hand—Pigou."[148] In a letter to Browning, Marshall asserted that it would be best if Pigou "should lecture for me next year. If after that the College [King's] likes to make him a College lecturer, I should be of course only too well pleased. They will then be able to judge better how far my high expectations with respect to him are justified."[149]

But Pigou himself was still divided between economics and more philosophical and literary pursuits. That year, he began to contribute short review essays to *The Economic Journal*, which was edited by Marshall's friend and Oxford professor F. Y. Edgeworth, but the works he covered revealed a decidedly mixed reading list. The first book he tackled was on economic crises, but just four months later, he reviewed one on the dispatches of a British ambassador to the court of Tsarina Catherine II.[150]

In 1901, he submitted his essay on Browning in an unsuccessful attempt to join the Fellowship at King's. Writing to Oscar Browning, with whom relations were still chilly, Pigou defended the topic as falling under Moral Sciences, since "the main part of [Browning's] religious teaching is simply a mixture of [British idealist T. H.] Green's Ethics and skeptical metaphysics." Still, in what may have been an attempt to save face, he claimed that he only submitted the Browning essay because he was writing on it anyway "for another purpose": "I never thought I'd have any real chance for a fellowship this year in any case, but intended to have a serious try next with a Dissertation on 'The Causes and Effects of Changes in the Relative prices of Agricultural Produce in the U.K. during the last 50 years.'"[151] But it was too late to convince Browning. In fact, at a meeting of the fellowship committee, Browning had unsuccessfully attempted to block Pigou from submitting a fellowship dissertation on Robert Browning at all.[152]

Immediately after Pigou's failed bid to become a fellow, Marshall hired him to teach and the following year, Pigou applied to King's again, this time submitting the lengthily titled analysis of agricultural production. This essay, as Pigou himself readily admitted, did not pioneer great new thought. But it aptly demonstrated his mastery of contemporary economic techniques learned, as he acknowledged, "from Professor Marshall's Principles of Economics."[153] Thus in 1902, with Marshall's support, Pigou became a fellow of King's College.[154]

Marshall's sponsorship and mentorship of Pigou came at a time when Marshall was building an institutional groundwork for the school of thought at whose center he stood.[155] Though Marshall himself was a fellow of St. John's College, he was principally concerned with the university-wide curriculum for the Moral Sciences Tripos, the examination that dealt with economic topics. In 1903, he successfully petitioned for the creation of an entirely new Tripos to cover his brand of abstract economic theory and not the economics of the historical school. Therefore, he took great pains to demonstrate that his star student and paid lecturer, Pigou, who started his training as a historian, was not a *historical* economist like Foxwell or Cunningham. In a heated letter to Browning after a meeting in which this topic arose, Marshall recounted: "You burst in with but Pigou studied economic history before economics. My answer was necessarily repressed: it was, 'he never came under Dr. Cunningham's influence at all:' he tried to listen to his lectures; but . . . found them . . . [a] waste of time for men who already knew how to read for themselves.' But I could not say that."[156]

When preparing a list of university-wide courses covering material for the new, independent Tripos in 1903, Marshall determined to have Pigou "give for me a set of lectures like that which he is giving this term." Marshall drafted "course titles vaguely, so that . . . [Pigou] may be free to pick out any part that he likes."[157] With the Economics Tripos established, Pigou quickly became a lecturer funded by the Girdlers' Company and was set in charge of the introductory course "treated from the scientific as distinguished from the historical and literary point of view," leaving Marshall free to teach advanced coursework.[158] The decision to relinquish a great deal of control over the program in which Marshall had invested so much time, energy, and hope spoke to the confidence he placed in his pupil.[159] Hopes were running high indeed. Marshall wrote privately of the potential for Cambridge's new system to overhaul British political life. "I shall not talk about the number of Chancellors of the Exchequer and Ministers . . . whom I [would] like to see educated during my life time on the new route: I fear the ridicule of the wicked," he wrote. "But I have not overlooked the fact that a Chancellor of the Exchequer may come from Cambridge."[160]

Thus, to a degree, the care and effort Marshall dedicated to Pigou's advancement was part of his larger effort to consolidate Cambridge as a base for modern economic theory. This is not, however, to suggest that Pigou and Marshall's relationship was merely instrumental or in any way insincere. Early in 1902, shortly after Marshall had hired Pigou to lecture, the former wrote to John Neville Keynes, another Cambridge economist, "I have had many pupils whom I have cared for: but only a few whom I have loved. Among those—of the male gender—you & Pigou have a special charm for me."[161] And for his part, Pigou would remain steadfastly loyal to Marshall and the Marshallian framework for the rest of his life. His writings on Marshall never lost the reverent admiration of a one-time pupil. As late as 1952, he wrote a short book titled *Alfred Marshall and Current Economic Thought*, in which he referred to Marshall as his "master"; the phrase, "it's all in Marshall" would, in time, become one of his professional mantras.[162]

Pigou was Marshall's student at a decisive moment, one at which Marshall was casting about for young disciples to become integrally involved in his new program. The result was that Pigou was personally plucked from the study of history and mentored by the greatest economist then working in Britain. His early connection with Marshall afforded him the imprimatur of the leader of British economists and enabled him to participate in the genesis of a new orthodoxy.[163] Yet unlike colleagues just a few years younger, Pigou was not educated exclusively as an economist. Instead, he was one of the last—perhaps the last—important economic thinker in Britain to come up under the old system in which politics, history, and moral science mingled with economic theory. Pigou's early economics, then, were almost unique in that they bore the clear marks of two systems. Though works of abstract theory, they took history, politics, and morality very seriously. And though forged in the crucible of a new science, they were clearly imbued with and inspired by ethical impulses.

CHAPTER TWO

Ethics, Politics, and Science

IN THE PREFACE to the first edition of *The Principles of Economics,* Alfred Marshall wrote that economic laws were "statements of tendencies expressed in the indicative mood, and not ethical precepts in the imperative." But, he went on, "ethical forces are among those of which the economist has to take account."[1] Marshall suggested that individuals, even "economic man," acted in accordance with a variety of moral codes and strictures, to which the economist needed to pay attention.[2]

Eighteen years later, in 1908, speaking in front of an assembled crowd, A. C. Pigou proposed a deeper relationship between economics and ethics. In expounding on the purpose and value of economics, he would "trespass beyond the domain of economic science itself" by making "an estimate of values in the ethical sense, and, therewith, an entrance into the province of moral philosophy."[3] Economic science, he claimed, did not exist as an end in itself. Neither its practice nor the knowledge it yielded was inherently good. Economics shed light on humankind in the "ordinary business of life," but it was "not in the ordinary business of life that mankind is most inspiring."[4]

Economics was useful, Pigou explained, only because of its ability to "bear fruit"—to do real, practical, ethical work in improving the conditions of human well-being. The impulse to do such work, he noted, was "a commanding one," for though great strides had been made in social reform, the "evil" that remained was still great. "The least imaginative among us sometimes sees with vividness the faces of the suffering and the degraded who have been worsted in the industrial struggle. The contrast between the luxury of some and the penury of others is evident."[5]

These words were delivered not at a political rally, though they would have resonated with both Liberals and an increasingly powerful labor movement. They were, instead, delivered to a distinguished audience at the Senate House, the ceremonial hall at Cambridge. The speech, titled "Economic Science in Relation to Practice," was Pigou's inaugural address as Professor of Political Economy.

The circumstances of the address's delivery underscored a major tension in Pigou's early work. Pigou was invested with an ethical desire to help the masses, but he suffered from an unwillingness to get near them. The content of the speech, however, revealed not a tension but a synthesis of scientific, political, and moral elements. In the first decade of the twentieth century, these elements were to publicly weave in and out of one another, leaving Pigou's politics, ethics, and economics not separate intellectual categories, but integrated components of a single mode of thought.

A Young Don's Life

In 1902 at the age of twenty-five, Pigou was a fellow of King's, a Cambridge lecturer in a burgeoning discipline, and the protégé of Britain's most famous economist. Though relations had somewhat cooled with Browning, he would soon begin lecturing at the latter's teachers' college.[6] But despite these responsibilities, Pigou was a don very much at ease, a man whose future stretched out languidly before him. He was a jovial fellow—and a jocular one. Recollections by his friends and students describe him as an animated bachelor who partook in lawn tennis and firework displays that went awry and left eyebrows "nothing to write home about."[7] He played tennis and golf as well as squash. On occasion, he would sneak into the gracious King's College chapel with friends to hold races, the somber air broken by the resonant footfalls of young men on marble.

FIGURE 3. Photographic Portrait of A. C. Pigou taken in the J. Palmer Clarke
Studio. Courtesy of the Cambridgeshire Collection, Cambridge Central Library.

With fellows and students alike, Pigou would take off for the Alps,
just as Browning had done. These were jaunty excursions, largely
consisting of climbing, but peppered with moments of luxury. Early
trips saw Pigou bring along dinner jackets as well as mountain gear.
On one such adventure, his tuxedoed party dined at the Schweitzer-
hof at Lucerne, a "first class occasion." And for the remainder of the
six-week holiday, the "wretched garments had to be posted on from
place to place," while the group "tramped with the more suitable
kit . . . in rucksacks."[8]

Pigou took more local mountaineering excursions with even
greater frequency. He first visited the Lake District in 1901 with his
friend Sclater from the Union to participate in "an institution called
a Lake Hunt in which 20 or 30 Cambridge people . . . [took] part."
"It ought," Pigou had anticipated in a letter to Browning, "be great

fun."[9] The yearly "Man Hunt" had been started just three years before by G. M. Trevelyan and two friends and was modeled on an
older game played at Harrow called "hare and hounds."[10] Bringing
together a collection of thirty or forty young men, many of whom
were progressive Liberals, the game took place over three days near
Keswick, a town in the Lake District and the ancestral home of
Pigou's Harrow housemaster, Frank Marshall. Pigou was immediately drawn to the Cumbrian landscape, and he would return for
the next fifty years, until infirmity made the 300-mile rail journey
from Cambridge too arduous.

Back at Cambridge, there was a fluidity and ease about the
young King's fellows. In a lazily self-indulgent "account of day's
events" from 1906, the young King's classicist John Tresidder Sheppard, wrote of breezing from strolls to philosophic conversations,
and finally to Pigou's rooms "to write." There, he found "nobody
+ A.C.P[igou]."[11] Though he himself taught and wrote, Pigou always set aside a good deal of time for less serious pursuits. He
hosted dinner parties whose invitations he composed elaborately
in French. One guest was John Maynard Keynes, the son of John
Neville Keynes and a King's undergraduate whom Pigou befriended
in 1904. Keynes was impressive even in youth. He managed, Pigou
wrote, "to be clear-headed without making muddle-headed people
hate him. That is a remarkable thing, which demonstrates that, besides the minor gift of cleverness, he has the major one of sympathy."[12] The result was that Pigou extended himself to the younger
man. "M. A.C. Pigou," one dinner invitation read, "demande le plai-
sir de la compagnie de M. J.M. Keynes en vêtements magnifiques."[13]

Magnificent clothes, extensive wine cellars, ritualized feasts:
such were the staples of the life of a King's fellow at the turn of
the century. The college was an intellectual and social hothouse. A
number of the fellows, including Pigou, lived within its walls, and
a good many more ate their meals at the High Table set on a raised
platform at the end of the college's neo-Gothic dining hall. When
Pigou joined the fellowship in 1902, it numbered about fifty, among
them Browning, of course, but also two economic historians: J. H.
Clapham and the "moustachioed and grave" W. F. Reddaway.[14] The
fellowship was bifurcated along the lines of age. A significant minority of scholars, Pigou included, were about to receive or had just

recently received their MAs, a degree Cambridge awarded six years after undergraduate matriculation without any additional coursework or examination. Fellowship, however, was for life, and the majority of King's fellows belonged to an older contingent whose presence helped preserve the timeless feel of the place. It was, in Pigou's words, a "museum of the antique."[15] With somber words lightened by the flicker of a smirk, he quoted Dante's *Inferno* to Donald Welldon Corrie, another King's undergraduate with whom he became close, on returning to the college from a vacation.

> As I came to the gates of the college, I saw written above it in letters of dull fire the words
>
> > Per me si va nella cita dolente; [Through me the way into the
> > suffering city]
> > Per me si va tra la perduta gente. [Through me the way to
> > everlasting pain]
>
> . . . Come, they said, let us at least dine; and they did consume the goodly duck and did ask me, the latest comer to that dim abode to tell them of the world that lay beyond the fastened gates. And so the days pass in Malebolge.[16]

But though Pigou might now have lived in a somber "museum of the antique," he was not one of the exhibits. Another Kingsman about Corrie's age, Hugh Dalton, later Chancellor of the Exchequer, recalled Pigou as "tall and handsome like a Viking, a mountaineer, already a strong intellectual and moral force in the College."[17]

Pigou was also now on his own, without strong family connections. His brother Gerard was far away, serving as a lieutenant in the navy and in 1904, his sister Kathleen married a first cousin, Arthur Hugh Oldham, also a naval officer, and shortly thereafter moved to Wales.[18] Pigou's mother died in 1902, and his father followed in 1905, leaving his entire estate, worth £8,184, to Pigou, the first son.[19] His parents' deaths brought new independence; their money ensured his ongoing solvency. But Pigou was discovering a different sort of freedom as well as he threw himself further into college life. Dalton remarked on Pigou's habit of choosing "a series of young men as they passed through King's to whom he gave unwavering sympathy and support. Good-looking, good on mountains, good moral tone. These were the gifts he most valued in them."[20] Pigou likely would not have identified himself as gay, either publicly or privately.[21] Homosexuality was a crime in Britain, and though Pigou's inclinations were a topic of gossipy discussion in the permissive atmosphere of King's, it remains unclear whether he was ever romantically involved. That said, thoroughly immersed in the homosocial world of his Cambridge college, he expressed little interest in women, around whom he was legendarily shy. As colleague D. G. Champernowne wrote, Pigou "would speak gallantly of the lovely Mrs. Smith, the gorgeous Mrs. Brown and the beautiful Mrs. Jones: but the photographs around his room proclaimed that his eye for beauty was rather concerned with mountains and men."[22] Keynes, while a postgraduate at King's in 1906, was less circumspect about Pigou's purported homosexuality. Pigou was "very nice but a little depressed and lovelorn." To Keynes, his interest in male undergraduates was "becoming a scandal."[23]

Early Political Involvement of the Marshallian Economist

Under the tutelage of Frank Marshall, Browning, and Alfred Marshall, all staunch Liberals, Pigou had long been immersed in a world of social reform. Indeed, his first academic publication evidenced the influence of a progressive strand of liberalism—the so-called new liberalism—on his early thinking. New liberalism emerged in the 1890s as part of an effort by Liberals to achieve gradualist socialist goals. As such, the movement generally took a softer line on the traditional Liberal priority of the individual over that of the social unit.[24] It also firmly stressed the priority of questions of ethics to those of scientific truth. But importantly, as Michael Freeden wrote in his classic study of the movement, economics was, for new liberals and positivists alike, "a scientific proving-ground of their ethical outlook, precisely because no contradiction was seen to exist between an economic science and humanism."[25] This outlook was certainly shared by Pigou.

Indeed, in 1901, just after he retired from active participation in the Union Society but before election to King's, Pigou contributed a chapter on private charity to a solidly new-liberal collection of essays dealing with urban poverty. The volume, titled *The Heart of the*

Empire: Discussions of Problems of Modern City Life in England,
was edited by a young and prominent new liberal, C.F.G. Masterman, with whom Pigou had become acquainted at the Union Society. Masterman, like Pigou, had been the Union's president and had
returned to the debating chamber throughout Pigou's undergraduate years to speak against imperialism.[26] But whereas Masterman
spent his time after Cambridge primarily in the slums of southeast
London, Pigou remained comfortably ensconced in his rooms in
King's. [27] Pigou was well aware of this difference, and he began
his contribution to Masterman's book with the disclaimer that he
was "unable to claim practical experience of life in the poorer parts
of London."[28] But though he was not fighting the battle on poverty from the trenches, his essay's publication took a clear political
stand for reform. He cited the existing "mass of misery and degradation" that comprised some 30 percent of London's population
as compelling reason to more systematically coordinate disparate
charity efforts into an effective program of moral and material up-
lift.[29] Moreover, *The Heart of the Empire* was published while the
Second Boer War continued to rage. In its implicit suggestion that
Britain's most pressing problems were social ills at home—at the
"heart of the empire"—the book challenged the increasingly unpop-
ular conflict, and by extension, the sitting government responsible
for it. For many new liberals, the expenditures of an imperialist war
in Africa ran diametrically counter to responsible social policy.[30]

Pigou embraced many of the ethical and social commitments
that characterized new liberals, with whom he rubbed shoulders at
events like the Hunt in the Lake District, but it should be remembered that he often found himself at odds with some of the thinkers
most closely associated with the term.[31] Figures like J. A. Hobson
and L. T. Hobhouse have been seen as intellectual opponents of the
early Cambridge economists, who considered them less rigorous in
their pursuit of social science.[32] Though Cambridge economists felt
the general pull toward more social forms of liberalism, Marshall—
and Pigou—stayed closer to traditional utilitarian doctrines. As
Freeden wrote, "two major aspects of utilitarianism were discarded
by the new liberals: its ahistorical approach and its exaggerated faith
in the power of the expert."[33] Cambridge economists at the turn of
the twentieth century might have challenged these tenets, but they

hardly abandoned them. In fact, the scientific expert was to remain central in Pigou's thinking for the better part of his intellectual life.

With fellowship and academic appointments in 1902, Pigou's writings, both economic and political, took on a more theoretical slant, one that would highlight his Cambridge affiliation. As Marshall's protégé, he was at the forefront of an intellectual movement that was rapidly gaining ground. The designation of "Marshallian" was an imprecise marker, but it was one that Pigou wholeheartedly embraced. Marshall had provided economics with a system, a comprehensive framework for approaching economic analysis. He presented a theory of how people operated "in the ordinary business of life," generally applicable across historical time and space.[34] And indeed, many of the most prominent features of this framework have persisted up to the present in economics curricula. The importance placed on rates of change in price, cost, and value; the notion of a "national income"; the importance of consumer surplus, which will be discussed later; and the now-ubiquitous supply and demand curves were key components of the Marshallian approach.

To be a Marshallian in the early 1900s, therefore, was to be someone who wielded these tools—these basic models of human behavior—in a manner that generally resembled Marshall's own systematic use of them. No one did so as faithfully as Pigou. It was Marshall's system of thought that Pigou taught in his lectures on foreign trade and on general economics that he billed as "not generally suitable for beginners."[35] Similarly, it was Marshall's system that he used in composing his articles for *The Economic Journal*, to which he contributed about two short articles per year starting in 1902. The very titles of Pigou's pieces marked his association with Marshall's theoretical approach, as opposed to the more statistically rooted historical school. He authored "A Point of Theory Connected with the Corn Tax" in 1902 and "Pure Theory and the Fiscal Controversy" two years later. Other articles of his from the period included "Some Remarks on Utility" and "Monopoly and Consumers' Surplus," both of which focused on elements central to Marshall's foundations: the analysis and measurement of utility and surpluses.[36] Though these early contributions were not groundbreaking, they demonstrated Pigou's easy facility in deploying Marshall's methods.[37]

As Pigou focused on economic theory for his academic responsibilities, he applied the same analytic approach to questions of politics. Despite his mentor's efforts to differentiate economics from older methods of political economy, Pigou found himself musing on the "parallel" nature of political and economic theory. In June 1902, he wrote a short comment in *The Economic Journal* in which he argued that the basic economic ideas of supply and demand as well as the difference between the short term and the long term had clear analogues in political science. His purpose, he explained, was "to suggest, by means of an analogy, that the more elaborate [economic] discussions are not so far removed from the sphere of real life as the impatient reader is inclined to suppose." In short, Pigou used politics as a means to explain foundational economic ideas. Focusing on the distinction between short- and long-run periods, he suggested that the same time horizons existed in the system of parliamentary democracy.

> From a short period point of view the idiosyncrasies of particular ministers will generally be the dominant factors in determining legislation, just as in economics temporary manipulations of the market may, for the moment, entirely overbalance in importance the deeper causes governing normal values.

In the long run, however, the young idealist thought it "quite clear" that "the will of the Cabinet . . . is itself dependent upon the more slowly moving will of the people."[38]

Pigou's words demonstrated not only his engagement with the Marshallian analytical framework but also a fundamental tension in his relationship with the common man, a stress that was to linger in Pigou's work for the next fifty years. On the one hand, he seemed to value the slow-moving equilibrium of popular sentiment—demonstrating an firm belief that it was the people, nebulously defined, who were the ultimate holders of political power. Their will, in a democracy, was the arbiter of legitimacy, and rightly so. Yet the note was intended, Pigou wrote, to educate the frustratingly slow "man in the street." Good economic analysis, he plaintively held, could "find but a small public, whereas expositions which are easy and short and obvious—and wrong—are perused with avidity and consecrated as the oracles of Science."[39] By using the simple

metaphor of politics, he sought to lower his language to a common denominator, to avoid the "fine-drawn academic subtlety by
which the practical man is so apt to be repelled."[40] Pigou, who so
respected the ultimate will of the people, was himself repelled by
the "practical men" who, in aggregate, composed its body.

The conflict between Pigou's admiration for democracy and his
contempt for everyday people "in the street" found striking expression in his continued and fervent participation in the debates over
tariffs. Free trade was one of the dominant political issues of late
nineteenth- and early twentieth-century Britain and a cause that
would captivate the public and energize the Liberal Party.[41] At its
heart was a commitment to openness and transparency, coupled
with a corresponding deep suspicion of protected special interests.
In the British context, tariffs effectively meant subsidizing large land-
holders while damaging the competitiveness of the large swaths of
Britain's industrial north that produced goods for export. Moreover,
it was argued that since protection drove up prices, it would also dig
into the consumer's pocketbook. Thus, for free traders, "protection"
was just the protection of a particular group of individuals—those
who supplied the home market—at the expense of everyone else.

In suggesting that tariffs would hurt "everyone else," the free
trade doctrine depended on a particularly Liberal understanding of
how the individual related to the social, namely, through consumption. As a movement, free trade was built around a figure that Frank
Trentmann has aptly called the "citizen-consumer."[42] To Liberal
eyes, consumers did not constitute a special, but instead, a general
interest group. For in a democratic market culture, such as the one
that was evolving in cities and towns across Britain in the late nineteenth century, *everyone* consumed. Tariffs, the argument went, directly assaulted the consumer by raising the cost of everyday life.
Pigou and other liberal economists heartily embraced the figure of
the consumer as representative of the public interest—it is not for
nothing that Marshall sought to maximize *consumer* surplus. But
although the consumer was understood to be a nearly universal category, it was also clear that some consumers were hurt more than
others by the higher prices that tariffs engendered. Because the poor
were disproportionately impacted by duties, free trade positioned
itself as inherently opposed to a regressive alternative.

Free trade had been an important issue in British politics during Pigou's time at the Union, but it became the country's central political flashpoint after the end of the Boer Wars in 1902.[43] Whereas the tariff debates had started as largely economic and social arguments, over the course of 1902 and 1903, they became increasingly tied up with questions of empire. The shift stemmed largely from the efforts of Joseph Chamberlain, a self-made businessman from Birmingham who had risen through government ranks to become Colonial Secretary. One of the driving forces behind the lengthy war in South Africa, he emerged from the costly conflict with a heightened taste for empire and an appreciation of the loyalty of the former colonies—a loyalty that had been paid for by Canadians, Australians, New Zealanders, and many others, in blood. With the end of the war, Chamberlain began casting about for ways of keeping the Empire unified. Absent blood, he settled on money. In his vision, tariffs that protected imperial trade between Britain and her colonies and dominions—that is, a system of "Imperial Preference"—would bind the empire together.[44]

Like other Marshallian economists and, indeed, many other Liberals, Pigou was unmoved by the new geopolitical rationale for protection. Still, he was reticent about engaging in public rhetoric. In 1902, as the debate heated up, Pigou penned a letter to the editors of *The Speaker*, a Liberal magazine, in response to an article about duties on grain. Though Pigou was strongly opposed to such tariffs, his principal contention was that economists should not directly enter into specific political discussions. It was not "the duty of our eminent professors to descend into the arena of politics and 'give counsel' to the Government through the public press." The rationale was simple: if professors "had spoken upon this matter they would have weakened their authority, which at the present time it is especially important that they retain."[45] Public perception of professorial objectivity was to be protected at all costs.

That Pigou would abstain early on from public debate because of his commitment to scientific detachment is particularly striking, given his continued belief in free trade. For, in truth, Pigou was chomping at the bit to argue against tariffs, as he had since 1898 at the Union Society. In 1902, he wrote popular articles for two liberal publications, the *Pilot* and *The Westminster Gazette*, in addition to a detached theoretical article on the subject.[46] In all three submissions, Pigou took a very reserved tone and couched his points as theoretical rather than practical. In 1903, in an article for the Liberal *Fortnightly Review*, he did list the various "plainly ill-considered" logical errors of tariff reformers, dismissing arguments for Neomercantilism and noting that tariffs on basic goods would disproportionately hurt the poor.[47] Still, his *Fortnightly Review* article did not overtly advocate for free trade but presented itself as only correcting popular misconceptions. Like the letter to the editors of the *Speaker*, the piece sought to maintain economic arguments as the exclusive legitimate preserve of technically trained practitioners. "Economic science," Pigou wrote, "is not a subject in which persons, however eminent, can expect, without special training, to negotiate an argument successfully."[48] He self-righteously continued: "If the public can be brought to see that even . . . [distinguished men] find themselves 'in wandering mazes lost' when they set out on predatory excursions into the domain of economics, the conclusions of 'the man in the street' may perhaps assume a less wild and confident tone."[49]

As ill-conceived economic arguments began to appear in the popular press with greater frequency, Pigou found his tenuous abstention from public advocacy ever harder to maintain. He finally caved in the summer of 1903, when he joined thirteen other economists in writing an open letter to the *Times* to offer academic, though hearty, support of free trade.[50] The list of signatories included many of the most prominent economists in Britain. Marshall signed, as did F. Y. Edgeworth, J. S. Nicholson, and L. R. Phelps, the then editor of the *Economic Review*. It went without saying that Pigou would stand with his teacher Marshall, for tariff reform was a highly divisive issue, not just nationally, but also locally among Cambridge economists. With Marshall and Pigou supporting free trade and H. S. Foxwell and William Cunningham (returned from America) backing tariffs, the issue added a political dimension to the widening split between the remaining historical economists and the increasingly dominant Marshallians.[51]

After the very public summer manifesto of 1903, Pigou engaged more and more in popular debate. Over the summer, he wrote his first book, a very short one, on trade barriers. *The Riddle of the*

Tariff, which was published in October, took a tone of analysis rather than argument, and Pigou claimed that he dwelt on economic aspects rather than political ones as he lacked "the practical knowledge needed for forming an adequate judgment." But though Pigou pitched the book as a heuristic enterprise, it was a tract intended for "the general reader," with political implications easily discernable beneath the veil of scientific inquiry.[52] Over the next four months, Pigou wrote five letters to the editor of the *Times,* all with a clear free trade agenda, in which he sparred with other contributors and even directly challenged Foxwell.[53] Still, he did not advocate in popular terms but in distinctly academic language, and in general, remained significantly more restrained than many of his colleagues, who shed their detachment. Edwin Cannan, a Liberal economist at the London School of Economics (LSE), declared that the statements of pro-tariff politicians made his "blood boil."[54]

Nevertheless, there was no question that Pigou was taking a public political stand. At the end of 1903, he wrote a scathing condemnation of tariff reform, in which he analyzed the monetary costs associated with the system of Imperial Preference put forward by Chamberlain. He estimated that the program would cost the United Kingdom £500,000 from higher prices alone.[55] He further calculated that the transfer from "general consumer to agricultural landlord" would be well over £3 million.[56] At home in Cambridge, Pigou returned to the Union's debating chamber alongside Trinity College philosopher J.M.E. McTaggart in October 1903 to unsuccessfully oppose "the reconsideration of our Fiscal Policy, as proposed by Mr Chamberlain."[57] Later, in response to Cunningham's decision to offer free public lectures in support of tariff reform, Pigou; McTaggart; and another fellow of King's, H. O. Meredith, began a lecture series of their own.[58] By the following summer, in a review of a pro-tariff book in *The Economic Journal,* Pigou was making fewer pretentions to objectivity. After characterizing the book as "disappointing," with a weak and inconsistent argument, he admitted that it was possible that "in forming this judgment, the reviewer may have been biased by his distaste for certain of the conclusions reached. If that is so, he can only ask pardon for a frailty that is not uncommon."[59]

In 1904, Pigou became the secretary of the newly formed Cambridge Free Trade Association, signing his name to the many announcements and invitations it circulated. The group's president, Arthur Elliot, was the editor of the staunchly Liberal *Edinburgh Review*, to which Pigou would contribute anonymous articles in 1904 and 1906.[60] As an entity organized to promote free trade candidates for Parliament, the Association faced an uphill battle. Until 1950, the University of Cambridge was a separate constituency supporting two members of parliament. Alumni, therefore, cast two ballots in elections: one in their home constituency and one for the University seats. The Cambridge Free Trade Association advocated in both the local and university elections, but since 1885, both the University's two seats as well as the borough's seat had been firmly in the landed Conservative camp and were to remain so throughout the first decade of the twentieth century. In spite of the relatively inclement political atmosphere, the group held meetings and hosted speakers in the Cambridge Guildhall—the politician George Goschen spoke in 1905, for instance—and by 1906, the Association boasted 280 members and 372 "sympathizers."[61]

That year, political agitations reached a feverish pitch just before the general election, in which the Association unsuccessfully backed the popular Conservative incumbent John Eldon Gorst, who had broken with his party and was running as the "Free Trade" candidate in the university race. The election provoked Pigou's most substantial academic effort in support of free trade: a new book titled *Protective and Preferential Import Duties*, published a few months before the vote that would decide the issue. By this point, he was so keen to get his ideas in print that he offered to publish at his own expense.[62] Inside the book, however, Pigou retained his academic tone and wrote in cautious language wrapped in economic theory that was more or less inaccessible to the lay reader. When he proposed the book to his publisher, Macmillan, he noted that it was "designed to be, not polemical, but scientific, and it does not deal except incidentally with popular arguments."[63] He reiterated these claims in the book's introduction, stipulating that he dealt only with economic issues related to tariffs. Of the other issues, Pigou wrote, "the economist has no peculiar knowledge; his science can tell him nothing, either of what they will be or, when their nature is given, of the relative importance belonging to them and to the economic effects proper."[64]

In theory, the economist's role was to be that of a technical consultant, one whose respected objectivity would translate into popular influence. Pigou recognized that though economics and politics were meaningfully related, they inhabited distinct spheres, and that of the two, the political was of greater immediate importance. Regardless of their merits, economic arguments for free trade would only be of use in so far as they affected political decisions. Indeed, Pigou recognized that his own economic justifications for keeping trade barriers open were not those "of first rate importance." Instead, what really provided the decisive case against Tariff Reform was that "in England, the supreme financial authority is, not a bureaucracy, but a Ministry subject to the control of Parliament. In view of the many and great interests which a protective tariff might affect, it is too much to hope that those who controlled it would be left unhampered in the contemplation of their intellectual task."[65] There simmered, in Pigou's words, a profound distrust for the machinations of democratic politics and popular administration. All of Pigou's rigorously justified economic arguments were superseded, even in his own mind, by a frank recognition of the limitations of popular rule. With a touch of sardonic irony, he adopted the tone of the detached academic, quite unconcerned with popular [mis]conceptions, interested only in ensuring that those in charge of the national economy were devoted to "their intellectual task" and not unduly influenced by more worldly concerns.

Ultimately, for all his political agitation, Pigou cherished a conception of the economist as truth bearer. Whether the general public chose to accept economic truths was, though important, not to be the immediate concern of the economist. But, of course, in presenting economists as noble scientists, Pigou worked to cement their authority and thereby improve the likelihood that the truths they presented would be recognized as such. Thus, though Pigou certainly sought to argue against trade barriers, he was quick to couch his assertions in academic qualifications. As he held in the 1902 letter to *The Speaker*, the legitimacy that the economist's opinion could carry was dependent on a perception of objective detachment. To make his economic argument convincing to a general audience, Pigou would need to set boundaries for his political engagement. More generally, as someone close to Marshall and thereby invested in the project of legitimizing a new breed of professional economists, Pigou did not want to make himself—or his Marshallian colleagues—appear merely partisan.

Formulation of Pigou's Ethics

Pigou's fears of tariff reform—and with them his public advocacy against the program–evaporated as voters delivered the Liberals, with their free trade agenda, to power in a landslide victory. In September 1906, after the election, Pigou penned another reflection on the connection between political and economic theory. His view had certainly evolved. Whereas the 1902 article had suggested a "parallel," the 1906 piece, published in *The Economic Journal*, claimed a "unity" to which the two fields both belonged. In its suggestion that the free working of a democratic system was a manifestation of a natural order, much like the forces of supply and demand, Pigou's piece was smug. Though "lagging" could occur in the short term, in the long run, supply and demand would perfectly equilibrate. So, too, Pigou wrote, when a piece of legislation was demanded, those "existing firms and ministers in power occupy a position of independence over against demanders. . . . In fact, the governing body is, as a rule, a unity, and its analogue is the industrial combine exercising the privileges of a temporary monopoly." Like a firm, the government in power might try to advertise, to generate demand for policy where there was none before. "Chamberlain's repudiation of Free Trade" was a "prominent illustration" of this effect.[66] In the end, however, the lag was resolved when the full weight of the demand for free trade was brought to bear on the current government. With that, the Conservatives lost control of the country for the first time in two decades, and national politics was restored to its natural equilibrium. The "people," after all, were not seen to be so incompetent when they voted for the right policies.

Pigou's article, "The Unity of Political and Economic Science," expressed a triumphal conception of legislative history advancing in an inexorable march toward progress. In it, Pigou ostensibly offered a positive theory about the way politics and economics functioned: although local phenomena might temporarily impede the general trends predicted by the laws of social science, in the long term, the laws held fast. But Pigou was making more than a value-neutral observation. He was thrilled that the Liberals had prevailed in the election, and it was obvious that article was precipitated by the pleasing victory at the polls.

In this light, Pigou's subject matter— the unity of political and economic science—is especially important. Pigou reacted to a political event by writing on political theory, which despite all claims to the contrary, was laden with extra-scientific emotion. And just as he had claimed in his article, Pigou's political and economic science functioned in similar ways. His economic analysis was no less motivated by normative commitments than was his analysis of politics. Indeed, throughout his life, Pigou never fully divorced his economic theory from his feelings on economic practice and economic consequences in society. The result was that his economics was always shot through with his ethical commitments. For Pigou, positive science and ethical theory were most useful when paired together. Ethics justified science and, in turn, science translated ethics into practice.

Pigou's first full-length book, *The Principles and Methods of Industrial Peace* (1905), demonstrated the extent to which his ethics and economics intertwined.[67] Emerging from a series of eight lectures Pigou delivered at University College, London, beginning in April that year, the book offered a rigorous analysis of the bargaining positions of industrial firms and trade unions.[68] It was, in the first instance, a mature expression of Marshallian thought applied to a typically reformist liberal problem: the determination of the most economically efficient and socially desirable ways to resolve labor disputes. Written by a man who earned his keep by teaching advanced courses on economic theory and foreign trade, the text was backed up with three appendices stocked with graphs and equations—careful analyses of wage fluctuations and bargaining diagrams, on which Pigou had collaborated with his friend J. M. Keynes.[69]

In the preface, Pigou profusely thanked Marshall "for the suggestion of this subject, ... for detailed criticism, for encouragement, and for general guidance."[70] It was, Pigou wrote, his "privilege" to be

Marshall's pupil. But though, as Pigou informed his publisher, the book's methodology was that of Marshallian "concrete economic analysis," its inquiry was "an ethical one," born from a reformist impulse. Its animating purpose was to serve as a "mild palliative of human ills."[71] In it, Pigou argued that in addition to the direct economic benefits—to workers, to employers, and to the general consuming public—industrial peace cultivated improved "moral," and "sympathetic" connection between management and labor.[72] Peace was to be affected, in principle, through an agreement to adjust wages according to an objective standard determined by economic science, one that took into account changes in labor supply and in consumer demand.[73] In practice, industrial peace was to be maintained by independent, impartial arbitrators, who ought possess both "practical knowledge" of the industry and "general economic knowledge," of the kind presented in Pigou's book.[74] As an ultimate backstop, Pigou argued that the state ought have the power to compel arbitration, at least with regard to important industries "whose interruption seriously injures the public." In advocating such a state-centered policy, both "safeguarded . . . against grave disasters" and open "to the future development of a gradual advance towards a better condition of life," he took the familiar line of a reformist Liberal.[75]

After *Industrial Peace*, Pigou continued to act the part of the Marshallian economist. In 1906, he took over teaching Marshall's advanced theoretical course at Cambridge on "Analytical Difficulties," and in the following year he began teaching as a lecturer at King's as well.[76] He wrote frequently and passionately as an economic commentator, ever attentive to maintaining and managing the public perception of the economic profession. Yet his interest in ethical issues also remained strong.

In 1907, Pigou was consulted as an academic expert by the Royal Commission on the Poor Laws, for which he composed a technical memorandum on the measurable economic costs associated with relief programs, both in terms of the size and distribution of national wealth.[77] Pigou argued that in the first instance, the poor laws "react upon the value of people as ethical personalities," and he expressed concern about relief curtailing industrious "economic virtues."[78] Though his memorandum, which he wrote in 1907 while traveling with Corrie, was less overt in its normative commitments than was his 1901 chapter on private charity on which it was based, his Liberal values were clearly on display. These values were in step with those of the Commission's subsequent Minority Report, compiled largely by the Fabian socialist Beatrice Webb and researched partly by a young William Beveridge, a rising Liberal reformer and future architect of Britain's National Health Service.[79] Like Webb and Beveridge, Pigou endorsed both a system of aid to the poor that was differentiated according to the recipient's opportunity to be employed and a national compulsory insurance scheme.

By 1908, he had also published several essays on issues in moral philosophy and was engaged in exploring the ethical questions that were anterior to economic considerations. In fact, nearly half of Pigou's publications before 1908 concerned topics that were not, strictly speaking, those of economic theory. Much of this was due to the general influence of reformist liberalism—the first decade of the twentieth century was a time of great ferment and success for Liberals and socialists interested in reforming a host of issues, including the Poor Laws, workmen's insurance, the burden of taxation, and the power of the aristocracy.[80] Yet a good part of the reason for Pigou's attention to ethics was also due to the changing landscape of Cambridge philosophy.

To a significant degree, Pigou's ethical writings responded to the 1903 publication of G. E. Moore's *Principia Ethica*.[81] One of the founders of analytic philosophy, Moore had suffered an early loss of Christian faith and brought a profound skepticism to his treatment of utilitarian as well as idealist ethics. Moore accepted the assertion of Henry Sidgwick that the good was to be known intuitively, but rejected Sidgwick's common-sense morality as well as his conventional utilitarian belief that pleasure was the sole good. For Moore and his followers, the most worthy states of mind had to do with human interaction, beauty, love, and truth.[82] Moore's ethics, as formulated in *Principia Ethica*, took Cambridge by storm. Historian Robert Skidelsky described their reception among the Cambridge Apostles, the intellectual secret society whose membership included philosopher Bertrand Russell, mathematician G. H. Hardy, and many future members of the Bloomsbury group, including

J. M. Keynes: "The Apostles were looking for an ethic which could direct attention to ends other than the duties set before the Victorian gentleman. This Moore provided for them. He unshackled contemporary ethics from its connection with social utility and conventional morality by locating its ultimate ends in goods which stood apart from the Victorian scheme of life."[83] Moore's moral system significantly changed what it meant to live rightly.[84] It seemed to liberate morality from strict conventions and open it to more sentimental pursuits like love and aesthetics. This changing sentiment was echoed in Pigou's own work. In an essay published in 1908, "The Ethics of Nietzsche," Pigou wrote, "what we [in ethical inquiry] want to discover is the nature of the *good life*."[85]

Pigou was not an Apostle, but as a young don himself in search of the "good life," he was not immune to Moore's allure. In his autobiography, Labour Party politician Hugh Dalton recalled the general excitement around the publication of *Principia* at Cambridge, noting that Pigou himself, like many others, had "accepted" Moore.[86] Certainly, Pigou read Moore and would have shared many acquaintances with the Trinity College philosopher just five years his senior. And he undoubtedly recognized the immensity of Moore's contribution to modern ethics. In a 1913 letter to Keynes concerning the formulation of his own ethical statements, Pigou inquired whether Moore had already addressed all of his ideas.[87]

Between 1905 and 1908, when he succeeded Marshall to the Chair of Political Economy, Pigou wrote and published several reflective articles that dealt principally with questions of ethics and of the "ultimate good." In their context, they largely staked out his opposition to the Oxford-based school of British idealism and its chief proponents, including T. H. Green and F. H. Bradley, which, given his Cambridge utilitarian training, was hardly surprising. The idealists were anti-empiricists, favoring a belief in an absolute reality to be accessed by the faculty of reason alone, an idea the self-consciously scientific Pigou would not countenance.[88] Yet in his challenges, Pigou also distanced himself from purely utilitarian lines of argument.

A glimmer of Pigou's discomfort with certain utilitarian categories appeared in *Industrial Peace*, in which he suggested that the causes of social realities were, "as Bentham held, in mental facts, though not of course, as he also held, in mere pleasure and pain."[89] It was not just, however, that Pigou rejected a hedonic sort of utilitarianism. In his 1907 essay, "The Problem of Good," he characterized Sidgwick and "the Utilitarians" as believing "that the only element upon which the goodness of a conscious state depends is the quantity of pleasant feeling that it contains."[90] Like Sidgwick in *The Method of Ethics*, Pigou proceeded to outline several other competing doctrines of the good. But unlike Sidgwick, Pigou did not conclude that the utilitarian position was the only logically correct one. Instead, he observed, "the only conclusion reached is that the goodness of any conscious state is, to use a mathematical phrase, a function of several variables."[91] He even shied away from the proposition that "the goodness of a total state is increased by an increase in the quantity of pleasant feeling contained in it." "States of deliberate evil-doing are conceivable," he noted, "which would be made worse and not better if they became happier."[92] Bringing an economic toolkit to the study of ethics, he elaborated on the nature of his "good function:"

> It may be held that pleasure is essential to a good state in the sense that any predominance, however slight, of pain over pleasure must always render the state as a whole bad. In my phrasing this would read that, whenever the sign of the variable pleasure is negative, that of the function is negative also. I do not accept this view, nor do I believe that it is in accordance with the ethical judgments of "plain men."[93]

Precise and analytical, Pigou argued that pleasure was not the ultimate determinant of the "good" and furthermore, that common sense morality—the ethical judgments of "plain men"—tended to support his claim. This was a clear signal of divergence from Sidgwick, from whom the term "plain men" came, and who relied on common sense morality to arbitrate utilitarian ethics.[94]

In "The Problem of Good" and in other works from the same time, Pigou seemed to adopt parts of Moore's ethics, emphasizing aesthetic ideals like love and beauty as important variables in the ultimate "good" function. Though he explicitly declared his disbelief that increasing the *pleasure* of a state would also always increase its overall goodness, Pigou was less skeptical about the variable of "good will." Indeed, the presence or absence of "good will" was, as an indicator of the goodness of a state, "much more plausible" than the presence or absence of pleasure.[95] Love, too, was an important variable in the "good function."[96] In short, Pigou—Keynes's "love-lorn" bachelor—treated ideals like love and good will with the same if not greater weight as that with which he treated pleasure or utility. In a different essay from the same period, he held up the gospels as a source of ethical meaning, noting approvingly that for Jesus, "goodness was to *be* and not to *do* something."[97] Pigou asserted: "His . . . teaching does not . . . suggest that righteousness can be based on selfish motives."[98] Rather, it was love—both of the divine and of one's neighbor—that lay at the very heart of the Christian conception of the good as laid out in the gospels. It was "love" that made the Christian doctrine worth remembering and Jesus a "conception, a life, a character, which the world might reverence more wisely, but can never love too well."[99]

Sidgwick had grown up as a practicing Anglican and although he rejected the orthodox strictures of religious belief, he was reticent to abandon religion, even if his ethics did not hinge on the existence of God. As Keynes once put it, Sidgwick "never did anything but wonder whether Christianity was true and prove that it wasn't and hope that it was."[100] For his part, though several of his friends ultimately took the cloth, Pigou was not a religious man. Still, in his early writings on religion and theism, he was interested in incorporating Christian values into a modern ethical framework.[101] Moore's emphasis on aesthetic ideals like love and beauty, though meant to serve as a separable alternative to religion, provided just such a structure. Christian righteousness, for example, could be conceived as leading not to physical pleasure, but instead to a higher state of goodness, through increased beauty, love, and good will.

But there was also a darker side to Pigou's Moorean-inflected multivariable "good function." In his discussions of the "quality of the people," and his treatment of eugenics, Pigou demonstrated a concern with an aesthetic calibrated to a scale of Darwinian biological fitness. Starting with a short article in 1907 and continuing throughout his works on welfare economics, Pigou rigorously engaged with eugenic arguments, a step Marshall had never taken.[102] Biological considerations, to Pigou's mind, overlapped considerably with economic ones. Like economics, eugenics was ultimately a tool to serve a particular moral end. This meant that biological facts—insofar as they were useful in the improvement of society—were themselves contingent on a question that was "wholly ethical": of "what kind of society is good."[103]

Pigou's answer to that question looked considerably different from that of more extreme social Darwinists like R. H. Lock and R. C. Punnett, both a two-minute walk away at Gonville and Caius College, who argued that human progress was entirely contingent on gametes.[104] In his 1907 article, Pigou issued a strong corrective to eugenic arguments: "The entity which biology declares to be unaffected by ancestral environment is a different entity from that to which the conception of progress applies."[105] Human "quality" could be improved through education and moral structures, which spanned generational lines. "The environment of one generation *can* produce a lasting result," he would later write, "because it can affect the environment of future generations. Environments, in short, as well as people, have children."[106] Still, like many other economists of his day, Pigou thought that in "extreme cases" of "tainted persons"—"the imbeciles, the idiotic, the sufferers from syphilis and tuberculosis"—policies of sterilization could be justified on grounds of "social improvement." Society was comprised of a highly heterogeneous—and stratified—populace, and Pigou was all for differentiating between the various strata.[107] He "tentatively" suggested that the "original properties of the poor as a whole are worse than those of the rich."[108] Certainly, the poor were the "morally and socially lowest classes in the community," and because they reproduced with greater rapidity than their social betters, steps might usefully be taken to limit their propagation.[109] But of course, eugenic considerations were only one element of Pigou's complex ethical framework, affecting only select variables in his function of the good.

In the final analysis, the most salient feature of Pigou's ethics was its imprecision. There was not one "good," but many. And Pigou was more concerned with moving in the right direction than he was with defining the parameters of a rigorous "good function." He made this intention explicit in *Industrial Peace*, in which he sought to offer a scientific solution to the problems of industrial strife between labor and management. Though he admitted that the project was an ethical one, he declared that it could "be conducted without reference to those fundamental controversies in which the science of the 'good' is involved." A true solution would be palatable to ethical thinkers of all stripes. For, "if only a scheme were found by which rich and poor could be bound together in closer unity, all schools of thought would welcome that result." Such an agreement would be "sufficient for our purpose, even though they immediately dispute as to whether it is good because it makes men happier, or because it is a step toward the moral union of the Kingdom of God."[110] This sort of pragmatic ethical pluralism would remain a hallmark of Pigou's thinking and serve as a basis for his decision to principally work on problems whose status as moral ills was universally acknowledged.

The Right Man at Hand: Marshall's Successor

For all his political agitations, Pigou had always argued that economics was to be a positive science, divorced from explicit political agendas. So if he had any reticence toward explicitly publicly discussing political issues before 1908, he was positively adamant to avoid such topics when he became a professor, which he did that year at the "preposterously" young age of thirty.[111] Pigou's ascent to the Cambridge Chair of Political Economy was a major juncture in his life, one that at once significantly narrowed the scope of his publications but also set him on a course to become the most respected academic economist in Britain. The new position carried great weight. In 1908 Britain, professorships were rare in any field but especially so in economics, for which there were only a handful in the country. And Pigou's chair held particular importance: it was Alfred Marshall's old position, the seat from which Marshall had shaped the discipline of economics as practiced at Cambridge and in universities across Britain and the empire. Not only did Pigou take Marshall's institutional place, he was Marshall's student and chosen man for the job. In his inaugural lecture, Pigou asserted: "It will be my earnest endeavour to carry on and develop . . . the work that . . . [Marshall] has begun, and to pass forward to others what I have learned from him."[112]

Despite its growing importance, the Marshallian line's continuation had not been a foregone conclusion at Cambridge. The process of appointing, or "electing," a new professor was left to a small committee, drawn from both inside and outside the university, and Pigou's own election proved especially political and hard fought, with the electors splitting along both ideological and methodological lines. His chief competitor for the position was H. S. Foxwell, one of Marshall's oldest friends and a lecturer at Cambridge since 1874.[113] Foxwell, however, was a stalwart of the so-called historical school and thus predictably came into conflict with Marshall on matters of theory.[114] There was also friction over national politics, as Foxwell was one of the few economists to have supported the cause of bimetallism (a system whereby currency was pegged to both gold and silver) in the late 1800s, as well as that of tariff reform in the early 1900s.[115]

Foxwell himself thought his public disagreement with Marshall over tariffs had cost him Marshall's support for his bid for the professorship and certainly, it widened the rift between the two men.[116] But a host of other factors affected the election's outcome. Pigou, after all, had long been mentored by Marshall, and Foxwell had chafed at Marshall's attachment to Pigou for just as long.[117] As early as May 1901, J. N. Keynes had noted in his diary, "Marshall is putting on Pigou as a Lecturer in Political Economy and the relations between him & Foxwell are very strained."[118] Jealous and hurt, Foxwell, who was known for his temper, vented to Keynes that Pigou was the "least qualified to deal with a general class, as he is such a prig!"[119] Matters were not helped by the fact that Pigou and Foxwell had decidedly different styles of economics; Pigou found the historical school outdated, and Foxwell objected to "smart fencing with abstract principles à la Pigou."[120] In 1906, in an effort to push Foxwell and Cunningham out of teaching for the Economics Tripos once and for all, Marshall suggested that Foxwell focus more on history and let other, younger colleagues (read: Pigou) take over his economics course load. In the lead up to his own retirement and the mid-1908 meeting of the men who would decide his successor, Marshall campaigned heartily for his student, "incensing" one elector, J. S. Nicholson, with his "maneuverings."[121] J. N. Keynes was also an elector, and to secure his support for Pigou, Marshall may have hinted at a conditional offer of a lectureship to his son, Maynard.[122] The pressure mounted until it was sufficient for the older Keynes to confide to his diary, "I very much wish that I were not an elector."[123] In the end, Pigou won a narrow majority of the votes.[124] With that, the delighted Marshall sent Foxwell what the latter described as a "very fulsome letter," in which Marshall freely admitted that "Pigou is . . . likely to be recognized ere long as a man of quite extraordinary genius: and I hoped that he would be elected to the Professorship."[125]

Ascending to Marshall's chair had an immediate effect on Pigou's self-fashioning. "Before I was elected professor, I used to do a certain amount of political speaking, chiefly in connection with Free Trade," he wrote to fellow economist Roy Harrod much later in life. "But after election, I decided to cut out politics altogether."[126] Ethics also receded from Pigou's scope of publication. At the time of his appointment, the manuscript for Pigou's collection of essays, *The Problem of Theism and Other Essays*, had been sent to print, but the book had not yet been released. Pigou, now a professor, found himself "in a position of some embarrassment as regards the publication of a book of philosophical essays immediately after my somewhat unexpected election to the Cambridge chair of political Economy."[127] In a letter to his publisher, Pigou noted that he had revised the preface of the book, which now stressed that the essays were "the result, not of my main work, but of a by-occupation, and that they do not pretend to deal with the subjects discussed in them from the standpoint of a professional student."[128] But editing the preface was evidently not enough. In light of his intervening election, he wrote, "I wish also to ask you, in any advertisement that you may publish, not to stress—if possible not to use—my title of Professor of Political Economy."[129]

Pigou's explanation for this request was that he did not want "to give the impression that I have rushed into print . . . essays on a different subject directly after my election and am using the fact of the election to push the sale of the essays."[130] Yet there was another rationale lurking behind the proffered one, related to honoring the value Alfred Marshall placed on the modern scientific tools of the newly formed economics profession. It was all well and good to claim in his inaugural lecture that ethics had an important place in economics, but to publish explicitly on moral philosophy was another matter entirely.

Pigou did not wish to tarnish his new title—Marshall's title—with anything that would leave so much as a smudge. He needed to carry on his teacher's commitment to the creation of a respected discipline of economics, not divorced but distinct from the moral sciences, from ethics, from anything that was not scientific. For the stakes of presenting such a scientific face to the general public were high. A bloody intramural battle had just been fought on this very issue. Writing to Foxwell, an avid book collector, Marshall had once noted: "Of course our ideals in economics are different. I have noticed that when a book or pamphlet pleased you greatly you describe it as 'scholarly' whereas I am never roused to great enthusiasm about anything wh(ich) does not seem to me thoroughly 'scientific.'"[131]

Marshall had ensured Pigou's election on the premise that his successor would be not merely a scholar but a scientist. Had Pigou continued to publish on politics and ethics, he would have failed to fully live up to Marshall's expectations of him. Marshall did not suggest that the economist operated with—or needed to possess—a fully scientific objectivity; as his biographer Peter Groenewegen notes, his "views on the objectives of economics were never constrained by a positivist agenda of normative/positive economics."[132] He was, however, keen to steer his fledgling discipline away from accusations of merely providing post facto justifications for given policy agendas.

It was for the same reasons that Pigou refused to wade into political debates after 1908. Pigou already had ample evidence of the damage politics could wreak on credibility and professionalism. Free trade had, after all, been a major issue in his own election. And although after losing out to Pigou, Foxwell recognized him as "a brilliant man," he lashed out at the former's partisanship in a letter to a friend: "he is young . . . and has been an extreme agitator on a side not popular either here or among influential people in the country."[133] It was in this context that, seeking to preserve his own legitimacy as well as that of his title, Pigou would limit himself to topics that could not be mistaken for anything except economics. He would become a pure economist of the chair.

CHAPTER THREE

Bearing Fruit
as Well as Light

PIGOU'S WELFARE ECONOMICS

AT THE TIME OF HIS ELECTION, Pigou was relatively untested and, despite Marshall's faith in his "quite extraordinary genius," the electors who voted for him were betting on future accomplishments. One such elector was F. Y. Edgeworth, the Drummond Professor of Political Economy at Oxford and one of Marshall's key ideological allies. Edgeworth did not have to wait long to see his bet pay off. In 1913, he glowingly reviewed a book by Pigou in *The Economic Journal*, of which Edgeworth had previously been the longtime editor.[1] "Originality," he wrote, "has set its unmistakable mark on Professor Pigou's work." "This treatise abounds in new ideas, but it is impossible by extracts to do justice to the author's logical arrangement of topics and lucid order." Edgeworth even used the word "brilliant."[2]

The book in question was *Wealth and Welfare*, which had appeared in shops in 1912. The treatise, some 500 pages long, served as the vindication of Marshall's and Edgeworth's faith in Pigou.[3] The precursor to the more famous *Economics of Welfare*, it also marked the formal start of Pigou's work on the economics of welfare and, arguably, the birth of the field of welfare economics. Though much greater in scope than any of his previous work, the book grew out of the same ethical and political commitments that had motivated Pigou since his days as an undergraduate. The American economist Allyn Young, in his own generally positive review, noted that in light of "recent proposals for social reform," the book took on "a distinctly fresh and unconventional flavor."[4] After all, like *Industrial Peace* before it, *Wealth and Welfare* was a book of economics with an obvious moral motivation. It concerned, as the *Times* commented, "largely a question of ethics and psychology."[5] In Edgeworth's words, Pigou drew from "two very high authorities on wealth and welfare." He borrowed a version of "Utilitarian philosophy" from Sidgwick and employed "the methods perfected by Dr. Marshall."[6]

Although the book had an ethical heart, it had a scientific head, evidence of Pigou's decision to "cut out" politics and abandon philosophical musings. In his work on welfare, Pigou, even more than Marshall, was inclined to classify economics as an *objective* science. As he noted in the first edition of *The Economics of Welfare*, it was a "positive science of what is and tends to be, not a normative science of what ought to be."[7] It was also to be an applied science. Like engineering, economics was intended, in Pigou's words, to "bear fruit" rather than just light—to yield "practical results in social improvement."[8] It was still, however, a science of abstract models, and Pigou refused to limit it "to those fields of positive scientific inquiry which have an obvious relevance to immediate practical problems." To do so, he wrote, would "shut out inquiries that might ultimately bear fruit."[9] In *Wealth and Welfare*, Pigou did not offer a collection of ad hoc solutions to temporary problems. Instead, he provided a comprehensive theoretical framework for understanding how economic welfare worked in society.

Wealth and Welfare and its successor, *The Economics of Welfare*, published in four editions between 1920 and 1932, were to do for welfare economics what Marshall's *Principles* did for economics as a whole. They would also make Pigou's name and, to a considerable degree, secure his place in history. Pigou's welfare economics was concerned with analyzing and correcting imperfections in the market that resulted in suboptimal levels of societal wellbeing. This premise—the idea that the market was not self-regulating—meant that much of the ameliorative potential of Pigou's welfare economics depended on the actions of a competent administrator located outside the market. Amid a surging public respect for science and a burgeoning pressure for government to take a more active role in the economy, Pigou's work not only made a major theoretical contribution, it was also able to provide a rigorous justification for state action at a propitious time. But Pigou's work offered another implication. By stressing his own objectivity and technical expertise, he suggested that the Marshallian professional economist was exactly the kind of enlightened authority that might help solve the economic problems he identified.

Wealthy and Well at Cambridge

Ascending to professorship at the age of thirty, Pigou had large shoes to fill, but in 1908, he was short on most credentials except potential. His publication record, while strong, was hardly what one might expect of the institutional leader of the Cambridge school of economics. Moreover, the program over which he presided, despite Marshall's guidance, was still in its formative years and in need of careful shepherding. And though Pigou had taught undergraduates for several years, he had little experience as an administrator. Student enrollment numbers had more or less stagnated since the introduction of the Tripos, and its nine instructors—to whom Marshall referred as the "brilliant, compact group of earnest men"—had widely varying degrees of economic competence.[10]

Therefore it was natural for Pigou, "the youngest professor in the youngest Tripos," to invest time in teaching, building enrollment, and establishing his discipline's position. To some extent, this is exactly what he did, taking over the general lecture course for second-year students in 1908 and offering a new course on the theory of value.[11] Though he relied on members of the older generation, including Marshall and J. N. Keynes, for support, under Pigou, the economics program expanded rapidly, with the number of enrolled students nearly doubling from thirteen in 1907 to twenty-four two years later.[12] In the words of Robert Skidelsky, Pigou supplied the faculty's "intellectual leadership."[13]

On other academic fronts, he was even more diligent. He revised an article written on land taxation in 1907 into a pamphlet that stressed the inefficiencies and "indirect costs" of taxing improvements made to land rather than the "inherent" or "public value" of the land itself. He noted that taxing improvements to the land had negative implications for social policy, as it pushed people out of the country into the cities, and for housing policy, as it incentivized cheaper construction.[14] "In both cases," he wrote, "the result is dirt, untidiness, and a general lowering of moral tone."[15] *The Policy of Land Taxation*, as the pamphlet was called, was a thinly disguised endorsement of the left wing of the Liberal Party's ambition to shift a greater burden of taxation onto large landowners in order to fund new social policies—an ambition that appeared in the famous, socially progressive People's Budget of 1909 and in the Liberal Party's platforms up until the start of World War I.[16] Despite his newfound professorial status, Pigou could not resist revisiting his 1907 article and expressing his view that the "public value of land is, economically speaking, an exceptionally good object of taxation," one that did not violate principles of equity.[17] Still, the pamphlet bore the hallmarks of Pigou's growing restraint. During a period in which the Liberal Party was successfully pursuing a host of policy priorities—social insurance, a more progressive tax scheme, labor exchanges, and the hobbling of the House of Lords—Pigou was careful not to explicitly advocate a political program, but to explore an argument. He never mentioned Asquith, the prime minister, as he had in his 1907 article, or Lloyd George, the Chancellor of the Exchequer, or even the Liberal Party itself. After revealing his support of a land value tax, he was quick to stress the "tentative" nature of his suggestions. The pamphlet thus ends on a cautious note, stressing the importance of the issue and calling for "those who advise the Government" to "devote to it much earnest consideration."[18]

A flurry of reviews written for *The Economic Journal* revealed a lengthy reading list of more specialized economic theory that drew extensively from foreign, especially Italian, authors.[19] He published a journal article on bilateral monopoly in 1908 and two more articles in 1910, one on calculating price elasticities and another on producers' and consumers' surplus.[20] The first marked the start of a limited but important body of empirical work on elasticities, which economist Angus Deaton later called "one of the best examples of indirect measurement by use of theory to be found outside the physical and biological sciences," and which Milton Friedman unsuccessfully assaulted some twenty-five years after its publication.[21] However, of the three articles, it was the last that was most striking.

Though significant in retrospect, the article presented itself as little more than a footnote to Marshall's sweeping theories of consumer surplus.[22] Marshall postulated that people only bought a good if they placed its value as equal to or greater than the money they spent on it. Thus, every time a consumer bought a good, he or she would gain a "surplus" of value. Similarly, producers only sold a good if they could derive some profit from it. This profit was also a "surplus." Inspired by utilitarian ethics and the liberal conception of the public as a collection of individual consumers, Marshall was concerned with maximizing consumer surplus, which he saw as a rough proxy for utility, throughout the economy.[23] In general, he reasoned that because of competition, the market would produce the most possible units at the lowest possible price so as to create the greatest possible surplus. However, Marshall recognized an important exception to the general rule that competition would yield "maximum satisfaction." Some industries, he suggested, were characterized by increasing returns to scale: the more they produced, the more efficiently they would be able to produce a successive unit of output. Others experienced decreasing returns to scale and found each successive unit of output increasingly costly to produce. Marshall proposed that taxing industries with decreasing returns and providing bounties to those with increasing returns could provide significant benefits to welfare. Though producers would be put at a slight disadvantage, consumers would face lower prices, resulting in a corresponding overall boost in consumer surplus.[24]

Pigou's 1910 article adopted Marshall's framework almost in its entirety, but added an important nuance: the potential divergence of individual and collective interests.[25] In a 1903 article that that had also drawn extensively from Marshall, Pigou had discussed how consumer taste for luxury items depended largely on the number of people who bought those items. Diamonds, for instance, were especially expensive, because the few people who possessed them were prestigious individuals. The price of top hats, in contrast, was kept up only because of their fashionability. The desire for a top hat, "is compounded of a desire for . . . the article and a desire to be 'in the swim.'"[26] Every purchase of a hat therefore had a first-order effect of signaling a particular level of demand for the good and a second-order effect of provoking further demand insofar as the wearing of the hat contributed to the hat's becoming popular. It was this second effect that caused private supply and demand curves to diverge from their collective counterparts. In other words, by contributing to a trend, the individual's purchase of a hat had social effects.

The 1910 article took this concept further and transposed it from consumption to production. It suggested that in industries where there were "*external economies* of improved general organization," the production of an additional unit would have a greater effect on an individual firm's supply price than on the industry's.[27] Where there were external diseconomies—as when the increased production of one firm raised the prices of raw material for all other firms in its industry—the changes to the cost of production would also be different for the individual firm and for its industry as a whole.[28] These "economies" and "diseconomies"—concepts Pigou borrowed from Marshall—led "to a conclusion of some importance in connection with the doctrine of *maximum satisfaction*."[29] Actual prices and therefore actual levels of consumption were determined by the decisions of individual firms, but these individual firms might be acting in ways that affected other firms in their industry. Because of the gap between the firm and the industry, industries might produce above or below the quantities that would be optimal for consumer surplus, or for "ophelimity," by which Pigou meant "economic utility."[30] If this were the case, Pigou asserted, the state might well take action by means of "the grant of a bounty . . . [or] the imposition of a tax on the production of the commodity" to affect a more "socially advantageous" level of production.[31] In essence, Pigou had reproduced Marshall's argument with the substitution of economies and diseconomies for increasing and decreasing returns to scale.[32] But importantly, in suggesting that because of external effects, public and private interests might diverge, the piece presaged some of Pigou's most important and original ideas.

In the autumn of 1910, as the Liberals were campaigning for a budget that would increase social welfare provision and land taxes, Pigou began work on what was to become *Wealth and Welfare*, the book in which those ideas would see their comprehensive expression. Pigou threw himself into the project; he sloughed off his main lecture course on Economic Principles to J. M. Keynes, whose father grumbled that "in many ways, [Maynard] seems to be taking Pigou's place as Professor of Political Economy."[33] The younger Keynes himself was a bit peeved that Pigou seemed to be shirking his duties and gave the latter "rather a pi-jaw" over the matter in 1911.[34] D. W. Corrie once noted that the "remarkable thing" about Pigou was how fast "he could relax from serious work and plunge with boyish enjoyment into any sort of harebrained spree and afterwards to assume the gravity of the professor of Economics."[35] Still, in spite of Pigou's ability to move seamlessly between work and leisure, Keynes had reason to grumble. Pigou was distracted from his duties at Cambridge not only by his book but also by a construction project he was overseeing in the Lake District. Between bouts of writing and supervision, he had commissioned a Cambridge friend and aspiring architect to design him a rustic lodge to be called Lower Gatesgarth, on the shores of Buttermere, just south of Keswick.[36] Thus, 1911 proved to be a busy but rosy year. As the Liberals successfully stripped the aristocratic House of Lords of its veto power and pushed through the People's Budget, Pigou was busy working on the book that would definitively establish his professional position and, at the same time, constructing the house that would serve as his refuge from the pressures of academic life.

By the first months of 1912, Pigou's house stood complete, an imposing structure set high on a bluff at the southern end of one of the most beautiful lakes in England. His book was also shaping up. In February, he wrote to tell his publisher that he had "now nearly completed" *Wealth and Welfare*, which Pigou "intended to be 'a contribution to learning,'" but one which "ought . . . to be intelligible to others than economists."[37] The spring and summer saw "the Prof" busy correcting proofs with the help of his friends Corrie and Keynes, and in the autumn, the book was released to significant enthusiasm.[38]

FIGURE 4. Lower Gatesgarth, Pigou's House in Cumbria. Courtesy of Roger Hiley.

Wealth, Welfare, and Welfare Economics

In the 500 pages of *Wealth and Welfare*, Pigou laid out his cohesive framework for considering questions of economic welfare. He would update the details of *Wealth and Welfare* for the better part of the next three decades—indeed, he began to revise it almost immediately after it was published "with the object of making it less difficult to understand and partly with that of including a number of topics not initially discussed in it." Just three years after the book's original release, these amendments and expansions were sufficiently extensive—they would double the size of the book— for Pigou to suggest a new title, "e.g. <u>The Economics of Welfare</u>."[39] But though the bulk of Pigou's welfare economics was layed out before 1915, because of World War I, the newly titled revision was not published until 1920, with subsequent editions released in 1924, 1928, and 1932. And though there were substantive amendments and changes in tone in the twenty years between 1912 and 1932—alterations that will be explored in chapter 5—the thrust of Pigou's welfare economics was never substantially altered. For this reason, the analysis of his welfare economics offered here focuses on the central, unchanging elements of his system, drawing not only from *Wealth and Welfare* but also from its significantly expanded, more systematic form, the first edition of *The Economics of Welfare*.[40]

From page one of *Wealth and Welfare*, Pigou's welfare economics was firmly rooted in ethics and imbued with optimism about Liberal reform. The book's first lines came directly from Moore's *Principia Ethica*: "If I am asked 'What is good?' my answer is that good is good, and that is the end of the matter. Or, if I am asked 'How is good to be defined?' my answer is that it cannot be defined, and that is all I have to say about it."[41] To this, Pigou added: "Welfare means the same thing as good." In setting out to study the causes and distribution of welfare, he was setting out to study the good— but, as he clarified in the next paragraph, his primary subject was not the good writ large, but only that part of the good measured in economic terms: "Of welfare in general economic welfare is one part . . . [that which enters] easily into relation with the measuring rod of money."[42] From the beginning, therefore, his welfare economics was to be a science, but a science self-consciously nested in an ethical justification.

After all, liberal social concern, shared by Pigou, Marshall, Sidgwick, and Browning, was a key force motivating Pigou's project, which in turn provided a basis for justifying redistribution from the rich to the poor. But welfare economics was not limited, as noted before, "to those fields of positive scientific inquiry which have an obvious relevance to immediate practical problems."[43] Pigou set out to create a systematic explanatory framework for what he would later describe in a letter to his publisher as "the use of productive resources."[44] *Wealth and Welfare* was correspondingly wide ranging in scope and its better-known successor, *The Economics of Welfare*, remained similarly sweeping. For Pigou, welfare economics had a deep and encompassing unifying ambition, one that had animated British economic thinkers since Jeremy Bentham and John Stuart Mill: the maximization of societal wellbeing.[45]

In this sense, welfare economics had a strong utilitarian pedigree.[46] Economists, especially those who followed a Marshallian lineage, took the utilitarian creed of quantified maximization to heart. Yet neither Marshall nor Pigou was willing to accept material prosperity or even hedonic pleasure as society's ultimate good. The "good" that Pigou was interested in maximizing resided in "states of consciousness only, and not material things or conditions." [47] Food, for example, could not be a "good," but the satisfaction that it elicited might be. This mental "good" could plausibly be thought of as a sort of utility, but for Pigou, it was not the same utility described by Sidgwick. Given the multivariable determinants of Pigou's "good function," he might be considered a utilitarian only in a loose sense of the term.

Nevertheless, driven by his ethics, Pigou's economics set itself at improving society. It did so by focusing on the maximization of a very particular part of wellbeing. An investigation into the causes of *general* welfare, as opposed to welfare of a specifically economic kind, he asserted in *The Economics of Welfare*, "would constitute a task so enormous and complicated as to be quite impractical."[48] Therefore, he sought to address only the "portion of the field in which the methods of science seem likely to work at best advantage": the part of social welfare that could be expressed in monetary terms.[49] Pigou took for granted that, all other things being equal, increasing material prosperity would make people happier and society better. This would be his goal. Though he addressed other variables in the "good function," including equality, human beauty, and good will, for the most part Pigou evaluated them only in terms of the economic, as opposed to the general, benefit they yielded. Of good will, for instance, he wrote that "if the gift of material aid is accompanied by the interest, sympathy and counsel of friends, willingness to work and save may be largely and permanently encouraged."[50]

When Pigou began writing about welfare, the principal framework in Britain for understanding distribution and maximization of economic welfare came from none other than Henry Sidgwick, who, in addition to playing a founding role in modern ethics, wrote extensively on issues of utilitarian political economy.[51] Sidgwick's key contribution to welfare economics was the assertion that the market acting by itself did not maximize a population's happiness. He had reached this conclusion by way of another: that the price of a good was not well correlated with the average utility it created. Following the work of W. Stanley Jevons, Sidgwick argued that price was determined by marginal utility, not average utility. That is, in Sidgwick's view as outlined in *The Principles of Political Economy* (1883), there were two ways of evaluating a given good: its price and its derived utility.[52] Though often conflated, these metrics were actually determined by different factors.[53] If price and utility were directly linked, anything that was free would have to produce as much disutility as utility, which clearly did not bear out in real life. The point was that if the goal set for society was to maximize utility—as it had been for utilitarians since Bentham and Mill—it was useless to rely simply on the price system to achieve the optimal distribution of resources, because the price system did not convey accurate information about levels of utility. For Sidgwick, this opened up the potential for useful and beneficial government intervention in the economy.

The idea of limited governmental intervention was not new to utilitarian circles. J. S. Mill had recognized that it was desirable for governments to provide certain goods—lighthouses, for example—that were not produced by private industry but would prove socially beneficial.[54] Sidgwick took the role of the government a step further. In particular, he was convinced that more equitably distributed wealth would prima facie increase the aggregate utility in a society. Sidgwick felt that the poor who would benefit from such a transfer would likely value money more than the rich would, an assumption dependent on the key premise that the utility preferences of all people were similar and generally comparable.[55] It is easy to see how this belief, coupled with Sidgwick's personal conviction that the general good was to be placed above the good of any given individual, would imply advocacy for redistributive government policies.[56]

Sidgwick, however, was not a radical but instead quite a tentative Victorian. Despite the acknowledged case for redistribution, he very much opposed drastic socialist programs, as he was convinced that the entire competitive capitalist system—in which he firmly believed—rested on the foundation of individual incentive. Extensive taxation schemes that put such an incentive (i.e., the prospect of great wealth) at risk could endanger the very mechanism that generated prosperity in the first place. Extreme redistribution, therefore, was out of the question, but moderate socialism that would not destroy the capitalist system was still a viable option. Gradual changes, Sidgwick argued, easily fell within the limits of economic sanity, preserving the incentive to participate in the economy while also allowing the poor a slightly larger slice of the pie.[57]

However, because of the uncertainty of reduced incentives to earn and the inability to precisely correlate utility with a metric like prices, Sidgwick's system was incapable of finding an "interior solution," a balance of redistribution and laissez-faire that would maximize or even definitively enlarge utility in a society.[58] As a result, his view on taxation in practice did not mark any significant departure from the views of more moderate Liberals like Mill or even the statesman William Gladstone. In short, Sidgwick's fear that a rigorous tax system could fuel class warfare led him, like the vast majority of his contemporaries, to conceive of it as a tool primarily for raising revenue rather than as an instrument of social change.[59]

Sidgwick, though only four years Alfred Marshall's elder, had been Marshall's mentor during the period of university reform of the 1860s and 1870s, and his work both on intuitional utilitarian ethics and on marginalism were to have a great influence on the latter's thought.[60] Though Marshall was keen to separate his own self-consciously scientific economics from that of Sidgwick, who explicitly conceived of political economy as an "art," Marshall's theoretical framework owed Sidgwick a great deal.[61] In an important sense, Marshall applied what he deemed scientific practices to Sidgwick's ethical impulses. The former's emphasis and rigorous mathematical work on marginalism made Sidgwick's prima facie case for some redistribution even stronger. Yet Marshall was also unable to find the "interior solution," the ideal balance of socialism and capitalism.[62] Both Sidgwick and Marshall had a yen for equality, but without the ability to determine all the effects of redistribution, they fretted about the loss of incentives.[63]

Like his teachers, Pigou did not locate the long-sought perfect balance between reduced incentives and a more equitable and ethically palatable distribution of resources. He did, however, provide a systematic theoretical framework for doing so, and his fundamental critique of the market left the door open wider than ever for state action. Pigou accepted that, though they were not the same metric, economic welfare and welfare often moved in parallel, meaning that *economic* welfare could serve as a useful proxy for welfare in general, at least for the purposes of his economic analysis. In doing this, he was able to quantify welfare, a luxury that Sidgwick never truly allowed himself.[64] Pigou himself recognized that using wealth as a proxy for welfare (or even utility) was riddled with uncertainties. As Amartya Sen has pointed out, Pigou's desire to link the material, commodity-based conception of economic welfare with general welfare led him "into a bit of a muddle."[65] Commodities could be only loosely linked to desire by way of money, the link from desire to satisfaction or happiness was even more nebulous, and happiness itself was only one variable in the overall "good" function. Still, Pigou's effort to quantify wellbeing came from a desire to be methodologically rigorous and was in sync with the more general movement toward the professionalization of economics as a discipline.[66] It was a move that profoundly transformed largely nebulous characterizations of wellbeing into much more easily quantifiable measures of material prosperity.

Yet Pigou, like Sidgwick, did not trust free market mechanisms to reach an optimal state of welfare, economic or otherwise. Indeed, since Pigou was more comfortable than was Sidgwick with conflating money and welfare, in important ways, Pigou's distrust of the market system went deeper than Sidgwick's. Sidgwick objected to the market system on the grounds that money prices did not fairly reflect average derived welfare. The market, because of inequalities in material prosperity, did not maximize satisfaction. Pigou agreed and, like Sidgwick, argued that this observation provided compelling grounds for redistribution. But Pigou went further. His welfare economics was predicated on the assumption that money could, at least to some degree, serve as a proxy for wellbeing. However, the market did not even maximize material prosperity throughout the economy. Thus, in his telling, it was deeply imperfect as an engine not just of utility—unsurprising in an age increasingly cognizant of the plight of the poor—but even of prosperity.

Much like Marshall and Sidgwick before him, Pigou set out to solve an optimization problem. He believed that there were three basic determinants, or criteria, of economic welfare, all related to the national dividend. The first determinant was the national dividend's overall size, the second was its distribution, and the third its variability.[67] In all arenas, he found the free market lacking. Pigou acknowledged that all other things being equal, the larger the national dividend, the greater would be the total economic welfare. One of his goals, then, was to enable the creation of the largest possible dividend. Like his intellectual mentors, Pigou held that the way to do this was to ensure that the marginal products of all resources used in an economy were equal—in other words, that no one resource's productive capacity could be improved more cheaply than another's.[68] Many of Pigou's suggestions for equalizing marginal products were highly conventional: monopolies were inefficient, as were political and physical barriers to the free movement of labor and other production inputs.

However, the market's problems ran deeper than mere impediments to the smooth operation of equilibrating forces.[69] There were what would come to be known as "externalities": economic activities whose costs and benefits operated in such a way that the price system alone could not necessarily maximize societal welfare.[70] There were already, of course, the "external economies" and "diseconomies" that existed in certain industries, about which Pigou had written in 1910. But compared to the ones on which he would focus in 1912, these were relatively small and localized—their effects mattered for the public only insofar as the public had an interest in buying the most possible at the smallest possible price.

In 1910, Pigou had followed Marshall in discussing effects external to firms but internal to industries. In contrast, in 1912, his hallmark example of an external diseconomy was pollution, a phenomenon that had effects outside any single industry. Pigou's first mention of pollution appeared in the introduction of *Wealth and Welfare* in connection with "Natural Beauty," which he deemed "the most important . . . condition of welfare other than the national dividend."[71] At the time, Britain had been undergoing a period of impressive industrial growth and urbanization for at least the past sixty years, a period of transition that threw the British idyll of green hills and pleasant pastures into stark relief with ash and soot and grime. Everywhere, industry spoiled natural beauty—"the hunt for coal or gold" destroyed scenery and, of course, there was "the desecration widely wrought by the uncontrolled smoke from factories."[72] The wanton pursuit of economic goals gave birth to a whole slew of noneconomic, even aesthetic, problems. Of course, it had provoked distinctly economic ones as well: "Smoke in large towns inflicts a heavy uncharged loss on the community in respect of health, of injury to buildings and vegetables, of expenses of washing clothes and cleaning rooms, of expenses for the provision of extra artificial light, and in many other ways."[73]

In an argument with a striking resonance to more recent debates over global warming, Pigou identified these "uncharged losses" as accruing insidiously as unseen by-products of the normal operation of industry.[74] Externalities (e.g., pollution) might cause a great deal of collateral damage (e.g., decreased health or damage to local flora and fauna), which could certainly be expressed in economic terms, but these losses were not explicitly catalogued as external effects on any balance sheet. Pollution thus silently supplemented the individual economic welfare of the factory owner at the expense of the social weal. Pigou's conception of externalities was built around an

understanding that no economic activity took place in a vacuum, so
that any economic transaction inevitably had an impact on others.
He recognized that many of those impacts were not only negative
but were also not priced by the open market. Moreover, they often
hurt wide swaths of individuals, and thereby society as a whole.

The next step was obvious. Acting as a professional scientific
economist, Pigou sought to quantitatively measure these inconsistencies and use the monetary values he found to determine
whether a given segment of the economy was operating in line with
the social good. As environmental economists have long recognized, valuing externalities was remarkably difficult, because the
costs associated with them were not always "readily brought into
relation with the measuring rod of money."[75] "Technical difficulties" of measurement prevented Pigou from offering an example
of someone successfully pricing "incidental uncharged disservices"
in *Wealth and Welfare* and the first editions of *The Economics of
Welfare*. Nevertheless his claim remained that, given sufficient time
and resources, it was theoretically possible to calculate externalities and use the result to quantify the relative benefits and costs of
an economic activity.[76] Sure enough, by the third edition, he had
found a perfect example of an effort undertaken to calculate an
"incidental uncharged disservice."[77] In 1918, the Manchester Air
Pollution Advisory Board had found that on laundry costs alone,
city residents spent conservatively £290,000 a year more than they
would have if the city had clean air.[78] This sort of quantification, in
turn, could be used to approximate an elusive interior solution, at
least a local one, and thereby justify moderate state intervention in
the form of a tax on polluters.

Pigou, like his contemporaries, only rarely used the term "the
market" to denote a force that moderated and directed economic
activity. More often, he referred to "natural" forces and phenomena: to "natural" wages, or prices, or equilibria. Implicitly, the in-
trusion of the state was in some sense artificial, unnatural. But,
for Pigou, "natural" was by no means "good," nor did it connote
tranquility. Ultimately, the market was a highly confrontational
forum—one in which an individual's wellbeing and society's wellbeing were often at odds. It did nothing to correct for "divergences
between marginal social net product and marginal private net

product": divergences between public and individual benefits.[79] That is, in seeking to make oneself better off, an individual might well, wittingly or unwittingly, compromise societal prosperity or, more generally, societal welfare. Pigou's division of social and individual wellbeing suggested that some individuals benefited materially at the general expense of society. In practical terms, then, Pigou's invention of what would subsequently become known as "externality theory" had great importance. It meant that governments could legitimately interfere in the economy to effect a better outcome with greater justification than what Marshall and Sidgwick had considered feasible.[80] Though Pigou did not advocate for any specific policy, he wrote that it was "possible for the State, if it so chooses, to remove the divergence in any field by 'extraordinary encouragements' or 'extraordinary restraints' upon investments in that field." For laudable examples of such action, Pigou turned to the tax on alcohol or the bounty for constructing housing in crowded areas.[81]

Pigou's point was that left to its own devices, the market's "natural" forces did not identify, evaluate, and take into account all the costs of an economic transaction. Practically speaking, therefore, a theoretical framework that rationalized externalities as regularly occurring instances of imperfect information or a lack of transparency in an otherwise functioning market was equivalent to a framework in which the market did not work to produce the most societally beneficial result. With hidden externalities, prices ceased to convey all the information they purported to, and the market, by itself, would not maximize welfare.[82]

This alone provided a new theoretical justification for reallocation of resources—for "bounties and taxes"—that was different from that of Marshall and Sidgwick.[83] But having held that the untended market would not necessarily produce the greatest national dividend, Pigou reprised the older justification, holding forth against extreme inequality of wealth as not maximizing the amount of enjoyment derived from a given national dividend. He wrote that inequality hurt society, because someone with very little would enjoy a given material benefit more than someone with a great deal. He also pointed out that economic welfare was derived from "the income . . . [a person] consumes rather than the income . . . [a person] receives," and since the poor spent a great deal more of their income than the rich did, redistributing to the poor would ceteris paribus increase economic welfare.[84] Rooting economic welfare in consumption rather than in overall wealth allowed Pigou to avoid part of the difficulty faced by Sidgwick and Marshall. The utility of the rich—and thereby their incentive to earn more money—would not be greatly damaged if redistribution did not negatively impact their consumption. That is, if redistribution only involved money that the rich were not going to spend on consumption, their own welfare would not be meaningfully hurt. Moreover, Pigou wrote, "of the satisfaction yielded by the incomes of rich people, a specially large proportion comes from their relative rather than their absolute amount, and, therefore, will not be destroyed if the incomes of all rich people are diminished together."[85] This line of thinking also sidestepped the old problem of incentives. As long as the rich still felt themselves to be on top, Pigou suggested, their welfare would not be meaningfully abated.

Trustee for the Poor: Pigou and Government House Utilitarianism

Pigou's welfare economics was motivated by a profoundly ethical goal: to help maximize social wellbeing. The primary beneficiaries of such a maximization would be the most disenfranchised and impoverished members of society. But though Pigou set out to help the poor, he did not respect them. Pigou, like Marshall and others before him, never made the assumption that the basic economic actor was particularly competent in pursuing his or her self-interest, and although Pigou's welfare economics predated the expression "rational economic actor," it clearly dismissed the notion out of hand. Late in life, after the term had come into use, Pigou laughingly quipped that "man is not a rational animal, and sometimes it's a good thing he isn't."[86] At the time that he formulated his welfare economics, he saw broad segments of the population as totally unfit to make even minor decisions. The masses needed leaders, or at the very least administrators, to help guide them. And few individuals, in Pigou's vision, were more qualified to guide than the economist, a figure distinguished largely by cultivated judgment and scientific detachment. In this way, Pigou fitted the model of a so-called "Government House Utilitarian."[87]

The term "Government House Utilitarianism," calling to mind the (at best) paternalistic practices of British colonial Government Houses, comes from a modern reading of Sidgwick's work by the philosopher Bernard Williams.[88] Williams paid special attention to a section of Sidgwick's *Methods of Ethics* that argued that any logical "enlightened Utilitarian" would recognize that certain utilitarian doctrines may, given existing conventions, be best propounded only to like-minded individuals and not to the general public. The utilitarian would understand that there were certain ethically valid exceptions to conventional, common sense morality, but may "doubt whether the more refined and complicated rule which recognizes such exceptions is adapted for the community in which he is actually living; and whether the attempt to introduce it is not likely to do more harm by weakening current morality than by improving its quality."[89]

At first glance, Sidgwick's conclusion was counterintuitive: utilitarians might "reasonably desire" that utilitarianism not be adopted or self-consciously embraced by a "vulgar" majority of "plain men" living in a society. The reason was that "the inevitable indefiniteness and complexity of [utilitarianism's] calculations render it likely to lead to bad results in their hands."[90] For instance, utilitarians generally believed that a more equal distribution of wealth was preferable to great inequality. A vulgar "plain man" who held this principle above intuitional, conventional ones, might be driven to steal in order to give to indigents, a course of action with undesirably chaotic results. Sidgwick's was the morality of an elite, whose membership would be determined not by wealth or political power, but by the ability to make "the distinction between theory and practice."[91]

Although no evidence suggests that Pigou consciously adopted Sidgwick's ethical theory to justify his attitude toward the general public and a differentiated subset of sophisticated thinkers, he himself was nonetheless a sort of "Government House Utilitarian." Instead of endeavoring to maximize utility, Pigou was concerned with good as a "function of several variables." But with this substitution, the model of Government House "Utilitarian" applies remarkably well to many parts of Pigovian theory as well as to his life. Pigou was a member of an academic elite insulated from financial pressures, and more than once he evinced a strong belief that the poor were not to be trusted with improving their own lot. He was, after all, raised in an age and an environment of sweeping paternalism and amidst calls to take up the "white man's burden" abroad. Hugh Dalton recalled that during one speech at the Cambridge Union, Pigou declared, "I often like to think that we here, with our greater opportunities, are trustees for the poor."[92]

It should also be recalled that Pigou's rationale in 1902 for economists' abstention from political debates was that if professors had taken a public stance, "they would have weakened their authority." This was precisely the sort of utility calculation that Sidgwick expected of his "enlightened Utilitarian." At that time, Pigou's ultimate goal was the preservation of free trade, a goal justified by his loosely utilitarian precepts. Yet in this instance, Pigou suggested that economists, the majority of whom were devout free traders, remain quiet on the issue in order to ensure that they retain their appearance of nonpartisan credibility. With this credibility—one very much linked to scientific objectivity—the professors would be able to advocate, whether publicly or privately, for free trade in the future. In short, Pigou had identified a Sidgwickian moment when it was justifiable from within a utilitarian framework not to propound utilitarian doctrine. It is not unreasonable to think of Pigou's shift away from noneconomic discussions after 1908 as the product, at least in part, of a similar calculation. Casting the veil of science over ethical questions itself suggested a moral calculation of sorts. By presenting himself as a scientist without an agenda, Pigou's ethical values remained hidden and did not interfere with the public perception of the economist as an objective observer, as someone in whom "plain men" could have full confidence. One of the reasons that Pigou decided to "cut out politics all together" was that if an economist were "an active politician, his economics will always be discredited."[93]

Pigou's theoretical work also reflected a form of Government House Utilitarianism. His economics was premised on the assumption that people—particularly the uneducated—required help from an external authority. His justification for redistribution implicitly hinged on the existence of a qualified individual or institution that could not only engage in the calculations necessary to justify intervention, but could also intervene correctly. The importance of such a figure stemmed directly from what Pigou perceived as the ignorance and stupidity of the general public, especially the poor.[94] In *Wealth and Welfare*, he pointed to several government reports that highlighted the financial mismanagement and general ignorance of the least advantaged segments of society. One report, for example, indicated that because poor parents were not knowledgeable about the relative financial merits of certain trades, they provided false information when encouraging their children to find work.[95] In a similar vein, another report, this one from the Board of Education, focused on undernourishment in children:

> It is probably no exaggeration to say that the improvement, which could be effected in the physique of elementary school children in the poorer parts of our large town if their parents could be taught or persuaded to spend the same amount of money as they now spend on their children's food in a more enlightened and suitable manner, is greater than any improvement which could be effected by feeding them intermittently at the cost of the rates.[96]

Pigou's argument was arresting. If poor parents could not even be relied on to satisfactorily spend their money on their children's food, could they, as economic actors, be relied on at all? Pigou's answer was a resounding no: "what has been said . . . should suffice to establish the thesis . . . that the poor, as entrepreneurs of investment in themselves and in their children, are abnormally incompetent." With respect to redistribution, this belief meant, as Pigou wrote in *Wealth and Welfare*, that "unless the transference of resources to the poor were accompanied by special conditions, the fund transferred would be almost entirely misspent."[97] This was a strong statement. Not only could the poor not be relied on to maximize social wellbeing (this was Pigou's assertion about *all* individual economic actors), but the poor also could not even be counted on to maximize their own wellbeing, a particularly striking assertion in a country whose working classes accounted for more than 70 percent of the population.[98] To use a more modern term, Pigou dismissed the rationality of a vast swath of the populace. Implicit in this critique was the presumption that his own rationality was of a higher order and that theorists like himself and some government officials drawn from the elite were better suited to determine the way redistributed money was utilized. It is true that Pigou's recommendations for state intervention were made in the abstract—he noted that "we cannot expect that any State authority will attain, or will even whole-heartedly seek" the ideal set out by economists.[99] But a strong "prima facie" case still remained, especially when the parameters of state action were determined by experts. These experts, presumably, would look a good deal like Pigou himself, whose welfare economics constituted one of the most sophisticated expressions of economic science produced to date, backed up by a variety of equations, graphs, and appendices.

CHAPTER FOUR

War, Peace, and Disillusionment

AFTER *WEALTH AND WELFARE* appeared in 1912, Pigou continued to direct his attention to theoretical welfare economics, working on revisions that added 300 pages to the tome's already substantial length. He also published a popular book on unemployment, drawn substantially from *Wealth and Welfare*, to positive reviews in 1913. He reviewed the latest book from the Swedish economist Knut Wicksell written in German and engaged in a debate with the Harvard professor F. W. Taussig on the finer points of monopolies and joint costs.[1] His tone, if anything, was becoming more authoritative. Yet Pigou's cultivated public face changed dramatically within two short years. World War I shook Pigou's work and his world; at no time in his life were his private thoughts about noneconomic values more public than between 1914 and 1918. Economists often grant that war is a period of exception: that policies and rules considered wise in peacetime are not applicable during wars. For Pigou, this exceptionalism applied not only to matters of economic policy but also to his own silence on policy and ethical imperatives.

The war's aftermath also affected Pigou, but in another way. Tapped to sit on a variety of government committees and commissions at its end, he eagerly boarded the train to London. This was a great chance; an association with Whitehall could enable his work to bear fruit in a way he had long imagined. Given the potential of this opportunity, the actual nature of Pigou's participation on committees was somewhat incongruous. Despite his moral outrage as the war raged, in London, his tone shifted back to one of subdued objectivity. To some extent, Pigou knew that he was expected to play the role of professor. But if, when he took on a public role, he imagined that he might be able to transcend his position and truly advise the government, he was mistaken. The war left Pigou disheartened by the human capacity for atrocity. The byzantine machinations of politics and bureaucracy left him disenchanted with something else entirely: the state apparatus, the very institution that would have to play the role of the "Government House" intervener. Thus, the war and its aftermath hollowed Pigou out; his youthful idealism was shaken, and his conception of the state as a fundamental theoretical agent in his system of welfare economics shattered.

Wartime Feelings

In 1914, two years after *Wealth and Welfare* came out, Pigou's career and fame were on the rise. Personally, he was thriving. Recollections by his friends and students describe him as an animated young bachelor. There was a garrulousness about his comportment, an energy that led Hugh Dalton to rhapsodize about the "Viking"-like mountaineer.[2] His friend Donald Corrie recalled several playful stories about "the Prof," with whom he shared rooms.[3] At one point:

> Keynes came in from a walk carrying a thick stick. He and the Prof got into an animated Economic argument and Keynes emphasizing a point brought his stick down on a parcel of Club matches on the table. The matches ignited and the Prof with lighting speed chucked the flaming exploding parcel out of the window and a shower of burning debris fell upon the head of the . . . [vice provost] walking below.[4]

With his position as professor, Pigou continued to live a sheltered and comfortable life. At the time of George V's coronation in 1911, he had paid a visit to Corrie, then living outside London. In Corrie's recollection, "the Prof" "suggested that to avoid all the fuss . . . we should hire a rowing boat + row down . . . to Oxford." Pigou bought fireworks and, after lighting them off from a bridge, "we discovered that the coloured fires had started the old wood smouldering + loads of smoke were rising from the river."[5]

"Professor Pigou," Corrie had written in a magazine profile the previous year, had "long since become one of the 'characters' of Cambridge. . . . His abstruse treatises on economics . . . have made him academically notorious at least; whilst his weakness for tattered garments and outdoor exercise of all sorts, and his oratorical outbursts at the Union have given him a status in the undergraduate world, which few fellows could hope to attain."[6]

"But," Corrie continued, Pigou was also notable for his "innate distaste for social conventionality. On solemn feast days he will desert the fellowship of his brother dons, to enjoy a simple chop and a glass of milk in the privacy of his own apartment." Pigou had never lost the "unconventional and eccentric" qualities observed by his schoolmate Jenkins. It was, perhaps, for related reasons that he "detest[ed] politics" and that not even "the prospect of high office would induce him to leave Cambridge and desert the Economic School, which he has done so much to foster." Even as a highly successful professor, Pigou would never be "widely popular."[7]

Though he wrote *Wealth and Welfare* and several articles as well as taught extensively in the period immediately before the war, he also set aside a good deal of time to spend climbing in the mountains. Pigou's supervisions were not onerous for him. In later life, his students were to be his closest friends, and he frequently invited them to travel with him. Corrie and he went to the English south coast, to the Alps, and to his house on Buttermere, to which Pigou would invite groups of Cambridge men. As an undergraduate at King's, Philip Baker (later Noel-Baker) wrote to his mother of one such "reading party" in the Lake District, noting, "we sh'd no doubt do a lot of work under the Professor's Eye. We sh'd also get valuable coaching from him: we sh'd likewise get set up physically for the term: + also have a good time."[8] From the time of its construction in 1911, Lower Gatesgarth, Pigou's handsome "cottage," provided a focal point for his extra-Cantabrigian social life. Though large, Gatesgarth was a spartan building, built of imposing local granite and devoid of creature comforts like central heating and electricity. It had only one bathroom, and the water supply came directly from a nearby stream.[9] It was to be a preserve, Pigou would later write, of "fresh eggs and all-male" life.[10] There he would entertain his students, obliging them, according to local stories, to run around the lake or up the mountain, or swim the lake before entry to the house.[11] Lower Gatesgarth would be Pigou's sanctuary for the rest of his life, a base camp for mountaineers and a retreat for friends. Yet at the time, it also represented a connection with a progressive crowd. The house sat on land belonging to a relative of Frank Marshall, Pigou's old housemaster from Harrow, who lived nearby in Keswick until his death in 1922.[12] Marshall was an outspoken pacifist and his daughter, for whom Pigou had once recommended a reading list, was a suffragette.[13] Many of the students Pigou invited were left-leaning as well.

Philip Baker certainly was. From an established Quaker family, Baker was also a pacifist, president of the Cambridge Union, and the star student of "the Prof," who, then in his early thirties, had strong feelings for him. Though the relationship was likely never romantic, its origins occurred at a period of time when "all-male" life, both at Cambridge—especially King's—and in the Lakes was a fact of existence. When the war broke out, Baker was instrumental in founding the Friends' Ambulance Unit, a volunteer organization that attracted idealists and others eager to participate in the war effort, including the historian G. M. Trevelyan, who had also been in Frank Marshall's house at Harrow and who would later also own property adjacent to Pigou's at Buttermere.[14] When Baker left for France in 1914, Pigou was anxious to "just see Phil off"; he would follow him into the Ambulance Unit a few months later during Christmas break.[15] Later, in the winter of 1915, when Pigou had returned to Cambridge, he was shocked and dismayed to discover that Baker had become engaged to Irene Noel, a friend of Virginia Woolf's some years his elder. Pigou was generally quite circumspect in expressing his feelings for Baker, but they shone through in a letter to Baker's younger sister, Josephine, then an undergraduate at Newnham College, Cambridge. Writing of the engagement, Pigou could barely contain himself, especially about the fact that Noel threatened to break off the engagement if they were not married immediately.

> To suspect oneself of being able more or less to forget Phil in three months!—and to have the chance of being with him for always. . . . It

was really that I was rather jealous—on the basis of thinking her to be quite a casual acquaintance. I shouldn't have been a bit jealous if I had though she really cared (I'm not a bit jealous of you!). . . . Oh well, she must be properly fond of him—how could she help it? . . . I'm so sorry, this is just rambling.[16]

Pigou was concerned enough to try to visit Josephine Baker, but these were the days when the all-women's Newnham College obliged male visitors to be accompanied by a chaperone, and Pigou was not about to share his feelings in the presence of a stranger. "I should like to talk to you before Wednesday," he lamented, but I suppose all the ways of doing it would be crimes!"[17] Philip Baker's wedding, at which a morning-coat-clad Pigou served as Baker's best man, took place in June 1915.[18] The marriage affected Pigou profoundly. Certainly it played a part in his decision to return to ambulance work not with Baker's unit, as he had originally done, but with Trevelyan's.

In any event, it was through his preserve at Buttermere, and his contact with Trevelyan, Baker, and Marshall, that Pigou entered the Great War. Pigou's objections, both public and private, to the fighting only grew after he joined the Ambulance Unit. He drove the wounded at Dunkirk, where, from his own funds, he bought a Ford for use as an ambulance. During the Easter and summer holidays, he would serve with Baker in Belgium and France and afterward with Trevelyan in Italy. Pigou's experiences in Europe hardened his antiwar convictions. He was horrified by the carnage he witnessed. "I have seen the shattered ruins of Ypres Cathedral," he wrote. "I have watched the mud-stained soldiery staggering homeward from their trenches; I have been near by when children in Dunkirk have been maimed and killed from the air."[19] The economic historian C. R. Fay, Pigou's friend and colleague at Cambridge, held that "World War I was a shock to him, and he was never the same afterwards."[20] Harry Johnson, a Cambridge colleague Pigou came to know after World War II, went further, asserting just after Pigou's death that "there can be no doubt that this experience was responsible for transforming the gay, joke-loving, sociable hospitable young bachelor of the Edwardian period into the eccentric recluse of more recent times."[21]

FIGURE 5. Pigou and Philip Noel-Baker at the latter's
wedding, 1915. Courtesy of King's College Archive.

Cambridge itself was radically transformed by the war. In 1910,
3,699 male undergraduate students were enrolled in the university. Just weeks after the war started, that number had fallen off by
nearly half. By the spring of 1916, there were only 575 male undergraduates in residence.[22] For a time, students were replaced by
soldiers and patients. Cambridge hosted the 6th Division of the
British Expeditionary Force, the unit's encampment spreading
over the surrounding fields all the way to the outlying village of

Grantchester. Soon, parts of Trinity College were transformed into a military hospital, as was the King's cricket ground, with a block of King's itself used to house the nurses.[23] Though not without pockets of dissent, Cambridge, like the rest of Britain, was mobilized in a burst of patriotic fervor that would wane only as the war dragged on.[24] By 1915, the town felt deserted. Everyone had gone to France.

When Britain initiated conscription under the Military Service Act in early 1916, Pigou, as an unmarried thirty-nine-year-old, was eligible for the draft. Yet Pigou was neither called up, nor did he join the ranks of conscientious objectors, a group highly stigmatized in British society, including by some of his colleagues.[25] As a teacher at Cambridge, Pigou was exempted from service, but only after it was argued by John Neville Keynes and others that his presence at Cambridge was indispensable, and that, due to other teachers being called to London, it would be "quite impossible" to carry on teaching economics without him.[26] The older Keynes's advocacy spared Pigou from military service, but it also bound Pigou to his teaching, despite his desire to return to the ambulance corps, in which he was decorated for valor.[27] He also briefly bowed to pressure to join the war effort as an economist, though he was less involved than many of his colleagues. Along with academics from other British universities, he authored a report for the Board of Trade, working part time from Cambridge as an advisor to the government on postwar employment and the reemployment of demobilized soldiers reentering the labor force.[28] Resistance to national wartime policy was not uncommon among progressive Liberals, many of whom were deeply uncomfortable with the prime minister, David Lloyd George, conscription, and the war itself.[29] Still, Pigou's sentiments put him distinctly out of step with popular sentiment. In an unpublished manuscript, he wrote that he had "been informed by one correspondent that, having thus proved myself a traitor to my country ought to be 'deported or shot with the least possible delay.'"[30] He later quoted another "brief and to the point" message he received: "May you rot for ever in the lowest cesspools of Hell!"[31]

His convictions hurt him professionally as well, repeatedly derailing his election to the British Academy.[32] In contrast, Pigou's brother had excelled in his rise through the ranks of the Royal

Navy. By the armistice in 1918, he was a commander and had been placed in charge of a cruiser.[33] By a similar series of events, his brother-in-law, Arthur Hugh Oldham, also became the acting captain of a battlecruiser.[34] Alfred Marshall, despite his own sympathy for German culture and his love of "the Germans through it all," also supported British belligerence.[35] Yet despite social, as well as likely personal and familial pressure, Pigou did not budge in his opposition to the war. In 1919, well after Germany had surrendered and Britain was basking in victory, he signed his name to a petition of notable individuals directed to Lloyd George on behalf of imprisoned conscientious objectors.[36]

The reasons for Pigou's opposition were spelled out in an unpublished manuscript written sometime between late 1915 and early 1916, after he had experienced war firsthand but before it had been decided whether he would be conscripted. Pigou explained his reticence, first in logical terms and then in more emotive language. He begged his would-be audience to recognize that the present war, like all wars, had become a "war of passion. . . . In the rich soil of an abysmal ignorance . . . [prejudice] scatters abundant seed."[37] Pigou decried the popular desire to punish Germany for atrocities "by another defeat on the field of battle." Employing stark, consequentialist language, he noted, "to anyone who reflects philosophically upon the matter to-day, it must be plain that mere revenge for its own sake and apart from its effects . . . is not a thing . . . [man] ought to pursue." Victory in the war would no longer serve as either a deterrent or a moral lesson for the Germans, since, for Pigou, by continuing the bloodshed, the Allies had already lost the moral high ground.[38] He also dismissed the promise of reparations as a justification for continued fighting. From a strictly economic standpoint, the cost of the war far outweighed the economic advantage of reparations. Yet, in the end, Pigou's most fundamental argument against the war did not make use of economics or even the cool rationality with which he dispatched popular justifications. Instead, he conjured the horrors of war, horrors that he himself had witnessed: the abject suffering and the loss of life:

> This to any humane mind must surely be conclusive—in the gamble . . .
> [of war], the stakes with which warring nations play are human lives.

Any man, be he statesman, journalist or simple citizen, who, in the hope of thereby winning an indemnity for his county, would cause the war to be prolonged by a week or by a day is bartering for money the blood of generous youths. How much agony in wounds and in disease, what array of homeless fugitives, what tale of widowed women, fatherless children, desolated friends, shall we balance against the chance of a penny off the income tax? That question it is an insult to ask.[39]

In "Terms of Peace," Pigou drew a vividly clear line between economic welfare and general welfare. In the face of so much human suffering, he found even the thought of reparations as a justification for war's continuation an insult. Some things were simply not meant to be brought into line with the measuring rod of money. It would be repugnant to value a human life, much less thousands or millions of lives, in monetary terms.

There was a profound humanity in Pigou's words. The war was perhaps the first time that he would have come into close personal contact with the "men in the street," to whom he had long condescended. The Ambulance Unit, though predominantly middle class, was composed of men from a range of social backgrounds, with "the poorest members drawing a small maintenance allowance from a special fund."[40] And, of course, Pigou would have been interacting every day with wounded and dying soldiers from across Britain and the empire. Coming face to face with "common men" in these circumstances, his reaction was deep and strong. In a rare burst of emotion, Pigou evoked of the power of unifying human experience: a reminder that pain, loss, and death affected all alike.

The war did not stop Pigou from thinking about economics or economic policy.[41] In fact, as will be discussed later, he published an important piece on the quantity theory of money in 1917.[42] War worked to further infuse Pigou's economics with both a concern for social issues as well as a fury that liberated him from his otherwise tempered positivistic objectivity. Though other economists, including the retired Marshall, wrote about the importance of capital and steeply graduated income taxes to equitably pay for the war, few were as direct or forceful as Pigou, especially on the topic of distributing the tax burden.[43] Sickened not only by the fighting itself but also by the hawkishness of the rich, he suggested in the pages

of journals and magazines a massive capital levy aimed at the very
wealthy in order to pay for the war once and for all, a proposal that
had also been made by organs of the left, including the Trades Union
Congress.[44] There was to be some justice, he suggested, in making
those who decided that Britain should go to war pay for it instead
of shouldering the innocents of future generations with a massive
debt obligation—something he discussed in a *Quarterly Journal
of Economics* article titled "The Burden of War and Future Generations."[45] It was not just the interest of the unborn that Pigou
sought to safeguard. In one version of his proposal, printed in *The
Economist*, he called for taxing individuals not at a percentage of
their income, but so as to leave all people with the same income:
"if a man with an income of £1,000 has to pay £500, one with an
income of £100,000 should pay, not £50,000 or even £80,000,
but £99,500."[46] For Pigou, the tax was appropriate as a wartime
measure not on economic grounds but on ethical ones. And those
grounds were rooted in principles of justice and equality. As he
wrote in *The Economist*:

> In this war young men are being asked to sacrifice—the strong and the
> weak together, those with full lives and those with little to live for—not
> equal fractions of their well-being, but the whole of what they possess.
> If this, in war, is the right principle to apply to the lives of men, it is also
> the right principle to apply to their money.[47]

The argument for the tax stressed the importance of making the
war hurt, not only for the poor who were invariably drafted, but
also for the rich, through their pocketbooks. Pigou recognized that
such a levy would not be enacted. "I do not, of course," he wrote,
"pretend that an arrangement of this kind could be practically
established. But it illustrates the principle and the ideal towards
which it is the duty of the government to approach."[48]

   In a different piece, not published but written before the end
of the war, Pigou argued that the levy should take the form of a
tax on wealth, not income, but as in the case of the tax proposed
in *The Economist*, asserted that it should penalize the rich, who
might have had low incomes but valuable holdings, more than it
would the poor. Again, the result was that all would suffer together
in comparable measure. "To impose such a levy," he wrote, "is not

merely not unfair, but considerations of fairness directly demand
it." And, here in this implausible theoretical case, it was clear that
the state was to be the instrument of rectitude. This unpublished
typescript bore the original title of "The War Debt and the Consumption of Wealth," which Pigou had crossed out and over which
he had written by hand the new title, "A Capital Levy after the War,"
much more obviously a policy suggestion.[49]

The war was a time of high emotion for Pigou and not coincidentally, it was also a time when he sought to make economics
serve social ends that were distinctly non-monetary. Just days after
the Armistice was signed in November 1918, Pigou wrote to his
publisher for the second time in three years. In addition to inquiring after the inventories of his books, he expressed his interest in
"collecting into a book a number of articles on social problems . . .
a dozen dealing with peace problems and another dozen dealing
with war problems."[50] Pigou had suggested a similar project "on
practical economic problems" three years earlier under the title of
"Economic Science in Relation to Practice."[51] This time, he proposed the title to be "something like <u>Economic Essays on Peace
and War</u>." The emphasis had also changed. The peace essays, at the
very least, were to "deal with housing . . . and social things," drawing from a lecture he had given in 1914, and signaling, perhaps,
a return to his early work on the problems of urban life. Though
Macmillan eventually accepted the war essays, which were published as *The Political Economy of War* in 1921, it rejected the
peace-centered ones on the grounds that they would be unlikely
to sell.[52] Even so, the essays in *The Political Economy of War* adopted an ethical tone as they argued for capital levies instead of
loans as a means of wartime funding and took note of war's "de-
struction of values outside the economic sphere: . . . the shatter-
ing of human promise, the accumulated suffering in wounds and
disease of many who go to fight, the accumulated degradation in
thought and feeling of many who remain at home."[53] Though he
might have "cut out" politics and pared his ethical writings in 1908,
Pigou had lost neither his moral compass nor his highly cultivated
sense of justice.

In 1923, two years after Macmillan rejected his proposal for
a volume on social issues, Pigou ultimately did publish such a

collection of work under the title *Essays in Applied Economics* with a different publisher, P. S. King & Son. In the book, which collected work undertaken over the past decade, Pigou again offered a firm reminder that questions of ethics underlay those of economics. There was a chapter on the problem for eugenics of employers subsidizing large families, an analysis of the "social malady" of unemployment with suggestions for government action, and a chapter bearing a strident appeal for employers to act with "economic chivalry."[54] But unlike some postwar commentators like William Beveridge, who stressed the benefits of greater state intervention, Pigou opened the book with an essay on the ethical dimensions of private economic activity.[55] "After the tax-gatherer has done his worst," he noted, "a large duty of private giving to social ends still remains for rich men to fulfill."[56] After all, "everybody would say that I ought to accept seven courses instead of eight if, thereby, I could save somebody else from dying of starvation."[57] These articles, for the most part, were directed at a nonacademic audience. Many of them had appeared in semi-popular periodicals, including the *Contemporary Review*, the *Eugenics Review*, and a supplement to the *Manchester Guardian*, the newspaper that would, in 1959, become simply the *Guardian*.

But *Applied Economics* contained other essays that had virtually no ethical language at all; nearly half were devoted to technical problems of public finance and exchange markets. The book was thus a synthesis of ethical and economic analysis, but not a neat one; the very first line of its introduction revealed its frictions: "though economics is a positive science and not a body of precepts, economists, in their unofficial capacity as human beings, frequently discuss the duty of Governments."[58] As a whole, *Applied Economics* was conceived by one man, but the neat partition of its constituent chapters revealed a bipartite mind. On one side was an economist; on the other was a morally and politically concerned observer. Though these two halves of Pigou briefly appeared together in *Applied Economics*, a short book with a small print run, in general, they were to remain clearly separated throughout the 1920s. Certainly, when Pigou advised the government in the years following the war, only the economist spoke. To politicians and civil servants, Pigou would only show the constructed front of a scientific practitioner.

Postwar Committee Involvement

In keeping with Edwardian Liberal tenets, Pigou's welfare economics had always been intended to "bear fruit," to serve a concrete ameliorative purpose. Its conclusions opened up the possibility for the state to be the instrument of positive change, and in *Essays in Applied Economics*, Pigou primarily addressed issues of public policy. Pigou had been building his credibility as a scientific economist in order to effect such change, presumably by implementing policy either himself or through someone already in the government. Soon after the war's end, Pigou had his chance. Despite his pacifist feelings and public vociferousness, Pigou was still arguably the most respected academic economist in the country, and in the years after the war ended, he was asked to serve on several government committees whose scope had direct bearing on the country's welfare. Pigou had earned his place at the table. His entire project of crafting a scientific theory of improving social wellbeing seemed to be building to this point, the point of being in direct contact with policymakers, the Government House administrators with whom he had been educated and in whom he had placed so much hope.[59]

It is surprising, then, that when serving on committees, Pigou reverted to his pre-war public stoic detachment, again consciously paring normative elements from his words.[60] Even when he was tapped to serve on the royal commission that was to rework the income tax—a prime opportunity to put his ethical beliefs into action—he remained distinctly apolitical, a technician who crunched numbers and approached economics as a science like physics or chemistry. With his experience in Whitehall, ethics slipped back into the shadows of Pigou's writing. By the middle of the 1920s, after scores of train trips to London, something had happened to Pigou. Something soured him on advocacy, turning him from a believer in the capabilities of governmental administration into a skeptic.

Even before the echo of the last gunshots faded in Europe, Britain was faced with a host of challenges. It had racked up massive debts to the United States, obligations that the latter country was unwilling to forgive and which, in turn, made the British desperate to extract massive reparations from the Germans. More immediately pressing was the problem of reinserting some 4 million men into the British labor force.[61] To make matters worse for Treasury officials anguishing over an ever-increasing debt burden, rising discontent among unemployed servicemen returning from years in the trenches made a costly social insurance program something of a political necessity. The labor market was also disconcertingly restive.[62] A returning army and scarcity at home, coupled with the debts, pushed prices up by 25 percent over the course of 1919 and 1920 while wages stagnated. With workers feeling the pinch, trade unions became ever more vociferous in clamoring for raises. Words soon turned to industrial actions. In 1919, 35 million days were lost in labor disputes. By 1921, the number had risen to 86 million. And as the Russian Civil War continued to rage, these developments carried an ever greater political urgency.

The Coalition government under David Lloyd George scrambled to tackle the wide array of problems set before it. It had formed a Ministry of Reconstruction during the war and, in proper bureaucratic fashion, convened a variety of commissions and committees. Pigou, the prominent and distinguished Cambridge professor, was actively sought as a witness and participant. Pigou willingly accepted his appointments, but when he arrived in London to serve on committees, he came off as an academic, a technical economist. Pigou was unpolished. Noted for his fraying tweed, he looked like the professor he was. According to Cambridge colleagues, "his only concession to sartorial elegance at the High Table was a double-breasted lounge jacket filched from a parcel of clothes which his aunt was sending to a Church Army shelter."[63] His appearance in London was little better. Pigou was not a presentable policy analyst like Keynes, who gained great fame for his book, *Economic Consequences of the Peace* (1919), which lambasted the Versailles Conference and settlement.[64] Keynes was active in the Treasury and the City (London's financial district), and he had, three years before, moved into a house at 46 Gordon Square in the fashionable neighborhood of Bloomsbury, just a few underground stops from the seats of British power. In contrast, Pigou stayed in King's, delivering his lectures, revising what would become *The Economics of Welfare*, and generally continuing to trudge in the unglamorous but highly erudite footsteps of Alfred Marshall, who lived just a 15-minute walk away. Edwin Cannan, the older Liberal London

School of Economics (LSE) professor, noted in 1919 that when giving economic evidence before a royal commission, "you must make
up your mind whether you're going to talk for the public, or for the
Bluebook [official parliamentary reports]. If the latter, you must
be prepared to make an apparently poor show, e.g. Pigou, who
made things worse by smiling at the Commissioners all the time."[65]
Pigou, then in his forties, was far more at home at the King's College High Table than he was in the corridors of power in Whitehall.
By 1920, he had spent the better part of his life living in King's and
with over two decades of teaching experience, it was understand-
able that Pigou would try to "talk for the Bluebook" but present
himself awkwardly in the rarified world of politics.

Of course, the proposals of government committees were, in no
small part, predetermined by the selection of the committee members, a process that was inherently political. Therefore the committee's activities were in no small part the formal deliberations that
would validate a decision that had already been reached by politicians and powerful bureaucrats. At the time of the war's end, those
civil servants, concentrated in the Treasury and the Bank of England, were armed with a basic understanding of economics, a deep
commitment to "sound finance," and highly developed connections
to the City.[66] Though Pigou was a natural choice for the committee, given his position as Cambridge professor, it was also true that
with his Harrow and Cambridge credentials and his long record of
support for free trade, he would have appeared as a natural ally to
these established civil servants.

In 1918, he was included as the only academic on the Cunliffe
Committee, a group charged with evaluating the war's effect on
Britain's capital and exchange markets.[67] The committee was intended to evaluate financial markets, and it was therefore natural
that it drew its members mostly from the City of London. But the
group's composition—it consisted of Bank of England Governor,
Lord Cunliffe, the Treasury's Sir John Bradbury, ten prominent
private bankers, and Pigou—highlighted the extent to which the
government was content to let financiers drive government policy
even over industrial interests concentrated in the country's north.[68]
Pigou, though hardly an industrialist, was also unconnected with
the world of finance and was clearly the odd man out. From the

very start of the proceedings, he served as the in-house academic; the records from the committee meetings show that he was referred to exclusively as "Professor Pigou." He was tasked with composing much of the committee's required background reading, and the resulting memoranda were thus intended to be both accessible and general.[69] The following passage, about the possibility of merging the bank and issue departments of the Bank of England, was typical of the tone he adopted:

> Suppose that under the present arrangement equilibrium is established, so that normally there is in the Issue Department x million £ of gold and in the Banking Department y million £ of notes. It is decided to transfer all the gold to the Banking Department and to do away with the Issue Department. The immediate effect obviously is that there will be in the Banking Department a reserve of x million gold plus y million notes instead of y million notes only.[70]

Pigou was not teaching—the bankers in the room would have been quite familiar with the content of Pigou's words. But he acted the professor, explaining concepts with variables rather than serving as a consultant about practice and asking relatively few questions of witnesses compared to his fellow committee members.[71]

It is hard to determine whether Pigou's presence made any major difference, except perhaps to pad out the credibility of the committee's reports. The group unsurprisingly found that tackling problems related to foreign trade, rather than industrial recovery, was the first and foremost national economic objective. Britain had effectively suspended adherence to the gold standard during the war, and the bankers were eager to return to it. "Nothing," they asserted in a preliminary report in August 1918, "can contribute more to a speedy recovery from the effects of the war, and to the rehabilitation of the foreign exchanges, than the re-establishment of the currency upon a sound basis."[72] To a group of financiers set on ensuring that Britain remained at the center of world trade and finance, the restoration of the gold standard and the stability that went with it was of primary concern.[73] With his own attachment to free trade and his liberal interest in international economic integration, Pigou was also supportive of such a recommendation, a position that would have been well known to the committee's organizers when they solicited his participation.[74] Together, the committee endorsed a traditional "sound money" solution to restoring Britain's prewar financial position. *The Economist* titled its review of the interim report "Back to Sanity."[75]

At first glance, it might be supposed that the next group on which Pigou served, the 1919–1920 Royal Commission on the Income Tax, would have offered a more obvious outlet for his energies.[76] Its organizer, N. F. Warren Fisher, the chairman of the Board of Inland Revenue (Britain's tax agency), half-heartedly sought to ensure that the group included commissioners who were not businessmen or career politicians: specifically, "7 members representing the taxpaying community as a whole (to include 1Woman 4 Labour, 1 Economist.)"[77] For the position of the economist, Fisher suggested only two options to the Chancellor of the Exchequer, then Austen Chamberlain: Edwin Cannan and A. C. Pigou. Chamberlain, who had been educated at Trinity College, Cambridge, and had been a vice president of the Union, chose Pigou, and in early 1920, the professor was invited to participate. On February 23, he wrote back that he would "be happy to serve as a member."[78]

But if Pigou was actually happy, he did not stay so for long. The commission met from May 1919 through the end of the year. And while Pigou was one of the most consistent attendees at the beginning of the process, he was not an active participant. In contrast to the Cunliffe Committee, the Royal Commission distributed reams of technical and contextual literature to its members, and it drew from a variety of economic analysts. The original plans called for Pigou to be the only economist on the panel, but after a few months, an authority on taxation, Josiah Stamp, joined its number, as did several others.[79] The review of the income tax, after all, was a massive undertaking, one with a comprehensive mandate to investigate all aspects of the tax, including scope, rates, allowances, administration, assessment, collection, and evasion.[80] The Commission noted in its report addressed to the king that it had met fifty times and interviewed some 187 witnesses.[81]

Although the minutes from those fifty meetings are spare and laconic, it was highly unlikely that Pigou was an advocate for any particular political interest. For one thing, by the beginning of the summer, he was becoming less invested in the work that the group was doing. Pigou noted that the Commission was not charged with examining sweeping questions of social interest like "the comparative advantages of a high income tax as against a capital levy or a special levy on war wealth," such as the one that Pigou had advocated. "Its function was a much more limited one": merely to iron out "the anomalies, and unfairnesses, and complications . . . [that] had grown up."[82] In other words, continuity of the established tax regime was at the heart of the Royal Commission's mission.[83] Pigou's only public comment on the Commission's proceedings came in June, when he registered his dissent about taxing profit sharing Cooperative Societies (co-ops) in *The Economic Journal*. The majority of his colleagues were in favor; Pigou, taking a more progressive stance, was not. But Pigou's statement came not so much out of moral outrage as out of academic interest. He noted that the subject raised "issues which are interesting theoretically as well as practical," but in practice, it was principally the theoretical side that Pigou discussed and with which he took issue.[84] The commission's chairman, Frederick Henry Smith, Lord Colwyn, would write to Austen Chamberlain to complain that "scientific thought on economic questions is hardly sufficiently represented on the Commission. It is true we have Professor Pigou, of Cambridge, but he has not been able to attend very regularly and has scarcely been the help that I hoped, as he does not combine practical methods with scientific thought."[85]

In July, Pigou showed his lack of concern for the Commission's work the most striking way yet: he left for Switzerland to climb in the Alps, with the result that he did not attend another of the weekly meetings until October 8.[86] It is difficult to square Pigou's absence from, and his half-hearted participation on, the commission with the lofty purpose he would claim for its work, "to make this tremendous engine of revenue . . . more equitable and less burdensome, but not less effective, than before."[87] It was as if Pigou had lost some of his spirit to continue. In his description of the Commission's ultimate recommendations, published in the *Quarterly Journal of Economics* in August 1920, his languid words betrayed a detached weariness. By and large, Pigou repeated several times, the Commission did not "feel it necessary to revise in any fundamental way" the existing tax structures and certainly not their underlying assumptions.[88] Those fifty meetings had, in the end, amounted to little more than the preservation of the status quo in terms of over-all structure and taxation levels, and they resulted in only small, if important, fixes to the current system. In his article, Pigou discussed the details of some of these adjustments—certain abatements and smoothings of income bracket gradations—but reiterated that there was little actual disagreement about fundamental principles like progressivity itself, which was "not now disputed by anyone."[89]

Pigou took no stand in his review. His ultimate conclusion was, in fact, perfectly milquetoast. "There can be no doubt," he wrote, "that, in the report, . . . there is a mass of raw material for the student of income tax principles and methods."[90] His distant tone stemmed partially from his self-perceived role as an objective professor; it was also, perhaps, related to his many absences during the proceedings. But the distance—both emotional and geographic— also seemed to herald a certain dismissal of the Commission's work, or at the very least, a growing disengagement.

But while he might not show it in the context of his role as a commissioner, on a fundamental level, Pigou was still concerned with economic welfare, particularly with that of the disenfranchised. After all, he had written three of the morally inflected essays on social issues like unemployment and housing shortages that appeared in *Applied Economics* during the first two years of the 1920s. And in surveying postwar Britain, Pigou would have had plenty to be concerned about. Since the end of the war, Lloyd George had struggled to appease the many political forces in his coalition government. Although the Treasury was dominated by officials close to the financial sector, the cabinet was much more concerned about industrial unrest. The pressure to return to the gold standard pushed the cost of living ever higher, even if, despite the recommendations of the Cunliffe Committee, the government delayed balancing the budget and removing trade barriers and agreed to suspend the gold standard until 1926.[91] These compromises, symptomatic of Lloyd George's efforts to be the "great conciliator" and stay a middle course on nearly everything from Irish Home Rule to housing, failed to satisfy anyone and in 1922, the Conservatives swept him out of power by a comfortable margin.[92]

In fact, the Liberals had been seriously divided for several years, a circumstance that also fundamentally sapped Pigou's enthusiasm for active reform. The war had marked the beginning of the end of the Liberal Party as Pigou had known it. War saw the definite rise of organized labor as a powerful political force, and it challenged the comfortable established imperial order. As importantly, it crushed the faith in the efficacy of liberal internationalism and ruined the world system in which free trade could function.[93] The coalition government that it precipitated provoked an identity crisis in the party. The pragmatic sacrifices—most notably conscription—that Liberals grudgingly made to meet wartime exigencies forced them to compromise principles for victory.[94] All this caused the party to split at the seams. In forming a coalition government with the Conservatives in 1916, Lloyd George and a collection of supporters broke with the more established element in the party, led by the Prime Minister H. H. Asquith. From that point on, the party that had long been the dominant force in British politics found itself increasingly pulled asunder, with rival factions gravitating to the competing poles of Labour and the Conservatives. What remained, under Lloyd George, no longer resembled the high-minded Edwardian party run by elite, patrician reformers that had so captivated Pigou in his youth.

The divided party was devastated in the 1922 election. Not only did the Conservatives wrest control of the government, the Labour Party also made major gains, picking up an additional eighty-five seats, in the process becoming the nation's official opposition. One of the principal elements of Labour's platform had been a proposed capital levy intended to pay off the war debts. This idea was hardly new; Pigou himself, of course, had called for one during the war in the pages of *The Economic Journal* and *The Economist*, and senior Labour politicians had been seriously considering the idea since 1920.[95] It remained, however, a bold message. In 1921, Labour elders chose Hugh Dalton, a former student of Pigou's, to draft the plan. The resulting proposal, which Labour published under the title *Labour and the War Debt*, called for taxes on wealth to be levied on a sliding scale "running from nothing on the first £5,000, and 5% on the next £1,000, up to 60% on all above £1 million."[96] After the 1922 election, Labour was still very much in the minority in parliament, with 142 seats to the Conservatives' 332, and their proposal for a levy lay dead in the water.[97] But the fierce public debate on Dalton's plan, which, though more dramatically gradu-ated, was similar to and likely influenced by Pigou's own proposals, inspired Pigou to revisit the subject.[98]

But this time, Pigou's discussion of the levy was a far cry from the emotive calls he had made five years earlier. For one thing, he began his efforts six months *after* the election that had already de-cided the levy's fate. In his two letters he wrote to the *Times* about the subject, Pigou evinced little more than an academic interest in the discussions about a one-off wealth tax. The farthest he ventured was to note in one letter that a proper consideration of a levy would take into account issues of both economics and "of the principles involved" and suggested that the matter might be investigated by a royal commission.[99] In the other letter, he only went so far as to suggest that people might do well to avoid polemical arguments against levies. [100] Given his prior agitations, it seems obvious that Pigou would have supported Labour's 1922 pro-levy agenda. Yet his contributions to the *Times* demonstrated that his interest in the subject was dwarfed by his desire to stay out of the political fray. In the second letter, in fact, he explicitly denied endorsing a political party or particular platform.[101] In tone, Pigou had made an about-face since the war, transforming from an impassioned ethical ad-vocate to an interested bystander, an academic who mused to little practical purpose on the theoretical aspects of practical policy.[102]

In 1924, after two years of teaching and writing at Cambridge and Lower Gatesgarth, Pigou reprised his role as in-house academic bystander, this time for the Chamberlain-Bradbury Committee (of-ficially the Committee on the Currency and Bank of England Note Issues). Like the Cunliffe Committee, this group was set up by ad-ministrators at the Bank of England and the Treasury to reach a predetermined internationalist conclusion about monetary policy. The time had come, the officials had determined, to once again make the push for a return to the gold standard. The reason had to do with developments in both domestic and international politics.

The previous year, in 1923, with the British economy still reeling from two years of recession, Conservative Prime Minister Stanley

Baldwin called for a general election to consolidate power and se-cure a mandate for his protectionist agenda. The returns were un-expectedly disastrous for Baldwin, leading to a hung parliament and the first ever Labour government, under Ramsay MacDonald. However, much to the relief of Treasury officials, MacDonald and his Chancellor of the Exchequer, Philip Snowden, did not press for the adoption of the capital levy that had been so central to their party's platform just a year before. Snowden, in particular, was somewhat in awe of the Bank of England's masterful governor, Montagu Norman, and generally acceded to the latter's orthodox policies.[103] But though their power was left intact, the mandarins of the Treasury and Bank had other concerns. At international ne-gotiations over what would emerge as the Dawes Plan for a massive American loan to debt-ridden Germany, British officials had be-come concerned that the dollar would replace the pound as the de facto currency of world trade, especially if Britain did not recommit to the gold standard.[104]

As in 1918, at the time of the Cunliffe Committee in 1924, such a return was considered a necessary step toward world economic recovery as well as toward reestablishing the sterling as the world's dominant currency and London as the world's financial center.[105] But though it would provide stability for Britain's overseas trade, adherence to the standard would also make money much scarcer at home. Thus, even though the standard would be helpful to creditors, financiers, and to those involved in international trade, it would hurt debtors and businesses that faced foreign competi-tion.[106] Therefore, despite Snowden's relatively conservative lead-ership at the Treasury and his sympathy with the City, the fact that Labour still occupied 10 Downing Street fostered a general hesi-tancy to launch a renewed push for gold. With such an inclement political atmosphere, Norman felt that the time had not yet come for him "to make this a question of practical politics."[107]

It was in this environment that the Chamberlain–Bradbury Committee emerged. Its stated purpose was "to consider whether the time has come to amalgamate the Treasury Note Issue with the Bank of England Note Issue, and, if so, on what terms and condi-tions the amalgamation should be carried out."[108] But the commit-tee had been arranged by Montagu Norman, one of the shrewdest power brokers of his day, with an ulterior motive. During the war, to cover government debts, paper Treasury notes had replaced circulating gold currency (in coin form) and were issued alongside Bank of England notes of larger denominations implicitly backed by gold. Integration of the two note issues, then, was a backdoor way of getting at the much greater question of returning to gold.

Working with his friend and colleague at the Treasury, Otto Niemeyer, Norman ensured that his new official committee was staffed with people sympathetic to his unstated goals. Of the five members of the new committee, three (Lord Bradbury; Gaspard Farrer; and Pigou, whom Norman requested by name) had served on the Cunliffe Committee, and a fourth member, Austen Chamberlain, had been the Chancellor of the Exchequer who had signed off on the Cunliffe report.[109] The fifth member was Niemeyer himself. Pigou somewhat hesitantly accepted membership, noting that he would be out of the country for most of the summer. But this did not faze Norman and Niemeyer; as before, Pigou's inputs mattered less than did his signature on the final report.[110]

Once the committee began meeting in June 1924, Norman, who was also the group's first witness, made certain that the members were well aware of his genuine motives.[111] Witness after witness was called over the summer and fall of 1924, most of them powerful bankers and nearly all sympathetic to the return to the gold standard. One of the few exceptions was John Maynard Keynes, now back at Cambridge after leaving his post at the Treasury in disgust in the wake of the Treaty of Versailles.[112] In the course of his testimony, Keynes built on his recently published *Tract on Monetary Reform* (1923), strenuously warning the commission about the dangers of returning to gold at a pre-war parity—a decision that could result in a "drastic credit restriction," which would gut the British export industry and cause a massive drop in wages.[113] Keynes's critique did not amount to a radical condemnation of the gold standard but a plea against revaluation. Even so, the Commission largely passed over his recommendations.[114]

For his part, Pigou was not an active force. During the better part of the summer, he was, as he had warned, absent, tramping through Alpine landscapes, though he did read and underline the transcriptions of the witness testimonies he missed.[115] On the occasions he was present in London and decided to participate in the meetings, Pigou's questions were, as usual, those of an economic scientist—probing but conscientiously stripped of politics.[116] In the end, despite harboring a deep sympathy toward the gold standard, Pigou was slightly less enthusiastic about the immediate return to gold than were the other members of the committee. In the view of a frustrated Gaspard Farrer, Pigou's feelings were, "I think too negative."[117] Part of Farrer's annoyance may have stemmed from the fact that Pigou always made his opinions known to fellow members with a key qualification, in both senses of the term: his academic status. As he wrote to Austen Chamberlain about the timing of returning to gold:

> On the main issue, which is one of practical politics rather than economics, . . . I am only just on balance in favour of a "wait and see" policy. *It would be very inappropriate for me as an academic person to press for heroism*; but if the rest of the Committee had been in favour of it, I doubt if I should have been opposed.[118]

Pigou certainly had political opinions—he, like much of the committee, wanted to "wait and see" if the pound could rebound further against the dollar before a return to gold (and pre-war British financial dominance)—but he felt uncomfortable with actively agitating for them, even in a confidential environment surrounded by like-minded individuals. What held him back, much to the consternation of his colleagues, was his institutional position as a professor.[119] Instead of using his position to advocate, Pigou sought to protect his reputation as an end in itself. Maintenance of scientific objectivity had turned from a tool to affect public policy into Pigou's personal policy for his own comportment, one that would brook no argument.

Again, while his behavior was affected by his perceived role as a detached academic, it also betrayed a certain dismissal of the Commission's work, perhaps even a lack of faith in the worth of his own participation. There were plenty of reasons Pigou might have felt discouraged. Britain was still recovering from a slump, and the Liberal Party was in fragments. But it is also possible that Pigou's behavior stemmed in part from a burgeoning recognition that his opinion—the opinion of one of the most respected academic economists in the world—mattered less than his title did. After all, given that Norman and Niemeyer had engineered the Chamberlain-Bradbury Committee to suit their purposes, Pigou never had to convince his fellow members of any truly important point; nor is it likely, had he been inclined, that would he have been able to counter the interests of the committee organizers.[120] If Pigou doubted his own relevance while on the Committee, the case for those doubts would have appeared just as strong—perhaps stronger—in retrospect. Ultimately, the Committee's report, which suggested "waiting and seeing" if rising American inflation would make the return to gold less painful, would prove more or less meaningless, as the decision was made by other agents keen to return. Norman was sufficiently eager to get back to the standard that he took matters into his own hands, and, in an effort to bring the pound closer to the pre-war dollar exchange rate of $4.86, raised the Bank of England's bank rate and the cost of discounting bills.[121] With this, and following a rousing Conservative electoral victory the next year, Britain returned to gold.[122]

New Conceptions of Authority

During and especially after his work on commissions in the early 1920s, Pigou began to grapple with the question of his own usefulness. Speaking in 1924, he suggested an uncomfortable new role for himself. "Though, for the economist," he wrote, "the goal of social betterment must be held ever in sight, his own especial task is not to stand in the forefront of attack, but patiently behind the lines to prepare the armament of knowledge."[123] This quartermasterly role was exactly the one Pigou had taken on. He withdrew from public debates and contributed far fewer letters and articles to the *Times* than he had before the war.[124] After the capital levy's failure at the polls in 1922, Pigou wrote only two additional letters until the Depression at the end of the decade. During his work on committees, he had published thirteen; in the decade before the war, sixteen.[125] Thus, in the face of a massive debt crisis stifling national prosperity, Pigou's involvement in public life was decidedly tepid. To the extent that this reflected a frustration with the common man, it was not new at all. His welfare economics, after all, constituted a project of helping the "abnormally incompetent" masses from a distance, not of trying to educate them. "Men in the street," he consistently noted, misunderstood economic theories and complained when technical economists were "intentionally and viciously obscure."[126]

But Pigou's absences and lack of vigor as a committee member demonstrated more than a distrust of the public. They revealed increasingly negative feelings about public officials and state apparatuses. Though Pigou had long ago stopped making overt references to politics, the war and the fall of the old Liberal Party of Asquith and Campbell-Bannerman disconcerted and disillusioned him, as it did many other Liberal intellectuals. Moreover, in London, he had witnessed a perverted realization of his aspirations for economics bearing fruit. Pigou was all in favor of economists wielding their scientific authority in the pursuit of implementing a socially useful policy. When serving on committees, however, it was clear he himself was not wielding his authority. It was instead being wielded by political forces entirely out of his control. It was a hard case to make that the economist as committee member was actually providing substantive "armaments of knowledge." Instead, the economist himself was the armament.

Like Marshall and Sidgwick before him, Pigou had long worried about the potential for corruption and inefficiency in government. Every public official, he wrote in *Wealth and Welfare*, "is a potential opportunity for some form of self-interest arrayed against the common interest."[127] His mistrust for politicians also ran deep. In the early 1920s, he wrote of the "falsehoods of charlatanry" committed by political campaigners, and he would later speak of the "continual danger . . . of attempts at exploitation" of economic ideas.[128] He recounted a story of how his own work was used for such an ill purpose, when a "Prime Minister of the day," Arthur Balfour, had misread and misused Pigou's statements.[129]

Pigou's old liberalism was loosely based on meritocratic noblesse oblige. Certainly, useful application of his welfare economics depended on an effective state operated by able civil servants. But his experience in government made him doubtful that such a state existed in practice. After his experience on the committees, Pigou did not seriously comment on the mechanics of government intervention until a short chapter called "State Action and Laisser Faire," published in 1935. In it, he reiterated his theoretical support of the state intervening to improve welfare conditions. But he also offered a vital caveat to his calls for intervention—one that had less to do with economics than it did with the mechanics of statecraft. State participation in the economy would only work, he held, if "the government is qualified to select the right form and degree of State action and to carry it through effectively." This depended on "the intellectual competence of the persons who constitute [a decision-making body], the efficacy of the organisation through which their decisions are executed," and administrators' "personal integrity" and "ability to resist the pressure of powerful interests."[130]

It takes no leap of the imagination to see how Pigou's time on committees might have soured him on "state action." His experience had demonstrated that there were often problems with the people who were in the position to play intervening roles. They might be the wrong ones for the job, or they might be beholden to political pressures that constrained their capacity for action. This, for the economist whose theory of welfare hinged on the competence of such bureaucrats, was powerfully disillusioning. It made the market imperfections, which in theory could be remedied by a skilled force that existed outside the market, seem like much greater obstacles to the achievement of a more prosperous and equitable economic world.

Pigou's postwar experience posed two difficult questions. The first was where welfare economics would be without a government willing or able to engage along Pigovian lines. The bleak answer to this question provoked another: who Pigou's audience would be. Until his involvement with committees, there was at least a model of how Pigou himself could contribute to societal good. By establishing his reputation and by investigating how the government should act, he put himself in a position from which he could advise the government—or at least have an influence on enlightened leaders—to help enact socially beneficial policy. However, committee work had sapped his faith in his would-be partners and their ability to act as skilled officers of the economic Government House.

How, then, was Pigou to affect the good? He recognized that economists would have to work with statesmen, since, as he contended well into the mid-1930s, "to *find* truth is not enough."

Somehow it needed to be "brought to the mind and utilized in the work of those persons who guide affairs."[131] But his vision of how he, as an economist, was to relate to policymakers would become much more distant than what he had envisioned just a few years before. Pigou had composed his economics of welfare during a period of surging optimism in the Liberal reformist project and at a point when the Liberal Party flourished under high-born and high-minded leaders. But after the war, that optimism lay in shreds. Pigou's role was necessarily amended. He would still provide the "armament of knowledge" for social betterment, but after the mid-1920s, his efforts to engage seriously with policymakers fell off dramatically. The passive, indirect form of influence to which Pigou resigned himself was a hollow echo of his former aspirations. And as his ambitions eroded, so too did the optimistic, proactive tone of his work on welfare.

CHAPTER FIVE

Retreat to the Ivory Tower

AS PIGOU DEVELOPED a new understanding of the country's leadership and his relationship with it over the course of the 1920s, his work retreated to the pages of academic journals and to those of books "suited for experts." As the Liberal Party and the Liberal intelligentsia waned in power, he confined himself to the fellows-only combination rooms and High Tables of Cambridge, to Buttermere, and to the Swiss Alps, surrounded by his colleagues and friends. The short experiment with popular outreach had reached its end. Even when among his friends, he spoke only rarely on "serious subjects."[1] Austin Robinson noted: "We talked climbing. We talked cricket," but not economics.[2] Pigou himself quipped that his "pen did all his thinking."[3] And that thinking was becoming less and less accessible to general audiences. By devoting greater attention to the mechanics of technical problems, Pigou may have still been seeking to "bear fruit" by furnishing an armament of knowledge. But the restriction of his audience was also a sign of defeat. His withdrawal to the academy at Cambridge did not just indicate a changing perception of the possibilities of government action. It signaled that the dream to engage in efforts that directly affected welfare was fading.

These developments occurred, however, during the period of Pigou's career that would prove the most productive, a period when he consolidated his reputation as the most eminent economic voice of his generation. As he stepped back from participating in issues of policy, he was ascendant as a scientist "of the chair."[4] It is not unlikely that Pigou himself took some satisfaction in this transformation. Tucked between the pages of his own copy of one of his later books was an anonymously published review by Joan Robinson that described him as "the most austerely professional of all economists."[5]

The 1920s were, after all, an austere time for Britain, for Liberals, and for Pigou. His generation had seen a golden era of nearly unchecked optimism—in British, imperial, and human progress—vanish, to be replaced with pervasive uncertainty.[6] Britain's economic future and her imperial dominance were in serious question, and liberalism itself was, in the words of Pigou's old friend C.F.G. Masterman, being "crushed between the upper and nether millstones of privilege and revolt."[7] And, for the first time in his life, Pigou began to feel his age. In 1922, in a rare display of postwar leisure, he played an exhibition match of fives with fellow Old Harrovian and Trinity classicist J.R.M. Butler against two boys from Harrow and lost soundly.[8] Indeed, being surrounded by young men at the height of their physical capacity in Cambridge put Pigou's own lack of vigor in striking definition. And, of course, many of his best friends were former students and thus significantly younger than he. During the early twenties, he became close to Tom Gaunt, a student at King's, a mountaineer and, like his school friend Jenkins, a future man of the cloth. Noel-Baker, with whom Pigou kept up, was also in peak physical condition; he won a silver medal at the 1920 Antwerp Olympics for the 1,500-meter race. In contrast, the twenties saw Pigou slowing down and laid up with a collection of physical ailments. A weak heart made climbing difficult, and digestive problems frequently confined the middle-aged mountaineer to bed. When he finally finished with his duties in London, Pigou was a changed man, older in both body and temperament.

Driven to Abstraction

As early as 1922, Pigou's optimism about the ability of welfare economics to be put to practical use had become significantly muted. That September, the economic historian J. H. Clapham wrote a short piece in *The Economic Journal* noting that economists tended to refer to conditions of "decreasing returns to scale" or "increasing returns to scale" "as if everyone knew what that was."[9] Clapham was referring to the Marshallian approach to industries as units of analysis. On a basic level, the theory had intuitive allure. Some industries, it suggested, were characterized by increasing returns: able to produce each additional item at a lower and lower cost. Others experienced decreasing returns and produced at ever mounting cost. Elegant or not, Clapham mused, in reality, it seemed as if the notions of increasing and decreasing returns were mere "empty economic boxes"—concepts that existed in theory but were not filled with any real, measurable content.

Clapham's piece was light hearted, filled with metaphors about economists wandering down the dusty aisles of hat-shops without looking inside the theoretical hatboxes. But for its humor, the article also had an edge. By suggesting that there was no compelling empirical evidence for particular firms or industries to be characterized as having increasing or decreasing returns, it challenged one of the most basic elements of the Marshallian framework.[10] Furthermore, in its critique, it especially confronted the work done by Pigou. Clapham noted that Pigou was one of these wandering economists, "less concrete in his treatment than Dr. Marshall, further from the clod and much further from the machinery."[11]

It is easy to imagine Clapham and Pigou themselves opening up dusty boxes for examination and hashing out the article's contentions across the High Table at King's. The pair had been colleagues for twenty years and friends for longer, so the matter may have been privately resolved well before Pigou's public response appeared three months later.[12] In his reply, also in *The Economic Journal*, Pigou worked with a soft touch, gently parrying Clapham's queries in an earnest attempt to preserve his abstract apparatus. Whether or not the theory bore direct applicability for action, Pigou held, it was certainly of some value, since the concepts in question were "not just boxes" but "part of the machinery" used for making sense of the world. Moreover, the former commissioner noted, the boxes were already of some use by dint of their mere existence, since they often exposed the falsity of political rhetoric.[13] Clapham, Pigou claimed, could "hardly deny that science may help practice by exposing the falsehoods of charlatanry."[14]

Nevertheless, Pigou acknowledged the massive gap between theory and practice, and he offered his modest claims for the boxes' usefulness with a set of hefty caveats. To be useful for constructive policy, the boxes would be need to be filled, not only with the vital piece of information concerning whether an industry was operating at increasing or decreasing returns to scale, but also with all sorts of other data. The economist would need to fill not just "bulky valises . . . but an intricate collection of little cases inside these" having to do with the particular shapes of demand and supply curves as well as elasticities.[15] But after laying out such a monumental task, Pigou, as a theorist, demurred from carrying it out himself. He noted that no one had, as yet, succeeded in such an endeavor, and he was "very far from wishing to underrate [its] difficulty."[16] This new position on the practicability of theory was substantively duller than the shining statements he had made years earlier in *Wealth and Welfare* and *The Economics of Welfare* about economics bearing the fruit of policy. Pigou would focus increasingly on perfecting the theory itself as opposed to its applications in the real world.

Over the 1920s, Pigou found himself embroiled in further discussions about the applicability of theory to practice. In 1924, he had a short debate with a younger colleague at Cambridge, Dennis Robertson, over the classification of certain external diseconomies.[17] Robertson raised a point that had nagged Pigou since Allyn Young's 1913 review of *Wealth and Welfare*: that there was a substantive difference between an external diseconomy like pollution and the phenomenon like the one brought about by agricultural production, wherein one farm's purchase of seeds might drive up the price of seeds for other farmers. Young had called this second kind not an external effect at all, but a "transference of purchasing power"; there was a market for seeds, but not one for pollution. Young claimed, in an argument echoed by Robertson, that it would not be useful to tax industries merely because of this effect.[18] In 1924, Pigou agreed—at least in the case of diminishing returns—and changed the second edition of *The Economics of Welfare,* published that year, to reflect the critiques of his past work. In the process, he further cut back the role assigned to the government in his theory.

Four months later, in the midst of these mounting challenges, Alfred Marshall died. Pigou, as his most loyal disciple, was "entrusted with the task of dealing with" his teacher's manuscripts and papers.[19] He duly sorted through Marshall's work at his late teacher's home, Balliol Croft, in Cambridge, and helped Mary Paley Marshall with the mountain of tasks precipitated by her husband's passing.[20] In the heavy months that followed, Pigou worked with Macmillan, Marshall's and his own publisher, to assemble a volume of selections from Marshall's writing prefaced by a series of remembrances and an introduction by Keynes.[21]

Marshall's death took a great deal out of his former student. In a moving memorial address delivered to students at Cambridge three months after his teacher's passing, Pigou was at his most emotional: "The Master whom we all revere is dead: full of honour, full of years, his life-work done. . . . If it were possible I should wish to stand as an interpreter of his spirit . . . and hand on some message, not unworthy of his thought and of his life.[22]

Pigou's interpretation was both uplifting and didactic. Marshall's work, he claimed, was inspired by the certainty that "the brief lives of multitudes of our fellow men are shadowed with sorrow and strained with want." And the message of Marshall's own life was to throw oneself headlong into a project that helped those in need. Recalling a fading prewar liberalism, Pigou urged the listening students: "Do not hoard your life: spend it; spend it on an aim outside yourselves, the worth of which you feel." Closing with a stanza from Tennyson's "Merlin and the Gleam," Pigou's words rang out with emotion:

> This is Merlin, and he is dying
> This is Merlin who followed the gleam.[23]

"After it," he exhorted, "follow it: follow the gleam."

Marshall had been something of a father figure and was probably the person Pigou had respected most. One of the most striking manifestations of that regard lay in his penmanship. By the 1920s, Pigou's once elegant handwriting had degenerated into a mass of nearly incomprehensible scratchings and blots. But in letters to Marshall, the lines and arcs corralled themselves into comprehensible, even neat words.[24] No other correspondent received such generous treatment from Pigou's pen; in fact, several of his correspondents transcribed his letters in the process of decoding them.[25]

Marshall's passing was thus a profoundly personal loss for Pigou, but the death also resonated for a man who, without a family of his own, was confronting his own failing health. In October 1925, Pigou was "laid up in a nursing home with a temporarily strained heart" and "off work for a month or more."[26] He spent that time in Marylebone in London, just a five-minute walk from the houses of both his brother and sister and only a short journey from the Kensington home of his friend Philip Noel-Baker, who had become Professor of International Relations at the University of London.[27] A penciled letter to Macmillan written during the stay at the rest home bore the writing of a feeble patient. After discussing his plans for future work after his strength returned, Pigou apologized. "I hope this is intelligible, but I'm not feeling up to much at the moment."[28]

Almost as importantly, the death of his teacher was also a deep professional loss, for now Pigou was indisputably the most prominent Marshallian economist alive. This position was soon heightened when F. Y. Edgeworth died in early 1926. As his teachers' generation faded away, Pigou himself increasingly emerged as a recognized elder of his discipline. Of the thirteen scholars who gave lectures in economics for the Tripos in the year of Marshall's death, only two, Clapham and the statistician Udny Yule, were older than Pigou, and neither of these men were theoreticians.[29]

Thus, when the Marshallian theoretical system came under fundamental attack in 1926, Pigou was particularly ready to defend it. The challenge arrived in the form of an *Economic Journal* article by the Italian economist Piero Sraffa, who would move to Cambridge the following year. Sraffa questioned the usefulness of the core Marshallian premise of free competition, which held that markets were sufficiently large and brisk to prevent individual firms from determining the prices of the goods they sold.[30] Sraffa argued that there was a tension between the reality of external (dis)economies on one hand and the commitment to conditions of perfect competition on the other. Either a firm's actions had major effects on the operations of other firms in the same industry by way of external effects, or if perfect competition held, they did not. The same reasoning, he contended, could be applied to industries.[31] Ultimately, Sraffa suggested that, according to the Marshallian system, demand did not play a part in setting a commodity's equilibrium price, a result that threw the entire system into question. The solution that Sraffa offered in his article was to abandon the conceptual framework of perfect competition for a type of monopolistic model wherein individual firms were not merely passive price takers, but were able to affect the price and quantity of industrial output.[32]

In his response, Pigou tried to achieve a compromise between perfect and imperfect competition, but the result was a clear espousal of orthodox Marshallian theory. In short, he held that the (dis)economies were external to individual firms but not to industries, thereby preserving the possibility of classifying whole industries as having increasing or decreasing marginal returns, which Sraffa had rejected in his article. This was, in some ways, a reasonable response, and one from which economists would later draw, but it did little to address and less to stem the tide of criticism attacking the basis of the Marshallian system, criticism that would only mount over the course of the decade.[33]

The theoretical disputes with Clapham, Robertson, and Sraffa grew into one of the major debates of the 1920s and ultimately resulted in the erosion of the Marshallian theory of value and a fundamental challenge to the established conception of supply and demand. For Pigou, they also mattered because of their implications for his welfare economics. Conceptualizing industries as practicable units that could be classified as bearing increasing or decreasing returns to scale allowed such units, in theory, to be manipulated by taxes and bounties to improve the social weal. Indeed, Pigou's system of bounties and taxes was fundamentally based on their existence.[34] However, his sparring with Clapham, Robertson, and especially with Sraffa was also largely motivated by concerns about preserving Marshall's legacy.[35] The "master" had left Pigou with a citadel, and it fell to him to defend it. Indeed, as time passed, and as he himself grayed, Pigou found himself with ever-weightier loads of responsibility, perceived and actual.

With responsibility came testiness. When Pigou encountered an ill-informed letter in the *Times* from a would-be economic commentator who had not undergone rigorous training, he replied, a task he considered his duty as "Chairman of the Faculty Board for Economics and Politics." In responding to *academic* challenges to his and Marshall's work, Pigou typically took a firm, though accommodating tone. But he was far less generous when defending economics from attacks made by outsiders, and his response to the *Times* seethed with cold anger. In the offending letter, which appeared in 1926, just months after the General Strike of some 1.7 million workers, Sir Ernest Benn, a publisher and an active critic of socialism, warned that there was "grave reason for suggesting that economics is in danger of degenerating as a science through the importation of a veiled political bias." Benn claimed that universities were "led by the nose by Socialists," and that the teaching, particularly at Cambridge (perhaps because of the presence of the communist Maurice Dobb), demanded greater scrutiny.[36] Pigou's response was quick and savage. In a few sentences, he countered the substance of Benn's claims, noting that the latter had not read the lists of lectures or examinations, and sarcastically noting that the external examiners included "the notorious Socialists Sir Josiah Stamp and the present editor of the *Economist* [Walter Layton]."[37] But the real message of Pigou's letter was that Benn was to be dismissed out of hand. Pigou's words burned with dismissive indignation at the fact that a layperson—especially a propagandizing publisher—would attempt to dictate academic policy and lecture scientists about the objectivity of their work. At Cambridge, Pigou fumed, teachers were appointed without "inquiry . . . into political opinions." Once appointed, teachers had a duty to "teach what is true, irrespective of whether Sir Ernest Benn . . . may happen to be aware of it." Pigou charged on:

> For an outsider, ignorant of our practice and an amateur in our subject, to charge us with violating it is an impertinence. For myself I make no answer to such a charge; of my colleagues with whose personality and qualifications I, unlike Sir Ernest Benn, happen to be acquainted, I flatly assert that it is untrue.[38]

The virulence with which Pigou responded was a result of more than just a Cantabrigian disdain. Benn's attack hit a nerve. Pigou's contention was that economics was scientific in large part because it was nonpartisan. Indeed, he saw his retreat from public life as consistent with a sort of apolitical insulation. This belief was reflected in his biting response to Benn in two ways. First, Pigou explicitly noted that at Cambridge, truth came before and above politics. And in directing Benn to mind his own business and his impertinences, Pigou also figured Cambridge as a closed citadel whose walls protected academics from an often misunderstanding public.

Major Works and the Height of Prestige

As Pigou resettled himself in academia after his forays to London, welfare—at least in abstraction—continued to preoccupy his thoughts. He revised *The Economics of Welfare* for second and third editions, which appeared in 1924 and 1928, and the two major new books he produced over the course of the decade, *Industrial Fluctuations* (1927) and *A Study in Public Finance* (1928), were both related to his canonical work. The tone of these two works, however, was somewhat different from that of *The Economics of Welfare*. They were the most academically rarefied of his books to date, and they employed a much greater quantity of technical and mathematical language, with the result that the reading public would have a much harder time accessing their meaning.[39] They were addressed to colleagues and no one else. As Pigou would write some years later, "conversation is fostered and knowledge advanced if Hindus are allowed to talk to one another in Hindustani. . . . Ought not some economist sometimes to have the privilege of these Hindus?"[40]

These were the words of a man who was slowly but surely retreating, in the words of Austin Robinson, "into the ordered life of a recluse." During the academic year, he continued to live inside King's, taking his dinner night after night in the college Hall. Every afternoon, he would walk west out of the college and through the fields surrounding Cambridge to the village of Coton, two and a half miles away. His routines would be broken only rarely: by visits from friends, holidays, and slightly more regularly by the lectures he delivered three times a week throughout the academic year. As Robinson noted, "the lectures cost him little effort."[41] He had taught the general course in economics for the better part of two decades, and the other topics on which he expounded were always related to his book project of the moment.

The books themselves provided Pigou's principal occupation. He worked on them constantly: at Cambridge during term time, at Lower Gatesgarth during vacations, and in the Alps over the course of his annual summer holiday. In writing and revising his books in the 1920s, Pigou saw his goal as the same as Marshall's: to contribute knowledge that, if successfully applied, might improve the societal lot by addressing the major social ills of the time. Unemployment, malnutrition, even unfair compensation were all problems that attracted the attention of reformers and politicians, but any potential action would require knowledge and understanding. In particular, at least in Pigou's estimation, they required *economic* understanding. Thus, after stepping back from direct discussions with policymakers, Pigou set himself a less proactive task: to develop a scientific theory that, by explaining economics as a whole, would be able to offer guidance in easing the major social problems confronting interwar Britain.

Like Marshall and other systematic thinkers of the late nineteenth century, Pigou believed that economics could provide a comprehensive set of theoretical models to describe the world, an "organon" universally applicable to practical questions. And indeed, Pigou envisioned all of his own major works as belonging to such a unitary corpus.[42] At its center was *The Economics of Welfare*, which entered its third edition in 1928. Considered the first and best theoretical explanation of economic growth at the time it came out, the tome was also held to be one of the premier comprehensive works on economics for students and scholars alike. American economist Frank Knight titled his review of the second edition "Economics at Its Best."[43] It was also economics at its more socially conscious. *The Economics of Welfare* was, after all, as its first pages laid out, meant to serve "the social sympathies."[44]

However, even his work on welfare did not prove immune to the changes that were narrowing Pigou's audience and dampening his tone. In the transition from *Wealth and Welfare* (1912) to *The Economics of Welfare* (1920), Pigou amended his purpose. Whereas he had begun writing for explicitly ethical reasons, by the 1920s, welfare economics had become much more of a technical project. In a letter written years later to Pigou, Hugh Dalton observed that the first and last paragraphs of *Wealth and Welfare* "have always been my ethical starting point for economic journeys, and I have been sorry that they dropped out from successive editions of E[conomics] of W[elfare]."[45] These omitted passages, which explicitly stated, "welfare means the same thing as good," were imbued not only with an optimism, but also with a certitude of purpose. In the introduction, Pigou wrote: "Whether the life of man ends with his physical death, or is destined to pass unscathed through that gateway, the good and the evil that he experiences here are real; and to promote the one and restrain the other is a compelling duty."[46] The conclusion was even more stirring. "First we must understand our task and prepare for it," Pigou wrote, "and then, in the glow of sunrise, by united effort, we shall at last, perhaps achieve."[47]

The four editions of *The Economics of Welfare*, published after the war in 1920, 1924, 1928, and 1932, never returned as explicitly to the original ethical origin. Instead, they were more observational, more reserved, more entwined with theoretical debates about measurement and prediction. Their introductions and conclusions, though still laced with ethics, took more pragmatic tones than did their predecessor. In the transition from *Wealth and Welfare* to *The Economics of Welfare*, the language of good and evil and the quotations from Moore were excised. Instead, *The Economics of Welfare* started with a description of the type of science economics was to be—a practical one—and how it would "elucidate . . . the actual world of men and women as they are found in experience."[48] The revision of the book's ending was more striking still. Whereas *Wealth and Welfare* concluded with a exhortation to "united effort," *The Economics of Welfare* ended without a formal conclusion, a striking parallel of Pigou's own unfinished task of putting his welfare economics into practice.

The new books Pigou penned in the middle years of the 1920s made even greater departures from the buoyant animating spirit of *Wealth and Welfare*. They were self-consciously observational and predictive, with much greater emphasis on statistical analysis. For the first time in one of his books, large inset graphs featured prominently in *Industrial Fluctuations*, which came out in 1927. Though they were not technical in the sense that the word is used today, Pigou certainly saw them as scientific, and their scholarship and "painstaking thoroughness" were widely noted. [49]

Pigou had started working on *Industrial Fluctuations* in 1925, and as he corrected proofs in late 1926 and early 1927, he began to see it as an addition to *The Economics of Welfare*: a sort of extended appendix that focused on the volatility of national income.[50] Just before embarking on his annual summer holiday in the Alps, he suggested in vain to his publisher that it might be published together with a new edition of *The Economics of Welfare* as a "sort of three-volume treatise," a reflection of how many pages the books together would run.[51] But though Pigou may have seen his new work as neatly dovetailing with his old, the books had decidedly different styles of exposition. *Industrial Fluctuations* showed off both data and mathematical modeling, with seventeen tables of statistics and twenty charts and graphs, features that barely appeared at all in *The Economics of Welfare*.[52] These nontextual elements and the corresponding glosses made the book feel as if it were at a further remove from the emotive and ethically founded prescriptions of past work.

That said, *Industrial Fluctuations* was nevertheless an expanded and revised version of part III of *Wealth and Welfare*.[53] Like its earlier iteration, *Industrial Fluctuations* was framed by ethics inasmuch as it was premised on the understanding that periods of booms and busts were socially harmful. Booms and busts tended to result in lower overall income than a corresponding period of stability, and the brunt of cycles was typically borne disproportionately by "the unfortunate few" who were often the least able to cope with them.[54] Moreover, the resulting unemployment brought "serious evils," like the "haunting sense of insecurity and danger" experienced by the unemployed poor.[55] But more than he had ever before, in *Industrial Fluctuations*, Pigou concentrated on the slew of *economic* costs and diseconomies associated with joblessness. "Considerable spells of unemployment," he wrote, might "damage a man's technical capacity and, what is much more important, the general make-up of his character." If "self respect" and the "habit of regular work" were lost, "the man, once merely unemployed is found to have become unemployable."[56] The result was that "industrial fluctuations . . . involve a substantial loss of economic welfare," both for the worker and the nation.[57]

In substance, *Industrial Fluctuations* offered a sweeping taxonomic exposition and a synthesis of various existing theories of the business cycles.[58] It argued that the expectations of businessmen, and nothing else, caused economic conditions to undulate. Specifically, businessmen responded to three sorts of impulses: real (e.g., a poor harvest), psychological (e.g., forecasting errors), and monetary (e.g., exogenous factors like changes in foreign debt). Cycles were precipitated and sustained not by one type of these impulses, but by a complex combination of them, and the "sum of their effects" was "something much bigger than the joint effect of all of them taken together."[59] This interplay made Pigou's conceptual framework for fluctuations almost impossible to model.[60] Despite this, and in marked contrast to past work on welfare, Pigou included a great deal of empirical work, mapping historical cycles in addition to developing a theoretical apparatus for describing how businessmen behaved. But while businessmen were at the center of Pigou's story of cycles, they were not his audience, as the technical and mathematical nature of his work limited its accessibility. In a letter to Hugh Dalton some years later, Donald Chapman, the general secretary of the Fabian Society (who had himself studied economics at Cambridge), confessed that he had stopped reading Pigou during this period as he feared subsequent work "might be as incomprehensible as some of his stuff on the trade cycle."[61]

Though comprehensive, the book was not groundbreaking, and its policy prescriptions were hardly extreme. Monetary policies were found useful in damping cycles of boom and bust, as were certain fiscal policies meant to create demand in depressions so as to stabilize demand throughout economic cycles.[62] Pigou, alluding to work of the British economic statistician Arthur Bowley, drew attention to the fact that government spending patterns mirrored the general cyclical fluctuations of national prices and argued that the government ought to shift its spending so that its own peaks aligned with the general market's troughs.[63] To some extent, municipal governments already employed this strategy of "setting up a small ebb and flow of its own to some extent counteracting the flow and ebb of private industry," a point that had been made in the Minority Report of the Royal Commission on the Poor Laws back in 1907 and echoed by Pigou in *Wealth and Welfare*.[64] However, Pigou's deep scorn for the general public kept him skeptical of state-directed relief programs. Works projects, after all, had to rely on "a miscellaneous collection of relatively inefficient people," untrained and undisciplined.[65]

As in his previous work, Pigou noted that "the old doctrine of the economic harmonies . . . that, in general, the pursuit by individuals of their private self-interest will make the sum of economic satisfaction a maximum" was "subject to large qualifications." Certain initiatives that were meant to align the individual and collective interest, he argued, could improve economic welfare.[66] But in recommending state action, Pigou trod very carefully, with significant skepticism of too heavy a government hand. The government was, at most, to watch the aggregate indicators of economic health and apply "a brake or a stimulant."[67] This could mean restricting or expanding credit, shifting its spending schedule, or providing bounties to certain nationally essential industries. Much of the lengthy section devoted to "remedies" concerned ways that the government could make the market function better. The state was to restore confidence and stability by adhering to the gold standard; it was to increase labor mobility; and, above all, it was to ensure that wages were able to adjust rapidly.[68] Thus, though Pigou put forward recommendations that were technocratic insofar as they would be implemented by state bureaucrats, by highlighting the importance of flexible prices, he circumscribed the role of the government in mitigating crises. In *Wealth and Welfare* and *The Economics of Welfare*, an ethical desire had motivated Pigou to create a conceptual framework that justified new sorts of ameliorative action to protect the social from the individual. Though *Industrial Fluctuations* justified state intervention on similar grounds, its message was much less provocative, and its exposition made for a considerably less strident call to action.

A Study in Public Finance, which appeared a year later, in 1928, continued in a similarly scholarly vein. Pigou noted in its preface that it was to be taken together with *The Economics of Welfare* and *Industrial Fluctuations*.[69] But though *Public Finance* was continuous with the tradition of Pigou's welfare economics, the new work was even less suitable for lay audiences than was *Industrial Fluctuations*. Readers not already familiar with Pigou's work would have significant trouble parsing the nuances of Pigou's meaning for, as

Hugh Dalton, writing in *Economica*, noted: "This third member of the trilogy . . . has less the appearance of a well-proportioned system and more that of a series of elaborations."[70] *Public Finance* also relied more heavily on equations than did its predecessors. "The abstract and, in spots, involved mathematical treatment," one reviewer observed in the increasingly important *American Economic Review* "makes the reading difficult."[71]

Difficulty, however, did not prevent academic reviewers from commending the work. Though Dalton compared it unfavorably to Pigou's past books, he also noted its "great merits relatively to the general body of modern writing on Public Finance." Pigou touched "no topic without illuminating it, and his logical skill in organising a discussion is unsurpassed among living economists."[72] Allyn Young was even more effusive. "Professor Pigou is constantly an explorer. His interest is always in the margins or frontiers where, by dint of painstaking analysis, new knowledge is to be had."[73]

In no small part, *Public Finance* responded to the unique economic problems that had arisen from the Great War. The first chapter concerned principles of compensation for commandeered materials, and the last discussed arguments for and against a massive capital levy of the sort that he had proposed nearly a decade before.[74] The book also reflected Pigou's own experience on government committees; the chapters on financing government expenditure through bank credits addressed the very problems the Cunliffe and Chamberlain-Bradbury Committees had faced, and in them, he provided justifications for several of the groups' conclusions.[75]

As a book primarily about taxation, *Public Finance* also drew from Pigou's experience on the Royal Commission on the Income Tax. Most of its pages studied specifics of tax schemes, calibrating tax levels and explaining how different types of taxes—land taxes, commodity taxes, or taxes on windfalls—might be implemented so as to take into account the distortions taxes caused in patterns of consumption.[76] Pigou's specific analyses were undergirded by a general principle of taxation: that taxes were to elicit the smallest possible aggregate sacrifice of general wellbeing across a society. This principle, he noted, was distinct from taxing people so as to make their sacrifices equal, though he also held that similar people should be made to sacrifice similarly. Each of these principles—"least sacrifice" and "equality" was important and, in resolving any tensions that arose between them, both "ultimate" principles were to "be brought before the tribunal of something more ultimate still, *i.e.* the principle of maximum good."[77] Fortunately, such a trial would not entail a messy optimization problem, since the two moral dicta overlapped. In practice, "tax arrangements that conform to the principle of least sacrifice always and necessarily conform also to the principle of equal sacrifice among similar and similarly situated persons."[78] This followed from conventional Marshallian reasoning. Sacrifices were minimized when the marginal sacrifice experienced by individuals was equal across the society.

Pigou, like his contemporaries, approached his subject with an unquestioned understanding that taxes were necessary because of their role in raising revenue; he made no comment on what might now be understood as macroeconomic policy. Pigou, at least in 1928, did not conceive of the purpose of government spending and finance as the improvement of overall national economic health, and the few pages he devoted to government expenditure focused largely on the determination of fair compensation for wartime appropriations.[79] *Public Finance* was not intended to advocate taxes as a way to directly improve social wellbeing. Instead it was meant to offer a heuristic analysis of tax forms and a framework for calibrating tax systems so they met existing revenue needs in the best possible way: a way that would take into consideration both fairness and efficiency.

Even on these grounds, Pigou was hesitant to make concrete policy recommendations. One notable exception concerned taxes on foreign trade, to which he remained firmly opposed on the grounds of faulty administration, though he admitted that "conditions may easily arise in which a country would benefit from restricting the importation of particular competitive goods." He also took a stance on unearned income; echoing the pre-war Liberal refrain, he called for higher taxes on unearned as opposed to earned income.[80] He similarly endorsed other old Liberal schemes: a graduated income tax, as the 1920 commission had recommended, and a system of death duties and taxes on monopolies and windfalls.[81] However, he concluded, all of these were "matters for technical experts" and "no final judgment can be passed upon the merits of the policy here sketched out except in collaboration with them."[82] Pigou himself, after all, was not a technical expert, but a theorist.

Though his work became more technical, as noted before, Pigou's output throughout the 1920s retained ethical elements. In this respect, *Public Finance* should be seen as it was intended: as a rigorous "supplement" to his work on welfare, a lengthy appendix concerned with the intricacies of fiscal policy.[83] But *Public Finance* was even less a call to action for the interventionist state than was *Industrial Fluctuations*. A comparison with one of the first works he wrote on taxation, the 1909 pamphlet on land taxes, is arresting. In 1909, Pigou had claimed that if a man were to find "an unexplained £100,000 in his garden, it is surely monstrous to vest the whole of this treasure-trove in the individual and none of it in the State."[84] There were no such decisive normative judgments in *Public Finance*.

Writing to Keynes in 1929, Pigou noted the recovery of his health: "My heart is now nearly as good as new" and joked "I plan to renovate my head next!"[85] The joke, however, was an apt metaphor for Pigou's transformation over the 1920s. By the end of the decade, Pigou was paying ever more attention to solving technical problems than to their ethical impetuses. Rather than the means to societal improvement, the creation and maintenance of his organon had become an end in itself. Moreover, it was an end that Pigou felt he had reached. With the completion of *Public Finance*, he declared to his publisher that he had covered "most of the subject matter of general economics."[86] But as his theoretical apparatus grew into its own, Pigou's hope for its practical application ebbed. By 1929, the year after *Public Finance* appeared in bookshops, he had entirely abandoned his long-held claim that the economist's central project was to bear fruit rather than light. In an address delivered at Oxford that spring, Pigou reversed his priorities. "The primary function of economic analysis ends with the provision of knowledge," he claimed, but "the knowledge that it provides may help in some measure—*not in great measure*, because many factors of a non-economic character are also relevant—to guide practice."[87] Pigou's comprehensive framework for understanding economic behavior was more or less complete, but it had been hollowed out. The organon lay ready to help understand economic reality but not to direct policymakers.

Within the academic community, however, Pigou's organon was almost universally respected. Moreover, the unity and influence of his own work was mirrored by that of his school. When Pigou succeeded Marshall to the Cambridge Chair of Political Economy in 1908, he inherited the position of power from which British economics had been shaped.[88] After Marshall's death in 1924, the forty-seven-year-old Pigou was the undisputed link back to the time of the Cambridge tradition's birth and the father figure for a flowering economics program. For the better part of the 1910s and 1920s, he presided over an ideologically and methodologically united economics faculty: a Marshallian consensus. The number of Tripos graduates tripled from around twenty in 1920 to nearly sixty a decade later.[89] The Departmental Library of Economics, which contained a good many books donated by Sidgwick and Marshall, grew out of its old home in the Divinity School and was moved to much larger spaces near the law schools on Downing Street in central Cambridge, the same building in which most economics lectures were held. There was growth in the faculty as well. Whereas six economists taught at Cambridge in 1910, there were twelve in 1925.[90] Of those, two, Keynes and Pigou, had been students of Marshall and one, C. W. Guillebaud, was Marshall's nephew.[91] Seven had taken the Economics Tripos at Cambridge, meaning that they had been Pigou's students.[92] The cohort responsible for the instruction of economics thus formed an identifiable and self-perpetuating "Cambridge School." And at the school's center was Pigou. Responsible for the general course on economic theory offered to second- and third-year students as well as a variety of other rotating courses, Pigou was by far the most important teacher of economics at the university during the period.[93]

The 1920s certainly witnessed economic debates in Cambridge— the articles by Clapham, Robertson, and Sraffa provide examples— but the serious disagreements arose between the "Cambridge School" as a unit and other schools of thought, among them the individualist-oriented "Austrian School" and a strain just beginning to take root closer to home at the LSE. Throughout the period, though Cambridge was home to a diverse array of economic think-ing, it displayed a generally unified front to the outside world.[94] When Pigou wrote to congratulate Dennis Robertson on a new book, his highest praise was that the work was a "great flower for the 'Cambridge School.'" And when Pigou himself had published an equation that led to a new conception of money demand in 1917, the concept became known not as the "Pigou k," but as the "Cam-bridge k."[95]

In and outside his home institution, Pigou's reputation in the 1920s was imposing; his scholarship earned him what one reviewer called the "high position which he occupie[d] among the world's economists."[96] In 1927, after two previous nominations in 1913 and 1917—both of which had been quashed by a group led by the em-bittered Foxwell and William Cunningham—he was finally elected to the fellowship of the British Academy.[97] The next year, he was elected as a foreign honorary member of the American Academy of Arts and Sciences. His 1929 delivery of the Sidney Ball Lecture, an annual talk at Oxford on social policy, showcased him as a thinker at the top of his field, one who fluently discussed the importance of the latest statistical tools to the analytical method.[98] Pigou could bask in the praise of his colleagues. In 1927, Josiah Stamp, the fel-low economist on the of the Income Tax Commission, noted that "a new work . . . from Professor Pigou bids fair to be itself an economic event of some importance." In the words of his reviewers, his work was "very scholarly," "most authoritative," and characterized by "or-ganic unity and massive solidity."[99] It was, in short, "worthy of a Professor of Political Economy in the University of Cambridge."[100] Pigou, to use the word of his friend Dennis Robertson, was a "giant."[101]

CHAPTER SIX

Paradigms Lost

IN 1932, JOAN ROBINSON, a young Cambridge economist, penned a short pamphlet titled *Economics Is a Serious Subject*.[1] It was a defensive work, meant to vindicate the economist's ability not only to produce rigorous scientific results but also to offer something concrete and helpful to the world. One of the reasons that Robinson's title was self-justificatory was that the discipline of economics was in the process of reevaluating itself. Books like *Lament for Economics*, a work published by another Cambridge economist, Barbara Wootton, and *An Essay on the Nature and Significance of Economic Science* (1932), by the LSE professor Lionel Robbins, raised questions about the stability of the discipline.[2] These titles were not merely a reflection on an interwar penchant for dramatic language; they were evocative of a growing uncertainty in the world of economic thought.

Robinson's pamphlet came in direct response to Lionel Robbins's *Essay*, which had produced strong waves in economics circles. Robbins's own story was a testament to how rapidly the discipline was changing. Though from a middle class background, Robbins was not Oxbridge educated and had, as Pigou would write of a young Eric Hobsbawm, "no old school tie."[3] Born in 1898, Robbins was part of a generation of economists who had received education in economics as such, a course of training whose existence owed a debt to figures like Pigou. Yet Robbins saw Pigou and other members of the older generation of economists as out of touch with modern methods, as falling short of the detached rigor required of the modern economic scientist. This was the view he expressed in his *Essay*, setting off a serious debate over the field's definition and purpose at a moment when economic thinkers of all political and ideological stripes were grappling with the general failure of their discipline to predict and combat the continued descent into economic catastrophe.

Yet whereas Robbins contended that that economics should (and, as a science, *could*) offer nothing but positive truth claims, Robinson, born in 1903, was still hopeful that her "serious" subject, if young and imperfect, was not only rigorous but also deeply inflected with the moral project of the betterment of humankind. In an unpublished note, she scrawled a list of thinkers to whom the pamphlet was indebted. Her husband, Austin Robinson, was mentioned, as was her mentor John Maynard Keynes and friends Dennis Robertson and R. F. Kahn. At the top, however, were the initials of A. C. Pigou, next to which Robinson had written, "the first serious optimist—with the gratitude of all who will follow him."[4] Such was the power and the importance of Pigou's welfare economics, explicitly animated by the desire to make things better and built on an optimism that it could actually bring about a happier, more just world.

However, by the time Robinson wrote her pamphlet in 1932, it was unclear whether Pigou could still be considered an optimist at all. Certainly, by the end of the decade, he was not. In a bitter 1939 presidential address to the Royal Economic Society, Pigou no longer held that economics was meant to help people, to bear fruit, but merely to theorize, to bear light. It was a pursuit that was, if not helpful, "at least not ignoble."[5] As Britain descended into the Depression, Keynes's theories emerged dominant at Cambridge, and economics redefined its conception of objectivity and its status as a rigorous science, Pigou himself slipped from dominance into pessimism.

Fissures in the Cambridge Front

The first hints of fundamental challenge to Pigou's ideas arose very slowly from within Cambridge itself. But early disputes, like the ones with Clapham, Robertson, and Sraffa, were amicable and, though significant, not cataclysmic. In them, Pigou largely took the position of the traditional defender of the Marshallian method, which was gradually coming under increasing scrutiny. When Keynes sent around an early draft of his *Treatise on Money*, Pigou was alone in his criticism that the new work "did not do justice to Marshall."[6] R. G. Hawtrey, an economics-trained civil servant, and Dennis Robertson also critiqued Keynes, but both found Pigou's responses lacking.[7] Still, it was generally accepted that intramural academic disagreements would be kept private, an acceptance derived in part from a shared stake in preserving a united Cambridge school. Though he disagreed with Pigou, Robertson wrote Keynes: "I don't want to give in public the impression of waging an all-round vendetta against the Prof! But I think it would be a good thing to send my note to the latter, so that he may see the objection occurred to two people independently."[8] The tone was conciliatory, hardly pointed.

Even in 1931, some six years after the circulation of Keynes's early draft of what would become the *Treatise on Money*, Cambridge maintained a fairly unified, generally Marshallian, front. For all the back and forth, Keynes's treatise, which came out early that year, still worked in the general tradition of Pigou's so-called Cambridge equation of money demand that he had written in 1917, which suggested that demand led supply.[9] Indeed, these early debates in Cambridge about monetary theory were largely over a minor issue.[10] When challenged by Pigou over a point in his *Treatise*, Keynes was at pains to note that the controversy stemmed from a misunderstanding—one due, he wrote to Pigou, "to your supposing that I held my equations to be in some way inconsistent with the Cambridge equation."[11] Nothing, Keynes held, could be further from the case.

The advent of the Great Depression in 1929, however, threw a spotlight on internal fissures that had been growing in the economics profession since Marshall's retirement in 1908. These cracks were not merely academic differences in theory, but divergences of a more general nature related to outlook and to the basic understanding of the economist's role. For Pigou, disenchanted with the government and with public life since his committee involvement in the early 1920s, the economist was to be an academic, a scholar who worked alone in an ivory tower. But another model of the economist had crept into the public consciousness: that of policy advocate.[12] This new proactive form was principally represented by Keynes, who had been an outspoken critic of government policies since the end of the Versailles Peace Conference. Keynes and his growing number of disciples shared none of Pigou's qualms about participating in government or about publicly supporting economic policies, even if it meant casting off a veil of nonpartisanship.[13] Both Keynesian and Pigovian theories called for the government to play a significant role in moving society toward a better state of economic affairs. But whereas Pigou conceived of government action as intended to reduce inequality and mitigate negative external effects, Keynes saw the government as acting so as to manage the overall health of the national economy, particularly the unemployment rate. With his government advisory positions and his city contacts, Keynes, much more than the disenchanted Pigou, still saw the government as a direct method of affecting ameliorative economic policy.

Certainly, Britain was in desperate need of ameliorative policy as global Depression descended on the heels of a decade of stagnant domestic economic performance. Immediately after the war, Britain had grappled poorly with the substantial problems of reinserting returning soldiers into the labor force and servicing its massive debts to the United States. The government severely cut spending from 1918 to 1920, contributing to a "slump" in 1921, and the 1925 decision to return to the gold standard had proved to be premature and stifling for Britain's export industries.[14] Throughout the 1920s, unemployment had dogged the British labor force, with levels hovering around 8 percent.[15] Largely because of this, the Labour Party, campaigning with the promise to provide "Work or Maintenance," was able to push the Conservatives from power in May 1929. But after the stock market crashed that October, American liquidity dried up overnight, leaving the new government unable to furnish either the work or the maintenance it had pledged in the election. Facing a massive contraction in world trade and continuing debt obligations, Labour found its actions constrained by "sound finance," the traditional wisdom of public policy. For though Labour had achieved its recent electoral success by blaming stagnant economic conditions on the excesses of capitalism, its own economic policy still reflected a fairly conventional economic outlook, based on a once-stable world order that now lay in ruins.[16]

For much of Labour's leadership—including the Prime Minister and Chancellor of the Exchequer—balanced budgets and the gold standard remained sacrosanct. But in a recession, these commitments had drastic consequences. Between them, they ensured that money was expensive and, despite rocketing unemployment, meant that only limited government support for the poor would be available. For generations, British prosperity had been built on world trade. But trade fell off precipitously after the crash in New York with the result that Britain, once "the workshop of the world," entered what Prime Minister Ramsay MacDonald would call an "economic blizzard," a downward spiral of sinking business confidence and shrinking national prosperity.[17] Joblessness soared, especially for workers living in the industrial heartlands of Labour's support. Unemployment figures for insured workers hovered just under 10 percent before the crisis, but rose steadily to a monthly average of 16 percent in 1930 and over 20 percent for the following three years.[18] The industrial north was particularly stricken, but wealthier areas of the country—even London and Cambridge—were hit as well. Southeast England, the administrative division that contained Cambridge, saw unemployment spike from 8.1 percent to 17.1 percent between 1929 and 1932.[19] Facing mounting economic and political pressure, MacDonald and Snowden found themselves with few options. They had campaigned on the promise to help the working poor, but the imperatives of sound finance and free trade, resolutely supported by City financiers and many Labour MPs alike, left them with their hands tied. In desperation, the government sought the advice of economists, specifically, an economist who had been willing to opine on matters of policy for many years: John Maynard Keynes.

It was in this way that Keynes came to be a driving force behind the 1930 creation of the government's Economic Advisory Council (EAC). Because the group was mostly composed of business leaders and policymakers, Keynes and a handful of like-minded, politically connected economists (including Josiah Stamp and H. D. Henderson), were in a position of drafting economic memos and making "any correction . . . [thought] essential" to material destined for the desk of the Prime Minister.[20] For Keynes, the EAC was a new sort of mechanism by which economists could exert direct influence on individuals at the highest levels of government and thereby shape policies related to economic management. He wrote to Prime Minister Ramsay MacDonald that "issues of economic diagnosis" were "the sort of thing for which economists, if they are any good at all, should be useful" and pushed for the creation of a secret "small committee, composed of leading professional economists" in the EAC that could "produce an answer."[21] He suggested only a few names. Henderson, Stamp, and he himself would represent the EAC and there would be a representative of the Bank of England, Professor Henry Clay. Finally, he suggested Pigou, Robbins, and Dennis Robertson "as leading academic economists."[22]

The difference between Pigou and Keynes's roles reflected a deep divide between the two men, which Hugh Dalton later described. "Keynes," Dalton wrote, "was a Man of the World . . . always on the move, with shining wings, from point to point, changing his opinions and prescriptions at short notice." In contrast, "Pigou was . . . fixed in Cambridge. His system never greatly changed. He gave the impression of using *one* machine, most beautiful and powerful in its construction, to solve a series of problems, the solutions all tending . . . to have a certain family likeness."[23] Though Dalton took poetic license, he captured two key differences. First, Pigou was the academic, "fixed at Cambridge," while Keynes was the policymaker, active and involved in Whitehall and the City. Second, whether warranted or not, to the contemporary observer, Pigou represented fixity; Keynes, dynamism.

In the summer of 1930, Pigou begrudgingly agreed to join Keynes's economists' committee. In August, on receiving inquiries about his participation, Pigou replied that he had "been asked," but was in no hurry to get down to London and still less eager to deal with the bureaucracy that such meetings entailed. Writing from the Alps en route to the Isle of Skye in Scotland and then Buttermere, he seemed to think of his participation as a favor or, perhaps more rightly, a chore. "I am planning to settle down in the Lakes and get on with my book till term. It's a great business getting up and down . . . so I think I might be let off the . . . procedure meeting. I would then come down for the week-end parts, and go back again to the Lakes till term or just before. Would that do?"[24]

On the committee, Pigou was a somewhat recalcitrant participant, just as he had been in the immediate postwar period, but his disinterest was overshadowed by a major disagreement between Keynes and Lionel Robbins, also a committee member, over trade policy. Led by Keynes, the committee submitted recommendations for a 10 percent tariff on all imports and a symmetrical bounty on exports until "abnormal unemployment" had subsided. The anti-protectionist and Austrian-influenced Robbins, however, balked and dissented, even after the rest of the committee agreed on the proposal.[25] Pigou, the old free trader, also had negative feelings about the plan, but unlike Robbins, he did not put up a fight. Pigou was less invested in the committee's work than Robbins was, but he also had another reason for signing on to Keynes's proposals.[26] Like many of the other economists on the committee, he was far more interested in presenting a unified front to government officials than he was with staying true to any particular agenda, even free trade.

This stemmed not so much from Pigou's Government House Utilitarianism as from an understanding shared by many committee members that the usefulness of their work depended on their unity in endorsing any recommendations they made. By resorting to the opinions of scientific "experts," the government was groping for terra firma—for concrete truth, or at least consensus, on which it could base its policies.[27] Without unity, the illusion of fact was lost. For this reason, the committee's secretary, A. F. Hemming, was loath to allow Robbins to publicly dissent and tried to hold him up on procedural precedent.[28] For his part, Pigou, sympathetic with Keynes's impulse to recommend definitive action and long cognizant of the power of the economist's perceived status as a scientist, refused to dissent along with Robbins and instead signed his name to Keynes's proposal, despite disagreeing with its ultimate recommendation for tariffs.[29] Hugh Dalton recorded that Pigou had tried to convince Robbins that writing a minority report would be ungentlemanly.

> "One never does that," said Pigou, "one tries to reach the greatest possible measure of agreement and then, if necessary adds a minute of dissent

on particular points." "If you want to make a row outside," said Pigou on another occasion, "can't you find some other way of doing it?"[30]

Pigou's insistence on agreement over conviction infuriated Robbins. "Lofty old woman," he privately wrote of Pigou. "Determined to be good committee man. Provided it was on record that Professor Pigou had recorded his dissent[,] who cared if the vulgar were swayed by the opposing arguments."[31] True to form, Pigou's divergence from the conclusions of the final report evidenced in a short paragraph of disagreement, where he noted his objections to tariffs on the grounds that they would not be repealed when economic conditions improved.[32] For him, a more comprehensive and public dissent would have damaged the reputation of his field, and Pigou was deeply committed to keeping that reputation intact.[33] His own was harnessed to it.

Indeed, for Pigou, the fact that economists were saying something definitively and with a degree of unanimity—even though the message was not very substantive—was particularly important in times of turmoil and uncertainty. In the autumn of 1932, in the midst of the Depression, the *Times* asked economists to comment on the "problem of private spending." Faced with the opportunity to confront an issue that could be solved without recourse to a deeply imperfect government, but solely by collective public action, Pigou hurriedly contacted colleagues from across the political and theoretical spectrum in the hope that they might together urge the public to spend more, a step that was widely accepted as vital for recovery.[34] Pigou drafted a deliberately uncontroversial statement warning that by saving too much, people would "be martyrs by mistake, and in their martyrdom, will be injuring others as well as themselves," which Keynes circulated.[35] Several economists, including Stamp, Walter Layton, and Arthur Salter, quickly signed on. The elderly Edwin Cannan, who had also been invited, however, published a set of caveats to Pigou's simple message, provoking a saddened response from Pigou, who had "thought [he] had left out all matters of controversy."[36] "The only effect of the various letters," he lamented, "has been to give the impression that economists never agree about anything at all, whereas I believe, as a matter of fact, we all do agree about the essentials.[37]

This may have been true, but disagreements in the discipline were steadily breaking out all over, even in Cambridge itself. Though Pigou and Keynes agreed that too much private saving was hurting the Depression-era economy, they disagreed strongly about the essentials of foreign trade and protectionism; Pigou maintaining his free trade stance and Keynes defending a more protectionist agenda.[38] More importantly, at the same time, Keynes was also beginning work on a new theoretical monetary model that would fundamentally challenge the traditional Marshallian one.

Meanwhile, economic conditions continued their downward spiral. Despite its promises to end unemployment, the Labour government had been able to do no such thing. As the country slipped into a deepening recession—the number of job seekers reached more than 3 million in 1931—Labour's struggling leadership broke with the large swath of the party that resisted coalition and formed a National Government with "men from all parties" in August 1931. The government, still led by MacDonald, left the gold standard in September 1931 and, responding to a compelling mixture of economic advice and political necessity, bowed to mounting pressures pushing for the institution of protective tariffs in 1932.[39] For by the mid-thirties, in the midst of economic winter, with Britain already off the gold standard, the great Liberal cause of free trade was dead.

As an affluent university town, Cambridge was relatively insulated from the economic and social turmoil engulfing the country, but every Briton living through the Depression felt the stress that gripped the nation and much of the world. With unemployment figures well into the double digits, restive social forces were bubbling over. Beginning in 1931, hunger marches and demonstrations became regular occurrences; the so-called Great Hunger March in October 1932 saw crowds of tens of thousands converge on London. Riots and heightened security measures became par for the course.[40] The "Hungry Thirties" were years of growing leftist sentiment and corresponding "Red Panic," and the popular press screamed warnings that the unemployed marchers were "pawns in a Communist game directed by master-intriguers of Moscow."[41] The Communist Party of Great Britain grew over the period, as did the leftist National Unemployed Workers' Movement. So too did the

British Union of Fascists. For Pigou—a devoted reader of the stolid *Times*—these developments were as frightening as their underlying economic cause. It is no surprise, then, that the Slump provoked him—as it did many economists from across the political spectrum—to again grapple with the phenomenon of unemployment.[42]

Pigou had started work on a technical treatise on the forces behind unemployment early in 1930, well before he joined the EAC. That fall, he began teaching a course on "Problems of Unemployment" to undergraduates and wrote to Keynes that he was "coming to the notion of making my next book a general discussion of unemployment."[43] Three years later, on April 24, 1933, he informed his publisher that the draft for this book, *The Theory of Unemployment*, was ready; that summer, it appeared in shops.[44] Continuing in the trajectory of *Industrial Fluctuations* and *Public Finance*, Pigou's new book was directed squarely at an academic audience. Its goal was to "clarify thought, not to advocate a policy," and Pigou offered "no apology . . . for publishing, in a period when the tragedy of unemployment is of unexampled magnitude, a book on that subject strictly academic in tone and content."[45] The result was Pigou's most mathematical and abstract tome to date, one that presented a highly complex model of the nature and causes of unemployment with the help of a great number of equations, references, and assumptions that would be understood only by those well versed in the literature of the time. For all its esoteric sophistication, however, Pigou's *Theory* bore a seemingly simple message, one that at points seemed out of keeping with his earlier progressivism: in theory, the course of depression was to be reversed first and foremost by cuts in the real wage of labor. At times, Pigou could sound callous. He noted that unemployment would probably be reduced "by contracting pensions and unemployment pay and remitting equivalent taxation on the well-to-do."[46] Transfers to the poor would likely harm national economic health more than help it, even if there were socially desirable reasons for maintenance of the indigent or out of work.[47] But Pigou's analysis of unemployment also suggested a significant role for "state action." Compulsory unemployment insurance would be helpful, as might "all sorts of State stimulation to employment in particular industries," notably bounties on the employment of new workers.[48]

In his previous academic books, Pigou had generally avoided making clear policy prescriptions and to put those that he did make in the hypothetical, nestled among a great many caveats. Such caution was equally if not more evident in *The Theory of Unemployment*, a tightly reasoned book that employed a collection of models and significant mathematical exposition over the course of its 319 pages.[49] For Pigou, unemployment was determined by a "complex," or "system of interconnected *factors*," including "employers' real demand functions for labour; . . . the set of real wage-rates stipulated for by the workpeople; the distribution of workpeople at different centres; and the degree of their mobility."[50] Still, at the very heart of the book was an exploration of the elasticity of the real demand for labor. In the short run, Pigou was convinced that the surest way of reducing unemployment was to lower the real wage, a topic to which he devoted part I of the book. Using accounting identities, basic differential calculus, and some estimation, Pigou arrived at the suggestive conclusion that the elasticity of the demand for labor was quite high. The implication was clear: "an all-around cut of 10 per cent in money rates of wages would lead, *other things being equal*, to a more than 10 per cent expansion in the aggregate volume of labour demanded, and so . . . in the volume of employment."[51]

The book's abstract rigor was widely noted and as a whole, it was generally hailed as "a valuable contribution to the academic study of the subject."[52] It was, in the words of one reviewer in the *American Economic Review*, "a keen, penetrating piece of analysis, worthy of the best Marshallian tradition." According to another in the *Quarterly Journal of Economics*, it was "one of the great books of recent years."[53] However, by the early autumn, Pigou's book had made a distinctly different sort of impression on Keynes and his growing cohort of followers. Much has been written about the degree to which Keynes and his supporters were fair in their pointed evaluations of the *Theory of Unemployment*, and more than one scholar has found Keynes's criticisms reductive and ultimately unfounded. From the beginning, though, it was clear that Keynes found the *Theory* both striking and deeply objectionable.[54] He asked Dennis Robertson: "Have you read the Prof's book carefully? I find it most disturbing. For if I haven't completely misunderstood it, it's simply nonsense from beginning to end."[55]

Keynes spoke as if he were surprised, but he likely was not. For as long as Pigou was working on his *Theory*, Keynes had been developing his own, the bulk of which would emerge in his 1936 *General Theory of Employment, Interest and Money*. And while on the EAC's committee of economists, Keynes had already come to loggerheads with Pigou over the causes of the Depression. Writing to his friend Ralph Hawtrey at the Treasury in 1930, Keynes had vented about an "attempt to explain to Pigou and Robertson the difference between excess hoarding and excess saving, about which they have been making obstinate misunderstandings."[56] By the time of the publication of Pigou's book, Keynes had strayed even further from traditional Marshallian precepts.[57] In a 1933 letter to John Hicks, an economist at the LSE, Keynes tantalizingly hinted that he had "put my finger on the fundamental point which, quite apart from saving and investment decisions, separates me not only from you and Pigou but from everyone since Ricardo."[58]

Over the next few months, in his responses to Pigou's *Theory*, Keynes painted it as overly optimistic and overly neat, the capstone of a classical tradition, according to which there would be no long-term involuntary unemployment and no long-term problems with the market self-regulating as long as it was allowed to run its course. Writing to Robertson, he lamented that the entirety of the *Theory* "turns on a completely bogus use of the mathematics of a single variable . . . [Pigou's] conclusion that employment (cet. par.) will only improve if real wages fall is only true in the same sense that it is true (cet. par.) that employment will only improve if more caviare [sic.] is consumed."[59] Here was a rupture, a gap between Pigou and Keynes so great that Keynes asserted the utter insanity of the older economist's ideas. "A.C.P. produces as great a sense of Bedlam in my mind, as [F. A.] Hayek does," Keynes exclaimed. "Are the undergraduates to be expected to take it seriously? What a subject!"[60] To Keynes, though the professor's earlier work on welfare was still seminal and his practical conclusions sound, his new output only continued in a dated vein.

Pigou's book was studded with nuances and caveats that made it significantly less traditional than Keynes had figured it to be. But unlike Keynes's work, Pigou's book focused on the real economy; he wrote in the preface that a recent emphasis on the monetary had led economists "to overstress somewhat the rôle that money plays," a line directed not least at Keynes and his recently published *Treatise on Money*.[61] Moreover, it was, at its heart, a Marshallian work and one, like *Industrial Fluctuations*, that did not make so strident a call for state action as Keynes's, which advocated that the government stimulate demand. Pigou held that unemployment was largely a result of fluctuations in the real demand for labor and that its solution was to be reached by lowering real wages, the wage adjusted for market prices.[62] To do this, Pigou argued that, in theory, real wages (or the actual purchasing power that workers received) would have to fall.[63] In contrast, Keynes had a broader conception of economic interactions, not only of how money wages related to real wages but also of how monetary forces in the economy affected unemployment. This led him to different conclusions about the importance of wage cuts. Moreover, much more than Pigou, Keynes focused on aggregate terms rather than on individual components of the economy.[64]

Still, it is critical not to overstate the differences between Keynes and Pigou, especially with regard to practical policy recommendations in the early 1930s.[65] Pigou hardly thought that the state ought to step aside and let the market self-correct. Though he held that there would be little "long-run effect of expansionist State policies," he saw "no argument against the State's *temporarily* adopting these devices as 'remedies' for unemployment in times of exceptional depression."[66] Such devices included "large-scale public works, . . . bounties, guarantees of interest," and even, "if successful in their purpose, protective duties."[67] Pigou had advocated a type of countercyclical spending since *Wealth and Welfare*, in which he endorsed proposals for municipalities and even the national government to make a greater number of their necessary purchases in times of depression rather than in boom times.[68] By 1933, his arguments had developed considerably. In one passage, strikingly reminiscent of what would later be known as Keynesian fiscal stimulus, Pigou expressed his support for public works spending when interest rates were unable to decline low enough to stimulate industrial investment:

> In times of deep depression, when industrialists see no hope anywhere, there may be *no* positive rate of money interest that will avail to get . . . money used. . . . In these circumstances, attempts to uphold the standard monetary system, so long as reliance is placed on purely monetary defenses, are bound to fail. If, however, . . . the Government adopts a policy of public works, the risk of failure is greatly reduced.[69]

An even more fundamental similarity existed between Keynes and Pigou's work on unemployment: both economists were concerned with finding a middle way between, to again use Masterman's terms, "privilege and revolt." Put in different terms, both were Liberals in a Britain that was increasingly torn between Tories and Labour. Both were moderates, and both had come a long way from prewar economic thought. But whereas Keynes stayed the Liberal course, Pigou had already begun to veer off it. It is striking, in historical retrospect, to consider the subject of Pigou's book: the "evil" of unemployment among wage laborers.[70] This was not a book about the individualist citizen-consumer. Instead, much more directly than Keynes's work, it was about the travails of the worker.

Keynes did not focus on Pigou's leftward-drifting liberalism but instead on the purportedly conservative implications of his model. And in Keynes's telling—as well as the tellings of many of his followers—his and Pigou's models were entirely unalike, as far apart as were his own and those of F. A. Hayek, an Austrian School economist at the LSE and a strident advocate for the free market.[71] Keynes's immediate reactions, which, as will be discussed later, he refined for his *General Theory*, were fairly extreme by the standards of the day. Two of the most famous careful readers of the book, Robertson, a traditional Marshallian who had worked closely with Keynes, and Ralph Hawtrey, a policy economist and the author of a leading textbook on monetary economics, both found his appraisal of the book somewhat unfair.[72] A third prominent economist to read it, Keynes's supporter Roy Harrod, offered many critiques, but ultimately hailed it as "a masterpiece of close and coherent reasoning."[73] Robertson, who along with Sraffa had revised drafts of the book for Pigou, responded to Keynes's emotive letter while "on brief holiday" to defend the work.[74] "I have always found the Prof's . . . method hard to get into," he wrote, "but I thought I was satisfied it worked out all right." Robertson, however, was less defensive of Pigou than he was saddened by the loss of consensus: "What a ghastly subject it is! Here you are saying wage-reductions are no good, and Pigou saying they are a lot of good, and Walter [Layton] saying they are no good at the beginning of a slump but some good at the end. . . . How I wish we could form a Cambridge front again!"[75] But in spite of Robertson's lamentations, and whether or not Keynes's critiques were valid or fair to Pigou's intent, the Cambridge front was fast disintegrating.

The next year, debate sprang up over who would fill a vacated University Lectureship in Economics. Perhaps the most favored candidate was Joan Robinson, the Cambridge economist who had written *Economics Is a Serious Subject* and had published *The Economics of Imperfect Competition*, an effort to extend Marshallian reasoning beyond perfect competition in response to Sraffa, to great acclaim the year before.[76] Pigou himself had provided some help with the revisions, joking to Robinson, "you will be amused to hear that I have just found in my proofs a greatly improved title for your book—The economics of improper competition."[77] Pigou maintained a friendly relationship with the Robinsons—on the birth of their daughter, Pigou wrote to Austin, "well done, Congratulations!" and invited the growing family up for "a spot of Buttermere." Inquiring as to the name of the infant, he suggested "Marginal Revenue Optimizer For Robinson!"[78] And, during the early 1930s, Joan Robinson was eager to secure the favor of Pigou. When Pigou took an active interest in a formal mathematical error in Robinson's work—he supposedly solved the problem while considering it one night in bed before going to sleep—both she and her close colleague R. F. Kahn were very pleased.[79] Nevertheless, both reacted with more than a hint of dismissiveness. Kahn wrote Robinson that "it is very good to hear the Professor acting as your mathematical handyman," and Robinson herself sought to downplay his contribution— "it doesn't add anything, but it is very beautiful"—even though she had at first failed to grasp its point.[80] For his part, Pigou was not ready to support Robinson for the lectureship, because by 1934, she was squarely in Keynes's camp, by now known as the Circus. Though she had referred to Pigou as "the first serious optimist," on the same list, Robinson described Keynes as "the optimist who showed that optimism is justified," the actual vindicator.[81]

Notwithstanding Pigou's friendly relations with the Robinsons and other economists of the rising generation, the younger Cambridge economists had largely flocked to Keynes.[82] Pigou was quite close to R. F. Kahn, for instance. He wrote glowingly of the latter's fellowship essay and was a source of advice in the 1920s. Indeed, the two remained friends until Pigou's death; they shared a passion for mountaineering, and as Pigou aged, Kahn managed the older man's finances.[83] Kahn would even bring imperfect competition to welfare economics, his work on the subject continuing in a Pigovian vein.[84] But Kahn was Keynes's star pupil, and it was clear where his intellectual loyalties lay. Robinson too sought to attach herself to Keynes's camp without alienating Pigou. When it came time, for instance, to review Pigou's *Theory of Unemployment*, she published an anonymous review in the *New Statesman* that painted the book, not as a major work but as a special case of Keynesian conclusions, an act she called "low cunning" that was intended to please Keynes.[85]

Of course, Robinson's candidacy for lectureship was suspect to many of her peers for a reason quite unrelated to her economics. She was a woman—one of three who taught economics at Cambridge before World War II—and her career was very much shaped by the prevailing sexism of the day. Pigou himself was by no means enlightened in this respect: he would later confide to Noel-Baker that when writing on the question of women's wages, "My huge principles and unfortunate sense of justice prevent me from the satisfaction of proposing that they should be made to work for nothing at all, chained together in gangs!"[86] However, Pigou's correspondence with Robinson revealed both an academic seriousness and a friendship, which together make it seem unlikely that Robinson's gender was the primary reason for his opposition to her appointment. Rather, it was the nature of Robinson's other friendships and the methodological inclination of her own academic seriousness that weighed on Pigou's mind when it came time to back a bid for the lectureship.

Instead, he supported John Hicks, the candidate out of the LSE, for the job.[87] To do so, Pigou joined with Dennis Robertson. Robertson was friends with Hicks, and though the former (along with most everyone else at Cambridge) was "a good deal out of sympathy with the extravagant [free market] dogmatism" of the LSE, Hicks was preferable to the Keynesian Robinson.[88] Robertson and Pigou were the only two prominent non-Keynesian theorists left at Cambridge, and they had a good deal in common.[89] Robertson, a fellow of Trinity since 1914, was a steadfast Liberal, had been president of the Union, and had even won the same award—the Cobden Prize—that the young Pigou had received for his Marshallian analysis of British agriculture. At Pigou's initiative, they had authored a book together three years earlier and, in Pigou's description, acted as "mutual catalysts . . . so as to keep one another going."[90] Together, the pair prevailed in blocking Robinson, and in 1934, Pigou had the grim pleasure of writing to Hicks with the offer.[91] Hicks was a rising star, and his *Theory of Wages*, published two years before, had been well received so that in several ways, his appointment represented something of a coup for Cambridge.[92] But it also indicated the extent of dramatic changes reshaping the Cambridge front. Appointing Hicks was, in a sense, a risky move, for though he was inspired by the Marshallian tradition, he was also influenced by the Austrian ideas gaining ground in London. Thus, his move to Cambridge was an indication that the gulf between Pigou and Keynes had become as great as that between Pigou and nearly any other prominent economist in Britain.

Keynes on the Rise: The Publication of The General Theory

Keynes's challenges to Pigou's position at Cambridge and in British economics culminated in his 1936 publication of *The General Theory of Employment Interest and Money*.[93] Although economists who were in contact with Keynes throughout the 1930s were familiar with many of the book's most contentious points, *The General Theory* was instantly understood as an immensely disturbing—and polarizing—work.[94] In it, Keynes presented a comprehensive, if sketchy, alternative to the established Marshallian system, building all his objections into a formal unified model. And this new model bore powerful implications for the role of the state in the economy. Keynes, a co-founder of the EAC and a frequent commuter to London, suggested that without decisive government action, the economy could stay in indefinitely prolonged stagnation.

Older economic models had never countenanced the potential for long-term involuntary unemployment, relying on forces internal to the market to bring the economy back toward full-employment equilibrium. Though in his welfare economics, Pigou had explicitly pointed out market failures, he never suggested that the market would fail so completely as to permit enduring unemployment on the scale witnessed during the Depression. And though he had argued for certain state relief measures, one of the central arguments of the *Theory of Unemployment* justified the reduction of money wages, a mechanism internal to the market that would push firms into hiring more workers and the economy back to prosperity.[95] Disenchanted with the government, Pigou had suggested that a great deal of damage could be rectified without recourse to an invasive state.

For his part, Keynes shifted attention from the failures of specific interrelated markets to the general failure of the economy. He suggested that if prices continued to fall, it was possible that the economy would enter a new equilibrium, one in which unemployment would persist indefinitely without decisive government action. *The General Theory* was largely a presentation of a set of monetary dynamics, but it reached a radically new conclusion: that after prices and interest rates had fallen past a certain level, monetary policies alone would do nothing to aid recovery. If the economy fell into this "liquidity trap," the government ought to engage in a program of spending—a "somewhat comprehensive socialisation of investment"—not just for the sake of purchasing goods, but with the purpose of injecting money into the economy, restoring confidence, and stimulating demand to boost production.[96] Fiscal policy was to treat the economy as a whole. This conclusion was shockingly new. So too was the dynamism that lay at the very heart of Keynes's model. In contrast, the year before, Pigou had written *The Economics of Stationary States*, a simplified textbook as a followup to his *Theory of Unemployment*, in which he made use solely of statics, to great acclaim.[97] In the words of a reviewer, Pigou's examination of one slice of time "displayed the white radiance of eternity" of the underlying elegant Marshallian principles that governed the marketplace.[98] Keynes's work took aim at both Pigou's stability and his certainty. In short, whereas Pigou conceived of economic remediation as a series of relatively small fixes, Keynes advocated for policies that would make much wider changes.

Keynes devoted a significant appendix of *The General Theory* to address Pigou's *Theory of Unemployment*, reiterating and expanding his previous criticism.[99] In Keynes's view, Pigou had passively accepted both the orthodox treatment of labor supply, in which the supply of labor was a function only of the real wage, and also the proposition that labor was "always in a position to determine its own real wage."[100] For one thing, this completely ruled out the possibility of involuntary unemployment. For another, it "assumed that the rate of interest always adjusts itself . . . in such a way as to preserve full employment."[101] In short, Keynes challenged, Pigou's title of "Theory of Unemployment" was "something of a misnomer. His book is not really concerned with this subject. It is a discussion of how much employment there will be, given the supply function of labour, when the conditions for full employment are satisfied."[102] In Keynes's reading, Pigou's *Theory* was an overly optimistic example of "classical" economics, one in which the market was always already in equilibrium and there was already full employment. Furthermore, by building his theory around the real wage of workers, Pigou ignored fluctuations in investment and, more generally, the effect of money. The result, per Keynes, was that "Professor Pigou believe[d] that in the long run unemployment can be cured by wage adjustments," not stimulation of demand or investment, as Keynes himself suggested.[103] Whereas Pigou focused on the correction of local problems and failures (wage adjustments, for instance, required a degree of local specificity), Keynes's solutions to the Depression treated the economy as a whole; they were general and sweeping.

Keynes well recognized the magnitude of his theoretical divergences, and he employed a host of rhetorical tools to convey his break with tradition. He adopted a flippant tone, claiming for instance, that to stimulate the economy, what was important was that the government spent money, not how it was spent. Burying banknotes in abandoned coal mines, he polemically claimed, would be approximately as helpful for recovery as investing it in housing stock.[104] He also presented a highly stylized version of the outdated "classical" school against which he was reacting. At its center was a straw man, A. C. Pigou, whose *Theory of Unemployment* was "the only detailed account of the classical theory of employment which exists."[105] This classical school epitomized by Pigou, Keynes claimed, was blatantly misleading, operating on the naïve assumption that the market would take care of itself.

Pigou's reaction was bitter and public. Writing, exceptionally, in *Economica*, the house journal of the LSE, he addressed what he considered personal attacks from a younger colleague he had, years before, recommended for a fellowship and whose undergraduate exams he had marked.[106] Pigou called attention to Keynes's effort to "lump" "classical" economists together so as to make "the shortcomings of one . . . attributed to all." With anger, Pigou paraphrased his antagonist: "Professor Pigou, in a book on Unemployment . . . has committed a variety of sins. Professor Pigou is a classical economist; therefore the classical economists have committed these sins!"[107]

Pigou objected to being painted with broad brushstrokes, snippily referring to himself in the third person and accusing Keynes of "misrepresentation," of choosing to pass over parts of his work that would have softened the differences between them. But he was doubly angered by "the patronage Keynes extended to his old master Marshall," from whom Keynes sought to signal his departure.[108] Keynes had great ambitions for his book, which he predicted in a letter to Bernard Shaw "would revolutionise . . . the way the world thinks about economics problems." To do so, he would, in his words, "raise a dust" in his departure from the classical Marshallian tradition.[109]

In Pigou's estimation, Keynes engaged in popular rhetoric and in so doing compromised his status as an economic scientist. Even as far back as 1919, when Keynes wrote *The Economic Consequences of the Peace*, he had abandoned the nobility that Pigou prized in academic economics. "For he discovered then, and his sub-conscious mind has not been able to forget since, that the best way to win attention for one's own ideas is to present them in a matrix of sarcastic comment upon other people. This method," Pigou wrote, "has long been a routine one among political pamphleteers. It is less appropriate, and fortunately less common, in scientific discussion."[110] This was the Professor reprimanding a wayward former student turned colleague, who, though only six years his junior, he saw as belonging to a younger generation that did not sufficiently honor the sanctity of economic science. Keynes's work was glib; it contained little of the ethical language that ran through Pigou's own writings on the "haunting evils" that the subject sought to correct. Keynes, Pigou seemed to suggest, had insufficient respect. "Einstein actually did for Physics what Mr. Keynes believes himself to have done for Economics," he wrote.[111]

Despite Pigou's ire and dismissiveness, *The General Theory*, with what came to be known as its macroeconomic approach, took economics by storm. Over the months after its publication, it spread to New Deal America and to former and current figures of the LSE—notably to Nicholas Kaldor and to John Hicks, who developed the IS-LM model, a formal representation of Keynes's ideas that still appears in standard economics textbooks.[112] For many at Cambridge, *The General Theory* soon became a touchstone, further fracturing what little remained of the old Cambridge unity.[113]

By 1937, correspondence between Keynes and Pigou was polite, but the two remained at theoretical odds.[114] While Keynes, exhausted by overwork, was on sick leave from his duties as editor of *The Economic Journal*, Pigou submitted a short article called "Real and Money Wage Rates in Relation to Unemployment," a piece that attacked the Keynesian position and constituted his first contribution to the debate on unemployment since his vitriolic review of *The General Theory*. Though the article was not as rigorous as much of Pigou's other work, Dennis Robertson, who was the *Journal*'s assistant editor, accepted it, much to the subsequent fury of Keynes and his circle. The article responded to *The General Theory*, again reiterating the traditional position that the money wage rate would need to decrease for employment to increase.[115] The responses from the Circus, both private and public, were strong and to a large degree coordinated so as to break Pigou's article apart.[116] To Kahn, Keynes wrote that the work was one "of a sick man, which no one would print who was in his right mind" and that Pigou was part of "a sort of Society for the Preservation of Ancient Monuments."[117] After receiving letters from Keynes and Kaldor, who had discussed the matter with each other and younger colleagues, Pigou gave in to the pressure placed on him by Keynes's circle. He wrote to Kaldor twice in short succession, first suggesting a different interpretation of his piece but then conceding that Dennis Robertson thought that "the arguments made in my article . . . were what you thought, and not what I said in the note. . . . Very likely he is right."[118] Pigou wrote almost diffidently, "I have been much preoccupied lately and not really composed to understand my own article!"[119] After several discussions with another of Keynes's students, D. G. Champernowne, he transformed the piece into a short comment and suggested that he might, in Keynes's words "return to the charge" and publish early the next year, something he did not do until 1941, by which time debates about the subject had moved in other directions.[120]

It has been suggested that Pigou's motivation for the withdrawal was worry over "upsetting the sick Keynes" and an effort to avoid confrontation.[121] Pigou *was* worried about confrontation, but not because of Keynes's health. In part, his decision was affected by his own ongoing medical troubles. The mid-to-late 1930s was an especially tenuous period for Pigou's health, and he was confined to nursing homes several times, making him an infrequent correspondent. His letters from the period displayed a shaking penmanship, often figured in pencil. "I have done another fibulation and have had to be descended here in state, because of the attack," he wrote Noel-Baker from the Swiss Alps in 1937. "It has stopped all night, but the patient is still feeble."[122] Beyond medical reasons, Pigou also wanted to avoid conflict because, despite his major differences with Keynes, he still cherished a desire to present economists as united. There was, however, a further rationale for his wavering: an erosion of confidence in his own writings. Once Robertson, Keynes, Kaldor, and Champernowne all combined against him, Pigou folded, expressing doubt in his work and even in his mental capacities. Though he had shown modesty before, the depth of this retreat was new. But it was to become increasingly common as he aged and grew more isolated in his own department, overlooked by his former students.

Having withdrawn from the public theoretical battle with Keynes, Pigou, in his late fifties and still in poor health, focused his efforts on playing an institutional role as a Cambridge elder. He faced the choice between a new Cambridge Consensus built not on Marshall's work but on Keynes's, and a more pluralist version of the Cambridge School, wherein Keynes's work would exist uncomfortably alongside more traditional approaches. Neither option was perfect, but Pigou was more predisposed against Keynesianism than he was for pluralism. Matters were complicated, however, by changes in the composition of the faculty. Despite (or perhaps because) he worked on topics similar to those that interested Keynes, Hicks had never been welcomed by the Circus, and he departed Cambridge for Manchester in 1938, just four years after he had arrived. With Hicks gone, Pigou worked even more vigorously to keep critics of Keynes, notably Robertson, at Cambridge and involved in the faculty.[123] But establishing any balance proved to be an uphill battle. Increasingly popular both with colleagues and students, Keynes, like Marshall before him, was filling Cambridge with supporters. For instance, he brought Michał Kalecki to the university from the LSE in 1938, setting him up with a project titled the "Cambridge Research Scheme of the National Institute of Economic and Social Research into Prime Costs, Proceeds and Output."[124] Statistical in nature, the scheme was supported by the expanding cohort of mathematically inclined practitioners, including Sraffa and Champernowne.[125] The growing institutional cohesion of Keynes's supporters left Robertson marginalized. Sensitive to this, Pigou interceded, asking Keynes to let him and Robertson sit on the Research Scheme's oversight committee. Keynes refused, and Robertson left Cambridge for the University of London in a huff, staying away until 1944.[126]

Robertson's departure spurred on Pigou in his efforts to prevent his beloved Cambridge from slipping further into the Keynesian grasp. He expressed "hesitance" to Joan Robinson about her lecturing on pre-Keynesian monetary theory. "In recent years the men have been put into a terrible muddle by having controversies," Pigou wrote, "about minor more or less verbal differences, emphasised to them." It would be, he intoned, "a great pity if you got the impression that everybody who wrote about money before Keynes was an imbecile and that his was a sort of sacred gospel of which every word was inspired."[127] Conscious of his own "more or less verbal differences" with Keynes, Pigou fretted about the dilution of Marshall's legacy and, increasingly, of his own. He continued somewhat testily to Robinson: "I hope very much that you will treat . . . [theories before Keynes] objectively. Of course, I don't suggest that you shouldn't criticise them or should suppress your own views. It's really a matter of degree."[128]

Pigou's words evinced his age as well as a fear of letting go of an institution he had helped build and of surrendering classic texts and foundational courses to Keynesians. Then again, for members of the rising generation, his own work would be labeled "classic." Already, the survey course on theory he had taught to every undergraduate for more than thirty years had been wrested from his control. In exchange, he was entrusted with a course of much lesser importance, a basic introduction to "elementary principles," which he would teach until his retirement.[129]

The publication traditionally favored by Cambridge economists, *The Economic Journal*, run by Keynes since 1913, was similarly a cause for concern.[130] In 1938, one of Keynes and Robertson's debates spilled over into the pages of the *Journal*. Seeking an impartial moderator, Keynes turned to Pigou, who seized on the opportunity to register his displeasure more generally with the tone and scope of the journal's content. He felt that there had been "much too much" about Keynesian conceptions of interest "in the *Economic Journal* recently." This was "particularly unfortunate as the topic is one that centres so much around the Editor. I have no doubt myself," Pigou wrote, "that the cause of this concentration lies in the character of the articles that are sent to you, but an unfriendly critic might easily attribute it to editorial bias . . . I think it important that the journal should continue to be 'the organ not of one school of economists but of all.'"[131]

Caveats aside, Pigou's response was an accusation that Keynes was turning *The Economic Journal*, even if passively, into his own personal space for debate. Keynes's reply was curt: "I am only too conscious of the large spaces given to what you call 'this sort of topic' and do my utmost to reduce it." However, he noted, "the truth really is that these and cognate topics are what everyone is thinking about and working at and where progress is being made and new things said."[132] Selection bias or no, Keynes was right. At Cambridge, "the Prof" was being eclipsed by his younger colleague and Keynes's Circus of admirers. Students Pigou had recommended and taught—including the Robinsons, Kahn, and Gerald Shove—embraced Keynes, who soon had an army of acolytes, many of whom themselves went on to teach at Cambridge. Pigou had hardly any. Keynes's, not Pigou's, were the economic views of the moment, and they would stay so for years to come. These developments would have emotionally jarring results. Pigou's authority was slipping not only in the faculty he had helped to found, but also in his own college, his home for the past four decades.

Methods and Objectivity

Despite the luster of Keynes's rising star, it was by no means the only challenge to Pigou's authority during the 1930s. The dissolution of the Cambridge Consensus and its reformation around Keynes was not the most dramatic transformation of the period for the economics discipline, or, arguably, even for Pigou himself. In the 1930s, the discipline's methodology changed in two fundamental ways, both of which worked to dislodge it from its heritage of political economy. First, the field received injections of increasingly sophisticated mathematics. Second, it renegotiated its relationship with ethics. Both developments had profound effects on Pigou and his work, but whereas he was able to accommodate the first, the second proved considerably more destabilizing. In the end, it would shake Pigou's world to its core.

Over the course of the 1920s, economists incorporated ever more mathematical reasoning into the text of their works. In large measure, this was a function of continuing curricular changes initiated by, among others, Pigou himself. In the years after its 1903 introduction, the Cambridge Tripos in Economics, originally set up in opposition to historical and narrative accounts of economic activity, began to offer training in statistics and formal modeling. This shift was concomitant with a greater concentration of mathematical knowledge among economists at Cambridge and across Britain.[133] In his 1907 application for election to a King's fellowship,

Keynes had submitted an essay on statistical probability, a topic whose mathematical components Pigou, an elector, felt unqualified to evaluate, but about which he was very enthusiastic.[134] Similarly, when R. F. Kahn, one of Keynes's protégés, came up for a fellowship at King's in 1930, Pigou heartily endorsed his economics, claiming that Kahn made "an exceedingly strong claim to fellowship," but deferred to others on evaluating the many mathematical elements.[135]

Until the mid-1920s, in the exposition of his books, Pigou had followed Marshall's personal "rule" of deriving economic principles mathematically but relegating the mathematics to endnotes and appendices and leaving the main text of the book the domain of words alone.[136] In *Industrial Peace*, for instance, he "endeavoured in the text to suppress this [technical] apparatus and to translate semi-mathematical reasoning into language intelligible to the ordinary reader."[137] He was, he later claimed, "looked at askance for occasionally putting a little algebra in a footnote."[138] But stylistic conventions were in flux during the 1920s, so that by 1928, one statistician suggested that even Pigou's flagship work would benefit from a more sophisticated mathematical expression. "The need for over eight hundred pages of sustained argument upon the one subject," British statistician L. R. Connor, wrote of the third edition of *The Economics of Welfare* (1928), "gives reasons for apprehension. Already, economic analysis taxes language to its uttermost, and it is a question how much longer mere verbal exposition will be able to control the swelling floods of observable data."[139]

The use of formal reasoning and econometrics was rapidly expanding during the period.[140] The journal *Econometrica*, which catered to both, rolled out its first issue in 1933 and the very term "model" was imported from physics to economics around the same time.[141] Pigou reacted throughout the 1920s, increasingly incorporating mathematical modeling in his work and making mathematics the explicit form of exposition for his 1933 *Theory of Unemployment*.[142] To no small extent, Pigou was successful in his integration of these elements; his books, as previously noted, met with great acclaim. So when the American economist Warren Persons wrote of *Industrial Fluctuations*, "so far as statistical data and methods are concerned, the book might have been written fifteen years ago instead of last year," Pigou could console himself with a host of other positive reviews.[143] Josiah Stamp asserted in his own review, for instance, that "the book will stand as almost a landmark in the development of method," because of its use of statistical verification.[144]

Pigou had a well-tuned mathematical mind. Not for nothing was he a chess partner of the computer scientist and mathematician Alan Turing, who joined the King's fellowship in 1935. While at Cambridge or at Lower Gatesgarth, Turing would play Pigou without so much as glancing at the board, a feat that impressed Pigou, a self-described "humble wood-pusher," immensely.[145] However, though he was hardly innumerate—his books exhibited an easy facility with differentials—Pigou was no mathematical wizard. His own education had been light in this area, and he relied on Muriel Barker Glauert, an aerodynamicist and the wife of a fellow of Trinity, to proof many of his equations.[146] Pigou also drew on colleagues for help. He turned to Piero Sraffa to review the mathematics of *The Theory of Unemployment* and to Kahn and Champernowne to do the same for his 1935 textbook, *Economics of Stationary States*.[147] He also consulted Turing to resolve a debate he was having, which "required some (to me) rather difficult mathematics."[148] Turing found that both Pigou and his interlocutor were wrong and, as Pigou reported, Turing "himself worked out what I presume was a valid argument, but would not let it be printed because he said, whatever it might be as economics, as mathematics it was 'not interesting.'"[149] But though Pigou made no pretensions that his comparative advantage lay in the province of mathematics, his overall treatment of mathematical concepts throughout the 1920s and early 1930s indicate that he was not significantly behind his peers in mathematical fluency.[150] Still, this hardly prevented Keynes, in his unrelentingly fierce criticism of the *Theory of Unemployment*, from portraying it as symptomatic of a general failing on Pigou's part: an example of his "pseudo-mathematical method."[151]

Economics was increasingly infused with mathematics, but the more sweeping shift in the discipline concerned the nature of economic objectivity. Perhaps unsurprisingly, the change had its origins in the era's furious political upheavals. The emergence of the Soviet Union had thrown the concept of central planning from the drawing board into the practical realities of daily life. Constantly in the headlines, the British Communist Party was a rising force, and notable public intellectuals—including Beatrice and Sidney Webb, whom Pigou met during his involvement in 1907 with the Royal Commission on the Poor Laws—were taking appreciative note of developments in Russia.[152] Closer to home, in the so-called Battle of Cable Street of October 1936, fascists and communists fought openly in the streets of London's East End. The conditions of the working poor and the hardships of the unemployed were poignantly depicted in widely read books, such as Fenner Brockway's *Hungry England* (1932) and George Orwell's *The Road to Wigan Pier* (1937). The Slump, in fact, provoked an entire genre, a "dole literature" of novels, memoirs, and documentaries. Many of these were distributed through the Left Book Club, a subscription service founded by Victor Gollancz, who, ironically, had previously worked for the publishing firm owned by the anti-socialist Ernest Benn. Bearing titles like *The Juvenile Labour Market* and *The Distressed Areas*, these books were often highly political and reached an ever-widening mass audience.[153]

There was, therefore, a sense of urgency in the ways planners and free-marketeers advocated for policies and for politically resonant ideas. Economics itself was becoming increasingly politicized; figures like Abba Lerner and Oskar Lange on the left and F. A. Hayek on the right were demonstrating that it was possible to be both a respected economist and an outspoken partisan commentator. Yet it was not just figures from the ends of the ideological spectrum that were participating in the political sphere. In Britain, organs like the Economic Advisory Council allowed more moderate thinkers, including Keynes and Josiah Stamp, to take increasingly active roles in government policy.

It was during this period, in the midst of the Great Depression, that Lionel Robbins wrote his seminal work on economic methodology, *An Essay on the Nature and Significance of Economic Science*. Part of Robbins's own motivation was local: an effort to stake out his own intellectual space and signal his departure from the aging and relatively staid older generation of LSE economists typified by Edwin Cannan.[154] Yet his work also offered a more generally applicable message. It was a biting response to the increased politicization of economics, arguing that the field was to be beyond ideology, beyond normative evaluations, even beyond ethics: a purely positive science that depended solely on what *was*, not on what should be. Robbins claimed to offer a powerful corrective for a discipline rechristened by figures like Pigou and Marshall as a science divorced from the old political economy, but one that was descending into political squabbles. However, Robbins's book carried implications that were easily as political as any of Pigou's work.

In the 1930 Oxford lectures that formed the basis for his *Essay*, Robbins grouped contemporary definitions of economics into four categories: "sociological definitions," definitions that "turn on the fact of exchange & money measurement," those that stressed the study of material welfare, and a fourth class that had to do with scarcity.[155] Of the four, the first three were the most common. Marshall's definition of the discipline as the study of the "ordinary business of life" was clearly sociological, while Edwin Cannan favored the material welfare definition.[156] In his own university lectures, Pigou took up the second category, holding that "economics is concerned with the activities of social groups which can be related directly . . . to a money measure."[157] Robbins, however, proposed a different definition that was in stark contrast to that of "Prof. Pigou."[158] For Robbins, economics was the "science which studies human behaviour as a relationship between ends and scarce means which have alternative uses."[159] This new, scarcity-centered conception, which is dominant today, expanded economics to realms not measurable in money: to *all* forms of choice.[160] However, in other respects it was also far more restrictive than previous definitions, as it precluded not only psychological investigations but also ethics. In the preface, Robbins wrote that economists were to "deal with policy like botanists deal with aesthetics," as something about which they might have an opinion, but not a *professional* opinion.[161]

Robbins was trying to detach economics from "political economy" by defining it as objective, as beyond claims of ideological inflection. He claimed Max Weber as his inspiration, borrowing the concept of *Wertfreiheit*, or ethical neutrality, the separation of analysis from normative evaluation.[162] Responding to one of his critics in the preface to the second edition, Robbins noted that the critic must "demolish, not me, but Max Weber: and I think Max Weber still stands." Though he had taught himself German and read Weber in the original, his German-language reading list was dominated by Austrian theorists like Hayek and Ludwig von Mises, Hayek's teacher in Vienna.[163] For the Austrians, and consequently for Robbins, what was to be taken from Weber was the notion of objectivity and of *Wertfreiheit*. But Robbins was himself caught up in another phenomenon described by Weber, the inherent tension in both observing a society and also inhabiting it.[164] As it was, despite his efforts to the contrary, Robbins himself participated in the advocacy of a distinct agenda.

For by redefining economics as a science of choice, Robbins was privileging the individual *chooser*, a bias that would have had resonance in the period of the Great Calculation debates over the efficacy of centralized planning to render efficient outcomes.[165] Robbins's new definition represented a turn away from both the materialism of Marxism and the embedded ethical commitments of an older generation of economists. What Robbins considered "scientific," "objective," or even "economic" was determined against a market-centered, choice-based definition.

Pigou was no Marxist, nor was he a participant in the socialist calculation debates. He was, however, ethically motivated, and his famous work on welfare displayed little hesitation about government administrators wresting basic choices from the hands of individuals for the greater good. Pigou was probably not Robbins's prime target in writing the *Essay*. In advancing his definition, Robbins most assertively challenged Edwin Cannan, not Pigou or Marshall, and in challenging the place of ethics in economics, it has been suggested that he took aim less at Cambridge than at more politically active economists working out of Oxford.[166] However, whether or not Robbins had Pigou in his crosshairs, the message of his *Essay* clearly applied to Pigou's work. One of the premises of the *Essay* remained a dismissal of that work, particularly *The Economics of Welfare*. Robbins was initially predisposed toward the book but "came to realize the extra-scientific nature of interpersonal comparisons used."[167] In other words, he took issue with what exactly Pigou meant by the common good and how such a conception was to be measured.[168] For Robbins, all previous work in welfare economics, of which Pigou's was the strongest and best known, had relied on interpersonal comparisons of utility as a basis for determining the socially optimal outcome.[169]

Robbins was, without question, right about this. Pigou's welfare economics, in seeking to use money as a proxy for happiness and therefore for welfare, assumed that the welfare of individuals could be compared. Pigou and other Marshallians generalized that since the marginal appreciation of wealth decreased with each added unit of capital, redistributions from the very rich to the very poor, ceteris paribus, would augment the total happiness in a society. These conclusions also assumed that the utility functions of the rich and the poor were roughly the same, a blurry claim that had caused friction since the days of J. S. Mill.[170] Robbins found these assumptions highly unscientific—there was no *proof* that utilities could be measured and no metric by which they could be rigorously compared. Even the great Marshallian "law of diminishing marginal utility . . . makes assumptions which, whether they are true or false, can never be verified by observation or introspection." Thus, Robbins concluded, any "arguments based upon it are lacking in scientific foundation."[171] Under his criteria, the theoretical apparatus of Pigou's foundational economics—particularly those dealing with welfare—were not up to modern scientific standards.

At a deeper level, Pigou's economics were objectionable because they were built around an ethical goal; Pigou himself had sought to draw a distinction between "positive economics" and "welfare economics" in his 1935 textbook, *The Economics of Stationary States*.[172] And because Pigou's loose brand of utilitarianism had motivated his early work, his welfare economics strove for the improvement of a very particular kind of welfare, one that was ethically rich and nuanced, laden with values like fairness and equality. In contrast, Robbins was concerned to stake out economic science as totally distinct from ethics. Even as early as 1926, Robbins had experienced misgivings about Pigou's use of ethical valuation in building welfare criterion. "Must economics include ethics?" he questioned in a note in 1926. "If not can it be urged that Economic Welfare has an ethical connotation. If so what can be substituted[?]"[173]

It is true that Robbins was not arguing for economists to stop making ethical valuations, nor was he opposed to political involvement. His intent, he wrote in the book's second edition, was merely to lay out what an economist as such should do, not what economists as people should do. "An economist who is only an economist and not a genius at his subject," Robbins wrote, "is a pretty poor fish."[174] Nevertheless, he took Pigou's own avowed commitment to the objectivity of economic science much further than Pigou himself did. For Robbins, who was writing at a time when economists played increasingly important roles in guiding government policy, the embedding of ethical norms in scientific practice was disingenuously stealthy and unquestionably objectionable.

Robbins intended his book to be polemical, and it immediately elicited a storm of commentary. Initial reviews in newspapers and periodicals were positive. To his friends and supporters, it was a masterful coup. Harold Laski, a Labour Party strategist and one of Robbins's teachers at the LSE, considered it a "brilliant piece of logical and systematic argument." Jacob Viner wrote from America that he was "in violent agreement," and in Vienna, Ludwig von Mises planned to incorporate it into his seminar.[175] But a more critical reception soon followed. There was an outcry over what many saw as Robbins's attempt to make the economist nothing more than a highbrow academic, a scholar unable to offer policy advice or to participate in political decision-making. Pigou had, in his own personal practice, seemingly accepted this model, but all sorts of economists, notably Keynes but also Robbins himself, were employed as advisors to the government. Many misread Robbins as suggesting that the economist would be unable to lobby and argue for policy, a restriction that appeared not only short-sighted but also implausible. "Economists cannot remain in the secluded contemplation of pure truth," one reviewer wrote. "If they are to help the community to solve its problems, they must themselves be counselors and advocates, perhaps also administrators and statesmen."[176]

Such practical objections to Robbins raised deeper, more philosophical ones, stemming from a hesitance to cleave ethics from economics.[177] What was the ultimate purpose of economists commenting on policy if not to improve social conditions? And did "improvement" not carry ethical valuation, as it had for generations of Liberals and reform-minded social scientists? Joan Robinson, in her short pamphlet, assumed that it did. So did Edwin Cannan, who, in defending his material welfare definition, noted that popularly, ethics were always part of economics: "when people ask the professor whether such and such a change will be good or bad, they will only find him tiresome if he pretends that he knows nothing of good and bad ends in economic matters and can only talk about the cheapness or dearness of different ways of attaining a given end."[178] From Chicago, Frank Knight, "protest[ed] that it is narrow and arbitrary to limit 'economic science' to the quasi mathematical theory of price and utility."[179] Others noted that Robbins himself had used the term "welfare," which carried ethical weight, so that "discussions of what is and of what ought to be are often linked together in the closest and most intricate manner . . . [in] Professor Robbins's own book."[180]

Yet for the criticism it provoked, the *Essay* made a significant impact. Most British economists active in the 1930s had been educated following a curriculum inspired by the efforts of Marshall and Pigou, one that had stressed the importance of scientific rigor. Academic theorists (especially those working on welfare) were therefore highly sensitive to accusations of deviation from positive science. Though many of the reviewers defended Pigou specifically by name from Robbins's assault on his scientific credibility, Pigou's reputation, particularly the image of scientific objectivity that he had cultivated throughout his professional life, had come under serious attack.[181] After all, Robbins had implicitly suggested that figures like Pigou, who were concerned with welfare economics, had if not a political agenda, then certainly an ethical one, which would inevitably color their economics.

Unlike Keynes's, Robbins's attack was primarily directed toward the works that had made Pigou famous—*Wealth and Welfare* and *The Economics of Welfare*—works written with a very clear moral end explicitly stated in the opening pages. Although Pigou had retreated somewhat over the years from explicit invocations of ethics, *The Economics of Welfare* was rife with references to greater ethical purposes, most of which depended on interpersonal comparisons of utility.[182] Thus, after Robbins's *Essay*, it was increasingly difficult for the middle-aged Pigou to be seen as a rigorous scientific economist, as the very conceptions of science shifted under his feet.

Prior to the 1930s, Pigou's only real brush with accusations of partiality had been about his attachment to *practical politics* during the free trade debates of the 1900s, when he was in his early twenties. After this episode, he made a conscious effort to cut out all politics and to stop any direct writing on ethics, with the partial exception of his wartime writings. Insulating himself in the increasingly Keynesian Cambridge, from 1908 until the mid-1930s, Pigou produced ever-more technical work; his original contempt for the public spreading first to politicians and then to bureaucrats in a rising wave of bitterness. As Pigou became more technical, he became increasingly removed from committees and policymakers, ever less involved with practical political considerations. This retreat from Whitehall would have been understood as essentially synonymous with a retreat from partiality to objectivity. But now, his own objectivity was coming under question from a respected source internal to economics, a source against which none of Pigou's tried and true retreats would prove effective.

In 1938, while he was recuperating from another bout of poor health, Pigou was confronted with another Robbinsian shock: the emergence of the so-called New Welfare Economics. Picking up on the *Essay*, John Hicks and Nicholas Kaldor had begun work on a theoretical framework for welfare economics that did not rely on interpersonal comparisons of utility. Embracing the concept of Pareto optimality as a distributional principle, Hicks and Kaldor suggested that although utility could not be directly compared across people, ordinal rankings of utility were still feasible.[183] Their methodology coalesced in two important articles that appeared in late 1939 after Hicks left Cambridge.[184] Central to their argument was the assertion was that even without interpersonal utility comparisons, an act of redistribution could in fact be deemed "better," but only if the lot of some members of society was improved while the lot of other members remained unchanged. Such an evaluation was possible only in cases where redistribution did nothing but eliminate inefficiencies. According to Hicks, Kaldor, and others, this gave economists a task without obliging them to make value judgments or directly compare individuals' psychological states, thereby satisfying Robbins's strict empirical imperatives. The name they chose for their method, "New Welfare Economics," heralded a break with the past: a fresh, rigorous take on old problems. In essence, the movement defined itself oppositionally to the "old," whose "standard representative," in Hicks's words, was "of course, Professor Pigou's *The Economics of Welfare.*"[185] In a quick rhetorical move, New Welfare Economics cast itself as a scientific advance.[186] Before long, it had spread throughout Britain and had won adherents in America.[187]

Pigou found himself beset from two directions. His most recent and most rigorous technical work was under attack from the Keynesians at his home base in Cambridge; they claimed it was theoretically flawed. At the same time, the work he had done early in his career, which the Keynesians (and all Cambridge school economists) had accepted as foundational and useful was now considered old and hopelessly outdated by other self-styled welfare economists. Even more troubling was the subtle charge that because he was ethically motivated, Pigou was not a scientist—as he had claimed to be for decades—but instead a partisan commentator of the sort he long disdained. In the case of Kaldor and Hicks, the very grounds on which Pigou could credibly respond had shifted. The increased use of statistics and advanced mathematics in economics, an ironic result of Pigou's own promotion of rigorous scientific method, had become conflated with the ideal of science in the field. Thus, a challenge to the philosophic foundations of Hicks and Kaldor's method would have only provided further evidence that Pigou was not acting as a modern scientist. Not that any response from Pigou would have mattered. By the 1940s, Robbins's views on interpersonal utility comparisons had reached deep into the British academy.[188] The age of the "old" Pigovian welfare economics seemed to be entering its final act.

Pigovian Responses: Bitterness and Publicity

The 1930s was a tumultuous, revolutionary time for economics and a professionally difficult one for Pigou. Not coincidentally, it was also the period when he began to cultivate a different audience. As the academic economic world moved past Pigovian thought, Pigou began to seek a new readership that could furnish the respect and reputation he had once enjoyed. In 1935, after Robbins's preliminary swipe and just before Keynes's coup de grâce, *The General*

Theory, Pigou took a radical step. Begrudgingly, he reached out to the general reading public.

Three years before, when he wrote to his publisher at Macmillan with the draft of the *Theory for Unemployment*, he described it as "not at all popular in character . . . like my other books, for serious students."[189] It was a significant reversal then, that in the late winter of 1934, he proposed a book "of a more or less popular kind," a book to be called *Economics in Practice*. Pigou was not entirely comfortable with the idea of having a popular audience, for whom he had not produced a book in nearly three decades. He noted that the impetus was not his own but had rather come from the University of London, where he had delivered a series of lectures, prompting his hosts to "express a wish" that the lectures should be put into print.[190]

In *Economics in Practice* (1935), Pigou oscillated between insulting and praising his new readership. Complaining that the typical member of the public thought "that every book written upon . . . [economics] shall be intelligible to him without any need for effort, as he reclines in his post-prandial arm-chair," Pigou compared the ignorant but falsely self-secure public to "accompanying herds, may I say, of goats!" But, Pigou wrote, the *general* public was not alone; no public really understood economics—not politicians, not even government administrators.[191] It therefore fell to "economists of the chair" to educate the public, a task that would both elevate political discourse and move the nation forward: "Nobody will deny that a wider spreading of . . . economic knowledge as already exists and of trained critical thinking on economic matters is an urgent public need; and that, so far as economists can promote this, they will by providing in their day and generation fruit of real value."[192] Pigou's conviction stemmed from his continued belief that the economist's "final justification . . . is the fruit of his practice."[193]

These were fine words, yet their graciousness bore an elective affinity with Pigou's saving face. He sought to elide the distinctions between methodological schools of economic thought just as his own star was waning. Indeed, he made a "plea" for "catholicity and tolerance": "Controversy for its own sake is a prodigious waste of time. More particularly, controversy about lines of approach . . . should long ago have been relegated to the scrap heap. Divergent methods are partners not rivals."[194]

How different these words were from those of the ascendant Pigou of 1908, who sought to cast Marshallian economics as the one true economics and a positive science, in a clear rejection of the historical methods of his competitors.[195] Now that his own methods were slipping out of favor, methodological divergence was a boon, not an atavism. However, it could only be so if the audience and the point of reference were the general public. To the untrained public eye, of course, Pigou was right that "among serious students, agreement on fundamental matters is enormously wider than the area of dispute." His lamentations that the public was being misled, discouraged, and let down by internal economic squabbles were true; the vast majority of economists *did* agree on fundamental points. But his were the lamentations of an underdog in those internal squabbles, who was arguing his case to a relatively uninformed arbiter. Certainly, his efforts to minimize the schisms of economics were not based solely on considerations of the public good. *Economics in Practice* was, as much as anything else, a political response to new modes of thinking in economics. For previous books he had written, Pigou had usually directed Macmillan to send copies to Cambridge colleagues—to Alfred Marshall when he was alive, to Keynes, to Kahn, Robertson, and the young economic statistician D. G. Champernowne. The author's copies of *Economics in Practice* were sent to a very different group—the new "scientific" economists of the LSE: Robbins, F. A. Hayek, John Hicks, and Arnold Plant.[196]

The book also reflected a changing national political landscape. By the mid-1930s, the Liberal Party was a shadow of its former self, and free trade had largely dissipated as a popular movement. But mass politics in general was very much on the rise, and insofar as *Economics in Practice* was intended for a popular audience, it was responsive to this trend. Pigou's treatment of tariffs in the book similarly demonstrated an unenthusiastic reconciliation to new political realities. In retrospect, he acknowledged that Keynes's 1931 proposal for a 10 percent duty on imports and a corresponding bounty on exports had been defensible as a way of stabilizing prices, and he recognized that there were new rationales for restrictions that had emerged after the end of the war.[197] For instance, a case could be made for stabilizing industries that had been disrupted because of war or temporary currency depreciation and also one for protecting industries in the interest of national defense.[198]

But though free trade as a broad-based civic movement had largely collapsed after the war and the abandonment of gold, Pigou remained committed to its animating values.[199] He held to the principle of comparative advantage, laughing away the idea of protection with a "caricature" of a Britain that produced its own unripenable bananas. "Glorying in this prosperity," he mocked, "England will assume the name Banana-land!"[200] He also condemned the potential for tariffs to privilege some industries over others and warned of the "more than equivalent cost to other people."[201] Perhaps most striking of all was Pigou's continued devotion to internationalist ideals. "When, being very clever, we think we have found a way to tax the foreigner—to compel him against his will to make a contribution to our national resources," he wrote, "are we to ignore altogether the fact that what we gain he loses?"[202] The only international restriction he endorsed was treaties limiting the production of armaments. In the case of weaponry, only relative advantage was important, so an agreement that would reduce all nations' spending would be economically beneficial. But for Pigou, this economic consideration was not, "of course, the main thing." The restriction of arms safeguarded against "what is, beyond doubt, the greatest of all public evils—war between modern States."[203]

Unnerved by the changing face of welfare economics and unwilling to engage Keynes in serious debate, throughout the second half of the 1930s, Pigou turned not just to a new audience but also to themes he never would have touched a few years before. "Stimulated" by noted Fabians Beatrice Webb and Sidney Webb's glowing book on Soviet Communism, Pigou wrote (though never delivered) a series of lectures about the economic implications of socialist planning.[204] These were not serious theoretical accounts of how the state might effectively manage an economy, but "some popular lectures," which Pigou, in a letter to Beatrice Webb, doubted "worth printing."[205] Pigou's personal diffidence was part of his persona, as was his high-handed surliness. When Webb enquired as to the origins of a certain turn of phrase, "economic calculus," he responded dismissively: "I don't believe [it] has a meaning. . . . It's just a jargon phrase to boost one's stuff like the scientific looking terms in advertisements of quack medicines!"[206]

Pigou ultimately turned the socialism lectures into a book, which he almost apologetically described as "popular," with a characteristically bold underline.[207] Half a century later, in the 1980s, amidst a national preoccupation with a ring of Soviet spies embedded at Cambridge, some cast *Socialism versus Capitalism* (1937) as proof of Pigou's latent communist sympathies, wildly suggesting that Pigou himself was a spy.[208] But even though the book demonstrated how he was increasingly willing to compromise liberal individualism for the sake of social welfare, it was hardly a leftist tract. Instead, it represented a logical continuation of the ideas he had been developing since the end of World War I, but this time directed at a general audience.

For Pigou, central planning offered what was in many ways a very appealing ideal: the possibility of enabling a publicly minded authority to correct the "existing inequalities of wealth and income and the serious evils with which they are associated." "The greater power of a socialist State . . . to enforce money rates of pay," he wrote, "must make it easier for it to control industrial fluctuations, and so unemployment."[209] Pigou outlined a system whereby socialist administrators could use a combination of tokens and internal "accounting prices" to mimic a market system through a series of "shuffling" "step-by-step" adjustments.[210] The payoff was clear. Without competition, a whole host of market imperfections would be obviated. Under a system of collective ownership enforced by a coercive state, divergences between private and public would, by definition, no longer exist.

But though central planning might in theory produce a superior economic result compared to generally laissez-faire capitalism, its success would require the coordination of an incredibly efficient and intelligent state mechanism. At the end of a chapter on the problems of central planning, Pigou called attention to "the immense multiplicity of adjustments that, in the actual world, would be called for." After all, "to solve a small number of simultaneous equations in a short time is one thing[;] to solve thousands and thousands of them is quite another."[211] Thus, at its core, *Socialism versus Capitalism* was about the slippage between theory and practice. And in practice, Pigou had already lost faith in the ability of a government to work in a well-oiled way.[212] For though the Webbs noted widespread enthusiasm among Soviet workers, Pigou remained skeptical of socialism's promise even in Russia, "in which in pre-socialism days the Civil Service was notoriously corrupt and popular education scandalously neglected."[213]

Socialism versus Capitalism serves as a testament to the ways in which Pigou's thinking was evolving. On the one hand, he still put stress on the limited abilities of administrators. But on the other, the book heralded a changing focus, a subtle move from Liberal toward Labour values. For although Pigou did not support a planned economy, he was strongly in favor of fundamentally modifying the current market framework. He called for "death duties and graduated income tax, not merely as instruments of revenue, but with the deliberate purpose of diminishing the glaring inequalities of fortune and opportunity which deface our present civilisation." These initiatives were to be supplemented with investment "in the health, intelligence, and character of the people," and potentially, gradual nationalization of certain public utilities and industries vital to the national interest. In short, Pigou took a social democratic course. He recommended "gradualness," but asserted "in large capitals" that "gradualness implies action, and is not a polite name for standing still."[214] Just as important as the content was the new style of presentation that *Socialism versus Capitalism* represented. Before, Pigou's project had been to convince persons he deemed sufficiently intelligent to act wisely on behalf of the masses. Now, with his diminished academic status, he inverted his Government House Utilitarian strategy and addressed the masses directly.

Many of the reasons Pigou turned to the public were on full display in his 1939 presidential address to the Royal Economic Society, in which he commented on the rapid evolution of the discipline.[215] He recalled, with some exaggeration, that in 1903, fourteen economists signed a letter condemning protectionism and "with some four or five exceptions . . . this list included all the economists with professional appointments in the United Kingdom."[216] How times had changed. The Economics Tripos at Cambridge, established in 1903, now had "150 to 200 students sitting for examination . . . every year": a grand realization of Alfred Marshall's dream of a professionalized corps of economists trained at Cambridge.[217] But though Pigou was president of his field's professional organization, by recalling "antediluvian" events, he was dating himself as part of a bygone age. For all his youthful agitations for progress, the older Pigou fondly referred to a halcyon past whose cohort of practitioners, though much smaller, had been studded with genius. "The great increase in the number of persons professionally concerned with economics ha[d] not," according to him, "been distributed evenly over all grades of ability. . . . Among men of really first-rate ability, . . . I much doubt whether in absolute numbers there has been any increase at all."[218] Moreover, he was unwilling to admit even that the practice of economics itself had improved, only that it had changed because of new global contexts. In the old days, "politics and economics alike were reasonably stable . . . the basic changes were gradual and slow working. There were no catastrophes," he intoned, speaking in the wake of a worldwide depression and on the eve of World War II. "How different is the experience of today!" It was "this fundamental difference of experience" that was "largely accountable" for the divergent ways in which old and new economists approached their problems. In what might sound to today's historians like a measured historicist move, Pigou claimed that "neither outlook can properly be called more right than the other. The two are not competitive: they are complementary."[219]

But in its context, this was as much a jibe as it was a naked attempt on Pigou's part to assert his own relevance. By claiming that there were only as many truly gifted economists now as before, he insulted a wide section of the audience. He did the same by claiming that new economics could not be "called more right" than old forms, the forms he implicitly associated with himself. Yet although the speech was pugnacious and defensive, more than anything, it was pessimistic.[220] Its implication, after all, was that economic science had not improved in forty years. In fact, the economics discipline had transformed from a Marshallian "centre of unity, of acquiescence, of quiescence" to a "turbulent sea."[221] Pigou admitted that such turmoil and confusion might "evoke life," a new synthetic theory to replace the lost consensus. "But if so," he wondered, "to what end?"

> The ambition . . . of most economists is to help in some degree, directly or indirectly, towards social betterment. Our study . . . provides for statesmen data, upon which, along with data of other kinds, they, philosopher kings, build up policies directed to the common good. How different from this dream is the actuality! How very unlike philosopher kings actual politicians are! To how small an extent the conduct of affairs is the result of thought!"

For Pigou, bringing the economist's goal to fruition depended on a broken link. The result was that by 1939, Pigou had abandoned the belief that economics could bear any fruit at all. Closing his speech, he pronounced to his colleagues, "we . . . follow, not thought, but an impulse—the impulse to inquire—which *futile* though it may prove, is at least not ignoble."222 In attempting to vindicate his generation, Pigou had also announced his own defeat. The man Joan Robinson had called "the first serious optimist" was no longer an optimist at all.

CHAPTER SEVEN

Another War and a Fresh Start

FOR PIGOU, AS FOR SO MANY OTHERS, the interwar years formed a period of uneasy intermission, over the course of which he grew increasingly reclusive and, until the late 1930s, directed himself toward an ever-narrowing audience. World War II itself served as the culmination of an extended period of loss. The war emptied Cambridge of friends and students, replacing them with affiliates of the LSE and decamped government agencies. And on reaching the age of mandatory retirement in 1943, he lost his post as professor.

These personal events unfolded against a global backdrop Pigou watched with disgust and horror. Though the war did cement the practical importance of economists as advisors to the government, everywhere else Pigou looked, cherished foundations of his comfortable life were threatened or crumbling. Pigou himself had reached an age at which he found his own energies waning. Nevertheless, with the arrival of war, he began to search assiduously for things to do. So reticent to work for the government during the first war, he asked for "any" job to help the war effort during the second, composing reports for the government and eventually teaching for a stint at Harrow. He wrote constantly, trying new subjects and tones, in the hope of widening his scope to appeal to a general audience, a move he made initially simply because he had no other option.

However, as the dust settled over Europe and Pigou confronted a changed Britain, he would find redemption, or at least consolation. And he would find it in a very unlikely place: the state. Moderated largely by his continuing friendship with Philip Noel-Baker, now a prominent Labour politician, Pigou took an active interest in politics and after years of disgust with the government, found himself again believing not only in a cause but also in a political program. He supported Labour, but more importantly, he came to believe that the party's sweeping policy initiatives would bear fruit. Remarkably, this seed of hope grew until it changed Pigou's very relationship with *people* as a category. Throughout the late 1940s and early 1950s, his disdainful tone changed. His words softened. As he came to terms with his own position as a professor emeritus and with the new government in power, Pigou demonstrated, both publicly and privately, an entirely new relationship with the common man.

The Home Front

When the war came to Cambridge, it found Pigou, then over sixty, in a state of great personal bitterness. From his rooms at King's, he was still fruitlessly fighting to prevent Keynesianism from becoming the school's dominant methodological approach, sniping at Keynes and Robinson over their zealousness and insufficient respect for older theories. To Noel-Baker, now a high-ranking member of the Labour Party, Pigou presented a different face, one acrimonious about different things, but hardened to his own lot and to the possibility of war. His first letters after the declaration of war in September 1939 were filled not with hope or fear, but `with bile laced with characteristic dismissiveness. In his private correspondence with his closest friends, the decorous prose reserved for his public writings vanished. Writing to Noel-Baker of the head of the Labour Party, Clement Attlee, Pigou noted, "I listened to your great leader last night on the wireless: a pleasant second-rater with no personality."[1] At the time, Pigou was grimly pessimistic about Labour's future. Attlee, he predicted, would "never make a prima donna."[2]

Complaints to Noel-Baker about Pigou's immediate situation at Cambridge soon followed: "Cambridge has been made (1) an evacuation area for other Universities and <u>children</u> to come to. (2) A First-class military objective by filling several colleges with air cadets and arranging to put the ministry of Economic Warfare into Trinity, instead of, as personnel would suggest, into Bedlam."[3]

Under Pigou's gruff exterior, however, was a much more sensitive and aching despair. In the epilogue written in November 1939 to a revised edition to his *Political Economy of War,* he excused himself for not treating topics of postwar recovery. The reason, he wrote, was that once again: "The young and gallant, our children and our friends, go down into the pit that others have digged for them. . . . We wait and watch and—those who can—we pray. As an economist I have not the power, nor, as a man, the heart, to strain through a night so black to a dawn I shall not see."[4]

The old Great War commitments to the work of the Quakers reemerged as well. Late in 1939, Pigou donated "£100 to help the friends" and reported to Noel-Baker that other, more recent former students (including Wilfrid Noyce, who would remain a lifelong friend) had joined the Ambulance Corps.[5] He also wrote on behalf of conscientious objectors, asking Noel-Baker to "<u>stand up" for non-combatives who would be forced into "Labour battalions just as . . . in the last war</u>," an assignment as good as suicide.[6]

As the war progressed, Pigou realized he had concerns much closer to home. Though the town of Cambridge prospered economically during the war, university life ground to a near halt. Cambridge was rarely bombed, but air raid sirens were a constant feature of wartime life. While others ran to shelters, the stubborn Pigou stayed above ground, hauling a deck chair out onto King's lawn and reading a newspaper in contemptuous defiance of the Luftwaffe.[7] Cambridge would play host not only to evacuated children but also to a number of distinguished scholars—many Jewish—fleeing Europe as well as to servicemen from a nearby American airbase.[8] King's became not only "an armed camp" but also the home of all sorts of displaced individuals. Keynes reported, "one has to expect to see in residence the LSE, the women, the blacks and a few other oddments." The Front Court was "full of military motor-cars."[9] Others were leaving the university, both to fight and to be interned. Keynes and Pigou anxiously corresponded about the fate of Sraffa, who as an Italian national, might be "pinched."[10]

To escape the hubbub, Pigou relocated to Lower Gatesgarth, but by mid-1940, he was restless, "sitting doing nothing in this funkhole." He wrote to Keynes to note that with Cambridge closed for the next term, "I must make a serious effort to get something to do: I can't just sit here and eat the . . . food."[11] He made enquiries about a job with the code breakers at Bletchley Park and about "teaching at a school," but these led nowhere. He was concerned enough to ask Keynes for a job doing "anything," to which Keynes replied sympathetically but not helpfully. "All Government Departments seem to be pursuing the same policy about employing people," Keynes wrote. "They are in a state of intense muddle, overwork and understaffing. But nothing will induce them to take anyone fresh."[12]

This may have been true, but it was also true that during World War II, economic knowledge was prized by state administrators, a lesson that had been learned slowly during the last war. Pigou finally landed a part-time position in 1941, writing economic analyses for Arthur Greenwood, the deputy leader of the Labour Party and a member of Winston Churchill's War Cabinet, which was formed in mid-1940 and included ministers from the three major political parties. Greenwood was intimately involved with the state's efforts to bring in and concentrate economic expertise. At first, he headed the Production Council and the Economic Policy Committee, but he proved a poor leader, and Churchill disbanded both groups. By the time Pigou joined him, Greenwood was working on reconstruction policy.[13] After long having sought a job, when Pigou finally landed one, he wrote with continual disdain of his work and his superior, to whom he alternatively referred as "Lord Alcohol" and "Whisky Arthur," jabs at Greenwood's alcoholism.[14] Still, he was glad of the activity. "Of course they won't make any use of the stuff," he wrote in October 1941, "but it's something to do."[15] But even this did not last long. Greenwood was sacked in 1942.

The war formed a period of profound dislocation for Pigou, professionally and personally. In the most obvious, physical sense, he was kept out of his usual haunts in Cambridge by Keynes's "collection of oddments." He spent much of his time in his "funkhole" in Buttermere with Ann Jackson, his long-time "formidable" housekeeper.[16] There, except for the occasional visitor, he stayed sequestered, alone, and cantankerous: a "hermit crab." In a letter

to F. A. Hayek, Pigou reported the scant news from the Lakes—
that a "4-engine Lancaster or something" had crashed somewhere
nearby. Mostly, however, his letter sighed heavily with boredom;
he was revising *Public Finance*, which he added, "gives me something to do."[17] Remembered in Cumbria for his spartan lifestyle
and his legendary thrift, Pigou would eat, in Noel-Baker's exaggerated account, "dead porridge and the crusts of yesterday's toast."[18]
His tendency to squirrel away food and not eat it provoked a wry
letter from Noel-Baker: "It became plain that Viscount Gatesgarth [Pigou], or his housekeeper, or both, were conspiring to
defraud the British people by hoarding food; and endeavouring
to make a Minister of the Crown an accomplice in that dastardly
manoeuvre!"[19]

From Buttermere, Pigou would almost beg his former students
and mountaineering friends, of whom Noel-Baker was probably
the closest, to pay him a visit. For even though Pigou would hardly
ever express anything but professional feelings to colleagues, to
his friends, he was emotive, even if proud. When he requested
company, he did so with a false bravado, ostentatiously referring
to himself as the "Viscount Gatesgarth" and extending invitations
with formality couched in layers of wit.[20] The fact remained, however, that in a preponderance of letters, he requested visits either to
Cambridge or Cumbria. In mid-1943, praising Buttermere's "fresh
eggs" and "all-male life," Pigou was asking Noel-Baker to commit to
what would be his fortieth visit.[21] He was imperious about receiving communiqués from Noel-Baker and other former students with
whom he had stayed friends, including Tom Gaunt and the young
Wilfrid Noyce, who would later be part of the first team to summit
Everest.[22] To secure visitors, he resorted to mock threats, especially
with Noel-Baker, who as a government minister, had several other
things on his mind. Still, Pigou instructed Noel-Baker that "Replies
to Cambridge [are] more important than to Albania!"

> It is quite certain that . . . you are doing nothing one-tenth as useful as
> it would be to keep in touch with the backbone of the country! There-
> fore in the Hitler manner I shall employ sanctions against your family.
> There is here a . . . Holy Roman Empire belonging to your son. Unless a
> letter of adequate length is received within the next few days, his name

will be erased from this book and it will be permanently incorporated in the Lower Gatesgarth library![23]

Pigou would only become more stringent. "<u>RSVP</u>," he wrote repeatedly, underlining the command twice or three times. "Conduct of self and dancing girl [Irene, Noel-Baker's wife] has been <u>disgraceful</u>," he wrote of a lull in correspondence.[24]

Practically every other letter contained some dismal projection about the future of the war. "The Admiralty should get . . . [battleships] ready," Pigou advised in August 1940, as Hitler would be coming.[25] "I give Crete 10 days before it's Dunkirked," he predicted in late 1941, "do you give it 10 years?"[26] Distrustful of the news, he continually questioned official reports: "Which is lying most?" he would ask.[27] The pair bet on how long the war would last, with Pigou, signing his letters "Strategist," polemically predicting the mid-1950s.[28] Despite Noel-Baker's optimism and his "series of prophecies," all of which came true, Pigou stuck to his gloom, writing of his dissatisfaction "with the handling of the Italian and Balkan strategy: also with your propaganda policy." Even when Operation Overlord opened a second front in Normandy, he remained skeptical. "I am inclined to fear that things are going much less well than the British public is being told," he grumbled.[29]

Academic Struggles

The war itself was partly responsible for Pigou's "blackest hours of despair," but it also reinforced an experience of disjuncture that had little to do with the conflict.[30] Professionally, Pigou was coming to the end of his tenure. The war removed him from teaching; from Cambridge; and, largely, from academic economics, many of whose practitioners were now in the employ of the state. This change was a mixed blessing. At times, it provided a distraction from his field's slow but certain shift toward Keynesianism and away from his own centrality. In 1942, for instance, he reported with typically inflammatory language, that he had "been working like a black for George [King George VI] and Lizzie [Queen Elizabeth] via Alcohol," on the report for Arthur Greenwood.[31] Though he complained constantly about his post, when it was over, Pigou was anxious to find another position with the government if only to remain occupied.[32] Out of boredom, he had dashed off *Lapses from Full Employment*, a quick 72-page "semi-popular book about unemployment of the same sort of grade as my little books about Socialism and Economics in Practice" and had resorted to writing articles on mountaineering, including one called "Night Life on High Hills" and sketches about popular affairs.[33]

Pigou continued to spar with Keynes, but by now he was tilting at windmills. His *Employment and Equilibrium* (1941) was largely passed over as economists had other, more pressing concerns at the time it was released.[34] When Kaldor reviewed the work with a light hand in *The Economic Journal*, Pigou responded in great length, picking apart small objections.[35] The book was actually quite modern in the exposition of its macroeconomic model; its methodology was "almost ideal" in the opinion of Paul Samuelson, who reviewed the book for the *American Economic Review*.[36] But despite it being "one of the most important books of recent years," in that it responded to Keynes by using Keynes's own "poetry," it was also "'classical,'" a word that connoted a bygone era.[37] Abba Lerner was even more explicit. By focusing the better part of his analysis on stable conditions and assuming long-term full employment, Lerner contended, Pigou demonstrated an "excessive loyalty to his school, his teachers, and their methods."[38]

Yet Pigou soldiered on with his defense of the classical approach. He resolutely titled a 1943 piece responding to the American Keynesian Alvin Hansen "The Classical Stationary State" at a time when the designation "classical" was fast becoming synonymous with "old" and when economists were increasingly interested in dynamics.[39] In it, he continued to uphold the well-worn position that even in the midst of a depression, if wages dropped sufficiently, the economy would return to a stable equilibrium. The article, which provoked a quick and definitive dismissal from Michał Kalecki, however, did achieve some subsequent fame for introducing what Don Patinkin would subsequently dub the "Pigou Effect," the idea that in times of falling prices, cash holdings would become worth more, causing an upswing in demand that could restore equilibrium conditions.[40]

The most substantive economic debate in which Pigou engaged during the war only further demonstrated the extent to which the

field was changing around him. The debate concerned a core bul-
wark of Pigovian welfare economics: the concept of national income. In his works on welfare, Pigou had adopted and expanded
Marshall's notion of the "national dividend," a term meaning national aggregate earnings, as an explanatory metric. In so doing,
he had established himself as one of its seminal theoreticians and
had helped pave the way for the modern conception of the gross
domestic product (GDP), a topic that attracted ever more attention throughout the 1930s and 1940s.[41] For Pigou, though national
income was necessarily measured in money, its value was rooted
in "objective services, some of which were embodied in commodities, while others are rendered direct"—in other words, in the real
economy.[42] In his major works, he relied on a concept of national
income as a proxy measure for wellbeing, and because of the importance of his works on welfare, he had a significant influence on the
burgeoning field of national income accounting. *National Income
and Outlay* (1937), one of the first comprehensive books on modern national accounting, by the Cambridge statistician Colin Clark,
began with an extended quote from Pigou:

> "Generally speaking," writes Professor Pigou in the *Economics of Wel-
> fare*, "economic causes act upon the economic welfare of any coun-
> try, not directly, but through the making and using of that objective
> counterpart of economic welfare which economists call the national
> dividend or national income."[43]

Clark was thus explicit about his field's debt to Pigou. Indeed, the
first chapter was essentially a defense of the latter's ethically oriented approach to economics and an explanation of how national
income measurements—"conceived in real, but measured in money
terms"—fit into a Pigovian program.[44]

But in 1940, Pigou's conception of national income was fundamentally challenged by F. A. Hayek, who, along with the rest of
the LSE, had decamped for the war to Peterhouse, Cambridge, just
a few blocks down Trumpington Street from King's College. One
of the Austrian economists who had a profound impact on Lionel
Robbins, Hayek had been based at the LSE since the early 1930s.
Unlike Robbins, Hayek was formally schooled in philosophy and
sociology, and his work was ideologically explicit. For him, choice

and individual agency were the ultimate defenses against the hor-
rific authoritarian regimes that had engulfed his native Austria and
the rest of continental Europe. But, Hayek held, agency was good
for people in a more tangible way; free markets were simply better
at improving societal wellbeing than any central planning board.
Hayek argued that such planners were unable to capture all the
information ordinarily held by individuals scattered throughout
the economy. Without perfect information—not only information
about preferences but also what Hayek would later call "knowledge
of the particular circumstances of time and place"—central planners would inevitably fail in their task of distributing resources effectively.[45] In this way, how individuals understood and used information was of key importance to economic prosperity. In *The
Pure Theory of Capital* (1940), Hayek argued that even real physical
capital, a core concept in income accounting, was subject to inter-
pretive flexibility; its meaning varied even for the same person in
different temporal contexts.[46] When calculating income, it would
therefore be useless to account for "maintaining capital intact," a
Marshallian concept of replacing physical productive capital (like
factory components that had been worn out with use) so that the
stock of physical capital remained undepleted. For Hayek, maintaining real capital in a physical sense meant nothing: it was how
the entrepreneur *thought* of the capital that mattered with respect
to its value.

Pigou was stirred by *The Pure Theory*, a copy of which Hayek
had given him. His marginalia shows he was paying close attention, especially to chapter 22, which dealt with maintaining capital intact.[47] At the chapter's end, Pigou scrawled a question about
Hayek's theory of both real capital and real income: "how [was it]
measured"?[48] He posed this challenge to Hayek in article in *Economica* in 1941, defending the old physical conception of capital
maintenance as a useful measurement tool.[49] Pigou defended what
J. R. Hicks would later call the "Materialist" or "volume" understanding of real capital on grounds of practicability of measurement. "Surely," he wrote, "it is proper for economists . . . while admitting that perfect definitions cannot be found, to try to make them
as little imperfect as they can."[50] Hayek again disagreed, stressing
that values, even of real capital, were fundamentally psychological

rather than material. "In a changing world, where different people, and even the same people at different times, will possess different knowledge, there can be no objective standards," he wrote, not even those rooted in seemingly unchanging physical objects.[51]

The stakes of this debate were high for both Pigou and Hayek. For Hayek, it was about keeping the ultimate locus of economic and market power located squarely in the minds of individual actors.[52] For Pigou, it was about holding onto a material and measurable conception of real capital—one that was rooted in the physical and tangible, terms in which he had long thought, terms in which Marshall had thought, and terms on which he had never been questioned.[53] But it should be noted that Hayek and Pigou's dueling notions of capital bore a striking implication for the usefulness or feasibility of state involvement in the market. Hayek's understanding implied that the only arbiter of value was the free market, in which the internal beliefs and valuations of individuals became manifest. In contrast, Pigou's materialist conception provided the wartime government, in the midst of readopting the planning functions developed in the Great War, with useable metrics for evaluating and managing economic performance.[54]

Now, however, these metrics were scrutinized, especially by the people who had questioned Pigou's status as a scientist. Writing in response to the debate, John Hicks granted that even though in practice statisticians would have to rely on materialist Pigovian conceptions of capital, Hayek was ultimately right—that individual perceptions and understandings of market actors were of final importance. The fact that Hicks, by then the new face of welfare economics, "came down mainly on Hayek's side" was indicative of a turn against the solid groundings that undergirded Pigou's work.[55] It was wrong—and more importantly, practicably useless—Pigou thought, to conceive of material capital as fundamentally changing in real value simply, as Hicks would later write, "by the mere admission of new information."[56] But this understanding was exactly what Hicks and Hayek maintained. They turned away from the concrete and moved toward a theory less connected to everyday physical experience or practical use, notably by agencies of the state. From Pigou's perspective, this meant that even the most fundamental physical realities were being replaced with nebulous concepts. Of course, many economists agreed with Pigou—applied economists found it impossible to actually account for national income by using the flexible Hayekian concepts, and Hicks himself noted that they were not "usable in practice"—but the debate itself suggested the dawning of a new age characterized by dramatically different economic thinking.[57] Pigou had long been among the most abstract of economic theorists, but he now found some of his own bedrock assumptions, even about what was concrete, significantly less stable than they had been a few years before.

Pigou's academic alienation peaked with his mandatory retirement from teaching in 1943 upon turning 65. As a fellow of King's, Pigou would remain at the college for the rest of his life, but his years as a professor had come to an end. The board of electors unanimously chose Keynes as his successor to the Chair of Political Economy, but Keynes, swamped with war work, was "unable to accept" because of "other demands on his time."[58] The post therefore went to Robertson, who returned from London to assume his new responsibilities. Pigou had battled Keynes for influence at Cambridge for nearly a decade and a half, but ultimately, when Keynes was offered the position that Pigou so valued, Keynes was too busy with tasks in London he considered more important to take it up. It was a cruel irony and a bittersweet victory that Robertson, Pigou's former ally at Cambridge, came back to the economics faculty only by default.

For his part, the retired professor was left with little to do. Writing to Noel-Baker in advance of his retirement, he noted: "It doesn't seem proper that a viscount should do absolutely nil while the war is on. . . . Obviously the thing one would be most competent for would be some sort of investigation on economic stuff. . . . But there might be something else useful. Do you know of anything?"[59] As time went on, Pigou became ever more serious. The following month, he returned to the issue. "Now about my job. This is a genuine enquiry. I don't want to be completely idle while there is all this rank about man-power, and there must be something that I am competent to do. . . . Therefore I am enquiring of you whether . . . you have acquired sufficient status to do a little nepotism."[60]

Noel-Baker was no nepotist. Instead of providing a job, he suggested that Pigou address himself to a different audience, one to which Pigou had already begun to turn: the general public. For Noel-Baker, the wartime optimist and purposeful reformer, was already thinking ahead to a time after the war. He replied, noting that after the war, Britain would need to make major changes in its economic policies. "There is admirable opportunity for making them," he wrote, "but the opportunity will only be taken if public opinion is instructed."[61] Moreover, he told Pigou, "It must be instructed by people like you." He ribbingly suggested that his friend write a "weekly article for the [popular, inexpensive, and generally conservative] *Daily Mail* or the *Daily Express*, at £50 a time" and that Pigou become an "economic commentator at £15:15 for the B.B.C." Tongue-in-cheek, Noel-Baker added, "in general, you should no longer give yourself, as in the last, to the acquisition of filthy lucre, but should set yourself a new ideal—namely, GOOD WORKS."[62] The response was a skillful deflection from providing the requested government post. It was, however, also a declaration of hope for a future in which people were instructed, not just directed.

Pigou's immediate reaction was to have none of it. As Noel-Baker had "done no nepotism with George and Lizzie," he would go "to Harrow to do a trial trip teaching a bit."[63] Unable to continue working as a scientist at a university, Pigou turned instinctively to a public school. Cast out of the faculty of economics and politics at Cambridge, the natural fallback was Harrow. Yet Noel-Baker's words gradually sank in, especially after the war. Even later that year, Pigou agreed to fill in for Keynes, then in Washington on government business, "to broadcast [on the BBC] a talk about whether we shall be poorer after the war (an idiotic subject)."[64] This is not to say that Pigou had yet embraced a new audience. As late as the middle part of 1943, he was still concerned with getting his ideas to the people already in power. Writing in April to Keynes, he enclosed a "rough" version of a plan for "conscription wealth"—a new version of a capital levy—"to pay off a large chunk of the war debt" with the hopes that Keynes would "put it in to someone at the Treasury."[65] When Keynes responded politely, but negatively, Pigou tried to save face by turning to the public. In his next letter to Keynes, he wrote that he was "thinking of printing this as an article for some paper," and criticized the channels through which he had originally hoped to contribute.[66] Royal commissions and other forms of bureaucracy, he asserted, were "highly artificial," merely "buzzing in a bottle."[67]

Thus, even after his semi-popular books of the late 1930s, the public was still a forum of last resort for Pigou. He turned to this audience only after being rebuffed as an academic and passed over as an advisor to politicians and bureaucrats. In this way, his decision to address the public was neither a genuine admission of its value in effecting change nor a statement of his renewed faith in humanity. Indeed, throughout the 1940s, despite his increasingly sanguine public face, Pigou privately maintained that "the limit is that the human race is a tick, and that, as I have long maintained, the only possible solution is the substitution for it of Lobsters."[68]

During the war, it was not the public, but the country's leaders who were the subject of Pigou's thoughts. This preoccupation was manifested by the constant stream of insults he hurled at them in his private letters. They were "rat-faced," and engaged in unfailing "claptrappery."[69] Political hacks had merely "petty souls," political organization was a "morass of muddle."[70] From the 1930s onward, specific politicians acquired Pigovian nicknames. There was, of course, Pigou's employer, Lord Alcohol, but also "Shifty" [Emanuel Shinwell]; "The Great Big Rat" [Clement Attlee]; "The Great White Chief" [Churchill]; "Fat little Morrie" [Herbert Morrison]; "The Welsh Vulgarian" or "Anaemia," [Aneurin Bevan]; and "Our Hugh," [Dalton], whom Pigou described as "a first-class tick."[71]

Yet, as in the 1920s, Pigou was not critical of *government* per se, but of the individual people who composed it. In his review of Hayek's *Road to Serfdom*, which appeared in bookshops in 1944, he took a mild tone toward big government and central planning. Disagreeing with Hayek's "historical thesis" that central planning necessarily led to fascism, Pigou suggested instead that fascism, as evidenced in Germany and Italy, might itself have led to central planning as a way of "directing . . . resources towards building up national power." "Is it fair," he asked, "to treat the means [central planning] as a cause of the end towards which it was in these cases directed?"[72] In the end, the review displayed Pigou's characteristic couched editorializing of the same sort that had appeared seven years earlier in *Socialism versus Capitalism*. Central planning was not an inherent evil, just a system that could be used for good or ill. As he had argued in *Socialism versus Capitalism* and his essay "State Action and Laisser Faire" in the 1930s, what was of key importance was not the political system but the people who wielded its power.

Reconcilings and the Public

By 1944, Pigou's criticisms of the government had become less about ineffectual work and more about backroom maneuverings that kept Noel-Baker from positions of greater authority. Pigou found fault not with the leaders of the country as leaders, but as politicians. A great deal of this change can be attributed to the fact that his world was turning around for the better.

Throughout the war, Pigou had always found solace in the friendships he had cultivated as a mountaineer and as an academic advisor, two roles whose worlds substantially intersected. He kept up with Wilfrid Noyce, Tom Gaunt, and Claude Elliott, a former Cambridge historian, member of the Friends' Ambulance Unit, and head master (later provost) of Eton.[73] Along with Noel-Baker, these were arguably his closest friends, and they spent many holidays together before, during, and after the war in the Lake District and the Alps. The waning of Pigou's professional star was a known fact, but it was one which was never brought up in alpinist circles, in an unspoken understanding that allowed him to maintain his status as "the Prof." His friends both idolized and cared for him, serving as a surrogate family for a retired don without close ties to relatives. They corresponded about him in tender terms; Wilfrid Noyce wrote, for example, to Noel-Baker that he had received "cheerful letters from the Prof . . . I am astonished at how well he keeps, pray only it may go on for many more years."[74]

Pigou's fast friendships were stable and reassuring, but there were other reasons for his change of mood in late 1944 and 1945. He began to reconcile himself to his retirement, resigning his unvalued membership in the politicized British Academy in 1945. Moreover, with the Axis on its last legs, he made fewer dismal predictions about the war's future and fewer criticisms of policy.[75] As the war ended and a blitz of electoral campaigning helped Britain return to a peacetime mentality, Pigou, along with the rest of the country, took an even more active interest in political machinations.[76] Approaching the June 1945 general election, he teased Noel-Baker, predicting that "O.S." (standing for "Old Schoolmate," Winston Churchill) would win, and lamenting that his friend, then a parliamentary secretary at the Ministry of War Transport, would be out of "an enormous salary, fine motor car, 50 gallons of petrol a month, [and] 6 dancing girls," by which Pigou meant secretaries.[77] This opinionated ribbing was one of many that Pigou would deliver in the years to follow. Once a victorious Labour Party formed a government, he bombarded Noel-Baker with questions about the cabinet, his place in it, his perks, and the behavior of "the rat," the new Prime Minister, Clement Attlee.[78]

But Pigou's interest in politics was spreading beyond backroom gossip. His post-war political commentary to Noel-Baker was voluminous and comprehensive, covering national and local elections, speeches, campaign strategies, and policies. Along with his analysis, for the first time in decades, Pigou expressed a modicum of hope. Despite the soaring popularity of "the Great White Chief," Winston Churchill, at the end of World War II, when the time came to rebuild the country, Britons put their faith in the Labour Party. In the July 1945 election, it won a landslide victory, capturing nearly 400 seats to the Tories' 200. Labour had stood on a platform of sweeping change outlined in its election manifesto, *Let Us Face the Future*.[79] With a clear mandate, the new government promised to reform education and health care, to nationalize major industries, and to put the so-called Beveridge Report, a blueprint for a social safety net, into practice. Labour proposed, in short, the creation of the modern British welfare state.[80] These developments excited Pigou, who was especially sympathetic to the Beveridge Report and to its architect, William Beveridge, whom he had known at least since his work for the Board of Trade during World War I.[81] In 1944, Pigou had publicly "cordially welcomed" Beveridge's suggestions for the government's "planned outlay" to curb unemployment and the "giant social evils of Want, Disease, Squalor and Ignorance." He did so "from the standpoint of employment, but also and not less for its more general implications" in furthering "more fair" distribution and fostering the "free development of all men's faculties."[82]

In sum, the platform of the elected Labour government deeply appealed to Pigou. The party proposed to intervene on behalf of the poor, and though it did not use Pigou's language specifically, it looked to remedy a great number of external diseconomies and damaging monopolies that existed in the national economy. Moreover, the presence of administrators of the caliber of Noel-Baker and Beveridge made the implementation of such programs appear feasible. Labour's rise to power, despite it being led by "the Rat" Attlee, reawakened Pigou's long-dormant hope that politicians could actually effect positive change. To Noel-Baker, he expressed optimism, albeit couched in sarcasm, for the first time in years, specifically about Labour's plan of nationalizing the coal industry.

> It's amusing that the Comrades' first great deed is to nationalise the B[ank] of E[ngland]. . . . This is a pure fake, which will make absolutely no difference to anybody. . . . On the other hand, if you deal with Coal properly, you may really do a little good! Even Comrade Emmanuel [Shinwell, the Minister of Fuel and Power] can't be worse than the Coal owners![83]

Soon Pigou would go much further. He wrote in October 1945 in support of Attlee, claiming that his words were "discussion, not mere flapdoodle like O.S. [Churchill's]. But no trace of prima-donna."[84]

Later in the year, Pigou drafted a plan for one of Noel-Baker's speeches, a work that, although ending on a humorous note, was for the most part a serious piece of political rhetoric and a strikingly public one at that. For Pigou, Labour's platform was about new beginnings. After the war,

> there was a case for concentrating on immediate difficulties—bombed houses, demobilisation, etc. in general restoring the status quo. This was the policy of the TORIES. . . . No time for fundamental change. The policy of the Labour party was different; and it was endorsed by the electorate (trumpets). For us no "safety first." L'audace, toujours l'audace![85]

Pigou noted that Labour *was* "dealing with the immediate post-war problems," including housing, worker reinsertion, inflation, rising interest rates, and industrial disputes.[86] Still, despite the importance of "immediate adjustments, compared with long-term policy, they . . . [were] secondary." For Pigou, the nature of Labour's long-term policy was to progressively bring about real good. Internationally, the party would work toward peace, cooperation, and disarmament, for which Noel-Baker was an outspoken campaigner and for which he would eventually earn the Nobel Peace Prize.[87] Pigou, however, was more excited about the domestic agenda. Here, he wrote, "on the one hand we want, in the widest sense, efficiency, so that the national cake may be as large as possible; on the other hand we want that cake to be so distributed that a reasonable minimum share is available for all."[88]

He justified Labour's program of nationalization of industries that had a "tendency towards monopoly"—"coal, transport, electricity, etc."—on the grounds of efficiency.[89] However, Pigou wrote, growing "the national cake" in this way was "not enough. . . . We want to help the underdog to get his share (Sob-stuff about the condition of the poor; muted music) . . . there is room for a good deal of useful action; of taxes on the rich for the benefit of the poor; which the public-spirited among the rich . . . would welcome."[90]

This responsible redistribution would be implemented through a slew of programs Pigou endorsed: "our social insurance policy, . . . milk in the schools, subsidies on essential foods and houses, the raising of the school-leaving age, state scholarships giving poor children similar opportunities with rich children, and so on."[91] For Pigou, hearkening back to his early work on welfare, these policies would go a long way toward removing external diseconomies and fostering economies. They were "not merely policies of redistributing the national cake." Instead, "so far as they keep people healthier and make them more intelligent, they induce them to produce more and so make the national cake bigger."[92] Pigou was returning to the basic tenets of his welfare economics. Picking up modes of thought he had put aside decades ago, he was reinvigorated by a concern for the poor and, however caustic he was about specific politicians, re-inspired by a government that was putting words into action. After all, in the first twelve months in power, Labour passed fifty-five bills and was well on its way toward nationalizing coal, communications, and civil aviation.[93]

Yet in some ways, the most striking passage of Pigou's speech draft was a short parenthetical that had little to do with actual policy. In summarizing the benefits of planning for the British economy, Pigou directed Noel-Baker to: "Make biased (!) summary of Socialism versus Capitalism and Economics of Welfare."[94] Pigou had long prickled at those who failed to grasp and honor the nuance of his theories.[95] Politicians who misused his ideas in the service of a political end annoyed him even more. Now, Pigou himself was telling Noel-Baker, a member of parliament, to make a selective reading of his own work for just such a purpose. Even if his exhortation was kept out of public sight, it still constituted a remarkable change in tack, one that could only have occurred with a new conception of the government's capacity to bring about positive change.

This is not to say that Pigou changed his mind about politics. Throughout the six turbulent postwar years of the Labour government, he repeatedly expressed his distaste for politics and individual politicians. He complained about "the wretched Hugh [Dalton]" and Labour Party strategist Harold Laski and plotted about "bumping off" Ernest Bevin with "a box of poisoned chocolates for X-mas" as "his figure makes it certain he will eat them."[96] He expressed "sadistic amusement" when Dalton, then the Chancellor of the Exchequer, had to step down in late 1947 for leaking a budget secret after making a careless comment about changes in the tax code. "Frightful bad luck," Noel-Baker responded to Pigou's glee, "but some people would think that he had been very lucky to escape so long!"[97] Briefed continuously by Noel-Baker about the cabinet's byzantine machinations, Pigou still maintained, "practically all politics are tricks on the make of the very blackest dogs. The moment they find anybody who'll do anything in the public interest their one idea is to exploit and swindle him! The only way to get proper treatment," he advised, "is to kick them repeatedly in the pants."[98] Members of the Labour Party, in particular, engaged in "appalling vulgarities and gaucheries."[99] An upper-middle class Liberal from a rapidly fading era, Pigou decried the savageries of the masses and instructed Noel-Baker to be a "gent."[100] Noel-Baker needed to stand out from a new class of politicians that comprised "tricks and arrivistes."[101]

However, Pigou laced his recriminations about Labour politics with hope of a future molded by a Labour government. "The

Comrades should not be merely a <u>section</u> to boost themselves," he wrote, "but a <u>political party</u> looking to the <u>interest of the country as a whole</u>."[102] Labour politicians were still, in his view, politicians—arrogant, stupid, and ignorant—but unlike their immediate predecessors, they could accomplish dramatic changes to the benefit of the whole country.

Increasingly, Pigou felt himself personally invested in that project of change. When speaking about the effects of one of Noel-Baker's speeches, he wrote of himself and the country together, holding that "*we* will be absolutely [lost] if at the conference you try to out-do Shifty [Shinwell] on his own muck-heap."[103] Describing a shift of influence in the party leadership, Pigou's tone was one of an insider, someone committed to the party's project. "It's a disgrace to the party," he wrote, "and it shows that it loves . . . tricks."[104] His hope had been rekindled. After so many years, a group in government had finally agreed not only to initiate sweeping economic reforms—to engage with the economy as active administrators along early Pigovian lines—but also had been elected with a mandate to carry out such policies.

Labour's promise relit in Pigou the spark that had animated his writings during the 1900s and 1910s. In this way, Pigou himself represented an unlikely through-line from the Liberal Party of the late nineteenth century to the postwar Labour Party. But Labour was different from the Government House that Pigou envisioned in his earlier works. It was not that Labour's leadership was much less rarefied than that of other more established parties—though some like Aneurin Bevan and Ernest Bevin came from working class backgrounds, many others (including Attlee, Dalton, and Noel-Baker) hailed from the upper-middle class and were products of elite education. The difference was that the party sought not only to help the downtrodden but also to represent them. Everyday people were not merely mechanical entities whose wants were to be satisfied, but living, breathing agents whose desires, feelings, and sensitivities were to be taken seriously.

For a variety of reasons, Pigou also began to take them seriously. In the mid-1930s, he had turned to the public, because there was no other audience left to him. At that time, the writings he intended for the public displayed scorn for the very readers they targeted.

Around the end of the war, however, Pigou's tone changed. Several months after Noel-Baker urged him to "instruct public opinion," he began work on a project unlike any previous one: a short, basic, introductory textbook of economics aimed not "at serious students" but at a populace increasingly bombarded with economic concepts. Pigou started work on the book in late 1944 and told Noel-Baker just after V.E. Day that he would "be pleased to hear that my great epic <u>Income: an Introduction to Economics</u> is now . . . with Macmillan."[105] Noel-Baker would indeed be pleased. Not only had the book kept his friend occupied, it was also an elucidating project, one that was very much in keeping with his earlier suggestion of addressing the common man.

When *Income* appeared in April 1946, Pigou was clear about its purpose. If members of the voting public learned the key concepts explained in the book, direct positive political outcomes would result: "their minister would not defend shutting out refugees on the ground that there are 250,000 unemployed!" Though the book was directed at the voter, Pigou also wryly recommended to Noel-Baker, "<u>all</u> the comrades [Labour Party members] should buy it to educate themselves."[106] They would be able to do so because the tone and content of *Income* was markedly different from his previous works. He had always placed a high premium on the clarity of his prose, but *Income* was especially lucid in its explanations and explicit in its endorsement of specific agendas. In *Income*, Pigou did exactly what he had recommended that Noel-Baker do in the speech draft of late 1945: he made a "biased summary" of his own corpus of work. Providing a quick overview of the central concepts of *The Economics of Welfare*, he explained the system of externalities and social costs before taking a clear political stand in support of the Labour government, particularly its policy of nationalization:

> For technical reasons [of economy], . . . services providing water, gas, electricity, telephones, tramways and railways, and communication, cannot be run as competitive enterprises, but must in the main, in each district, function as monopolies. . . . [These industries require] great government oversight or ownership.[107]

Nationalization on the grounds of efficiency was by no means the most radical of Pigou's positions in *Income*. Commenting on inequality of income, he noted that a distribution curve in the shape of a "cocked hat" might exist for inherited traits like height or mental faculty, but "not for income." Bemoaning income inequality, Pigou decried that half the children in the country belonged to families whose income did not furnish them enough food, and three quarters to families whose income was unlikely to provide enough. "These very small incomes of the many," he wrote, "stand in sharp and challenging contrast with the very large incomes enjoyed by a fortunate few."[108] A few years before, Pigou might not have drawn attention to the "challenging" nature of the contrast. Now, he conveyed his own skepticism about the morality of "one per cent of the persons aged twenty-five and over in England and Wales . . . [possessing] 55 per cent of the total property in private hands."[109]

Pigou advocated leveling the playing field. He favored large death duties and called for educational reform so as to afford people of all backgrounds an equal chance of financial success.[110] He recognized that "in recent times the State and the Universities have done a good deal to alter this state of things by educational grants, scholarships and so on; and they are proposing presently to do a good deal more." Still, he wrote, "investment in expensive education is in great part concentrated on the comparatively small number of children whose parents are well-to-do. . . . The sons of rich parents even if they are practically morons are given . . . [elite] kinds of training and education."[111] For Pigou, members of the general public were functioning not just as audience members or as mere objects of aid but as deserving individuals and potential equals.

Over the following years, Pigou undertook more and more public outreach efforts. He grumblingly acquiesced in 1945 to speak at the Cockermouth Rotarian show near Buttermere. "I have been tricked by a dentist," he claimed. "He had his drill so I didn't dare refuse."[112] He was also asked the next year to organize an event "to publicize [the] U.N.O. [United Nations Organization] and stir the great heart of the Cambridge public," for which he asked Noel-Baker, then part of Britain's UN delegation, to speak.[113] Throughout the late 1940s, he toyed with writing a full-length introductory economics textbook, but "found it so incredibly boring" that he "certainly couldn't do it."[114] Instead, he penned another small popular book, this time on the theory of money.[115] Between 1947 and 1957,

Pigou was published thirteen times in the *Times*, something that had not happened once in the preceding six years. His messages were mostly technical correctives, but they demonstrated both a renewed concern with educating the public about economic matters as well as a loosening restriction on nonpartisanship, with one article implicitly crediting the Labour government with postwar economic recovery.[116] Inspired by Labour and Noel-Baker, who became chair of the party in 1946, Pigou embraced a more open Britain, a democratic Britain in which political power was ultimately held by a general public to which he increasingly reached out.

CHAPTER EIGHT

To "Really Do
a Little Good"

A REDEMPTIVE CONCLUSION

THERE IS A PHOTOGRAPH of an elderly Pigou walking in the King's grounds with another aging fellow, Frank Adcock, a retired professor, fittingly, of Ancient History. Pigou and Adcock had been fellows together at King's for more than forty years.[1] Though not particularly close in their youth, in old age, the pair had taken to perambulating the grounds. Captured in mid-stride on a steely day in March 1954, the two of them were strolling through the college toward the River Cam. Pigou had donned a battered tweed jacket, a scarf, and worn woolen mittens, one of which was wrapped around the handle of a cane. His frame less straight than in his youth, Pigou had about him the softened lines of age. He had become one of the "dark shades" of the "museum of the antique" whom he had playfully figured over fifty years before.

Even in his retirement, Pigou stayed ensconced in Marshall's chair. This was not the Chair of Political Economy, but a physical armchair given to him by Marshall's wife, "in which Marshall used to seat people who came to see him."[2] The chair, however, was just one of the many laurels on which Pigou could rest. In the 1950s, Pigou, now in his seventies, began to take his retirement to heart. He still traveled up to Lower Gatesgarth at every opportunity,

[194]

FIGURE 6. Pigou and Frank Adcock in King's College, 1954.
Courtesy of Richard Cormack and King's College Archives.

though by this point, he shared the house with Claude Elliott. Elliott served as president of the Royal Alpine Society from 1950 to 1952, and in that capacity, planned a good deal of the first successful ascent of Everest from the dark sitting room overlooking Buttermere.[3] Pigou also still journeyed to the Alps, traveling "in safety by air in a <u>Swiss</u> plane," and bringing along Tom Gaunt's son (also Noel-Baker's godson), David, for "instruction in mountaineering under the guide, Tom, but <u>not</u> his wife."[4] Pigou was also a frequent visitor at his friends' houses, where he was a first class curmudgeon. He directed Noel-Baker that "you are to come visit me here . . . or to receive me, without any 'entourage de cochons [pigs].'"[5] When visiting Tom Gaunt, he pilfered his friend's stationery.[6] When planning to attend Wilfrid Noyce's wedding, he bragged that he would be robed in "a claret-colored tie, jumper, socks, and handkerchiefs," a picture of sartorial splendor.[7]

Pigou's penchant for complaint and grumbling about politics persisted as well. As Noel-Baker relayed the internal bickering among Labour Party ministers, Pigou responded with sympathy and cynicism, announcing during a visit to Tom Gaunt that Lower Gatesgarth would "secede from the Commonwealth." And when Noel-Baker was passed over for a position of leadership, Pigou commiserated and urged him to "abandon the doomed vessel and return to the gowns of Academia."[8] He took to composing poems about politicians. In one, he imagined the nation's leaders reveling during a time of postwar rationing:

> Champagne for us; though there's coal for none
> And meat for none and the nuts are done!
> Champagne for us; let the vermin pay!
>
> . . .
>
> Till the sun goes down we will make our hay!
> We shall keep our jobs; hip hip hooray![9]

In another, this one for Francis Noel-Baker, Philip's son and Pigou's godson, he commemorated a Labour Party conference on the Isle of Wight:

> The rats went down to the Isle of Wight,
>   The little rats and the great Big Rat!
>
> . . .
>
> They talked all day and they dreamed all night
>   Of whom to expel and whose back to pat.[10]

But despite all the vitriol Pigou spewed during the late 1940s and 1950s, he was hardly as despairing or as resentful as he had been over the preceding one and a half decades, especially after Noel-Baker was named Minister of Fuel and Power in 1950.

Nor was there ever any doubt of his affection for his friends or theirs for him. In the early fifties, Pigou began composing short stories for Wilfrid Noyce's son, whom he called "Gaters," the boy's middle name being Gatesgarth. Featuring Gaters and his "girl friend Tiger Lily," the tales were the product, in the words of Gaters's mother, of the "Prof. at his most whimsical and far too clever for children."[11] Pleased with himself, he submitted a manuscript to Macmillan. "Bits of it have been tried out successfully on several children," Pigou bragged, "and several parents (female) have said, 'O Professor Pigou, why don't you publish your delightful stories?'"[12] The editors were unmoved, but those personally close to Pigou were not. After all, Pigou was a devoted friend and, in the words of one of his longtime colleagues, his "young friends were indeed what he lived for."[13] In the end, not one family member inherited from Pigou. Although he had originally considered leaving a tidy sum to one of his nephews, he changed his mind when he discovered that the nephew in question was "well-to-do." Therefore, his wealth—£27,290 according to probate records—was left to his friends, the people who had ensured his personal welfare, by cutting through his pervasive ire and disillusionment.[14]

Back in Cambridge, Pigou was finally feeling at ease. Certainly, his softening toward the public and his general change in outlook were naturally concordant with a late-blooming acceptance of his waning position in academic economics. It was not that Pigou retired completely from academic circles. He continued to contribute to organs like *The Economic Journal* and *Economica*, and between 1947 and 1954, he published twelve journal articles, several of which were quite technical.[15] But he also began to explore new topics and relaxed his standards on political advocacy in economics journals as he was doing in his submissions to the popular press. Harkening back to his pre-professorial days, he wrote on historical political economy and current affairs. In 1948, he used a review of Lionel Robbins's *The Economic Problems of Peace and War* to muse on central planning. Again, he advocated limited but rigorous planning, a position consistent with his support for Labour's postwar policies. "The doors are wide open," he wrote, "through which the State may claim, as a good neighbour, to step in."[16] The next year, he authored a short piece in *The Economic Journal* about J. S. Mill on wages.[17]

What was of key importance was that at this stage in his life, Pigou was under no illusion about contributing groundbreaking work. Writing to R. F. Kahn, he asked for candid edits. "Please tell me without camouflage whether it is bunk. The brain having softened, I can no longer distinguish between bunk and non-bunk, and so must rely on comments not buttered."[18] By the late 1940s, Pigou readily admitted his own fallibility to younger economists. To Richard Stone, a colleague in his thirties working heavily in statistics and national accounting, he wrote in 1948 of uncompleted projects with the apology that he was "too gaga to do it now."[19] Later, in response to being sent one of Stone's articles, he ruefully noted: "It is possible, though not likely that I shall eventually understand it! Now . . . economics is becoming a branch of mathematics—which, so far as I ever knew any, I have completely forgotten! Alas for 'progress'! I feel like St. John, 'like a sea-jelly' left astrand at Patmos."[20] Even to Hugh Dalton, the "first-class tick," Pigou admitted that he was "no longer on the active list as an economist." Welfare economics, he complained, had "now become mixed up with highly complicated mathematical arguments about utility . . . with which I'm not now, if I ever was, competent to cope."[21]

It was not just in private correspondence that Pigou acknowledged his own limitations. His articles sounded a deferential tone. He wrote to R. F. Harrod, now one of the editors of *The Economic Journal* in 1949, claiming, "having become too stupid to contribute, I'm becoming a commentator."[22] He even softened somewhat on Keynes's work. In 1949, three years after Keynes's death, Pigou wrote a short book on Keynes in which he praised the latter's "fundamental conception" of how the market worked, bringing "all the relevant factors, real and monetary at once, together in a formal scheme." Though he warned that "Keynesianism" was "in danger of becoming a new orthodoxy," he acknowledged that he had "failed to grasp its significance" in his earlier critical review.[23]

Throughout the late 1940s and 1950s, Pigou found his earlier work invoked and critiqued, often by unfamiliar and distant voices, many from the ever more important academic centers of the United States. Pigou and his work now existed in a fundamentally altered world order. The British Empire no longer ruled the waves, and Pigovian economics no longer represented the cutting edge of academic thought. When Pigou responded to invocations and references to his work, he did so principally to correct minor instances of misinterpretation or merely to comment on a new idea. "It is a misfortune of longevity," he wrote, "that things which one wrote long ago survive in . . . later versions of one's books. When errors are found in these things . . . it is only with extreme difficulty that the antiquated author can bring his mind—what is left of it—to bear on them again.[24] Despite the difficulty, Pigou did bring his mind to bear on new ideas, especially those related to his early work on welfare. His goal, however, was not to critique or defend, but to explain his original intent to scholars who may not have been out of school when the piece in question had first been published. Responding in 1951 to an article by the American economist Paul Samuelson, which positively but critically invoked his "classic" treatment of national income in light of new developments in welfare economics, Pigou, then in his seventies, wrote:

> It is not surprising that serious defects in my treatment have been revealed. I do not want to challenge Professor Samuelson's argument on any substantial matter. The most useful way, I think, in which I can comment is by saying in my own language—his tools come unhandily to me—how these things seem to me to stand now.[25]

Pigou would use his own tools, but even in their use, he would not fundamentally challenge any new work done on the subject on which he had labored decades before, avoiding any controversy around interpersonal comparisons of utility.[26] Four months later, in a retrospective on welfare economics written for the *American Economic Review*, he acknowledged that he was very much out of the currents of contemporary work. "A great deal has been written on this subject in recent years," he noted, "and most of it I have not read."[27]

In 1952 and 1953, Pigou delivered the Marshall Lectures at Cambridge, a yearly lecture series that had been launched in 1946 in honor of his teacher. In his first, he "welcomed the chance" of "escaping for a moment from that shadowed land where departed spirits dwell."[28] Finding a topic on which to declaim was no simple task, Pigou explained, "for in that land memories fade and powers of concentration dwindle." Ultimately, he came to the conclusion that as one of the "few survivors" of those whom Marshall taught, perhaps the most useful thing he could do was to "act as a liaison officer" between his long-departed teacher and the current generation of economists that knew the master only through his portrait in the library. The resulting lectures, published in 1953 as *Alfred Marshall and Current Economic Thought*, offered a commentary on current economic debates as he felt Marshall might have delivered it, covering a ride range of topics, including mathematical methods, utility, and socialism. For an aging Pigou, the work was a natural one to write. For though he had not given up academic economics, he had openly stopped trying to forge new thought. He was, instead, an elder statesman of his field whose age and experience were to be valued on their own terms.

With this new role, Pigou commented with increasing transparency on his ethical motivations. Reinvigorated by the possibility for meaningful political change, he returned to the positions for which Joan Robinson had referred to him as the "first serious optimist." In a 1951 letter to Dalton, his ethical commitments were back on display. "The point about economics being not a normative science is, of course, only one of methodological convenience," Pigou wrote. "Nobody suggests that an economist shouldn't <u>have</u> ethical opinions; only it's convenient not to call them economics."[29]

In the retrospective article for the *American Economic Review*, Pigou was explicit that the raison-d'être for welfare economics was "to suggest lines of action—or non-action—on the part of the State or of private persons that might foster . . . the economic welfare of the world."[30] Without great argument, he stolidly reiterated his commitment to interpersonal comparisons of utility, not only because he thought that such measurements that existed could be compared but also out of a theoretical necessity: "if economic welfare were not something to which the notion of greater or less were applicable, welfare economics would vanish away."[31]

The world needed welfare economics, and so did Pigou. With the rise of the Labour Party and more activist governments in countries around the world, the social significance of his economics of welfare reemerged as his final justification, a system whose truth and usefulness stood as his lasting contribution to the world. Keynes had overturned his work on unemployment, but his contributions about welfare, despite the concerted attacks of Robbins and his followers in the 1930s, were to live on.

Welfare economics, however, was not just a former project whose resuscitation gave Pigou a sense of fulfillment. It also lent him fame and validation. Throughout the fifties, he would be recognized for his contributions, perhaps most notably by the Academia Nazionale dei Lincei in 1955, which elected him a foreign member and awarded him a 5 million lira (about £3,000) prize.[32] More importantly, however, his welfare economics seemed to acquire a new luster in the age of the burgeoning welfare state. Pigou's welfare economics may not have directly precipitated the welfare state, but it participated importantly in a liberal turn toward increasingly social and communal thinking—consider, for instance, Hugh Dalton's assertion that *Wealth and Welfare* was his "ethical starting point for economic journeys." And though the roots of the welfare state were multifarious, it was certainly a product of this broad intellectual movement.[33]

Throughout his career, Pigou had called for greater government intervention in the operation of the market. In retrospect, it is especially notable that he had specifically endorsed more steeply graduated tax regimes, more extensive state-mandated social insurance, and even the nationalization of key industries. In the postwar period, Pigou recognized the ethical impulses that motivated Labour Party leaders to be very similar to his own. Thus, Labour's ability and wherewithal to implement its 1945 manifesto gave Pigou both real hope, and, on some level, vindication. And despite his continued mockery of party leaders in his private letters to Noel-Baker and others, the success of Labour's enduring reforms ensured that that hope would be sustained even after the party's electoral defeat in 1951.

With hope came a new sense of promise, a heightened resolve to commit himself to justice and "GOOD WORKS." Despite continuing surliness, Pigou reinvested himself in questions of fairness and justice. These ethical considerations, which had lurked in the shadows of his economics for decades, reemerged into the light of publication. In 1954, for the first time since 1907, Pigou wrote a piece, "Some Aspects of the Welfare State," for a philosophical journal, and not just any journal, but *Diogenes*, a new international journal of the social sciences that was simultaneously printed in French, English, and Spanish. Other early contributors included the French anthropologist Claude Lévi-Strauss; the American historian Oscar Handlin; and the German theorist Gerhard Ritter, whose piece on totalitarianism appeared just pages after Pigou's. The setting of Pigou's article thus reflected the extent to which Pigou himself had changed. Even a few short years before, he was a man who referred to foreign languages as "Wop, Frog, Jap, Hun," and who, after impugning "talking to Yanks and Yank food," referred to San Francisco as a "film-star ridden inferno."[34] Now he was seemingly embracing a more international public sphere.

Pigou was introduced by the editor of *Diogenes* as having "had a decisive part in the genesis of [the] great intellectual and moral mutation" of an "almost universal demand for the 'Welfare State.'" Speaking from this elevated podium, Pigou launched into an authoritative overview, outlining tasks for which the welfare state was responsible.[35] It was to intervene to provide public goods like roads, and it was to look out for people who might not have their own best interests in mind by, for instance, providing mandatory basic education. It might also step in to regulate people like factory owners, whose activities yielded "uncovenanted damage on other people whose . . . losses do not enter into the[ir] calculations." In a moment of self-congratulation, Pigou noted that "these gaps . . . between private and public costs were not much in people's minds until fairly recently. Now everybody understands about them."[36]

Pigou offered up time-honored ideas, condensed into reflection on a life's work in welfare. His words, however, had taken on a new kind of tone. Like his early pieces from the time before he became a professor, "Some Aspects of the Welfare State" manifested a fusion of ethics, politics, and economics. This resurrected and retooled synthesis was, by turns, earthy and soaring. Pigou grumbled about politicians and the ease with which democratic ideals could be corrupted. Elected officials were "not philosopher kings and a blueprint [for beneficial State action] might quickly yield place on their desks to the propaganda of competing pressure groups." "'Fancy' finance," he continued, "like a fancy franchise, whatever its theoretical attractions, has, at all events in a democracy, dim practical prospects."[37] But despite the regrettable incompetence and weakness of certain officials, Pigou was still firm in his desire for the state to be, in Marshall's phrase, "up-and-doing." Citing the absence of perfect competition, he dismissed the "thesis that Government should stand aside because private individuals know their own business and their own wants better than officials." "The Welfare State," Pigou defiantly declared, "will certainly not stand aside."[38]

This was a manifesto many years in the making, one that incorporated both the hopeful, idealistic theories of the young don and those of an old man, tempered by decades of experience. The result was arresting. Here, Pigou, for so long an apolitical commentator, loudly declared that the Welfare State, with all of its left-leaning connotations, was ultimately an instrument of social justice.

> The [Labour] slogan *fair shares*, though a meaningless noise so long as *fair* is undefined, illustrates the benevolent, if muddled, aspirations of many enthusiasts for welfare. These seem at first sight so obviously right that to discuss them is a waste of time. But they were not always deemed obvious.[39]

In the past, Pigou claimed, popular perception held that to help the poor was to render them "idle and thriftless." To prevent mill owners from employing children for fourteen-hour days was also considered wrong. "To be poor was one's own fault, a crime fitly punished by suffering." These commonly held sentiments had, after so many years, been debunked and dismissed. "Other people's poverty is no longer a crime; that is now the fate of other people's wealth!" In this new, more morally sensitive context, redistribution was both natural and right. Besides, Pigou claimed, satisfaction was in large part social—after a certain point it had more to do with relative wealth than with absolute wealth.[40] "If everybody else is flaunting a pearl necklace and I, being for the purpose of the argument a lady, am not, I am grieved. But if nobody has a pearl necklace, I shall be equally content with glass beads." At long last, the mature Pigou had arisen, a Pigou who moved naturally from theory to humor to moral dictum.

With a nod toward the internationalism of his friend Noel-Baker, Pigou even looked beyond domestic social welfare policy. The pair worked together over the summers of the mid-1950s on Noel-Baker's book called *The Arms Race: A Programme for World Disarmament*, a project that helped Noel-Baker win the Nobel Peace Prize in 1959. In Noel-Baker's words, Pigou "read everything I read and discussed it enthusiastically with me. After I was getting in great difficulties about how to arrange my material and make the argument of my book hold together, he made a complete plan for a book in 7 parts." This plan was adopted, Noel-Baker claimed, "in toto."[41] The 1954 *Diogenes* article also reflected Pigou's collaboration with Noel-Baker. "To reduce international tension, and therewith the need for armaments," Pigou wrote, "is probably the greatest . . . contribution that a statesman could make to the development of the Welfare State." Moreover, in it, he evinced a sharp ethical concern with global inequality and wondered whether it would not be hypocritical for a welfare state to ignore "the distresses of less fortunate parts of the world," an important statement made during a long decade of decolonization.[42]

At the time of his final book's publication in 1955, Pigou was at his most openly egalitarian. This last book, *Income Revisited*, was the sequel to *Income*, his popular textbook from 1946, and in both its exposition as well as its ethical claims, it continued along the lines set by its predecessor. Like the first, it was aimed at "the plain man," but it was even more explicit in its democratizing method and its efforts at inclusiveness. "The plain man confronted with recent refinements in economic theory, often expressed in mathematical language," Pigou wrote, "may be tempted to think that the subject is one entirely for specialists and not for such as him." However, "economic happenings *affect* the plain man in his private life and, maybe, have a bearing on his political judgment."[43] Twenty years before, in a book intended to be generally accessible, Pigou had likened the public to goats. Now he welcomed his readership warmly, offering that "behind the complications of advanced analysis there is a central core of economic truth which can, I think, be made intelligible to any educated person who chooses to take a little trouble."[44] The book, like its predecessor, endeavored to help make economics intelligible and was clearly set out with simple chapter titles like "Money," "How Capital Is Built Up," and "Social and Private Cost."

Yet *Income Revisited* was not just a reference for armchair economists but also an inherently political work with clear ethical arguments. Four years before his death, in the final chapter of his final book, Pigou threw off the cross he had borne for five decades. He observed that economics was a study of what tends to happen rather than what ought to happen.

> Questions about what is just or fair lie beyond its scope, and the law-abiding economist will not trespass among them. Definitions, however, are made for man, not man for definitions, and I do not propose to be law-abiding.[45]

Pigou broke the law with a splash. He titled the book's concluding chapter "Fair Shares for All," the former Labour Party slogan. And in the chapter itself, Pigou set out the most radical ethical opinion he had ever espoused.

In *Income*, Pigou had argued for equality of opportunity. In *Income Revisited*, he went much further. Fairness, he wrote, meant "equal shares for all" qualified first "by reference to differences in objective needs," and second (and less importantly), "by reference to difference in contributions of service." Pigou had, after years of avoiding moral philosophy, come out as an egalitarian, and a very strong one at that. On the second qualification—difference in contribution—he wrote:

> A man may put more into a pool either because he is stronger or more intelligent or possesses a kind of skill which at the moment is in specially keen demand, or because he works for longer hours or more intensively or has devoted more time and labour to training and improving his faculties than others have.[46]

Inequalities that resulted from ability or intellect, however, were hardly fair. "Greater strength or natural intelligence creates an obligation, not a claim!" Even rewards gained from luck, especially those made on the stock market, were unearned, and therefore unfair.[47] In any event, Pigou wrote, "we should not . . . consider it fair for differences in contribution to be associated with anything like equal differences of reward." Thus, "very large differences of disposable income, whatever their cause, are on this plane of thinking not fair."[48] The political message was clear. Redistribution of the sort expected of the welfare state was as much an ethical imperative as it was an economic one.

Income Revisited displayed the nature of Pigou's ethical thinking more clearly than any of his work since his taking the Chair in Political Economy. His ethics had changed considerably since then, shedding both their classism and their Government House mentality. With the hindsight of his own loss of status and his continued distaste for government hacks, Pigou had developed a democratized concept of fairness that stressed equality. This new egalitarianism, though idealistic, was still, in an important sense, pragmatic. It stemmed not only from his disenchantment with elites but also from Pigou's renewed hope that politicians and economists could, in some synergistic enterprise, change the world for the better.

In the broadest of brushstrokes, Pigou's changing relationship with the state depended on the rising importance of economic expertise in state management throughout the early twentieth century. Yet Pigou's story demonstrates that the new scientific experts were often independent thinkers and not always eager participants in state projects.[49] For Pigou, politics and personal experience played vital roles in his understanding of the state. His move from Liberal to Labour mirrored Britain's; like Britain's, it was forged in the crucible of World War I. But his was also, to a large extent, made possible by his own particular intellectual and professional experiences of disciplinary shift and loss. Without having been overtaken by his professional colleagues, it is dubious that he would ever have turned to the public. Without having known professional hardship in the 1930s and the traumas of war, he would never have been able to rekindle the hope of his youth.

But a large part of the credit for the shift in Pigou's thinking should be claimed by the Labour Party itself. Pigou's ethics were able to shrug off its Government House mentality because of the success of Labour's commitment to and execution of a limited form of central planning. Labour's accomplishments reawakened Pigou's dream of a competent intervener. This time, however, the nature of the intervener reflected Labour's vision of a just future based on equality, not on mere management. At the end of his life, A. C. Pigou had come more than full circle. He had returned to a broad, multivalent practice of political economy, one in which his ethics took a prominent public role. More than that, he had discovered a new hopeful vision of a more democratic future. Ironically, only as a surly old don considered by many to be a recluse, did Pigou truly embrace people.

Epilogue

PIGOU DIED OF AN ABDOMINAL DISORDER in March 1959 at the age of eighty-one. He was buried in the churchyard in Grantchester, the small village just south of Cambridge. The graveyard stands in the shadow of the fourteenth-century parish church, just across from meadows owned by his beloved King's College that stretch down to the River Cam. It is an idyllic English landscape, with thatched roofs and grazing livestock. Just down the road is the bend in the river where Lord Byron used to take his swims.

It is a fitting resting place for a man who spent his entire adult life in Cambridge, but a somewhat ironic one for an economist whose name would be associated with the economics of pollution for the next seven decades. Little more than a year after Pigou's death, Ronald Coase published his famous essay called "The Problem of Social Cost." Coase set out to investigate "those actions of business firms which have harmful effects on others . . . the standard example is that of a factory the smoke from which has harmful effects on those occupying neighbouring properties." He noted that the economic analysis of such a situation customarily "followed the treatment of Pigou."[1] Coase went on to dispute this treatment, arguing that externalities arose not from a major divergence of public and private interests, but because of barriers to negotiation and poorly defined property rights. Nevertheless, the fact remained that Pigou set the stage for all subsequent discussions about external diseconomies.

Today, Pigou's ideas seem more germane than ever, and a renewed understanding of his influence is coming into clearer focus.

In an age beset by increasingly arresting predictions of climate change, the external effects of the normal operation of the economy have never been more headlined. For it is widely recognized that the ramifications of pollution extend far beyond those "occupying neighbouring properties." Historians of the Anthropocene now chart the unintended impact of human activity on truly massive planetary, geological scales.[2] Climate change and its accompanying existential anxieties have provoked a realization that externalities will not resolve themselves without some sort of intervention.

In this way, much of the world has awakened to the fact that it is, and has been for some time, in a post-Pigovian age. In 2006, a Harvard economist, N. Gregory Mankiw advertised himself as a Pigovian and subsequently labeled scores of other prominent figures from the left and right alike as the same. Pigou's suggestion to tax industries that produced socially undesirable effects was just "good sense" according to Mankiw. The *Economist* seemingly agreed. So too did the *Washington Post*. So did the Obama administration. The future of environmental policy in the United States looks less certain after the 2016 presidential election, but it is likely that calls to treat climate change as a negative externality will only continue to grow in number and in intensity.

Many in the public sphere have recognized and called attention to the fact that Pigou stands behind these suggestions. A web search for Pigou turns up droves of editorials suggesting that one of the most sensible ways to deal with the climate crisis—to tax it out of existence—was thought up by a largely forgotten English economist with "wavy hair and a luxuriant moustache."[3] "One way to think about global warming," the *New Yorker* intoned in 2012, "is as a vast, planet-wide Pigovian problem."[4] The *New York Times* argued that "taxes on activities with harmful side effect" were "one of the few realistic hopes for progress." These taxes, the *Times* noted, "are known as Pigovian taxes, after the British economist Arthur C. Pigou, who advocated them."[5] Other commentators have found Pigou's work useful in confronting different contemporary challenges. The *New Yorker* staff writer John Cassidy suggested, for instance, that Pigou's work "provides a guide to the financial crisis." Failures in the financial system, Cassidy argued in the *Wall Street Journal* and his book *How Markets Fail*, should be seen as massive market failures that require a Pigovian solution.[6] Amartya Sen, writing in the *New York Review of Books*, invoked Pigou's own treatment of financial crises as well as his stress on the importance of distribution.[7] Others, writing in the *American Prospect* and the *New York Times* have claimed that excessive inequality itself is a market failure and that as such, it calls for a hefty corrective Pigovian tax.[8]

It is tempting to look back on Pigou's life and work to find lessons for our current predicaments. There is a tendency to worship long-dead economists as sages who presaged the crises of the future. And, in light of Pigou's work on external diseconomies, his analysis of the costs of pollution, his distaste for massive disparities in wealth, and even his preference for a stable financial sector, there is a powerful urge to review his corpus of work and conclude that he was ahead of his time—that quite simply, he got things right.

Pigou certainly endowed future generations of economic thinkers with a powerful set of tools, tools that current economists may do well to reexamine. There is, however, something uncomfortable about the conclusion that Pigou was "correct" or that he presaged some of the developments after his death. The principal lesson of Pigou's life is that his work grew out of a specific historical moment. It emerged from personal interactions with government officials, from conversations with his friends, from contemporary economic and political conditions, and from the shifting sands on which economic ideas rested. Pigou responded to a growth in heavy industry that was destroying the environment, to a growing national perception of inequality, and to a major financial crisis. Is it any wonder that his ideas resonate today?

But whether or not Pigou's ideas are borne out in reality, there is a clear lesson to be drawn from his life's work. Pigou, like almost all of his contemporaries, was an ethical economist. He set himself to explaining and solving the most pressing crises of his day. And he did not shirk in his diligence. His justification for his career, maybe even for his very existence, was to serve a moral end. Perhaps it is this part of Pigou's systematic framework—its self-conscious motivation—that present-day economists would do best to revisit. The world is today faced with a host of economic crises, but they are equally moral crises. Returning to a truly Pigovian way of thinking would mean honoring this fact and acknowledging it publicly. It would mean accepting what Pigou had declared in 1908, that "Ethics and Economics are mutually dependent," and that "economics cannot stand alone."[9]

Introduction: History and Economics

1. E. A. G. Robinson, "Pigou, Arthur Cecil (1877–1959), Economist," *Dictionary of National Biography* Archive, 1971, http://www.oxforddnb.com/view/olddnb/35529.

2. See Austin Robinson to Mark Blaug, November 10, 1992, Archives of the London School of Economics (hereafter LSE), London, United Kingdom, Blaug Papers, Blaug/3.

3. See Notes on Pigou's Family, Austin Robinson Papers, Marshall Library of Economics, Cambridge, UK (hereafter MLE), EAGR 6/6/2 and EAGR 6/6/5.

4. Austin Robinson to D. W. Corrie, October 7, 1964, Austin Robinson Papers, MLE, EAGR 6/6/6, 151.

5. E. A. G. Robinson, "A.C. Pigou," *Times* (March 9, 1959): 12.

6. For examples of this general trajectory of the Liberal disillusioned and discomfited by World War I, see the excellent biographies of G. M. Trevelyan and William Beveridge. David Cannadine, *G.M. Trevelyan: A Life in History* (New York: W. W. Norton & Company, 1992); José Harris, *William Beveridge: A Biography* (Oxford: Clarendon Press, 1977).

7. See John Maloney, *The Professionalization of Economics: Alfred Marshall and Dominance of Orthodoxy* (New Brunswick, NJ: Transaction, 1991): 91–119.

8. See the correspondence of librarians in 1959 in "Academic and Tutorial Records," King's College Archive, Cambridge (hereafter KCA) KCAC 6/1/11/36.

9. Richard Deacon, "The British Connection 2," *Guardian* (May 30, 1979): 16.

10. N. Gregory Mankiw, "Smart Taxes: An Open Invitation to Join the Pigou Club," n.d., http://www.economics.harvard.edu/files/faculty/40_Smart%20Taxes .pdf. The Pigou Club's manifesto was published in the *Wall Street Journal* in 2006. N. Gregory Mankiw, "Opinion: Raise the Gas Tax," *Wall Street Journal* (October 20, 2006), http://online.wsj.com/article/SB116131055641498552.html?mod=opinion _main_commentaries; N. Gregory Mankiw, "Rogoff Joins the Pigou Club," September 16, 2006, Greg Mankiw's Blog, http://gregmankiw.blogspot.com/2006/09/rogoff -joins-pigou-club.html.

11. In *The General Theory*, Keynes identified Pigou's *Theory of Unemployment* as "the only detailed account of the classical theory of employment which exists." J. M. Keynes, *The General Theory of Employment, Interest and Money* (New York: Harcourt, 1964): 7. See Gerhard Michael Ambrosi, *Keynes, Pigou and Cambridge Keynesians: Authenticity and Analytical Perspective in the Keynes-Classics Debate* (Houndmills, Basingstoke, UK: Palgrave Macmillan, 2003).

12. R. H. Coase, "The Problem of Social Cost," *Journal of Law and Economics 3* (October 1, 1960): 1–44. See also Nahid Aslanbeigui and Steven G. Medema, "Beyond

the Dark Clouds: Pigou and Coase on Social Cost," *History of Political Economy* 30, no. 4 (Winter 1998): 601–625; Steven G. Medema, *Ronald H. Coase* (London: Macmillan, 1994).

13. The term "Pigou Effect" was coined in 1948. See Don Patinkin, "Price Flexibility and Full Employment," *American Economic Review* 38, no. 4 (September 1948): 543–564. For more on subsequent support for the Pigou Effect, see Serge Coulombe, "A Note on the Pigou Effect and the Liquidity Trap," *Journal of Post Keynesian Economics* 10, no. 1 (October 1, 1987): 163–165; S. C. Tsiang, "Keynes's 'Finance' Demand for Liquidity, Robertson's Loanable Funds Theory, and Friedman's Monetarism," *Quarterly Journal of Economics* 94, no. 3 (May 1, 1980): 467–491; and Jacques Melitz, "Pigou and the 'Pigou Effect': Rendez-Vous with the Author," *Southern Economic Journal* 34, no. 2 (October 1, 1967): 268–279.

14. David Collard was editor of a 1994 collection of Pigou's works and a further 2002 two-voume set of some of Pigou's journal articles. Collard's introductions serve as good starting points for understanding Pigou's work. Collard also produced other articles and chapters on Pigou. Nahid Aslanbeigui has written on Pigou since the early 1990s, alone and with Guy Oakes and Steven Medema. Aslanbeigui and Oakes published a book on Pigou in 2015. Gerhard Michael Ambrosi's 2003 book, *Keynes, Pigou and Cambridge Keynesians* is a more technical reconstruction of Pigou's thinking. There is also a burgeoning Japanese literature on Pigou, notably by Ryo Hongo and Norikazu Takami. Karen Knight and Michael McLure at the University of Western Australia, Perth, have also recently contributed to Pigovian literature. For lists of works by these scholars, see the Bibliography.

15. Donald Winch's application of Cambridge School methods to the history of economics remains a touchstone. See Donald Winch, *Riches and Poverty: An Intellectual History of Political Economy in Britain, 1750–1834* (Cambridge: Cambridge University Press, 1999); Donald Winch, *Wealth and Life: Essays on the Intellectual History of Political Economy in Britain, 1848–1914* (Cambridge: Cambridge University Press, 2009). So too does Robert Skidelsky's three-volume biography of John Maynard Keynes, published between 1983 and 2000. Emma Rothschild's work in broadening contexts has similarly been influential, especially *Economic Sentiments: Adam Smith, Condorcet, and the Enlightenment* (Cambridge, MA: Harvard University Press, 2002). Other examples of recent work in this vein include Jeremy Adelman, *Worldly Philosopher: The Odyssey of Albert O. Hirschman* (Princeton, NJ: Princeton University Press, 2014); Angus Burgin, *The Great Persuasion: Reinventing Free Markets Since the Depression* (Cambridge, MA: Harvard University Press, 2012); Erik Grimmer-Solem, *The Rise of Historical Economics and Social Reform in Germany, 1864–1894* (Oxford: Clarendon Press, 2003); Fredrik Albritton Jonsson, *Enlightenment's Frontier: The Scottish Highlands and the Origins of Environmentalism* (New Haven, CT: Yale University Press, 2013); Nicholas Phillipson, *Adam Smith: An Enlightened Life* (New Haven, CT: Yale University Press, 2012); Timothy Shenk, *Maurce Dobb: Political Economist* (Houndmills, Basingstoke, UK: Palgrave Macmillan, 2013). Daniel Stedman Jones, *Masters of the Universe: Hayek, Friedman, and the Birth of Neoliberal Politics* (Princeton, NJ: Princeton University Press, 2012).

Chapter 1: Beginnings

1. "Marriage of Miss Lees," *Isle of Wight Times*, November 23, 1876. See also "Tying the Knot," *Beyond the Graves*, Ryde Social Heritage Group Newsletter 5, no. 4 (October 2010): 3.

2. Austin Robinson to Sir Harcourt Lees, n.d. [after 1959], MLE, EAGR 6/6/4. The former resident, Sir James Caldwell, (1770–1863), was a general in the service of the East India Company. R. H. Vetch, "Caldwell, Sir James Lillyman (1770–1863)," rev. Roger T. Stearn, *Oxford Dictionary of National Biography* (Oxford: Oxford University Press, 2004), http://www.oxforddnb.com/view/article/4385.

3. The unit was the Fifteenth (The East Yorkshire Riding) Regiment of Foot.

4. "Marriage of Miss Lees."

5. The uncle was William Nassau Lees (1825–1889). H. M. Chichester, "Lees, William Nassau (1825–1889)," rev. Parvin Loloi, *Oxford Dictionary of National Biography* (Oxford: Oxford University Press, 2004), http://www.oxforddnb.com/view/article/16333.

6. Pigou's ancestors came to England in the 1680s. An early ancestor, Frederick Pigou, was the chief "supercargo," or trader, of Canton for the East India Company and later a director of the company. Another relative, Frederick John Pigou, was also a director of the company and of its bank. Marika Sherwood and Kathy Chater, "The Pigou Family across Three Continents," *Proceedings of the Huguenot Society* 28, no. 3 (2005): 408–413.

7. The disinherited uncle was Frederick John Pigou (1815–1847). Knowledge of early Pigous has benefited from an active genealogical interest on the part of their descendants. See "The Pigou Family," last modified 2011, http://www.piggin.org/charts/pigou.htm. M. G. Dauglish and P. K. Stephenson, eds. *Harrow School Register 1800–1911* (London: Longmans, Green, and Co., 1911): 132.

8. Oldham married Clarence's eldest sister, Ella Frances Emma Pigou. *The Army List* (London: Royal Stationers, September 1902): 1405.

9. Sherwood and Chater, "The Pigou Family Across Three Continents," 410–411.

10. "Marriage of Miss Lees." After short service as a lieutenant starting in 1869, there is no indication that Clarence worked. In census records, Clarence's profession is listed as "Late 15th Regiment." *Census Returns of England and Wales, 1881*, Kent, The National Archives of the United Kingdom, Kew, United Kingdom (hereafter TNA), RG11/923/28, 8. "India-Office, March 7," *Morning Post, t*March 8, 1876, 6.

11. Austin Robinson thought Pigou's "Christian name" was probably Cecil and that his first name, Arthur, was merely a way of differentiating C(ecil) from his father, C(larence). Austin Robinson to Mark Blaug, November 10, 1992, Blaug Papers, LSE, Blaug/3.

12. The Leeses were among Ryde's wealthiest residents, and Beachlands was furnished with "VALUABLE CONTENTS," including nine gilt Louis XVI armchairs, "a massive ormolu inkstand from the Tuileries, Crown Derby, Dresden, and Oriental China, and 1100 ounces of silver plate." "Beachlands," *Isle of Wight Observer*, August 1892, http://www.historicrydesociety.co.uk/history/royal-victoria-arcade/ryde-houses/beachlands/.

13. *Census Returns of England and Wales, 1881*, Kent, TNA, RG11/923/28, 8.

14. *Census Returns of England and Wales, 1891*, Kent, TNA, RG12/683/114, 3.

15. At the time of publication, The Larches was known as "Sunhill Court" and was part of a retirement community. See also, Tunbridge Wells Borough Council, "Draft Review: Pembury Conservation Area Appraisal," August 2007, accessed Feburary 14, 2014, http://consult.tunbridgewells.gov.uk/portal/planning_information/spp/drp/.

16. "Those in Authority: Arthur Cecil Pigou," *Granta* 13, no. 281 (April 28, 1900): 656.

17. A.C. Pigou, "F.E.M." *Harrovian* 35, no. 6 (October 21, 1922): 78.

18. Christopher Tyerman, *A History of Harrow School 1324–1991* (Oxford: Oxford University Press, 2000): 377.

19. See Colin Shrosbree, *Public Schools and Private Education: The Clarendon Commission, 1861–64, and The Public Schools Acts* (Manchester: Manchester University Press, 1988): chapter 6.

20. "Notices," *Harrovian* 2, no. 1 (February 7, 1889): 135. Originally housing seven boys, Newlands grew over Pigou's tenure at Harrow, becoming home to forty-two by 1904. "Newlands: History of the House," accessed January 20, 2014, http://www.harrowschool.org.uk/1702/boarding/newlands/history-of-the-house.

21. Tyerman, *Harrow School*, 359–360.

22. Ibid.

23. Ibid., 358, 376. This did not mean that all its students came from upper class backgrounds. Indeed, earning potential was becoming increasingly important for new graduates. Of the 1890 entrants to Harrow, 37 percent went into military service; 17 percent into law; and 23 percent into business, banking, or trade. Ten years later, 25 percent went into the service, 14 percent into law, and 30 percent into business or banking. On the connection of earning and the concept of the gentleman, see Martin J. Wiener, *English Culture and the Decline of the Industrial Spirit, 1850–1980* (Cambridge: Cambridge University Press, 1981).

24. Tyerman, *Harrow School*, 376.

25. J. W. Jenkins to Austin Robinson, September 27, 1964, MLE, EAGR 6/6/6.

26. Pigou, "F.E.M," 78.

27. "Harrow in the Holidays," *The Harrovian* 6, no. 2 (March 25, 1893): 13.

28. Pigou, "F.E.M.," 78.

29. Francis Edward Marshall (1848–1922) came from a prominent family that split its time between Leeds and Keswick in the Lake District. W. N. Bruce, "F.E.M.," *Harrovian* 35, no. 6 (October 21, 1922): 77–78.

30. Edward Graham, *The Harrow Life of Henry Montagu Butler, D.D.* (London: Longmans, Green and Company, 1920): 275.

31. Life at Harrow was dramatically depicted by Old Harrovian Arnold Lunn in his 1913 novel, *The Harrovians: A Tale of Public School Life* (London: Smith, Elder and Co., 1913).

32. "Founder's Day," *Harrovian* 8, no. 8 (October 19, 1895): 97.

33. J. W. Jenkins to Austin Robinson, September 27, 1964, Austin Robinson Papers, MLE, EAGR 6/6/6.

34. Ibid. Jenkins misremembered that Pigou's mother had died and that Pigou was "the only son . . . without women's company." Pigou's mother did not die until 1902, and Pigou had both a sister and brother, though both might have been at school when Jenkins visited.

35. Pigou won the Rev. R. Davies, Matfield Grange, and Staplehurst prizes. "Honours and Prizes," *Harrovian* 4, no. 3 (April 30, 1891): 27. "Those in Authority: Arthur Cecil Pigou," 656; "Honours and Prizes," *Harrovian* 5, no. 3 (April 9, 1892): 25.

36. Mary Moorman, *George Trevelyan: A Memoir* (London: Hamish Hamilton, 1980): 23–24.

37. "Here and There," *Harrovian* 7, no. 4 (May 8, 1894): 30.

38. On Pigou's bout with pugilism, see "Gymnasium," *Harrovian* 7, no. 2 (March 17, 1894): 25. On cricket, see J. W. Jenkins to Austin Robinson, September 27, 1964, Austin Robinson Papers, MLE, EAGR 6/6/6.

39. "Debating Society," *Harrovian* 8, no. 9 (November 21, 1895): 112; Debating Society," *Harrovian* 9, no. 1 (February 22, 1896): 10.

40. "Debating Society News," *Harrovian* 7, no. 8 (November 15, 1894): 103.

41. See chapter 14 of Tyerman, *Harrow School*, 355–402.

42. Edward Whymper (1840–1911), who led the first ascent of the Matterhorn in 1865, spoke at Harrow in early 1894. "Lecture on Mountaineering," *Harrovian* 7, no. 2 (March 17, 1894): 20–21. For the Royal Navy talk, see "Royal Navy," *Harrovian* 7, no. 9 (December 14, 1894): 110. The debating society held a debate inspired by the talk, on whether, if war were declared with France, the Mediterranean were to be evacuated. "Debating Society News," *Harrovian* 8, no. 3 (April 6, 1895): 27.

43. Gerard Clarence Pigou "Pigou, Gerard Clarence," Executive Officers' Services. Dates of Entry: 1893–1896, TNA, ADM 196/45/61; *Navy List* (February 1896): 252.

44. "Debating Society News," *Harrovian* 7, no. 8 (November 15, 1894): 103.

45. Aslanbeigui rightly suggests that contemporary evaluations of Pigou's misogyny should be tempered by historical circumstance. As will be outlined later, however, Pigou's opinion of women was unusual even in his context. Nahid Aslanbeigui, "Rethinking Pigou's Misogyny," *Eastern Economic Journal* 23, no. 3 (Summer 1997): 301–316.

46. "Debating Society," *Harrovian* 9, no. 2 (March 27, 1896): 19.

47. Although such debates had political implications, many others were much more explicitly concerned with contemporary politics. For instance, five days before the discussion on Charles I there was a debate—"the most animated of the term" on the motion that "Lord Salisbury's action as Foreign Secretary during the present administration is worthy of severe censure." The motion was rejected by fourteen votes to eight, showing support for Salisbury's Conservative administration.

48. At the end of his penultimate year, Pigou was first in his form and recited a speech by Lord Beaconsfield on conservative principles to the school and a visiting member of the royal family, the Duchess of Teck. Pigou also won the Fortescue Prize and the Clayton Prize. "Here and There," *Harrovian* 8, no. 6 (July 3, 1895): 70; "Prize List," *Harrovian* 8, no. 4 (May 23, 1895): 48. "Speech Day," *Harrovian* 8, no. 7 (July 27, 1895): 85.

49. "Here and There," *Harrovian* 8, no. 8 (October 19, 1895): 97.

50. On the appointments, see "Here and There," *Harrovian* 8, no. 9 (November 21, 1895): 112; "Musical Society," *Harrovian* 8, no. 8 (October 19, 1895): 104. On Pigou's tone deafness, see J. W. Jenkins to Austin Robinson, September 27, 1964, MLE, EAGR 6/6/6.

51. The Mission was founded in Nottingdale, West London, in 1883. Few Harrovians were actively involved, but many contributed money. Tyerman, *Harrow School*, 183.

52. "Debating Society," *Harrovian* 8, no. 9 (November 21, 1895): 112.

53. Ibid.

54. "Debating Society," *Harrovian* 9, no. 1 (Februrary 22, 1896): 10. After Pigou was no longer president, he commented that because of low participation, the Debating Society "seems to be in a very bad way indeed." Remarking that "forced debates are as insipid as forced strawberries," he suggested new formats and rules. "To the Editors of the Harrovian," *Harrovian* 9, no. 9 (December 19, 1896): 112.

55. "Debating Society," *Harrovian* 9, no. 1 (Februrary 22, 1896): 10. Leander Starr Jameson, a colonial administrator of the Cape Colony in what is now South Africa, had launched a botched raid at in late 1895 on the Boer-controlled Transvaal Republic to incite an uprising of British workers. Jameson did not succeed in destabilizing the Afrikaaner-controlled state, but he mobilized nationalistic sentiment.

56. Ibid.

57. "Founder's Day," *Harrovian* 8, no. 8 (October 19, 1895): 97.

58. The speech was "The Slavonic Provinces of the Ottoman Empire," which Gladstone delivered at Hawarden, Wales, on January 16, 1877. At Speech Day, Pigou shared the stage with classmate Maharaj Singh (1878–1959), an Indian prince who became the first governor of Bombay State and who recited a piece by the Whig, Lord Macaulay (1800–1859). "On Speech Day," *Harrovian* 9, no. 6 (July 25, 1896): 66.

59. Pigou won the Neeld Prize, the Problem Prize, the Lady Bourchier Reading Prize, the Mix Copies Prize, and the "On Leaving Harrow" Prize. See "Here and There," *Harrovian* 9, no. 3 (May 23, 1896): 30; "Here and There," *Harrovian* 9, no. 5 (July 1, 1896): 56; "Prize List," *Harrovian* 9, no. 7 (October 24, 1896): 81.

60. See Sheldon Rothblatt, *The Revolution of the Dons: Cambridge and Society in Victorian England* (Cambridge: Cambridge University Press, 1981).

61. Christopher N. L. Brooke, *A History of the University of Cambridge, Volume IV, 1870–1990* (Cambridge: Cambridge University Press, 1993), 247.

62. Brooke, *A History of Cambridge*, 240–252.

63. Quoted in Brooke, *A History of Cambridge*, 289.

64. Elisabeth Leedham-Green, *A Concise History of the University of Cambridge* (Cambridge: Cambridge University Press, 1996), 181.

65. Ibid., 162. These were Theology, Semitic Languages, Indian Languages, Oriental Languages, Medieval Languages, Modern Languages, and Mechanical Sciences. Only one (the splitting of History and Law) had been introduced in the previous twenty years.

66. By 1900, the number of graduates passing the Natural Science Tripos was 20 percent higher than the number passing Classics. Leedham-Green, *A Concise History of Cambridge*, 162.

67. See Leedham-Green, *A Concise History of Cambridge*, chapter 5; Rothblatt, *The Revolution of the Dons*. On women, see Brooke, *A History of Cambridge*, chapter 9.

68. Brooke, *A History of Cambridge*, 293.

69. Ibid., 229. The Cambridge grading system of undergraduate degrees has five tiers. At the bottom, there is an ordinary degree, or a "pass." Then, in ascending order, come third-class honors (Third); second-class honors, lower division (2:2); second-class honors, upper division (2:1); and first-class honors (First).

70. Brooke, *A History of Cambridge*, 229–230.

71. Ibid, 232. See also P. R. H. Slee, *Learning and a Liberal Education: The Study of Modern History in the Universities of Oxford, Cambridge and Manchester, 1800–1914* (Manchester: Manchester University Press, 1986), 71–83.

72. Brooke, *A History of Cambridge*, 36. On Browning and teachers' colleges, see Pam Hirsch and Mark McBeth, *Teacher Training at Cambridge: The Initiatives of Oscar Browning and Elizabeth Hughes* (London: Woburn Press, 2004). For a biography of Browning, see Ian Anstruther, *Oscar Browning: A Biography* (London: John Murray, 1983).

73. Brooke, *A History of Cambridge*, 36.

74. Leedham-Green, *A Concise History of Cambridge*, 173; Anstruther, *Oscar Browning*, 55–66.

75. Brooke, *A History of Cambridge*, 89.

76. Ibid., 465. See also P. Searby, *The Training of Teachers in Cambridge University: The First Sixty Years, 1879–1939* (Cambridge: Cambridge University Press, 1982), 36–37.

77. "Union Notes," *Granta* 10, no. 193 (October 24, 1896): 20–21.

78. Pigou to Oscar Browning, June 24 [n.d.], The Papers of Oscar Browning, KCA, OB/1/1281/A.

79. Pigou to Oscar Browning, n.d. [1897–99], Browning Papers, KCA, OB/1/1281/A.

80. Pigou to Oscar Browning, n.d. [1897–99], Browning Papers, KCA OB/1/1281/A.

81. Browning was a diligent correspondent, writing from his lengthy holidays in Florence or the Alps. Though he cut a wide figure, The O.B. was also a nominal mountaineer—a member of the Alpine Society—and Pigou was invited to join his expeditions. Pigou to Oscar Browning, September 23, [1897–99], Browning Papers, KCA, OB/1/1281/A.

82. Pigou to Oscar Browning, April 5, [1897–99], Browning papers, KCA, OB/1/1281/A.

83. Ibid.

84. Pigou to John Tresidder Sheppard. July 24, 1903, The Papers of John Tresidder Sheppard, KCA JTS/2.160.

85. A.C. Pigou, "Undergraduate History Notes," n.d., Arthur Cecil Pigou Papers, MLE, Pigou 1/2.

86. Ibid. Alfred Marshall admired Herbert Spencer and other social Darwinists and, unlike Sidgwick, thought of ethics as inherently evolutionary along the lines of Hegel. On Marshall and evolutionary theory, see Peter Groenewegen, *A Soaring Eagle: Alfred Marshall 1842-1924* (Aldershot, UK: Edward Elgar, 1995): 479-485, 499, 510-511. On Marshall's evolutionary ethics, see Donald Winch, *Wealth and Life: Essays on the Intellectual History of Political Economy in Britain, 1848-1914* (Cambridge: Cambridge University Press, 2009): 242-243.

87. E. A. G. Robinson, "Pigou, Arthur Cecil (1877-1959), Economist," *Dictionary of National Biography* Archive, 1971, http://www.oxforddnb.com/view/olddnb/35529. "Lectures Proposed by the Special Board for History and Archaeology," *Cambridge University Reporter* 29, no. 2 (October 8, 1898): 17-18. John Rawls described *The Methods of Ethics* as "the outstanding achievement in modern moral theory . . . the first truly academic work in moral theory, modern in both method and spirit." Yet as Sidgwick scholar J. B. Schneewind observed, *Methods* was very much "also a mid-Victorian work." John Rawls and Samuel Richard Freeman, *Lectures on the History of Political Philosophy* (Cambridge, MA: Harvard University Press, 2007): 378; J. B. Schneewind, *Sidgwick's Ethics and Victorian Moral Philosophy* (Oxford: Oxford University Press, 1977). See also Roger E. Backhouse, "Sidgwick, Marshall, and the Cambridge School of Economics," *History of Political Economy* 38, no. 1 (Spring 2006): 15-44.

88. Henry Sidgwick, *The Methods of Ethics* (London: Macmillan, 1907): 89.

89. Sidgwick warranted that other ideals might be conceptualized as related to the ultimate end; he specifically mentioned "Goodness, Perfection, or Excellence of Human Existence." Yet Sidgwick did not see these more nebulous values as having a claim to being "ultimate goods." Instead, he fitted them into a utilitarian framework by suggesting that they were constitutive of pleasure, the one true good. Ibid.,102; Schneewind, *Sidgwick's Ethics*, 322-327.

90. "Concerning Speaking at the Union," *Granta* 12, no. 252 (February 11, 1899): 178.

91. Austin Robinson to J. W. Jenkins, September 24, 1964, Austin Robinson Papers, MLE, EAGR 6/6/6.

92. "Union Notes," *Granta* 12, no. 262 (May 27, 1899): 344-345; "Union Notes," *Granta* 13, no. 270 (November 18, 1899): 470-471; "Union Notes," *Granta* 13, no. 277 (February 17, 1900): 578-579

93. "Those in Authority: Arthur Cecil Pigou," 656.

94. "Union Notes," *Granta* 12, no 254 (February 18, 1899): 198-199.

95. "Union Notes," *Granta* 13, no. 273 (January 20, 1900): 517.

96. "Those in Authority: Arthur Cecil Pigou," 656.

97. Ibid.

98. On the monarchy, see "Union Notes," *Granta* 12, no. 262 (May 27, 1899): 344-345; on democratic government, see "Union Notes," *Granta* 12, no. 258 (April 27, 1899): 283-284; on the theater incident, see "Union Notes," *Granta* 13, no. 270

(November 18, 1899): 470–471. Pigou called for the university authorities to close the theater as many "intoxicated" undergraduates were making "obscene remarks." The offenders were men who wished to "prove they were men by showing they had ceased to be gentlemen."

99. On the issue of colleges (whether Oxford and Cambridge should not seek to reduce the autonomy of individual colleges), see "Union Notes," *Granta* 13, no. 277 (February 17, 1900): 578–579; on the Dreyfus Affair, see "Union Notes," *Granta* 11, no. 228 (February 12, 1898): 183–184; "Union Notes," *Granta* 12, no. 245 (October 29, 1898): 38–39.

100. "Union Notes," *Granta* 13, no. 277 (February 17, 1900): 578–579; "Union Notes," *Granta* 13, no. 278 (February 24, 1900): 593–594.

101. This may have been hyperbolic and self-consciously provocative, since relations between Pigou and Browning had frayed by this point, as explained below. From *Cambridge Review,* May 30, 1901. Quoted in Alon Kadish, *Historians, Economists, and Economic History* (London: Routledge, 1989): 192.

102. "Union Notes," *Granta* 12, no. 259 (May 6, 1899): 296. On China, see "Union Notes," *Granta* 10, no. 193 (October 24, 1896): 20–21; "Union Notes," *Granta* 10, no. 195 (November 7, 1896): 54–55.

103. The supporter in question was S. C. Cronwright-Schreiner. "Union Notes," *Granta* 13, no. 279 (March 10, 1900): 620–621.

104. "Union Notes," *Granta* 13, no. 286 (June 2, 1900): 731–732.

105. Opposition to imperialism was one of the key elements of the so-called new liberalism, discussed below. For an overview, see Peter Clarke, *Liberals and Social Democrats* (Cambridge: Cambridge University Press, 1978): chapter 3. On liberal imperialists, see H. C. G. Matthew, *Liberal Imperialists: The Ideas and Politics of a Post-Gladstonian Elite* (Oxford: Oxford University Press, 1973). See also Jennifer Pitts, *A Turn to Empire: The Rise of Imperial Liberalism in Britain and France* (Princeton, NJ: Princeton University Press, 2005).

106. On popular support for free trade, see Frank Trentmann, *Free Trade Nation: Commerce, Consumption, and Civil Society in Modern Britain* (Oxford: Oxford University Press, 2008), especially 27–33.

107. Marshall wrote Browning that Pigou "did not come to my lectures in his first year: but before coming to them in his second year he had read my Principles [*The Principles of Economics*], through; & he adds that he had read my Economics of Industry . . .'some time ago.'" At the top of the same letter, Marshall scrawled: "Pigou has just come in. He tells me that the entry 'some time ago' . . . means 'at school'" Alfred Marshall to Oscar Browning, October 28, 1903, Browning Papers, KCA, OB/1/1062/C. This scrawling is not noted in the letter published in *The Correspondence of Alfred Marshall, Economist,* 3 volumes, ed. John Whitaker (Cambridge: Cambridge University Press, 1996): III, 67–68.

108. Pigou wrote that he was reading "Political Economy." It is likely that he meant Sidgwick's *Principles of Political Economy* (1883), which he found "not nearly as bad as" the other book he was reading, Henry Hallam's *Constitutional History of England.* Pigou to Oscar Browning, September 23, 1898, Browning Papers, KCA,

OB/1/1281/A. On Ashley, see Pigou to Oscar Browning, June 22, 1898, Browning Papers, KCA, OB/1/1281/A.

109. Pigou to Oscar Browning, September 22 [1898], Browning Papers, KCA, OB/1/1281/A.

110. "Union Notes," *Granta* 10, no. 205 (February 27, 1897): 218–219.

111. "Union Notes," *Granta* 10, no. 203 (February 13, 1897): 184–185; "Union Notes," *Granta* 10, no. 213 (May 29, 1897): 352–353. The first debate of Pigou's second year, in which he did not take part, was also about trade unions. "Union Notes," *Granta* 11, no. 218 (October 23, 1897): 25-26.

112. "Union Notes," *Granta* 11, no. 225 (January 22, 1898): 135–136.

113. Ibid.

114. Alfred Marshall to Herbert Foxwell, February 14, 1902, in *The Correspondence of Alfred Marshall*, II, 359.

115. Pigou won the Chancellor's gold medal for English verse. Harry G. Johnson, "Arthur Cecil Pigou, 1877–1959," *Canadian Journal of Economics and Political Science / Revue canadienne d'Economique et de Science politique* 26, no. 1 (February 1, 1960): 150–155.

116. Alfred Marshall to Oscar Browning, May 15, 1903, in *The Correspondence of Alfred Marshall*, III, 10–11.

117. The letter was written from Hotel de France, Saint-Pol-de-Léon, Brittany. Pigou to Oscar Browning, August 2, 1899, Browning Papers, KCA, OB/1/1281/A.

118. The books recommended for the Political Economy syllabus were Bagehot, *Lombard Street*; Bastable, *Theory of International Trade*; Dunbar, *The Theory and History of Banking*; Jevons, *Money and the Mechanism of Exchange*; Keynes, *Scope and Method of Political Economy*; Marshall, *Principles of Economics*, Vol. 1; Plehn, *Introduction to Public Finance*; and Sidgwick, *Principles of Political Economy*, Introduction and Book III. There was a much longer list of books "which may be read with advantage." See appendix B to chapter 15 of Groenewegen, *A Soaring Eagle*, 563–564.

119. "Those in Authority: Arthur Cecil Pigou," 656.

120. J. M. Keynes, "Alfred Marshall, 1842–1924," in *The Memorials of Alfred Marshall*, edited by A. C. Pigou (London: Macmillan, 1925), 2. See also chapter 18 of Groenewegen, *A Soaring Eagle*, 660–701.

121. Keynes, "Alfred Marshall, 1842–1924," 2.

122. Pigou to Oscar Browning, April 12, 1900, Browning Papers, KCA, OB/1/1281/A.

123. "Lectures Proposed by the Special Board for History and Archaelogy 1898–1899," *Cambridge University Reporter* 29, no. 2 (October 8, 1898): 17-18; "Lectures Proposed by the Special Board for History and Archaelogy 1899–1900," *Cambridge University Reporter* 30, no. 2 (October 7, 1899): 18–19.

124. Herbert Foxwell referred to the movement as characterized by "the historic feeling." H. S. Foxwell, "The Economic Movement in England," *Quarterly Journal of Economics* 2, no. 1 (October 1887): 89. On the meanings of "the historical school," see Erik Grimmer-Solem, *The Rise of Historical Economics and Social Reform in Germany 1864-1894* (Oxford: Clarendon Press, 2003), chapter 1; Erik Grimmer-Solem

and Roberto Romani, "The Historical School, 1870–1900: A Cross-National Reassessment," *History of European Ideas* 24, nos. 4–5 (1998): 267–299; Gerard M. Koot, *English Historical Economics, 1870–1926: The Rise of Economic History and Neomercantilism* (Cambridge: Cambridge University Press, 1987); and A. W. Coats, "The Historist Reaction in English Politicial Economy, 1870–1890," *Economica* 21, no. 82 (May 1954): 143–153.

125. On the disputes between schools of economic thought in Cambridge and Britain, see Kadish, *Historians, Economists, and Economic History*.

126. See Koot, *English Historical Economics*.

127. On Foxwell's status as an English Historical Economist, see Gerard M. Koot, "H.S. Foxwell and English Historical Economics," *Journal of Economic Issues* 11, no 3 (September 1977): 561–586.

128. On Marshall's German philosophical influecnes, see Simon Cook, *The Intellectual Foundations of Alfred Marshall's Economic Science: A Rounded Globe of Knowledge* (Cambridge: Cambridge University Press, 2009), especially chapter 6, "A Philosophy of History." On evolution in Marshall's thinking, see Tiziano Raffaelli, *Marshall's Evolutionary Economics* (London: Routledge, 2003). On Cunningham, see Koot, *English Historical Economics*, 135–155; John Maloney, *The Professionalization of Economics: Alfred Marshall and Dominance of Orthodoxy* (New Brunswick, NJ: Transaction, 1991), 91–119.

129. On the professionalization of Marshallian economics, see Maloney, *The Professionalization of Economics*.

130. Alfred Marshall, *Principles of Economics*, eighth ed. (London: Palgrave Macmillan, 2013 [1920]): xxi.

131. For an overview of English historical school and Marshallian economics, see Roger E. Backhouse, *The Penguin History of Economics* (London: Penguin, 2002): 177–182. See also Koot, *English Historical Economics*, especially chapters 6 and 7.

132. Marshall's influence grew as his intellectual rivals left the country. Ashley departed for North America in 1888 for several years, and Cunningham followed in 1899. See Katherine Harris, "The Rise and Fall of the Practical Man: Debates over the Teaching of Economics at Harvard, 1871–1908" A.B. thesis, Harvard University, 2010; Tiziano Raffaelli, Giacomo Becattini, Katia Caldari, and Marco Dardi, eds., *The Impact of Alfred Marshall's Ideas: The Global Diffusion of His Work* (Cheltenham, UK: Edward Edgar, 2010).

133. H. S. Foxwell, "The Economic Movement in England," *Quarterly Journal of Economics* 1, no.1 (1887): 92. On Marshall and the Cambridge school, see Groenewegen, *A Soaring Eagle*, 753–762.

134. Marshall was the father of the concept of substitution at the margin. See Keynes, "Alfred Marshall, 1842–1924," 39.

135. Marshall, *Principles of Economics*.

136. A. C. Pigou, "Looking Back from 1939" in *Essays in Economics* (London: Macmillan, 1952): 7.

137. This is the thesis of Roger E. Backhouse and Tamotsu Nishizawa, eds. *No Wealth but Life*, (Cambridge: Cambridge University Press, 2010). According to

Groenewegen, Marshall's "life . . . illuminates Victorian middle-class reactions to socialism, alternatively recoiling in horror from its more extreme prescriptions while revealing simultaneous fascination with the new intellectual and social visions it opened up." Groenewegen, *A Soaring Eagle*, 4.

138. For a concise treatment, see Dorothy Ross, "Changing Contours of the Social Science Disciplines," in *The Cambridge History of Science Volume 7: The Modern Social Sciences*, ed. Theodore M. Porter and Dorothy Ross (Cambridge: Cambridge University Press, 2003): 203–237. See also Grimmer-Solem, *The Rise of Historical Economics*; Andrew Jewett, *Science, Democracy, and the American University: From the Civil War to the Cold War* (New York: Cambridge University Press, 2012); Reba N. Soffer, *Ethics and Society in England: The Revolution in the Social Sciences, 1870–1914* (Berkeley: University of California Press, 1978); Rothblatt, *The Revolution of the Dons*; Peter Wagner, Bjorn Wittrock, and Hellmut Wollmann, "Social Sciences and Modern States," in *Social Sciences and Modern States: National Experiences and Theoretical Crossroads*, ed. Peter Wagner, Carol H.Weiss, Bjorn Wittrock, and Hellmut Wollmann (Cambridge: Cambridge University Press, 1991): 28–85.

139. On ideology and Marshall's economics, see Maloney, *The Professionalization of Economics*, chapters 9 and 10.

140. Marshall developed a cautiously optimistic position on the state's role in providing assistance to the poor and aged and in 1910, after retirement, wrote a proposal for a Cambridge program in social work, sharing it with Pigou privately, who in turn shared it with John Maynard Keynes and others. J. M. Keynes to Alfred Marshall, July 10, 1910, in *The Correspondence of Alfred Marshall*, III, 253. On Marshall's attitudes toward state assistance, see Peter Groenewegen, "Marshall on Welfare Economics and the Welfare State," in Backhouse and Nishizawa, *No Wealth but Life*, 25–41. In a 1907 article titled "Social Possibilities of Economic Chivalry," Marshall called for the state to be "up and doing" in providing services that anticipated those of Britain's postwar welfare state. Groenewegen, *A Soaring Eagle*, 570–611; Winch, *Wealth and Life*, 237–241.

141. Alfred Marshall, *Industry and Trade* (London: Macmillan, 1919): vii. Writing to F. Y. Edgeworth after the publication of the latter's *New and Old Methods of Ethics*, Marshall noted: "I think there is room for question whether the utilitarians are right in assuming that the end of action is the sum of the happiness of individuals rather than the vigorous life of the whole." Alfred Marshall to F. Y. Edgeworth, March 28, 1880, in *The Correspondence of Alfred Marshall*, I, 124.

142. Marshall defined the national dividend as the sum of a country's production of goods and services in a given year, while the American Irving Fisher counted only those goods and services that were consumed in a year. The descendents of these approaches remain alternative measures of GDP. On economic statistics, especially in America, see Thomas A. Stapleford, *The Cost of Living in America: A Political History of Economic Statistics, 1880–2000* (Cambridge: Cambridge University Press, 2009).

143. Marshall, *Principles of Economics*, 714.

144. "Moral Sciences Tripos, Part II, 1900," *Cambridge University Reporter* 30, no. 40 (June 12, 1900): 1039. Pigou was one of three sitters, out of six, who took a

First. He took the examinations in Ethics and Political Philosophy and in Advanced Political Economy.

145. In the preface, Pigou wrote, "[I have made] no attempt to distinguish Browning's religion from his philosophy, but have interpreted the phrase 'religious teacher' in the widest possible sense." Drawing from Browning's poetry and essays, Pigou evaluated Browning's philosophy on internal consistency. A. C. Pigou, *Robert Browning as a Religious Teacher: Being the Burney Essay for 1900* (Cambridge: C. J. Clay and Sons, 1900). Michael McLure suggests that in dealing with "states of consciousness," the Browning essay is consistent with Pigou's later assertion that "welfare" was to be found in states of consciousness only. Michael McLure, "Assessments of A.C. Pigou's Fellowship Theses," Discussion Paper 10.22 (Perth: Business School, University of Western Australia, 2010), http://www.business.uwa.edu.au/__data/assets/pdf_file /0015/1326111/10-22_Assessments_of_AC_Pigous_Fellowship_Theses.pdf.

146. Pigou's essay on Browning won the Burney Prize, awarded "on some metaphysical subject." His essay on economics, "The Causes and Effects of Changes in the Relative Values of Agricultural Produce in the United Kingdom during the Last Fifty Years," won the Cobden Prize, given every three years for work relating to political economy. Robert Potts, *Cambridge Scholarships and Examinations* (London: Longmans, Green, and Co., 1883): xii, xxii. One of the three examiners for the Cobden Prize was Alfred Marshall. See "The Cobden Prize, 1901," *Cambridge University Reporter* 30 no. 37 (1304) (May 29, 1900): 922.

147. Pigou to Oscar Browning, n.d. [1900–1901], KCA, Browning Papers, OB/1/1281/A. Kadish, *Historians, Economists, and Economic History*, 192.

148. Letter from Alfred Marshall to J. N. Keynes, March 4, 1900, in *The Correspondence of Alfred Marshall, Economist*, II, 269–270.

149. Alfred Marshall to Oscar Browning, October (24?), 1900, in *The Correspondence of Alfred Marshall*, II, 289–290.

150. A. C. Pigou, "*Economic Crises* by Edward D. Jones," *Economic Journal* 10, no. 40 (December 1900): 523–526; A. C. Pigou, "*The Despatches and Correspondence of John, Second Earl of Buckinghamshire, Ambassador to the Court of Catherine II of Russia, 1762–5* by Adelaide D'Arcy Collyer," *Economic Journal* 11, no. 41 (March, 1901): 77. In 1900–1901, Pigou reviewed a total of eight books for *The Economic Journal*, ranging from *The Science of Civilization* (Cecil Balfour Phipson) to *Social Justice* (Westel Woodbury Willoughby) to *Government in Switzerland* (John Martin Vincent).

151. Pigou to Oscar Browning, n.d. [1901], Browning Papers, KCA, OB/1/1281/A.

152. Electors to Fellowship Committee Meeting Minutes, October 13, 1900, KCA, KCGB/6/14/1/1. Seven candidates submitted dissertations, and four were nominated. Arthur William Hill, a botanist, and Charles Edward Inglis, an engineer, were elected with thirteen and eleven votes, respectively. Pigou came in third with five votes. Electors to Fellowship Committee Meeting Minutes, March 16, 1901, KCA, KCGB/6/14/1/1.

153. A. C. Pigou "The Causes and Effects of Changes in the Relative Values of Agricultural Produce in the United Kingdom During the Last Fifty Years" (Cambridge: King's College, 1901), Arthur Cecil Pigou Papers, MLE, Pigou 1/3, ii.

154. Four candidates were nominated by fellows in 1902, of which three, the logician William Ernest Johnson, music scholar Edward Joseph Dent, and Pigou, were elected. Pigou and Johnson both received fifteen votes; Dent received eight. A Mr. Filon received only seven and was not elected. Electors to Fellowship Committee Meeting Minutes, March 15, 1902, KCA, KCGB/6/14/1/1.

155. See Groenewegen, *A Soaring Eagle*, 443–493, 531–561; see also the final three chapters of Kadish, *Historians, Economists, and Economic History*, 128–245; and Maloney, *The Professionalization of Economics*, 226–229.

156. Alfred Marshall to Oscar Browning, October 28, 1903, in *The Correspondence of Alfred Marshall*, III, 67.

157. Alfred Marshall to Joseph Robson Tanner, May 20, 1903, in *The Correspondence of Alfred Marshall*, III, 13.

158. Marshall to J. N. Keynes, January 8, 1901, quoted in Kadish, *Historians, Economists, and Economic History*, 193. See also "Lectures Proposed by the Special Board for Economics and Politics, 1904–1905," *Cambridge University Reporter* 35 no. 2 (October 8, 1904): 21–22.

159. In Alon Kadish's words, "Pigou was safe, loyal and unquestionably competent." Kadish, *Historians, Economists, and Economic History*, 193.

160. Alfred Marshall to Oscar Browning, May 1, 1901, in *The Correspondence of Alfred Marshall*, II, 311–312.

161. Marshall married a former student, Mary Paley. Alfred Marshall to J. N. Keynes, January 30, 1902, in *The Correspondence of Alfred Marshal*, II, 350.

162. A. C. Pigou, *Alfred Marshall and Current Economic Thought* (London: Macmillan, 1952): 64; Robinson, "Pigou, Arthur Cecil (1877–1959), Economist."

163. A. C. Pigou, "Presidential Address," *Economic Journal* 39, no. 194 (June 1939): 219.

Chapter 2: Ethics, Politics, and Science

1. Alfred Marshall, *Principles of Economics*, eighth ed. (London: Palgrave Macmillan, 2013 [1920]): xix.

2. On the history of "economic man" see Mary Morgan, "Economic Man as Model Man: Ideal Types, Idealization, and Caricatures," *Journal of the History of Economic Thought* 28, no. 1 (March 2006): 1–27.

3. A. C. Pigou, *Economic Science in Relation to Practice* (London: Macmillan, 1908): 8.

4. Ibid., 11.

5. Ibid., 12.

6. Pigou to Oscar Browning, n.d. [1905–6], KCA, The Papers of Oscar Browning, OB/1/1281/A.

7. D. W. Corrie to John Saltmarsh, February 19, 1960, Papers Relating to A. C. Pigou, KCA, ACP/1/Corrie.

8. Ibid.

9. Pigou to Oscar Browning, n.d. [1901], Browning Papers, KCA, OB/1/1281/A.

10. Avner Offer, *Property and Politics 1870-1914: Landownership, Law, Ideology and Urban Development in England* (Cambridge: Cambridge University Press, 1981): 337.

11. "Account of a day in 1906," July 12, 1906, The Papers of John Tresidder Sheppard, KCA, JTS/1/8.

12. Pigou commented on Keynes's performance at the Union: "Clear-headedness more than human; a petrifying logicality; judicial impartiality worthy of a Rhadamanthus." Taken from *The Granta*, June 4, 1904. Quoted in Robert Skidelsky, *John Maynard Keynes: Hopes Betrayed 1883-1920* (London: Macmillan, 1983): 125.

13. [Mr. A. C. Pigou requests the pleasure of the company of Mr. J. M. Keynes in magnificent clothes.] Pigou to John Maynard Keynes, October 3, 1907, The Papers of John Maynard Keynes, JMK/PP/45/254.

14. Another fellow was the Scottish idealist philosopher William Ritchie Sorley, whom Pigou referenced in his early work. A. C. Pigou, "The Unity of Political and Economic Science," *Economic Journal* 16, no. 63 (September 1906): 372-380.

15. Pigou to D. W. Corrie as quoted in D. W. Corrie to John Saltmarsh, February 25, 1960, Pigou Papers, KCA, ACP/1/Corrie.

16. The lines in Italian are those written above the Gates of Hell, according to Dante's *Inferno*. Pigou to D. W. Corrie as quoted in D. W. Corrie to John Saltmarsh, February 25, 1960, Pigou Papers, KCA, ACP/1/Corrie.

17. Hugh Dalton, *Call Back Yesterday: Memoirs 1887-1931* (London: F. Muller, 1953): 57-58.

18. *Census Returns of England and Wales, 1911*, Pembrokeshire, TNA, RG14/33146, 158.

19. Notes, Austin Robinson Papers, MLE, EAGR, 6/6/5, 26.

20. Ibid.

21. See Deborah Cohen, *Family Secrets: Living with Shame from the Victorians to the Present Day* (London: Viking, 2013), chapter 5. Aslanbeigui and Oakes assert that there is "no evidence" that Pigou had sexual encounters before World War I, but they take too strong a line in suggesting that all of Pigou's male relationships were platonic. See Nahid Aslanbeigui and Guy Oakes, *Arthur Cecil Pigou* (Houndmills, Basingstoke, UK: Palgrave Macmillan, 2015): 247-252.

22. D. G. Champernowne, "Arthur Cecil Pigou 1877-1959," *Statistical Journal* 122, no. 2 (1959): 264.

23. Donald Moggridge, *Maynard Keynes: An Economist's Biography* (London: Routledge, 1992): 82.

24. See the introductory chapters in Michael Freeden, *The New Liberalism: An Ideology of Social Reform* (Oxford: Clarendon Press, 1978) and Peter Clarke, *Liberals and Social Democrats* (Cambridge: Cambridge University Press, 1978).

25. Freeden, *The New Liberalism*, 21.

26. Masterman and Pigou both spoke in "sympathy" with Greece's struggle against Turkey in May 1897. They spoke for opposing positions on two occasions. In one, Masterman argued for the House to support Zola, while Pigou, unpopularly, demurred. In the other, Pigou supported Spain's position early in the Spanish-American

War, while Masterman and Trevelyan took the side of the Yankees. "Union Notes," *Granta* 10, no. 210 (May 8, 1897): 302–303; "Union Notes," *Granta* 11, no. 228 (February 12, 1898): 183–184; "Union Notes," *Granta* 11, no. 234 (May 7, 1898): 278–280.

27. H. C. G. Matthew, "Masterman, Charles Frederick Gurney (1874–1927)," *Oxford Dictionary of National Biography* (Oxford: Oxford University Press, 2004, rev. 2011), www.oxforddnb.com/view/article/34927.

28. A. C. Pigou, "Some Aspects of the Problem of Charity," in *The Heart of the Empire: Discussions of Problems of Modern City Life in England*, ed. C. F. G Masterman, rev. ed. (New York: Harper & Row, 1973): 236. Ryo Hongo suggests that this piece reveals the social inclinations behind the creation of welfare economics. Ryo Hongo, "On the Origins of Pigou's Welfare Economics: Poor Law Reform and Unemployment Problem," working paper, Kwansei Gakuin University, Nishinomiya, Japan, 2013, http://www.ier.hit-u.ac.jp/extra/doc/Hongo_p.pdf.

29. Pigou, "Some Aspects of the Problem of Charity," 237, 258–259.

30. Bentley B. Gilbert, "Introduction," in Masterman, *Heart of the Empire*, xi. That government was a coalition between Conservatives and a collection of "Liberal Unionists" committed to keeping Ireland. See Freeden, *The New Liberalism*, 139–140.

31. See Freeden, *The New Liberalism*; Clarke, *Liberals and Social Democrats*, and Avital Simhony and D. Weinstein, eds., *The New Liberalism: Reconciling Liberty and Community* (Cambridge: Cambridge University Press, 2001). On Marshall and new liberalism, see Eugenio F. Biagini, "New Liberalism," in *The Elgar Companion to Alfred Marshall*, ed. Tiziano Raffaelli, Giacomo Becattini, Katia Caldari, and Marco Dardi (Cheltenham, UK: Edward Elgar, 2006): 554–558.

32. See A. W. Coats, "Sociological Aspects of British Economic Thought (ca. 1880–1930)," *Journal of Political Economy* 75, no. 5 (October 1967): 706–729; Yuichi Shionoya, "The Oxford Approach to the Philosophical Foundations of the Welfare State," in *No Wealth but Life*, ed. Roger E. Backhouse and Tamotsu Nishizawa (Cambridge: Cambridge University Press, 2010): 91–113. On the antipathy between Cambridge and Hobson, see Peter Clarke, "Hobson and Keynes as Economic Heretics," in *Reappraising J.A. Hobson: Humanism and Welfare*, ed. Michael Freeden (London: Unwin Hyman, 1990): 100–115.

33. Freeden, *The New Liberalism*, 15.

34. Alfred Marshall, *Principles of Economics*, 1.

35. "Lectures Proposed by the Special Board for Economics and Politics, 1904–1905," *Cambridge University Reporter* 45, no. 2 (October 8, 1904): 21.

36. A. C. Pigou, "A Point of Theory Connected with the Corn Tax," *Economic Journal* 12, no. 47 (September 1902): 415–420; A. C. Pigou, "Pure Theory and the Fiscal Controversy," *Economic Journal* 14, no. 53 (March 1904): 29–33; A. C. Pigou, "Some Remarks on Utility," *Economic Journal* 13, no. 49 (March 1903): 58–68; A. C. Pigou, "Monopoly and Consumers' Surplus," *Economic Journal* 14, no. 55 (September 1904): 388–394.

37. See David Collard, "Introduction," in *A.C. Pigou, Journal Articles 1902–1922*, ed. David Collard (London: Macmillan, 2002): xiv–xvii.

38. A. C. Pigou, "A Parallel Between Economic and Political Theory," *Economic Journal* 12, no. 46 (June 1902): 276.

39. Ibid.

40. Ibid., 277.

41. On free trade and liberalism, see Anthony Howe, *Free Trade and Liberal England, 1846-1946* (Oxford: Clarendon Press, 1997); on free trade as a political movement, see Frank Trentmann, *Free Trade Nation: Commerce, Consumption, and Civil Society in Modern Britain* (Oxford: Oxford University Press, 2008).

42. Trentmann, *Free Trade Nation*, 69-80.

43. Tariff reform had many implications (for social reform, for Empire, and for Ireland), and it split British political constituencies in a number of ways. See Alan Sykes, *Tariff Reform in British Politics 1903-1913* (Oxford: Clarendon Press, 1979).

44. See "Hands Off the People's Food," the first chapter in Peter Clarke, *Hope and Glory*, rev. ed. (London: Penguin, 2004). See also Peter T. Marsh, *Joseph Chamberlain: Entrepreneur in Politics* (New Haven, CT: Yale University Press, 1994), chapter 19.

45. A. C. Pigou, "Professors and the Corn Tax," *Speaker* (June 14, 1902): 306. This was consistent with Marshall's own less explicit "rule" against "taking active part in the discussions in the market place." Marshall to W. A. S. Hewins, July 14, 1903, quoted in A. W. Coats, "The Appointment of Pigou as Marshall's Successor: Comment," *Journal of Law and Economics* 15, no. 2 (October 1972): 487 n.1.

46. Pigou, "A Point of Theory Connected with the Corn Tax." See the preface to Pigou's *Protective and Preferential Import Duties* (London: Macmillan, 1906), in which Pigou referenced several articles that he wrote for popular magazines.

47. A. C. Pigou, "Free Trade and Its Critics" *Fortnightly Review* 435 (March 1, 1903): 542-554.

48. Ibid., 542-543.

49. Ibid.

50. F. Barnstable, A. L. Bowley, Edwin Cannan, Leonard Courtney, F. Y. Edgeworth, C. K. Gonner, Alfred Marshall, et al., "Professors of Economics and the Tariff Question," *Times* (August 15, 1903): 4. See Nahid Aslanbeigui and Guy Oakes, "The British Tariff Reform Controversy and the Genesis of Pigou's *Wealth and Welfare*, 1903-12" *History of Political Economy* 47, annual supplement (2015): 23-48.

51. On Foxwell and Cunningham at Cambridge, see Gerard M. Koot, *English Historical Economics, 1870-1926: The Rise of Economic History and Neomercantilism* (Cambridge: Cambridge University Press, 1987), chapters 6 and 7.

52. A. C. Pigou, *The Riddle of the Tariff* (London: R. Brimley Johnson, 1903): v-vi.

53. A. C. Pigou, "Professors of Economics on Fiscal Policy," *Times* (August 24, 1903): 4; A. C. Pigou, "The Economics of Mr. Balfour's Manifesto," *Times* (September 18, 1903): 6; A. C. Pigou, "Consumers and Producers," *Times* (November 10, 1903): 15; A .C. Pigou, "Consumers and Producers," *Times* (November 14, 1903): 14; A. C. Pigou, "To the Editor of the Times," *Times* (December 3, 1903): 5.

54. Edwin Cannan, "Letter to the Times," *Times* (November 28, 1903): 14, quoted in A. W. Coats, "Political Economy and the Tariff Reform Campaign of 1903," *Journal of Law and Economics* 11 (1968): 213.

55. A. C. Pigou, "The Known and the Unknown in Mr. Chamberlain's Policy," *Fortnightly Review* 445 (January 1, 1904): 46-47.

56. Ibid., 47.

57. The motion carried by 255 votes to 195. Alon Kadish, *Historians, Economists, and Economic History* (London: Routledge, 1989): 217.

58. Ibid. Pigou also wrote a note on the usefulness of economic theory for resolving practical disputes over free trade. Pigou, "Pure Theory and the Fiscal Controversy."

59. A. C. Pigou, "*Free Trade and the Empire* by William Graham," *Economic Journal* 14, no. 54 (June 1904): 268.

60. A. C. Pigou, "Mr. Chamberlain's Proposals," *Edinburgh Review* 200, no. 310 (July–October 1904): 449–475. A. C. Pigou, "Protection and the Working Classes," *Edinburgh Review* 203, no. 415 (January–April 1906): 1–32.

61. "Cambridge University Free Trade Association Agenda for the Annual Meeting," 1906, Browning Papers, KCA, OB/1/1281/A.

62. Pigou to Macmillan, April 10, 1908, Macmillan Papers, British Library, London, United Kingdom (hereafter BL), Add. MSS 55199, 20.

63. Pigou to Macmillan, August 25, 1906, Macmillan Papers, BL, Add. MSS 55199, 12–13.

64. Pigou, *Protective and Preferential Import Duties*, 2–3.

65. Ibid., 80.

66. Pigou, "The Unity of Political and Economic Science," 378.

67. This was Pigou's first book with Macmillan, which published the overwhelming majority of his subsequent books. Fifty years later, Pigou wrote that Macmillan "have been quite good with me, though some people think them uninspiring." Pigou to Philip Noel-Baker, n.d. [January–February 1955], The Papers of Baron Noel-Baker, Churchill Archive Centre, Cambridge, UK (hereafter CAC), NBKR 9/69.

68. Pigou to Macmillan, November 19, 1904, Macmillan Papers, BL, Add. MSS 55199, 1–2.

69. "Schedule of the Jevons Memorial Lectures: Associations of Employers & Employed, Arbitration and Conciliation," The Papers of James Bonar, MLE, Bonar 3/35.

70. A. C. Pigou *Principles and Methods of Industrial Peace* (London: Macmillan, 1905): vii.

71. Pigou, *Industrial Peace*, 3–4; Pigou to Macmillan, November 19, 1904, Macmillan Papers, BL, Add. MSS 55199, 1–2.

72. Pigou, *Industrial Peace*, 22–28.

73. Ibid., 92–103.

74. Ibid., 161–162.

75. Ibid., 207–208. Though automatic arbitration would "involve too large an interference with individual liberties," selective arbitration was desirable.

76. The course met Saturday mornings to supplement Marshall's advanced economic theory course. Peter Groenewegen, *A Soaring Eagle: Alfred Marshall 1842–1924* (Aldershot, UK: Edward Elgar, 1995), 551–552.

77. A. C. Pigou, "Memorandum on Some Economic Aspects and Effects of Poor Law Relief," in *Minutes and Evidence of the Royal Commission on the Poor Laws and Relief of Distress*, Appendix vol. 9, 1910 [Cd. 5068]: 981–1000. For general background on the Commssion, see David Englander, *Poverty and Poor Law Reform in*

Nineteenth-Century Britain, 1834–1914 (London: Addison Wesley Longman, 1998): 73–78. See also Clarke, *Liberals and Social Democrats*, 118–121; José Harris, *William Beveridge: A Biography* (Oxford: Clarendon Press, 1977), chapter 6; Aslanbeigui and Oakes, *Arthur Cecil Pigou*, 57.

78. *Minutes and Evidence of the Royal Commission on the Poor Laws and Relief of Distress*, [Cd. 5068], 982.

79. Pigou to Oscar Browning, n.d. [1906–7], Browning Papers, KCA, OB/1/1281/A. The Commission produced two reports. The majority report stressed the importance of individual responsibility. The minority report argued for greater state involvement. Hongo argues that Pigou's contribution, together with his other early work on social issues—especially unemployment—was foundational for the development of his welfare economics. Hongo, "On the Origins of Pigou's Welfare Economics." In contrast, John Maloney observes, "the battle to professionalise economics was primarily a battle between those who saw it as a discipline comparable to the natural sciences and those who saw it as an adjunct to immediate social reform," and Pigou was a professionalizer, not a reformer. John Maloney, *The Professionalization of Economics: Alfred Marshall and Dominance of Orthodoxy* (New Brunswick, NJ: Transaction, 1991), 232. See also Harris, *William Beveridge*, chapters 5 and 6. The binary distinction between minority and majority reports is challenged in A. W. Vincent, "The Poor Law Reports of 1909 and the Social Theory of the Charity Organization Society," *Victorian Studies* 27, no. 3 (Spring 1984): 343–363.

80. See Freeden, *The New Liberalism*; Clarke, *Liberals and Social Democrats*; Bruce K. Murray, *The People's Budget 1909/10: Lloyd George and Liberal Politics* (Oxford: Clarendon Press, 1980). On the international context, see Daniel T. Rodgers, *Atlantic Crossings: Social Politics in a Progressive Age* (Cambridge, MA: Harvard University Press, 1998); James T. Kloppenberg, *Uncertain Victory: Social Democracy and Progressivism in European and American Thought, 1870–1920* (New York: Oxford University Press, 1986).

81. G. E. Moore, *Principia Ethica*, rev. ed. (Cambridge: Cambridge University Press, 1993).

82. Ibid., 238–251; Skidelsky, *John Maynard Keynes: Hopes Betrayed*, 133–141; Yuichi Shionoya, "Sidgwick, Moore and Keynes: A Philosophical Analysis of Keynes's 'My Early Beliefs'" in *Keynes and Philosophy*, ed. Bardley Bateman and John Davis (Northampton, MA: Edward Elgar, 1991): 6–29; Roger E. Backhouse, "Sidgwick, Marshall, and the Cambridge School of Economics," *History of Political Economy* 38, no. 1 (Spring 2006): 15–44.

83. Skidelsky, *John Maynard Keynes: Hopes Betrayed*, 140. J. M. Keynes wrote that Moore's "influence was not only overwhelming; it was exciting, exhilarating, the beginning of a new renaissance, the opening of a new heaven on a new earth."

84. Bart Schultz argues that Moore's departure from Sidgwick was less dramatic than is often understood. Bart Schultz, *Henry Sidgwick: Eye of the Universe: An Intellectual Biography* (Cambridge: Cambridge University Press, 2004): 5–6, 160–163.

85. A. C. Pigou, "The Ethics of Nietzsche," in *The Problem of Theism and Other Essays* by A. C. Pigou (London: Macmillan, 1908): 124. This excerpt is taken from a

section in which Pigou dismissed what Derek Parfit later called the "Repugnant Conclusion," the idea that society would be best off maximizing the number of people in the world, even if each person was trivially happy. Derek Parfit, *Reasons and Persons* (Oxford: Clarendon, 1984), chapter 16. Pigou noted: "its inadequacy, I think, is obvious. Mere quantity of life does not present itself to our consciousness as the only good thing; it may not even present itself as necessarily good at all."

86. Dalton, *Call Back Yesterday*, 54.

87. Pigou to J. M. Keynes, n.d. [1913?], Keynes Papers, KCA, JMK/PP/45/254.

88. See W. J. Mandler, *British Idealism: A History* (Oxford: Oxford University Press, 2011).

89. Pigou, "The Unity of Political and Economic Science," 372.

90. A. C. Pigou, "The Problem of Good," in *The Problem of Theism and Other Essays*, 85. The essay was originally published in 1907 in the *International Journal of Ethics* as "Some Points of Ethical Controversy."

91. Pigou asked Keynes (then at the India Office), "if not obscured by Indian bollocks" to comment on whether people had already addressed "the notion of the goodness of a . . . state as a function of many of variables." Pigou to J. M. Keynes, n.d. [1913?], Keynes Papers, KCA, JMK/PP/45/254/18.

92. Pigou, "The Problem of Good," 87.

93. Ibid., 88.

94. Henry Sidgwick, *The Methods of Ethics* (London: Macmillan, 1907), 489–490.

95. A. C. Pigou, "The Problem of Good," 88.

96. Pigou tempered this claim as he did for "pleasure," noting that love "certainly adds to this goodness if the object, as conceived in consciousness, both is and is thought to be worthy." Ibid., 88–89.

97. A. C. Pigou, "The Ethics of the Gospels" in *The Problem of Theism and Other Essays*, 99.

98. Pigou, "The Ethics of the Gospels," 96, 100.

99. Ibid., 108. Pigou was quoting Sidgwick's 1866 review of Nietzsche's *Ecce Homo* in the *Westminster Review*.

100. J. M. Keynes to B. W. Swithinbank, March 27, 1906, quoted in R. F. Harrod, *The Life of John Maynard Keynes* (New York: Harcourt Brace, 1951): 116. Sidgwick resigned his Trinity fellowship over adherence to Anglicanism. On Sidgwick and religion, see Jerome Schneewind, *Sidgwick's Ethics and Victorian Moral Philosophy* (Oxford: Oxford University Press, 1977): 17–20, 26–39. See also Steven G. Medema, "'Losing My Religion': Sidgwick, Theism, and the Struggle for Utilitarian Ethics in Economic Analysis," *History of Political Economy* 40, no. 5 (2008): 189–211; and Schultz, *Henry Sidgwick: Eye of the Universe*, chapter 2.

101. Pigou's work on Robert Browning and his essay on the gospels show respect for religion. However, in another early essay, he identified theism as a major problem. A. C. Pigou, "The Problem of Theism" in *The Problem of Theism and Other Essays*, 18–64. He discussed religion with the vicar in Buttermere, the Lake District town where he summered, and had Macmillan send the vicar a copy of "The Problem

of Theism." Pigou to Macmillan, March 18, 1929, Macmillan Papers, BL, Add. MSS 55199 [140]. In his late years, he joked about joining the church:

> I have been contemplating this final paragraph in my obituary notice: "But the Professor! . . . in his 71st year, he accepted a stop-gap appointment to the deanship of King's College. . . . When the college council promptly met to make a permanent appointment, the whole college assembled in the court, chanting in unison: 'Pigou, Pigou, we want Pigou!' . . . [Since] by tradition the dean should be a clergyman . . . [the] Professor [was asked] whether he would consider taking holy orders. 'Salus populi suprema lex' was the instant answer. In a few days he had passed his bishop's examination with flying colours."

Pigou to L. P. Wilkinson, n.d. [after 1948], The Papers of Lancelot Patrick Wilkinson, KCA, LPW/8/4/7.

102. See part I, chapter IV of A. C. Pigou, *Wealth and Welfare* (London: Macmillan, 1912): 52–65; part I, chapter X of A. C. Pigou, *The Economics of Welfare*, fourth ed. (London: Macmillan, 1932): 106–122. Although Marshall did not discuss eugenics, he was influenced by biological and evolutionary thinking. See, for instance, Tiziano Raffaelli, *Marshall's Evolutionary Economics* (London: Routledge, 2003) and Tiziano Raffaelli, Giacomo Becattini, Katia Caldari, and Marco Dardi, eds., *The Elgar Companion to Alfred Marshall*, (Cheltenham, UK: Edward Elgar, 2006), particularly chapter 28 of that volume by Geoffrey M. Hodgson, "Economics and Biology."

103. A. C. Pigou, "Social Improvement in the Light of Modern Biology," *Economic Journal* 17, no 67 (September 1907): 359.

104. See R. H. Lock, *Recent Progress in the Study of Variation, Heredity, and Evolution* (London: John Murray, 1907); R. C. Punnett, *Mendelism* (London: Macmillan and Bowes, 1905). On eugenics, see Lucy Bland and Lesley A. Hall, "Eugenics in Britain," in *The Oxford Handbook of the History of Eugenics,* edited by Alison Bashford and Philippa Levine (Oxford: Oxford University Press, 2010): 213–227. See also Andre Pichot, *The Pure Society: From Darwin to Hitler* (London: Verso, 2001): 109–173.

105. Pigou, "Social Improvement in the Light of Modern Biology," 361.

106. Pigou, *Wealth and Welfare*, 58–59. In *The Economics of Welfare*, he added: "For, whereas each new man must begin where his last ancestor began, each new invention begins where its last ancestor left off." Pigou, *The Economics of Welfare*, 114. See also David Collard, "Pigou and Future Generations," *Cambridge Journal of Economics* 20 (1996): 585–597.

107. Eugenic elements in economic theory indicated a conception of a heterogeneous population. See Sandra J. Peart and David M. Levy, "Denying Human Homogeneity: Eugenics & The Making of Post-Classical Economics," *Journal of the History of Economic Thought* 25, no. 3 (September 2003): 261–288. See also Thomas C. Leonard, *Illiberal Reformers: Race, Eugenics and American Economics in the Progressive Era* (Princeton, NJ: Princeton University Press, 2016), especially chapter 7.

108. Pigou, "Social Improvement in the Light of Modern Biology," 365.

109. Pigou's treatment of eugenics changed in his later work, as he discussed genetic traits principally in terms of their effect on economic productivity and thus

economic welfare. However, Pigou still treated biological quality as more than just a means to an economic end. He asserted not only that "ability, moral character, good health, physical strength and grace, beauty and charm" were "desirable qualities," but also that they were determined at least in part by hereditary factors. Pigou, *Wealth and Welfare*, 53. This marked a departure from his earlier work. In *Principles and Methods of Industrial Peace*, Pigou's valuation of fitness was instrumental and not solely inherited. He stressed the importance of biological fitness for the quality of labor as a technical input. "With increased nourishment, leisure, and so forth," Pigou wrote, "the work done may gradually become a different commodity. . . . In short, the biological law of functional adaptation supervenes upon the mechanical laws of equilibration." Pigou, *Industrial Peace*, 47.

110. Ibid., 4.

111. Copy of the *Gownsman*, May 26, 1910, Austin Robinson Papers, MLE, EAGR 6/6/4. Aslanbeigui and Oakes argue that 1906, rather than 1908, marked the turning point in Pigou's extra-academic involvement. Pigou did comment less on politics after 1906, but this is attributable to the decisiveness of the Liberal victory in that year rather than to any change of heart on Pigou's part. Aslanbeigui and Oakes, *Arthur Cecil Pigou*, 58. See also Aslanbeigui and Oakes, The British Tariff Reform Controversy," 45.

112. A. C. Pigou, *Economic Science in Relation to Practice* (London: Macmillan, 1908): 8.

113. On Marshall and Foxwell's friendship, see Groenewegen, *A Soaring Eagle*, 670–679.

114. On Foxwell and the historical school, see Gerard M. Koot, "H.S. Foxwell and English Historical Economics," *Journal of Economic Issues* 11, no.3 (September 1977): 561–586.

115. Donald Winch *Wealth and Life: Essays on the Intellectual History of Political Economy in Britain, 1848–1914* (Cambridge: Cambridge University Press, 2009): 260–263.

116. See Coats, "Political Economy and the Tariff Reform Campaign," 226–228; Coats, "The Appointment of Pigou as Marshall's Successor," 487–495. See also Winch, *Wealth and Life*, 263.

117. R. H. Coase, "The Appointment of Pigou as Marshall's Successor," *Journal of Law and Economics* 15, no. 2 (October 1, 1972): 473–485. Groenewegen argues that Marshall decided to name Pigou as his successor sometime in 1905-1906. Groenewegen, *A Soaring Eagle*, 625.

118. Coase, "The Appointment of Pigou," 476.

119. H. S. Foxwell to J. N. Keynes, October 6, 1900, in *The Correspondence of Alfred Marshall*, II, 289 n.7.

120. H. S. Foxwell to J. Bonar, November 22, 1903, quoted in Winch, *Wealth and Life*, 265.

121. Coase, "The Appointment of Pigou," 477–479; See also Aslanbeigui and Oakes, *Arthur Cecil Pigou*, 23–24.

122. Trevor W. Jones, "The Appointment of Pigou as Marshall's Successor: The Other Side of the Coin," *Journal of Law and Economics* 21, no. 1 (April 1978): 235–243.

123. John Neville Keynes, Diaries, April 30, 1908, cited in Jones, "The Appointment of Pigou as Marshall's Successor," 240.

124. Pigou's electors were the Vice Chancellor, Ernest Stewart Roberts, Lord Courtney, J. N. Keynes, Inglis Palgrave, F. Y. Edgeworth, J. S. Nicholson, Vincent Henry Stanton, William Ritchie Sorley, and Arthur Balfour. There are no surviving records of how the electors voted, and the election has been the subject of speculation. Balfour did not attend the proceedings, citing Pigou's participation in the free trade debates. See Coats, "Politial Economy and the Tariff Reform Campaign," 226–229. Balfour may have supported Pigou, as Walter Layton (1884–1966) suggested, though this is unlikely. The letter in which he expressed his opinion to the Vice Chancellor has been lost. See W. T. Layton, *Dorothy: The Story of the Married Life of Dorothy and Walter Layton* (London: Collins, 1961): 32–33; A. W. Coats to Austin Robinson, January 18, 1968, Austin Robinson Papers, MLE, EAGR 6/6/6, 19. See also Coase, "The Appointment of Pigou," 478. Courtney was an active free trader and likely voted for Pigou, and Edgeworth was public about his support of Marshall's protégé. Sorley also likely supported his fellow Kingsman, and Foxwell believed Stanton also voted for Pigou. Coase, "The Appointment of Pigou as Marshall's Successor," 493–494. On the other side were Nicholson, Palgrave, and J. N. Keynes, who found the process "like a black cloud throwing its shadow over the whole of the term." Diary of Keynes, June 14, 1908, quoted from Coase, "The Appointment of Pigou," 480.

125. Alfred Marshall to H. S. Foxwell, May 31, 1908, in *The Correspondence of Alfred Marshall*, III, 190.

126. Pigou to R. F. Harrod, n.d. [1949], The Papers of Sir R. F. Harrod, BL, Add MS 72764, 235.

127. Pigou to Macmillan, June 5, 1908, Macmillan Papers, BL, Add. MSS 55199, 22.

128. Pigou, *The Problem of Theism*, vii.

129. Pigou to Macmillan, June 5, 1908, Macmillan Papers, BL, Add. MSS 55199, 22.

130. Ibid.

131. Coase, "Pigou as Marshall's Successor," 477. Quoting Letter from Marshall to H. S. Foxwell, February 7, 1906, *The Correspondence of Alfred Marshall*, III, 48.

132. Groenewegen, *A Soaring Eagle*, 761.

133. Letter from H. S. Foxwell to C. E. Collet, June 8, 1908, quoted in Coats, "Pigou as Marshall's Successor," 494.

Chapter 3: Bearing Fruit as Well as Light

1. At the time, the editor was J. M. Keynes. Edgeworth gave up his duties in 1911 but returned as a joint editor in 1919.

2. F. Y. Edgeworth, "*Wealth and Welfare* by A.C. Pigou," *Economic Journal* 23, no. 89 (March 1913): 62, 63, 67.

3. Marshall, though pleased with Pigou's work, took issue with the abstract treatment of increasing and decreasing returns. He recorded his critiques of Pigou's work in his own copy of *Wealth of Welfare*. See Krishna Bharadwaj, "Marshall on Pigou's *Wealth and Welfare*," *Economica* New Series 39, no. 153 (February 1973): 32–46.

4. Allyn Young, "Pigou's *Wealth and Welfare*," *Quarterly Journal of Economics* 27, no. 4 (August 1913): 672.

5. Sir John Macdonell, "New Phases of Political Economy." *Times Literary Supplement* (January 9, 1913): 10.

6. Edgeworth, "*Wealth and Welfare* by A.C. Pigou," 62.

7. A. C. Pigou, *Economics of Welfare*, first ed. (London: Macmillan, 1920): 5.

8. Ibid. On engineering and economics, see Mary Morgan, "Economics," in *The Cambridge History of Science Volume 7: The Modern Social Sciences*, ed. Theodore M. Porter and Dorothy Ross (Cambridge: Cambridge University Press, 2003): 275–305.

9. Ibid.

10. Peter Groenewegen, *A Soaring Eagle: Alfred Marshall 1842–1924* (Aldershot, UK: Edward Elgar, 1995): 553; See Robert Skidelsky, *John Maynard Keynes: Hopes Betrayed 1883–1920* (London: Macmillan, 1983): 209. The group consisted of Pigou, Leonard Alston, John Clapham, Lowes Dickinson, C. R. Fay, W. E. Johnson, John Maynard Keynes, Walter Layton, and H. O. Meredith. Dickinson was an economist only by the loosest definition, and Johnson's credentials were also shaky. Fay and Clapham were economic historians.

11. A. C. Pigou, "Obituary [John Neville Keynes]," *Economic Journal* 60, no. 238 (June 1950): 408. He would continue to teach the general lecture course until 1930. "Lectures Proposed by the Special Board for Economics and Politics, 1910–11," *Cambridge University Reporter* 41 no. 3 (October 8, 1908): 55.

12. Groenewegen, *A Soaring Eagle*, 553. "Lectures Proposed by the Special Board for Economics and Politics, 1908–9," *Cambridge University Reporter* 39, no. 3 (October 10, 1908).

13. Skidelsky, *John Maynard Keynes: Hopes Betrayed*, 211.

14. This distinction, as Pigou pointed out, came from Ricardo. A. C. Pigou, *The Policy of Land Taxation* (London: Longmans, Green, and Co., 1909): 10. The article was A. C. Pigou, "Local Taxation," *Edinburgh Review* 206 (July, 1907): 88–109. On the economics of land taxation, see Nahid Aslanbeigui and Guy Oakes, *Arthur Cecil Pigou* (Houndmills, Basingstoke, UK: Palgrave Macmillan, 2015), 105–107.

15. Pigou, *The Policy of Land Taxation*, 29.

16. See Avner Offer, *Property and Politics 1870–1914: Landownership, Law, Ideology and Urban Development in England* (Cambridge: Cambridge University Press, 1981), chapter 22; Bruce K. Murray, *The People's Budget 1909/10: Lloyd George and Liberal Politics* (Oxford: Clarendon Press, 1980): 44–50, 131–147, 296–300; Roy Hattersley, *David Lloyd George: The Great Outsider* (London: Little, Brown, 2010), especially chapters 15 and 22.

17. Pigou, *The Policy of Land Taxation*, 32. Pigou advocated for heavily taxing appreciation in the value of land due to changes in the market. Pigou also argued for the superiority of taxing the public value of land rather than the capital value of land as Lloyd George proposed. See Murray, *The People's Budget*, 133–135.

18. Ibid.

19. Pigou reviewed five Italian books between 1907 and 1913. See A. C. Pigou, "*Emigrazione di Uomini ed Esportazione di Merci* by L. Fontana-Russo," *Economic*

Journal 17, no. 65 (March 1907): 114; A. C. Pigou, "*Commercio Internazionale* by G. de Francisi Gerbino," *Economic Journal* 17, no. 66 (June 1907): 262–263; A. C. Pigou; "*Trattato di Politica Commerciale* by Luigi Fontana-Russo," *Economic Journal* 17, no. 67 (September 1907): 414–415; A. C. Pigou, "*L'Imposta sul Trasporto Degli Emigranti* by Pasquale Jannaconne," *Economic Journal* 18, no. 69 (March 1908): 95; A. C. Pigou, "*Intorno al Concetto di Reddito Imponibile e di un Sistema d'Imposte sul Readdito Consumato* by Luigi Einaudi," *Economic Journal* 23, no. 90 (June 1913): 260–263.

20. A. C. Pigou, "Equilibrium Under Bilateral Monopoly," *Economics Journal* 18, no. 70 (June 1908): 205–220; A. C. Pigou, "A Method of Determining the Numerical Values of Elasticities of Demand," *Economics Journal* 20, no. 80 (December 1910): 636–640; A. C. Pigou, "Producers' and Consumers' Surplus," *Economic Journal* 20, no. 79 (September 1910): 358–370.

21. Angus Deaton, "The Measurement of Income and Price Elasticities," *European Economic Review* 7 (1975): 261–274, quoted in David Collard, "Introduction," in *A.C. Pigou, Journal Articles 1902–1922*, ed. David Collard (London: Macmillan, 2002): xvi. See also Milton Friedman, "Professor Pigou's Method for Measuring Elasticities of Demand from Budgetary Data," *Quarterly Journal of Economics* 50, no. 1 (November 1935): 151–163; A. C. Pigou, Milton Friedman, and N. Georgescu-Roegen, "Marginal Utility of Money and Elasticities of Demand," *Quarterly Journal of Economics* 50, no. 3 (May 1936): 532–539. Pigou would also correspond briefly with the econometrician Jacob Marschak (1898–1977) in the mid-1930s about this topic. See Arthur Cecil Pigou Papers, MLE, Pigou 2/2/4 and Pigou 2/2/7.

22. It expanded on topics that Pigou had explored in 1903. See A. C. Pigou, "Some Remarks on Utility," *Economic Journal* 13, no. 49 (March 1903): 58–68. Alfred Marshall, *Principles of Economics*, eighth ed. (London: Palgrave Macmillan, 2013): 103–110; or, in the edition Pigou would have used, Alfred Marshall, *Principles of Economics*, fourth ed. (London: Macmillan, 1898): 199–208.

23. Marshall's ethics were not entirely utilitarian, though he drew on utilitarian ideas. By the 1870s, Marshall's ethics involved a synthesis of various systems, notably Darwinian evolutionary ethics. See Tiziano Raffaelli, *Marshall's Evolutionary Economics* (London: Routledge, 2003): 96–102.

24. Marshall, *Principles of Economics*, fourth ed., 532–533. This analysis was reproduced largely unchanged in the definitive eighth edition. See Marshall, *Principles of Economics*, eighth ed., book V, chapter XII, 462–476. Peter Groenewegen, "Marshall on Welfare Economics and the Welfare State," in *No Wealth but Life*, ed. Roger E. Backhouse and Tamotsu Nishizawa (Cambridge: Cambridge University Press, 2010), 30–31.

25. Pigou wrote on the divergence of private and public supply and demand schedules. See Nahid Aslanbeigui, "The Cost Controversy: Pigovian Economics in Disequilibrium," *European Journal of the History of Economic Thought* 3, no. 2 (Summer 1996): 275–295.

26. A. C. Pigou, "Some Remarks on Utility," *Economic Journal* 13, no. 49 (March 1903): 60.

27. Pigou, "Producers' and Consumers' Surplus," 360.

28. This change in price would not be considered a negative externality today. Pigou changed his mind about what constituted an external diseconomy in the 1920s, as will be discussed in chapter 5.

29. Ibid., 365. Marshall suggested in *Principles of Economics* that external economies could be related to increasing returns to scale in an industry (and thus could push markets away from the theoretical ideal), but his discussion was not as explicit as Pigou's. See Marshall, *Principles of Economics*, fourth ed., 393–397.

30. The term ophelimity came from Italian economist Vilfredo Pareto, who associated optimizing ophelimity with a pure form of bargaining and exchange. Ibid., 359. See also Michael McLure, "Pareto and Pigou on Ophelimity, Utility, and Welfare: Implications for Public Finance," Discussion Paper 09.13 (Perth: Business School, University of Western Australia, 2009).

31. Pigou, "Producers' and Consumers' Surplus," 366.

32. Marshall disputed some of Pigou's assertions. See Bharadwaj, "Marshall on Pigou's *Wealth and Welfare*," 41–43.

33. Skidelsky, *John Maynard Keynes: Hopes Betrayed*, 211.

34. Ibid.

35. D. W. Corrie to John Saltmarsh, February 19, 1960, Papers Relating to Arthur Cecil Pigou, KCA, ACP/1/Corrie.

36. The architect was A. M. Moberley, who signed the menu card for the dinner celebrating Pigou's professorship. See "Menu Card," June 6, 1908, Academic and Tutorial Records, KCA, KCAC/1/2/6/1/Pigou1. See also Plans for Lower Gatesgarth, 1911, Cumbria Archive Centre, Carlisle, United Kingdom, SRDC/3/2/709.

37. Pigou to Macmillan, February 10, 1912, Macmillan Papers, BL Add. MSS 55199, 30.

38. Pigou to Macmillan, July 11, 1912, Macmillan Papers, BL, Add. MSS 55199, 44.

39. Pigou to Macmillan, November 7, 1915, Macmillan Papers, BL, Add. MSS 55199, 47.

40. In general, citations to Pigou's works on welfare reference the latest edition then published. In this chapter, which concerns *Wealth and Welfare* and the first edition of *The Economics of Welfare*, an effort has been made in the footnotes to register if an idea or phrase was not original to one of these books. Here, a general overview of the evolution of *The Economics of Welfare* may be helpful. The first edition of the book, which ran over a thousand pages, was criticized for its length. Therefore, as will be explained below, in subsequent editions, Pigou removed the book's final section, dealing with fluctuations in national income, to an independent volume, *Industrial Fluctuations*. He also condensed a three-sided distinction between individual, social, and trade net product into a "single distinction between social and private net product;" see A. C. Pigou, *The Economics of Welfare*, second ed. (London: Macmillan, 1924): vi. As treated below, the third edition (1929) was edited so as to respond to the so-called cost controversy, notably Piero Sraffa's critique of the Marshallian theory of value. The fourth edition contained only minor revisions. See Nahid Aslanbeigui, "Introduction," in *The Economics of Welfare*, by A. C. Pigou (New Brunswick, NJ: Transaction, 2001): xxxiv.

41. A. C. Pigou, *Wealth and Welfare* (London: Macmillan, 1912): 3.

42. Ibid. The term "measuring rod of money" was originally Marshall's.

43. Pigou, *The Economics of Welfare*, first ed., 5. The language of positive science did not appear in *Wealth and Welfare*.

44. Pigou to Macmillan, September 9, 1923, Macmillan Papers, BL, Add. MSS 55199, 78.

45. On the economic implications of utilitarianism, see Steven G. Medema, *The Hesitant Hand: Taming Self Interest in the History of Economic Ideas* (Princeton, NJ: Princeton University Press, 2009), chapter 2.

46. Pigou himself has been cast as a utilitarian. See C. J. Dewey, "'Cambridge Idealism': Utilitarian Revisionists in Late Nineteenth-Century Cambridge," *Historical Journal* 17, no. 1 (March 1, 1974): 63–78; Roger E. Backhouse, "Sidgwick, Marshall, and the Cambridge School of Economics," *History of Political Economy* 38, no. 1 (Spring 2006): 15–44, 35–38; Margaret G. O'Donnell, "Pigou: An Extension of Sidgwickian Thought," *History of Political Economy* 11, no. 4 (1979): 588.

47. Pigou, *Wealth and Welfare*, 3.

48. Pigou, *The Economics of Welfare*, first ed., 11.

49. Ibid.

50. Pigou, *Wealth and Welfare*, 362–363 and Pigou, *The Economics of Welfare*, first ed., 785. In an exam Pigou prepared for Cambridge undergraduates in 1910 or 1911, he asked students to examine "how . . . provision [should] be made for . . . [good will] in the balance sheet." Gerald Shove, Class Notes, c. 1909–10, Gerald Frank Shove Papers, MLE, Shove 1/1 [9–10].

51. Backhouse, "Sidgwick, Marshall, and the Cambridge School of Economics;" Martin Daunton, "Welfare, Taxation and Social Justice: Reflections on Cambridge Economists from Marshall to Keynes," in *No Wealth but Life*, ed. Backhouse and Nishizawa, 62–90. See also C. J. Dewey, "Cambridge Idealism;" Medema, *The Hesitant Hand*, 42–50.

52. Backhouse, "Sidgwick, Marshall, and the Cambridge School of Economics," 22; Roger E. Backhouse and Tamotsu Nishizawa, "Introduction: Towards a Reinterpretation of the History of Welfare Economics" in *No Wealth but Life*, ed. Backhouse and Nishizawa, 2.

53. In Sidgwick's words, "when the supply of any article has been increased and its price consequently fallen, it is not really correct to reckon the total utility of the article as having increased in proportion to the decrease in value." Henry Sidgwick, *The Principles of Political Economy* (London: Macmillan, 1883): 75.

54. Mill wrote, "it was the proper office of government to build and maintain lighthouses, establish buoys, &c., for the security of navigation: for since it is impossible that the ships at sea which are benefited by a lighthouse, should be made to pay a toll on the occasion of its use, no one would build lighthouses from motives of personal interest, unless indemnified and rewarded from a compulsory levy made by the state." John Stuart Mill, *Principles of Political Economy: With Some of Their Applications to Social Philosophy* (London: Longmans, Green, Reader, and Dyer, 1866): 589. Ronald Coase challenged this position in 1974, noting that lighthouses in Britain

were traditionally maintained by the private sector. See R. H. Coase, "The Lighthouse in Economics," *Journal of Law and Economics* 17, no. 2 (October 1974): 357–376. For a more full discussion, see Medema, *The Hesitant Hand*, 33–42.

55. See Daunton, "Welfare, Taxation and Social Justice," 66. This utilitarian assumption was disputed by several economic thinkers of the late nineteenth century, notably Vilfredo Pareto, who questioned the possibility of interpersonal comparisons of utility. See Vilfredo Pareto, *Manual of Political Economy* (Oxford: Oxford University Press, 2014), particularly chapters 3 and 6.

56. Sidgwick, *Principles of Political Economy*, 511.

57. Backhouse, "Sidgwick, Marshall, and the Cambridge School of Economics," 27. On Sidgwick's Victorian values, see Jerome Schneewind, *Sidgwick's Ethics and Victorian Moral Philosophy* (Oxford: Oxford University Press, 1977). On Sidgwick's tentative support for government intervention, see Medema, *The Hesitant Hand*, 49.

58. Backhouse, "Sidgwick, Marshall, and the Cambridge School of Economics," 26–27.

59. Ibid., and Daunton, "Welfare, Taxation and Social Justice," 67.

60. Groenewegen *A Soaring Eagle*, 275.

61. Marshall praised the third chapter of *Principles of Political Economy* on the functions of government as "by common consent, far the best thing of its kind in any language." "Report of Marshall's Speech at the Meeting to Promote A Memorial For Henry Sidgwick," November 22, 1900, in *The Correspondence of Alfred Marshall*, II, 442. On Sidgwick's designation of economics as an art, see Sidgwick, *Principles of Political Economy*, 27.

62. Marshall, *Principles of Economics*, eighth ed., 713–714. See also Backhouse, "Sidgwick, Marshall, and the Cambridge School of Economics," 28–33; Groenewegen, "Marshall on Welfare Economics and the Welfare State," 25–41.

63. See Daunton, "Welfare, Taxation and Social Justice," 68. Medema suggests that both Sidgwick and Marshall evinced dim views of government effectiveness. Sidgwick noted the potential for waste; Marshall was especially worried about corruption. Medema, *The Hesitant Hand*, 49, 57; Roger E. Backhouse and Steven G. Medema, "Economists and the Analysis of Government Failure: Fallacies in the Chicago and Virginia Interpretations of Cambridge Welfare Economics," *Cambridge Journal of Economics* 36 no. 4 (July 2012): 981–994.

64. Because there was "no precise line between economic and non-economic satisfactions," Pigou saw money as a viable proxy for utility, which itself was just one of many variables in an "ultimate good" function. But Pigou recognized that money was not utility and, in fact, that utility itself was *not* happiness, pleasure, or satisfaction, but instead a "measure of desire," as classical utilitarians had held. Pigou, "Some Remarks on Utility," 58; Pigou, *The Economics of Welfare*, first ed., 11, 23–30. This definition, inherited from Marshall, made monetary quantification of utility much easier. According to it, people spent money on what they wanted, not necessarily on what would bring them the most happiness. Desires and satisfactions were not assumed to be perfectly in sync, even if they served as approximations of each other. Though he recognized that "the elements of welfare are states of consciousness,"

Pigou still sought to link material prosperity to desire and thereby to satisfaction and welfare.

65. Amartya Sen, "The Living Standard," *Oxford Economic Papers* 36 (November 1984): 80.

66. John Maloney, *The Professionalization of Economics: Alfred Marshall and Dominance of Orthodoxy* (New Brunswick, NJ: Transaction, 1991): 176–185.

67. The third criterion, the variability of the dividend, disappeared from the second edition of *The Economics of Welfare*.

68. See especially part II, chapter III of Pigou, *Wealth and Welfare*, 104–108, which became part II, chapters II and III of Pigou, *The Economics of Welfare*, first ed., 114–130. For Marshall on marginal costs and values, see Marshall, *Principles*, 403–438.

69. Medema, *The Hesitant Hand*, 62–64. Pigou's use of money as a rough quantifier of wellbeing led some economists after his death to incorrectly conclude that Pigou conceived of externalities as accounting errors. They read Pigou as believing that the market would not *necessarily* lead to imperfections, but only that it operated without full transparency due to the difficulty of identifying and calculating the costs and benefits of an economic activity. U. Hla Myint, *Theories of Welfare Economics* (New York: Reprints of Economics Classics, Augustus M. Kelley, 1965): 178–183. Thinkers who equated Pigou with the quantification of Marshall included Lionel Robbins, and Talcott Parsons in *The Structure of Social Action* (New York: McGraw-Hill, 1937): 134. See also J. N. Tewari, "What Is Economics?" *Indian Journal of Economics* (April, 1947), and Israel Kirzner, *The Economic Point of View: An Essay in the History of Economic Thought* (Auburn, AL: Ludwig von Mises Institute, 1976): 95–96. See also Steven G. Medema, *Ronald H. Coase* (London: Macmillan, 1994).

70. In his attack on externality theory, Ronald Coase called Pigou's *The Economics of Welfare* the "fountainhead" of externality theory. See R. H. Coase, "The Problem of Social Cost," *Journal of Law and Economics* 3 (October 1, 1960): 3, 28. Francis M. Bator was the first to use the term "externality." Francis M. Bator, "The Simple Analytics of Welfare Maximization," *American Economic Review* 47, no. 1 (March 1957): 22–59. See also Backhouse and Medema, "Economists and the Analysis of Government Failure."

71. Pigou, *Wealth and Welfare*, 7. In the third edition of *The Economics of Welfare*, Pigou used the example of a factory to illustrate an externality, but not that of pollution. He wrote of a case wherein "the owner of a site in a residential quarter of a city builds a factory there and so destroys a great part of the amenities of the neighbouring sites; or, in a less degree, when he uses his site in such a way as to spoil the lighting of the houses opposite." A. C. Pigou, *The Economics of Welfare*, third ed. (London: Macmillan, 1929): 187–188.

72. Ibid., 8. On industry as destructive of the English landscape, see Martin J. Wiener, *English Culture and the Decline of the Industrial Spirit, 1850-1980* (Cambridge: Cambridge University Press, 1981), chapter 4.

73. Pigou, *Wealth and Welfare*, 159

74. Just as there could be uncharged losses, there could also be profits that went unaccounted. Pigou claimed that establishing new forests had a hidden benefit; railway

developments bore untold dividends for connected communities; and good building arrangements might improve "general organization of steadiness in the employment of labor." Ibid. Through his work on externalities, Pigou has been influential in the history of environmental economics. William Baumol and Wallace E. Oates note that Pigou "showed why the performance of a profit system in supplying social amenities is apt to be less satisfactory," and that this was key to understanding the economics of environmental protection. William J. Baumol and Wallace E. Oates, *Economics, Environmental Policy, and the Quality of Life* (Englewood Cliffs, NJ: Prentice-Hall, 1979), 72. Agnar Sandmo, "The Early History of Environmental Economics," *Review of Environmental Economics and Policy* 9, no. 1 (January 2015): 43–63.

75. Pigou, *The Economics of Welfare*, first ed., 11, 160.

76. The first edition of *The Economics of Welfare* passed over the specific ways of calculating such economic costs and benefits, noting that calculability was "of formal as opposed to real importance." Ibid., 160–161.

77. Pigou, *The Economics of Welfare*, third ed., 160.

78. Ibid., 185–186n. See also Sandmo, "The Early History of Environmental Economics," 23.

79. Pigou, *Wealth and Welfare*, 148–171.

80. See Medema, *The Hesitant Hand*, 60–65.

81. Pigou, *Wealth and Welfare*, 164.

82. See Nahid Aslanbeigui and Steven G. Medema, "Beyond the Dark Clouds: Pigou and Coase on Social Cost," *History of Political Economy* 30, no. 4 (Winter 1998): 601–625; Medema, *The Hesitant Hand*, 60–65.

83. Pigou, *Wealth and Welfare*, 164.

84. This turn of phrase first appeared in the second edition of *The Economics of Welfare*, but it was implied in the first edition. Pigou, *The Economics of Welfare*, second ed., 79; Pigou, *The Economics of Welfare*, first ed., 52–53.

85. Pigou, *The Economics of Welfare*, first ed., 53. In the first edition, Pigou cited the contemporary Italian philosopher Eugenio Rignano for this idea. By the fourth edition, he cited Mill. Pigou, *The Economics of Welfare*, fourth ed., 89–90.

86. Pigou to Philip Noel-Baker, n.d. [March 1955], The Papers of Baron Noel-Baker, CAC, NBKR 9/58/1.

87. This is distinct from (but not inconsistent with) Aslanbeigui and Oakes's assertion that Pigou saw his relationship with the government as "whispering into the ear of the prince." Aslanbeigui and Oakes, *Arthur Cecil Pigou*, 132.

88. Bernard Williams, "The Point of View of the Universe: Sidgwick and the Ambitions of Ethics," in *Making Sense of Humanity* by Bernard Williams (Cambridge: Cambridge University Press, 1995).

89. Sidgwick, *Methods of Ethics*, quoted in Williams, "The Point of View of the Universe," 165.

90. Ibid., 166.

91. Ibid. This is a necessarily reductive sketch of Sidgwick. Sidgwick was also convinced that humanity would become more like an ideal community of utilitarians, thereby reducing the gap between elites and the rest of society. See Bart Schultz,

Henry Sidgwick: Eye of the Universe: An Intellectual Biography (Cambridge: Cambridge University Press, 2004): 264–272.

92. Hugh Dalton, *Call Back Yesterday: Memoirs 1887–1931* (London: F. Muller, 1953): 59.

93. Pigou to R. H. Harrod, n.d. [1949], Harrod Papers, BL, Add. MS 72764, 235.

94. See Daunton, "Welfare, Taxation and Social Justice," 71. Pigou drew inspiration from B. Seebohm Rowntree's study *Poverty*, which noted poor families' "purchase of food is not always spent in the most economical way," even when family budgets were strained. B. Seebohm Rowntree, *Poverty: A Study of Town Life* (London: Macmillan, 1901): 260.

95. Pigou, *Wealth and Welfare*, 357. This report was "Mr. Jackson's Report on Boy Labour," *Royal Commission on the Poor Laws*, Appendix vol. 20 [Cd. 5068], 1910. Pigou drew extensively from the Minority Report of the same royal commission, for which he had given evidence in 1907.

96. Pigou, *Wealth and Welfare*, 357. The report was that of the Working of the Education (Provision of Meals) Act 1906 up to 31 March 1909, 1910, Cd. 5131. Although this particular passage did not appear in *The Economics of Welfare*, its sentiment did. In *The Economics of Welfare*, Pigou argued that for a transference to be successful, the poor should not receive money, but already purchased goods. The implication was the same as in *Wealth and Welfare*—that the poor should not be trusted to spend redistributed funds. In *The Economics of Welfare*, Pigou made clear that transferring money to the poor was also problematic, as money transfers gave the poor an incentive to work less. Pigou, *The Economics of Welfare*, first ed., 756–760. Moreover, in *The Economics of Welfare*, Pigou was in favor of mandating the ways in which the poor spent any sort of guaranteed real income. See ibid., 787–798.

97. Pigou, *Wealth and Welfare*, 358.

98. Ross McKibbin, *Classes and Cultures: England, 1918–1951* (Oxford: Oxford University Press, 1998): 106.

99. Pigou, *Wealth and Welfare*, 248. See also Roger E. Backhouse and Steven G. Medema, "Economists and the Analysis of Government Failure: Fallacies in the Chicago and Virginia Interpretations of Cambridge Welfare Economics," *Cambridge Journal of Economics* 36 no. 4 (July 2012): 984; For more on the economic expert in America, see Thomas C. Leonard, *Illiberal Reformers: Race, Eugenics and American Economics in the Progressive Era* (Princeton, NJ: Princeton University Press, 2016).

Chapter 4: War, Peace, and Disillusionment

1. A. C. Pigou, *Unemployment* (London: Williams & Norgate, 1913). A. C. Pigou, *"Vorlesungen uber Nationalokonomie auf Grundlage des Marginalprinzipes* by Knut Wicksell," *Economic Journal* 23, no. 92 (December 1913): 605–606; F. W. Taussig and A. C. Pigou, "Railway Rates and Joint Cost," *Quarterly Journal of Economics* 27, no. 3 (May 1913): 535–538; F. W. Taussig and A. C. Pigou, "Railway Rates and Joint Costs," *Quarterly Journal of Economics*, 27, no. 4 (August 1913): 687–694.

2. Hugh Dalton, *Call Back Yesterday: Memoirs 1887–1931* (London: F. Muller, 1953): 58–60.

3. The pair shared a bedroom with two beds while Pigou was a fellow and Corrie an undergraduate, an arrangement that provoked C. R. Fay, the King's economic historian, to call the pair "Mr. and Mrs. Pigou." See Nahid Aslanbeigui and Guy Oakes, *Arthur Cecil Pigou* (Houndmills, Basingstoke, UK: Palgrave Macmillan, 2015): 247–248.

4. D. W. Corrie to John Saltmarsh, February 19, 1960, Papers Relating to A.C. Pigou, KCA, ACP/1/Corrie.

5. Ibid.

6. Copy of the *Gownsman*, May 26, 1910, Austin Robinson Papers, MLE, EAGR 6/6/4.

7. Ibid.

8. Philip Baker to Elizabeth Balmer Moscrip, n.d., The Papers of Baron Noel-Baker, CCA, NBKR 9/45/8.

9. Nicholas Elliott, *Never Judge a Man by His Umbrella* (London: Michael Russell, 1991).

10. Pigou to Philip Noel-Baker, n.d. [June 1943], Noel-Baker Papers, CCA, NBKR 9/58/2.

11. Information from author's conversations with the present owners of Lower Gatesgarth, October 31, 2012.

12. "Copy Duplicate of Conveyance of Freehold Farm Cottage and Land known as Gatesgarth, Buttermere, Cumberland," W.M.W. Marshall, Esq. to Professor G.M. Trevelyan, O.M., July 30, 1935, Private Collection, Buttermere, United Kingdom.

13. Pigou to Catherine Marshall, February 27, 1906, The Letters of Miss Catherine E. Marshall, Cumbria Archive Centre, Carlisle, United Kingdom, DMAR/2/23. For more on Catherine Marshall, see Jo Vellacott, "Marshall, Catherine Elizabeth (1880–1961)," *Oxford Dictionary of National Biography* (Oxford: Oxford University Press, 2004), http://www.oxforddnb.com/view/article/38527.

14. On Philip Baker's early years, see D. J. Whittaker, *Fighter for Peace: Philip Noel-Baker 1889–1982* (York, UK: William Sessions, 1989): 1–31. On Trevelyan in Cumbria, see Elliott, *Never Judge a Man by His Umbrella*, 66–67. On Trevelyan in Italy, see David Cannadine, *G.M. Trevelyan: A Life in History* (New York: W. W. Norton & Company, 1992): 80–81. Trevelyan was neither a pacifist nor a conscientious objector; he joined a Red Cross ambulance unit because of poor eyesight.

15. Pigou to Josephine Baker, n.d. (1914), Noel-Baker Papers, CCA, NBKR 9/45/4.

16. Pigou to Josephine Baker, n.d. (March 1915), Noel-Baker Papers, CCA, NBKR 9/46/2.

17. Ibid.

18. Photos of Pigou, June 12, 1915, Pigou Papers, KCA, ACP/3/1.

19. John Saltmarsh and Patrick Wilkinson, *Arthur Cecil Pigou, 1877–1959, Fellow and Professor of Political Economy* (Cambridge: King's College, 1960): 8–9.

20. Ibid.

21. Harry G. Johnson, "Arthur Cecil Pigou, 1877–1959," *Canadian Journal of Economics and Political Science / Revue canadienne d'Economique et de Science politique* 26, no. 1 (February 1960): 153.

22. Christopher N. L. Brooke, *A History of the University of Cambridge, Volume IV, 1870–1990* (Cambridge: Cambridge University Press, 1993): 331.

23. Ibid., 333–334; G. R. Evans, *The University of Cambridge: A New History* (London: I. B. Tauris, 2010): 25–26.

24. See Brooke, *A History of Cambridge*, 335–340.

25. Dennis Robertson (1890–1962), who joined up, wrote to J. M. Keynes, that "Of some of one's other friends one feels that death was the most useful thing of which they were capable." Robertson saw even passive acceptance of Germans as treacherous. "I wish L-G [David Lloyd George] had put a heavy tax on any further mention in print of the names Nietzsche, Treitschke or Berhardt." Dennis Robertson to J. M. Keynes, November 19, 1914, The Papers of John Manyard Keynes, KCA, JMK/L/R 6.

26. Pigou's exemption was a close call and attracted national media attention. Aslanbeigui suggests that departmental politics fomented debate over whether Pigou was needed at Cambridge, with a disgruntled Foxwell stirring up unrest. Nahid Aslanbeigui, "Foxwell's Aims and Pigou's Military Service: A Malicious Episode?" *Journal of the History of Economic Thought* 14 (1992): 96–109. Maloney suggests that Foxwell only felt snubbed that others thought him incapable of substituting for Pigou. John Maloney, *The Professionalization of Economics: Alfred Marshall and Dominance of Orthodoxy* (New Brunswick, NJ: Transaction, 1991): 224–225.

27. "Medal Card of Pigou, Arthur C." 1920, War Office, TNA, WO 372/16/6394.

28. Pigou served on the "Committee of Economists Appointed by the Board of Trade to Consider the Probable State of Industry after the War with Special Reference to Employment." Other economists included William Ashley and Edwin Cannan. Each was assigned a set of industries to analyze. Pigou's were "building trades, quarries, brick and cement trades, wood and furniture trades." He also devised the general scheme for the report and, together with his friend J. H. Clapham, wrote an introduction and assembled the full document of 89 folio pages. "The General Report of the Committee of Economists Appointed by the Board of Trade to Consider the Probably State of Industry after the War with Special Reference to Employment," Sir William Ashley Papers, British Library, Add MS 42247, 245–289. See also William Ashley's papers relating to the committee. Sir William Ashley Papers, British Library, Add MS 42247, 158–244. See especially "Minutes of the Second Meeting," Feburary 9, 1917, Add. MS 42247, 212, and J. H. Clapham to W. J. Ashley, March 5, 1917, Ashley Papers, BL, Add. MS 42247, 217.

29. See Michael Bentley, *The Liberal Mind, 1914–1929* (Cambridge: Cambridge University Press, 1977), chapter 1; and Trevor Wilson, *The Downfall of the Liberal Party, 1914–1935* (London: Collins, 1966), chapter 3.

30. A. C. Pigou, "Terms of Peace," unpublished manuscript, c. 1915–16, Arthur Cecil Pigou Papers, MLE, Pigou 1/5/2, 6.

31. Of this letter, Pigou would comment, "Not Dante himself devised for his enemies a punishment less enticing!" A. C. Pigou, *Economics in Practice* (London: Macmillan, 1935): 153.

32. Donald Winch, "Keynes and the British Academy," *Historical Journal* 57, no. 3 (September 2014): 760–763.

33. *Navy List* (February 1919): 729.

34. *Navy List* (January 1919): 386; *Navy List* (June 1919): 767.

35. Peter Groenewegen, *A Soaring Eagle: Alfred Marshall 1842–1924* (Aldershot, UK: Edward Elgar, 1995): 643.

36. The petition appeared in a memorandum prepared by Winston Churchill, then the secretary of state for war. Winston S. Churchill, "Conscientious Objectors." Memorandum prepared for the Prime Minister, 1919, Cabinet Papers and Minutes, TNA, CAB 24/75, 6873.

37. Pigou, "Terms of Peace," 5, 8–9.

38. Pigou was dismissing the so-called Naturalistic Fallacy—the notion that because something occurred naturally, it was worthy. Moore had engaged the naturalistic fallacy "and of it . . . endeavor[ed] to dispose." G. E. Moore, *Principia Ethica*, rev. ed. (Cambridge: Cambridge University Press, 1993): 62, 65–66.

39. Pigou, "Terms of Peace," 16.

40. Michael Barratt Brown, *The Evolution of the Friends' Ambulance Unit* (1914 and 1939) (London: Friends' Ambulance Unit, July 1943): 5. See also Meaburn Tatham and James E. Miles, eds., *The Friends' Ambulance Unit, 1914–1916: A Record* (London: Swarthmore Press, 1919): 249–250. About half of the unit consisted of Quakers. See Thomas C. Kennedy, *British Quakerism, 1860–1920: The Transformation of a Religious Community* (Oxford: Oxford University Press, 2001): 315–316.

41. Pigou published on wartime economics over the course of the war. Much appeared in *The Political Economy of War*, which came out in 1921. A .C. Pigou, *The Economy and Finance of the War* (London: Dent, 1916); A. C. Pigou, "Interest after the War and the Export of Capital," *Economic Journal* 26, no. 104 (December 1916): 413–424; A. C. Pigou, "The Economics of the War Loan," *Economic Journal* 27, no. 105 (March 1917): 16–25; A. C. Pigou, "Inflation," *Economic Journal* 27, no. 108 (December 1917): 486–494; A. C. Pigou, "A Special Levy to Discharge the War Debt," *Economic Journal* 28, no. 110 (June 1918): 135–156; A. C. Pigou, "Government Control in War and Peace," *Economic Journal* 28, no. 112 (December 1918): 363–373.

42. A. C. Pigou, "The Value of Money," *Quarterly Journal of Economics* 32, no. 1 (November 1917): 38–65.

43. On taxation as a tool of justice, see Martin Daunton, *Just Taxes: The Politics of Taxation in Britain, 1914–1979* (Cambridge: Cambridge University Press, 2007), especially chapter 3. See also Groenewegen, *A Soaring Eagle*, 644–646; William Harbutt Dawson, ed. *After-war Problems* (London: Allen & Unwin, 1918).

44. Nahid Aslanbeigui and Guy Oakes, *Arthur Cecil Pigou* (Houndmills, Basingstoke, UK: Palgrave Macmillan, 2015): 108.

45. A. C. Pigou, "The Burden of War and Future Generations" *Quarterly Journal of Economics* 33 (1919): 241–255. Future generations were important in Pigou's work. David Collard, "Pigou and Future Generations," *Cambridge Journal of Economics* 20 (1996): 585–597.

46. A. C. Pigou, "The Need for More Taxation." *Economist* (December 9, 1916): 1087. Pigou favored a special wartime tax but strongly opposed it only being levied on the men of military age as it was in Italy. Pigou asserted: "It has often been said that this is a young man's war, and for the work of actual fighting, that is, of course,

true. Young men embody the main part of the nation's physical strength. *But old men embody a great part of its financial strength.* They are largely instrumental in making others fight; ought they not themselves be made to pay?"

47. Ibid.

48. Ibid.

49. A. C. Pigou, "A Capital Levy after the War," Undated typescript, in "Essays on Government Indebtedness," Keynes Papers, KCA, JMK/T/22, 40. See also Daunton, *Just Taxes*, chapter 3.

50. Pigou to Macmillan, November 23, 1918, Macmillan Papers, BL, Add. MSS 55199, 49.

51. Pigou to Macmillan, November 7, 1915, Macmillan Papers, BL, Add. MSS 55199, 47. This is the same title as Pigou's inaugural address as professor.

52. Pigou to Macmillan, December 20, 1918, Macmillan Papers, BL, Add. MSS 55199, 50.

53. A. C. Pigou, *The Political Economy of War*, second edition (New York: Macmillan, 1941): 47. On taxes and loans, see chapter VII, 72–94.

54. This referenced Marshall's 1907 call for "economic chivalry." Alfred Marshall, "Social Possibilities of Economic Chivalry," *Economic Journal* 17, no. 65 (March 1907): 7–29. The eugenics chapter, "Eugenics and Some Wage Problems" appeared first in the *Eugenics Review* in April 1923. A. C. Pigou, *Essays in Applied Economics* (London: P. S. King & Son, 1923): 80–91. This piece concluded that eugenicists could not engineer a perfect society and that it was similarly impossible to predict the outcomes of policies on genetic quality. On economic chivalry, Pigou noted there were financial as well as moral benefits to treating workpeople well. Good conditions maintained worker health and prevented costly strikes. Workplace philanthropy fostered a spirit of cooperation rather than mere patronage. Citing the work of utopian socialist Robert Owen, Pigou concluded, "it is through comradeship, not through autocracy, that the good life grows." Pigou, *Essays in Applied Economics*, 23.

55. See, e.g., William Beveridge, *British Food Control* (Oxford: Oxford University Press, 1928); E.M.H. Lloyd, *Experiments in State Control at the War Office and the Ministry of Food* (Oxford: Clarendon Press, 1924); Leo Chiozza Money, *The Triumph of Nationalization* (London: Cassell, 1920).

56. A. C. Pigou, "The Private Use of Money," in Pigou, *Essays in Applied Economics*, 2.

57. Ibid., 1–2. Pigou retained his multivariable good function. "It is true, no doubt, that the things which money can buy are not the best things—kindness and youth under open skies, comradeship of true friends in pleasure or difficulty or danger, a word, a silence, a smile, love that moves the sun and other stars. But, though the best things are not purchasable, they . . . need some modicum of purchasable things as a foundation."

58. Ibid., 1.

59. Though Marshall gave evidence to several committees over the course of his life, he was an infrequent member of such bodies. See Groenewegen, *A Soaring Eagle*, chapter 11; Aslanbeigui and Oakes, *Arthur Cecil Pigou*, 132.

60. See *Reports and Minutes of Evidence on the Second Stage of Inquiry of the Coal Industry Commission* [Cmd. 360], 1919, 423, cited in Aslanbeigui and Oakes, *Arthur Cecil Pigou*, 261. Aslanbeigui and Oakes argue that Pigou's framework of pros and cons and "guarded, and hedged, and qualified" judgments were central to what they call his theory of policy analysis. See ibid., 97.

61. See Barry Eichengreen, "The British Economy Between the Wars," in *The Cambridge Economic History of Modern Britain*, ed. Roderick Floud and Paul Johnson (Cambridge: Cambridge University Press, 2004): 314–343.

62. On Lloyd George and labor, see chapter 3 of Kenneth O. Morgan, *Concensus and Disunity* (Oxford: Clarendon Press, 1979): 46–79; Peter Clarke, *The Keynesian Revolution in the Making, 1924–1936* (Oxford: Clarendon Press, 1988): 106–108.

63. Saltmarsh and Wilkinson, *Arthur Cecil Pigou*, 18.

64. J. M. Keynes *Economic Consequences of the Peace* (London: Macmillan, 1919).

65. Cited in Dalton, *Call Back Yesterday*, 113–114.

66. See chapters 2 and 3 of Clarke, *The Keynesian Revolution in the Making*, 28–69. See also Robert W. D. Boyce, *British Capitalism at the Crossroads: A Study in Politics, Economics, and International Relations* (Cambridge: Cambridge University Press, 1987): 30–31.

67. The vast majority of the committee, which was chaired by Bank of England Governor Walter Cunliffe, worked in the financial industry. Members included Charles Addis of the Hongkong and Shanghai Banking Corporation; George Goschen, a businessman who had been Chancellor of the Exchequer; and Gaspard Farrer, a chairman of Baring Brothers. Minutes of the First Meeting, February 2, 1918, Committee on Currency and Foreign Exchange (Cunliffe Committee), TNA, T185/1, 82.

68. Boyce, *British Capitalism at the Crossroads*, 31. See also Martin J. Wiener, *English Culture and the Decline of the Industrial Spirit, 1850–1980* (Cambridge: Cambridge University Press, 1981).

69. "Memorandum prepared by Professor Pigou on Fiduciary Note Issue after the War," March 6, 1918, Cunliffe Committee, TNA, T185/1, 96–102; "Note by Professor Pigou on the Proposal to Prohibit Gold Import Except to the Bank of England and to Sell Gold for Use in the Arts at a Premium," March 6, 1918, Cunliffe Committee, TNA, T185/1, 103–104; A. C. Pigou "The Effect of Amalgamating the Issue and Banking Departments of the Bank of England," 1918, Cunliffe Committee, TNA, T185/1, 143–144.

70. A. C. Pigou "The Effect of Amalgamating the Issue and Banking Departments of the Bank of England," 1918, Cunliffe Committee, TNA, T185/1, 143–144.

71. Pigou rarely asked witnesses questions. For some of the few examples, see the questioning of Walter Leaf in Minutes of the Fifteenth Meeting, May 27, 1918, Cunliffe Committee, TNA, T185/1, 300–302; of Sir James Hope Simpson, in Minutes of the Eighteenth Meeting, June 3, 1918, Cunliffe Committee, TNA, T185/1, 341; of Drummond Fraser, in Minutes of the Nineteenth Meeting, June 4, 1918, TNA, T185/1, 362; and of Felix Schuster in Minutes of the Thirty-Second Meeting, October 16, 1918, Cunliffe Committee, TNA, T185/1, 732. One area about which Pigou was uncharacteristically vocal was that of reserve ratios. Pigou worried that banks, especially the Bank of England, were exposing themselves to too much risk, and he expressed

interest in ensuring that the Bank of England maintained significant gold reserves. See Minutes of the Second Meeting, February 25, 1918, TNA, T185/1, 86, and Minutes of the Fourth Meeting, March 4, 1918, Cunliffe Committee, TNA, T185/1, 104. See also A. C. Pigou, *Industrial Fluctuations* (London: Macmillan, 1927), part II, chapter VII, "Problems Connected with the Supply of Currency."

72. Boyce, *British Capitalism at the Crossroads*, 31. The Committee received 21 submissions of evidence. Only one was arguably the "expression of industrial opinion." Though the report did not stress the return to gold, the Committee noted, "we are glad to find that there was no difference of opinion among the witnesses who appeared before us." Cunliffe Committee, *First Interim Report*, [Cmd. 9182], 5.

73. Charles Maier contends that the search for stability was one of the key political economic issues of the twentieth century. Charles Maier, *In Search of Stability: Explorations in Historical Political Economy* (Cambridge: Cambridge University Press, 1987). On the uncertainty of the period, see Harold James, *The End of Globalization: Lessons from the Great Depression* (Cambridge, MA: Harvard University Press, 2001).

74. In the only memorandum he wrote for the League of Nations, Pigou supported gold as a way of keeping world economies together. See A. C. Pigou, "Memorandum on Credit, Currency, and Exchange Fluctuations," in *Documents de la conférence: Conférence financière internationale, Bruxelles, 1920: Memoranda d'experts en matière économique*, League of Nations (London: Harrison, 1920). See also Aslanbeigui and Oakes, *Arthur Cecil Pigou*, 128.

75. "Back to Sanity," *Economist* (November 2, 1918): 618–620.

76. See Fuad Shehab, *Progressive Taxation: A Study in the Development of the Progressive Principle in the British Income Tax* (Oxford: Clarendon, 1953).

77. N. F. Warren Fisher, "Memorandum on the Royal Commission on the Income Tax," prepared for the Chancellor of the Exchequer, February 6, 1919, Royal Commission on the Income Tax, TNA, T 172/985.

78. Pigou to N. F. Warren Fisher, February 23, 1919, Royal Commission on the Income Tax, TNA, T 172/985.

79. Austen Chamberlain to N. F. Warren Fisher, August 8, 1919, Royal Commission on the Income Tax, TNA, T 172/985.

80. On the tax commission, see B. E. V. Sabine, *A History of Income Tax* (London: Allen and Unwin, 1966): 157–162.

81. *Report of the Royal Commission on the Income Tax* [Cmd. 615], 1920, 1.

82. A. C. Pigou, "The Report of the Royal Commission on the British Income Tax" *Quarterly Journal of Economics* 34, no. 2 (August 1920): 607.

83. Daunton, *Just Taxes*, 105–106.

84. A. C. Pigou, "Co-operative Societies and Income Tax," *Economic Journal* 30, no. 118 (June, 1920): 156. Pigou noted that though Cooperative Societies (especially retailers) did produce non-monetary income (for the consumer), in general, non-money incomes were not taxed, and the amount of money that was in the balance was not enough to justify a deviation from the rule. See also A. C. Pigou, "Mr. and Mrs. Webb on Consumers' Co-Operation," *Economic Journal* 32, no. 125 (March 1922): 53–57.

85. Frederick Henry Smith, Lord Colwyn, to Austen Chamberlain, August 7, 1919, Royal Commission on the Income Tax, TNA, T 172/985.

86. Minutes of Meeting, July 2, 1920, Royal Commission on the Income Tax, TNA, IR 85/4, 109; Minutes of Meeting, October 8, 1919, Royal Commission on the Income Tax, TNA, IR 85/8, 223.

87. Pigou, "The Report of the Royal Commission," 607.

88. Ibid., 619.

89. Ibid.

90. Cheekily, he added: "He may even, if he so chooses, discover in these records hints of devices by which he himself may evade payment to the Revenue of moneys that are properly due!" Ibid., 625.

91. Boyce, *British Capitalism at the Crossroads*, 32–33.

92. On Lloyd George's thinking during this period, see Roy Hattersley, *David Lloyd George: The Great Outsider* (London: Little, Brown, 2010), chapters 32 and 33. See also of Kenneth O. Morgan, *Consensus and Disunity: The Lloyd George Coalition Government 1918–1922* (Oxford: Clarendon Press, 1979), chapter 11.

93. Frank Trentmann, *Free Trade Nation: Commerce, Consumption, and Civil Society in Modern Britain* (Oxford: Oxford University Press, 2008): 189–190.

94. On the war and the Liberal Party's decline, see Wilson, *The Downfall of the Liberal Party*; Bentley, *The Liberal Mind*.

95. Dalton, *Call Back Yesterday*, 122–129. See also F. W. Pethick Lawrence, *The Capital Levy: How the Labour Party Would Settle the War Debt* (London: Labour Party, 1920).

96. Labour Party, *Labour and the War Debt: A Statement of Policy for the Redemption of War Debt by a Levy on Accumulated Wealth* (London: Labour Party, 1922). See also Richard Whiting, *The Labour Party and Taxation: Party Identity and Political Purpose in Twentieth-Century Britain* (Cambridge: Cambridge University Press, 2000): 25–34; and Dalton, *Call Back Yesterday*, 129.

97. Fear of a levy gripped the financial community. Immediately after Labour formed a government in 1923, the Governor of the Bank of England, Montagu Norman, relaxed restrictions on capital movement so that the wealthy would be able to shelter their assets.

98. In 1918, Pigou had suggested doubling the rates for the current estate tax, which would make the top bracket taxed at 40 percent. See Pigou, "A Special Levy to Discharge War Debt," 154–155.

99. A. C. Pigou, "Capital Levy: Matters for a Royal Commission," *Times* (May 1, 1923): 9; Dalton, *Call Back Yesterday*, 122.

100. A. C. Pigou, "Capital Levy," *Times* (May 7, 1923): 8.

101. Ibid.

102. Pigou's letters to the *Times* appeared before Andrew Bonar Law (1858–1923) resigned as prime minister and his successor, Stanley Baldwin, announced a new election scheduled for 1923. Thus, Pigou's words should not be taken as endorsing a Labour position in the 1923 election.

103. On Norman, see Liaquat Ahamed, *Lords of Finance: The Bankers who Broke the World* (New York: Penguin, 2009), especially chapter 12.

104. Boyce, *British Capitalism at the Crossroads*, 64–66. See also Charles P. Kindleberger, *The World in Depression, 1929–1939* (Berkeley: University of California Press, 1973), chapter 2. Adam Tooze sees the rivalry between Britain and the United States around World War I in stark terms. Adam Tooze, *The Deluge: The Great War, America and the Remaking of the Global Order* (New York: Penguin, 2015).

105. See, for instance, Pigou's 1920 memorandum for the League of Nations: Pigou, "Memorandum on Credit, Currency, and Exchange Fluctuations," in *Documents de la conférence: Conférence financière internationale, Bruxelles, 1920: Memoranda d'experts en matière économique*, League of Nations (London: Harrison, 1920).

106. See D. E. Moggridge, *British Monetary Policy, 1924–1931, The Norman Conquest of $4.86* (Cambridge: Cambridge University Press, 1972), especially chapter 3.

107. Boyce, *British Capitalism at the Crossroads*, 66–67; Richard Sidney Sayers, *The Bank of England, 1891–1944, Volume 1* (Cambridge: Cambridge University Press, 1976): 136.

108. Moggridge, *British Monetary Policy*, 38. Moggridge offers a comprehensive overview of the committee's work on 37–51.

109. Montagu Norman to Otto Niemeyer, April 16, 1922, Committee to Consider Currency, Note Issues, and the Gold Standard, TNA, T 160/197 F 7528, 10.

110. Norman and Niemeyer were still keen to have Pigou serve even after he notified them that he would be abroad for much of the summer. Pigou to Otto Niemeyer, May 22, 1924, Committee to Consider Currency, TNA, T 160/197 F 7528, 19; Pigou to Otto Niemeyer, June 12, 1924, Committee to Consider Currency, TNA, T 160/197 F 7528, 30.

111. Moggridge, *British Monetary Policy*, 38; Boyce, *British Capitalism at the Crossroads*, 66–67.

112. Another witness, the Liberal politician Reginald McKenna, was opposed to the return to gold. Ibid., 42.

113. Not only would it "absolutely cut from under our feet" the British export trade, it would cause a collapse in credit. Keynes prioritized stable domestic prices over stable exchanges. Testimony of John Maynard Keynes, July 11, 1924, Committee to Consider Currency, TNA, T 160/197 528/02/2, 14. Also published in *The Collected Writings of John Maynard Keynes*, vol. XIX, 257. See also Robert Skidelsky, *John Maynard Keynes: The Economist as Saviour 1920–1937* (London: Macmillan, 1992): 153–160, 191–193; Moggridge, *British Monetary Policy*, 42–43; John Maynard Keynes, *A Tract on Monetary Reform* (London: Macmillan, 1923).

114. Skidelsky, *The Economist as Saviour*, 193.

115. Pigou's Copy of the Minutes of the Meetings of the Committee on the Currency and Bank of England Note Issues, Pigou Papers, MLE, Pigou 4. See Michael McLure, "A.C. Pigou's Membership of the 'Chamberlain-Bradbury' Committee Part I: The Historical Context," Discussion Paper 14.04 (Perth: Business School, University of Western Australia, 2014); Michael McLure, "A. C. Pigou's Membership of the 'Chamberlain-Bradbury' Committee Part II: "Transitional" and "Ongoing" Issues," Discussion Paper 14.05 (Perth: Business School, University of Western Australia, 2014).

116. Pigou was interested in the extent to which businessmen were swayed by general sentiment as opposed to concrete economic indicators. Revised Proof of Minutes

of the Committee on the Currency and Bank of England Note Issues, June 27, 1924, Committee to Consider Currency, TNA, T 160/197 F 7528/02/1, 16–21.

117. Compare to Aslanbeigui and Oakes, *Arthur Cecil Pigou*, 125–130. Notwithstanding Pigou's hestitation, the committee's final report strongly recommended "that the early return to the gold basis should forthwith be declared the irrevocable policy of His Majesty's Government." *Report of the Committee on the Currency and Bank of England Note Issues* [Cmd. 2393], 1925, 6. Gaspard Farrer to N. E. Young, September 6, 1924, Committee to Consider Currency, TNA, T 160/197 F 7528/01/2, 2–3.

118. Emphasis added. N. E. Young to Sir John Bradbury, September 12, 1924, Committee to Consider Currency, TNA, T 160/197 F 7528/01/2, 32. N. E. Young was the Committee's secretary. See also Moggridge, *British Monetary Policy*, 48–49.

119. In the same letter from N. E. Young to Sir John Bradbury, Young referred to Pigou's declaration of political detachment as "flabbiness." The "wait and see" policy was the one urged by Keynes and others, who predicted American inflation, which would make returning to gold less painful. Boyce, *British Capitalism at the Crossroads*, 70. See also Moggridge, *British Monetary Policy*, 47–51.

120. Ibid. See also Boyce, *British Capitalism at the Crossroads*.

121. Boyce, *British Capitalism at the Crossroads*, 70.

122. Ibid., 71–78; Moggridge, *British Monetary Policy*, chapter 3.

123. A. C. Pigou, "In Memoriam: Alfred Marshall, a Lecture Delivered in Cambridge Oct 24, 1924," in *Memorials of Alfred Marshall*, edited by A. C. Pigou (London: Macmillan: 1925): 84.

124. After he left the committees, Pigou published only two letters until the Great Depression. A. C. Pigou "Economics at the Universities," *Times* (November 19, 1926): 15; A. C. Pigou, "Safeguarded Industries," *Times* (November 17, 1928): 8.

125. This does not include a letter he wrote as part of his official capacity as a member of the Bradbury Commission. See John Bradbury, Gaspard Farrer, O. E. Niemeyer, and A. C. Pigou, "Return to Gold Standard," *Times* (April 19, 1925): 11.

126. A. C. Pigou, "An Economist's Apologia," in *Economics in Practice: Six Lectures on Current Issues*, by A. C. Pigou (London: Macmillan, 1935): 7–8.

127. A. C. Pigou, *Wealth and Welfare* (London: Macmillan, 1912): 70. See also Roger E. Backhouse and Steven G. Medema, "Economists and the Analysis of Government Failure: Fallacies in the Chicago and Virginia Interpretations of Cambridge Welfare Economics," *Cambridge Journal of Economics* 36 no. 4 (July 2012): 981–994.

128. A. C. Pigou, "Empty Economic Boxes: A Reply," *Economic Journal* 32, no. 128 (December 1922): 462. See also Pigou, "An Economist's Apologia," 8–9.

129. Pigou, "An Economist's Apologia," 7–10. The letter to the *Times* in question was likely A. C. Pigou, "The Economics of Mr. Balfour's Manifesto," *Times* (September 18, 1903): 4.

130. A. C. Pigou, "State Action and Laisser Faire," in *Economics in Practice: Six Lectures on Current Issues* by A. C. Pigou (London: Macmillan, 1935): 125. Steven Medema argues that this essay—which suggested that the state was always already invested in a laissez-faire system—is vital to understanding Pigou's stance on market

interventionism. See Steven G. Medema, "Pigou's 'Prima Facie Case': Market Failure in Theory and Practice," in *No Wealth but Life*, ed. Roger E. Backhouse and Tamotsu Nishizawa (Cambridge: Cambridge University Press, 2010): 42–61; Steven G. Medema, *The Hesitant Hand: Taming Self Interest in the History of Economic Ideas* (Princeton, NJ: Princeton University Press, 2009): 65–72.

131. Pigou, "An Economist's Apologia," 25.

Chapter 5: Retreat to the Ivory Tower

1. Philip Noel-Baker to Austin Robinson, October 21, 1964, Austin Robinson Papers, MLE, EAGR 6/6/4, 32.

2. Quoted in Christopher N. L. Brooke, *A History of the University of Cambridge, Volume IV, 1870–1990* (Cambridge: Cambridge University Press, 1993): 469.

3. Philip Noel-Baker to Austin Robinson, October 21, 1964, Austin Robinson Papers, MLE, EAGR 6/6/4, 32.

4. A. C. Pigou, "An Economist's Apologia," in *Economics in Practice: Six Lectures on Current Issues*, by A. C. Pigou (London: Macmillan, 1935): 8.

5. Anonymous [Joan Robinson], "Professional Economics: The Theory of Unemployment," *Statesman and Nation* (August 26, 1933): 240–241, Arthur Cecil Pigou Papers, MLE, Pigou 2/2/3. A copy of this review from an unknown source was found in Pigou's own copy of *The Theory of Unemployment*, published in 1933.

6. Richard Overy explores interwar Britain's preoccupation with "crisis of civilization." Richard Overy, *The Twilight Years: The Paradox of Britain Between the Wars* (New York: Viking, 2009).

7. C. F. G. Masterman, *The New Liberalism* (London: L. Parsons, 1920).

8. "Harrow v. Cambridge in Fives," *Harrovian* 35, no. 2 (April 1, 1922): 26–27.

9. J. H. Clapham, "Of Empty Economic Boxes," *Economic Journal* 32, no. 127 (September 1922): 305. Aslanbeigui and Oakes provide an overview of Pigou's involvement in the so-called cost controversy, which they trace back to the 1910s. Nahid Aslanbeigui and Guy Oakes, *Arthur Cecil Pigou* (Houndmills, Basingstoke, UK: Palgrave Macmillan, 2015), chapter 5.

10. Aslanbeigui and Oakes assert that before Clapham's article, debates at Cambridge had been settled privately, but with the article, "public airing of dissent became a legitimate and institutional feature of its culture." Aslanbeigui and Oakes, *Arthur Cecil Pigou*, 137.

11. Ibid., 311. See also Carlo Cristiano, "Marshall at Cambridge," in *The Impact of Alfred Marshall's Ideas: The Global Diffusion of his Work*, ed. Tiziano Raffaelli, Giacomo Becattini, Katia Caldari, and Marco Dardi (Cheltenham, UK: Edward Elgar, 2010): 22–23.

12. Pigou inherited Clapham's college rooms early in his tenure as a fellow. Pigou to Oscar Browning, n.d. [1902–4], The Papers of Oscar Browning, KCA, OB/1/1281/A.

13. For instance, Pigou noted, "when we are informed that a tax always raises the price of the taxed article by the amount of the tax, we know that our informant . . . is tacitly assuming that all articles are produced under conditions of constant return."

A. C. Pigou, "Empty Economic Boxes: A Reply," *Economic Journal* 32, no. 128 (December 1922): 461–462.

14. Ibid., 462.

15. Ibid., 464.

16. Ibid. The only recourse was to "endeavour to train up more men of the calibre of Jevons" who might unite both theory and firm-level content. Clapham was unsatisfied that he was being "paid with a cheque drawn on the bank of an unborn Jevons." J. H. Clapham, "The Economic Boxes," *Economic Journal* 32, no. 128 (December 1922): 562.

17. A. C. Pigou and Dennis Robertson, "Those Empty Boxes," *Economic Journal* 34, no. 133 (March 1924): 16–31.

18. Allyn Young, "Pigou's *Wealth and Welfare*," *Quarterly Journal of Economics* 27, no. 4 (August 1913): 683. Young claimed many of the factors of production (e.g., land in an agricultural setting) that contributed to higher prices when production increased were not "used up," which meant that there were higher monetary, but not real, costs. See also Nahid Aslanbeigui, "The Cost Controversy: Pigovian Economics in Disequilibrium" *European Journal of the History of Economic Thought* 3, no. 2 (Summer 1996): 281–285; Roberto Marchionatti, "The 'Increasing Returns and Competition' Dilemma: From Marshall to Pigou," in *The Elgar Companion to Alfred Marshall*, ed. Tiziano Raffaelli, Giacomo Becattini, Katia Caldari, and Marco Dardi (Cheltenham, UK: Edward Elgar, 2006): 617–624. Jacob Viner later dubbed these effects later pecuniary external economies, or diseconomies. See Jacob Viner, "Cost Curves and Supply Curves," *Zeitschrift für Nationalökonomie* 3, no. 1 (February 1932): 23–46.

19. Pigou to Macmillan, October 20, 1924, Macmillan Papers, BL, Add. MSS 55199, 87.

20. See Pigou to Macmillan, October 28, 1924, Macmillan Papers, BL, Add. MSS 55199, 89.

21. A. C. Pigou, ed. *Memorials of Alfred Marshall* (London: Macmillan, 1925).

22. A.C. Pigou, "In Memoriam: Alfred Marshall," in A.C. Pigou, ed. *Memorials of Alfred Marshall* (London: Macmillan, 1925): 90.

23. Ibid.

24. For example, see Pigou to Alfred Marshall, January 25, 1923, Marshall Papers, MLE, Marshall 1/168.

25. They included Edwin Cannan and Piero Sraffa.

26. Pigou to Macmillan, October 9, 1925, Macmillan Papers, BL, Add. MSS 55199.

27. Pigou stayed at 33 Beaumont Street. Gerard Pigou lived in St. Andrews Mansions in Dorset Street. Electoral Register for St. Marylebone, Westminster, London, 1928, ss 2010; Pigou's sister lived at 8 Weymouth Street. Outwards Passenger List of the *Ranchi*, Feburary 3, 1928, Records of the Board of Trade, TNA, BT 27, Digital Images Ancestry.com, July 8, 2014. *Electoral Registers*, Parliamentary Borough and Parish of St. Marylebone, London, London Metropolitan Archives, 1928, LCC/PER/B/1882, 120, Digital Images Ancestry.com, July 9, 2014. For Noel-Baker's address, see Parliamentary Borough of Westminster, St. George's Division London,

London Metropolitan Archives, 1924, LCC/PER/B/1776, 77, Digital Images Ancestry
.com. July 9, 2014.

28. Pigou to Macmillan, October 9, 1925, Macmillan Papers, BL, Add. MSS 55199.

29. "Lectures Proposed by the Special Board for Economics and Politics, 1925–
26," *Cambridge University Reporter* 56, no. 5 (October 9, 1925): 71.

30. Piero Sraffa, "The Laws of Returns under Competitive Conditions," *Economic
Journal* 36, no. 144 (December 1926): 538. Sraffa's article was a revision of a longer
piece he had published in Italian the previous year. Piero Sraffa, "Sulle relazioni fra
costo e quantita prodotta," *Annali di Economia* 2, no. 1 (1925): 277–328.

31. Echoing Clapahm's argument of four years before, Sraffa cited the "hetero-
geneousness" of a given industry and argued that "to classify the various industries"
as having increasing or decreasing returns was functionally impossible. Sraffa, "The
Laws of Returns under Competitive Conditions," 538.

32. There is an extensive literature on Sraffa's attack on Marshall. See Cristiano,
"Marshall at Cambridge," 23–27; Scott Moss, "The History of the Theory of the Firm
from Marshall to Robinson and Chamberlin: The Source of Positivism in Economics,"
Economica 51, no. 203 (August 1984): 307–318; Neil Hart, "From the Representative
to the Equilibrium Firm: Why Marshall Was Not a Marshallian," in *The Economics
of Alfred Marshall*, ed. Richard Arena and Michel Quéré (Basingstoke, UK: Palgrave
Macmillan, 2003): 158–181. Aslanbeigui and Oakes cover the material with attention
to Pigou: Aslanbeigui and Oakes, *Arthur Cecil Pigou*, 157–164. Maria Cristina Marcuzzo and Annalisa Rosselli argue that Sraffa's fundamental objection was to marginalism itself. Maria Cristina Marcuzzo and Annalisa Rosselli, "Sraffa and His Arguments Against 'Marginism,'" *Cambridge Journal of Economics* 35 (2011): 219–231.

33. A. C. Pigou, "The Laws of Diminishing and Increasing Cost," *Economic Journal* 37, no. 146 (June 1927): 188–197. See also David Collard, "Introduction," in *A.C.
Pigou, Journal Articles 1902-1922*, ed. David Collard (London: Macmillan, 2002):
xxii. The next year, Pigou returned to the theoretical underpinnings of the supply
curve in an agnostic survey of possible theories of supply. It included a conciliatory
gesture of replacing Marshall's notion of the "representative firm" with the "equilibrium firm" which was at equilibrium when its industry was. Collard, "Introduction,"
2002, xxiii; A. C. Pigou, "An Analysis of Supply," *Economic Journal* 38, no. 150 (June
1928): 238–257. Scott Moss writes, "Pigou's equilibrium firm has become the exclusive subject of analysis in the conventional theory of the firm." Moss, "The History of
the Theory of the Firm," 313. On subsequent theorizing at Cambridge, see Dennis P.
O'Brien, "The Theory of the Firm after Marshall," in *The Elgar Companion to Alfred
Marshall*, ed. Tiziano Raffaelli, Giacomo Becattini, Katia Caldari, and Marco Dardi
(Cheltenham, UK: Edward Elgar, 2006): 625–633. See also Nahid Aslanbeigui and
Guy Oakes, *The Provocative Joan Robinson* (Durham, NC: Duke University Press,
2009), chapter 2.

34. Sraffa recast local external effects as having to do with monopoly situations
and had thereby undercut a basic part of Pigou's apparatus of welfare economics.

35. There has been debate over the extent to which Joan Robinson's book, *The
Theory of Imperfect Competition* (1933), was Marshallian. Cristina Marcuzzo sees it

as broadening Marshallian theory to apply to cases of imperfect competition and as a defense against Sraffa's attack on marginalism. See Maria Cristina Marcuzzo, "Joan Robinson and the Three Cambridge Revolutions," *Review of Political Economy* 15, no. 4 (October 2003): 545–560. See also Marcuzzo and Rosselli, "Sraffa and His Arguments Against 'Marginism.'" Others see Robinson as less Marshallian. See Aslanbeigui and Oakes, *The Provocative Joan Robinson*, 93–100; George R. Feiwel, "Joan Robinson Inside and Outside the Stream," in *Joan Robinson and Modern Economic Theory*, ed. George R. Feiwel (London: Macmillan, 1989): 4–10. Dennis P. O'Brien sees Robinson's book as a fundamental break with Marshall. O'Brien, "The Theory of the Firm after Marshall;" D. P. O'Brien, "The Evolution of the Theory of the Firm," in *Methodology, Money and the Firm I* (Aldershot, UK: Edward Elgar, 1994): 254–258.

36. Sir Ernest Benn. "The Teaching of Economics," *Times* (November 17, 1926): 15–16. On Dobb, see Timothy Shenk, *Maurce Dobb: Political Economist* (Houndmills, Basingstoke, UK: Palgrave Macmillan, 2013).

37. A. C. Pigou. "Economics at the Universities," *Times* (November 19, 1926): 15.

38. Ibid.

39. This is Karen Knight's contention. Karen Knight, "A.C. Pigou's *The Theory of Unemployment* and Its Corrigenda: The Letters of Maurice Allen, Arthur L. Bowley, Richard Kahn and Dennis Robertson," Discussion Paper 14-08 (Perth: Business School, University of Western Australia, 2014), http://www.business.uwa .edu.au/_data/assets/rtf_file/0010/2478916/14-08-A.C.-Pigous-The-Theory-of -Unemployment-and-its-Corrigenda.rtf. See also Norikazu Takami, "Pigou and Macroeconomic Models in the 1930s: Models and Math," CHOPE Working Paper 2011–06 (Durham, NC: Center for History of Political Economy, Duke University, August 2011), http://lupus.econ.duke.edu/HOPE/CENTER/Working%20Paper%20Series /takami-pigou-workingpaper2.pdf.

40. A. C. Pigou, "Newspaper Reviews, Economics and Mathematics," in *Essays in Economics* (London: Macmillan, 1952): 117. This essay was originally published in 1941.

41. E. A. G. Robinson, "Pigou, Arthur Cecil (1877–1959), Economist," in *Dictionary of National Biography* Archive, 1971, http://www.oxforddnb.com/view/olddnb /35529.

42. See Robert Skidelsky, *John Maynard Keynes: The Economist as Saviour 1920– 1937* (London: Macmillan, 1992): 405–406.

43. Frank Knight, "Economics at Its Best," *American Economic Review* 16, no. 1 (March 1926): 51–58. On Knight's own complex ethics and politics, see Angus Burgin, "The Radical Conservatism of Frank H. Knight," *Modern Intellectual History* 6, no. 3 (November 2009): 513–538.

44. A. C. Pigou, *The Economics of Welfare*, third ed. (London: Macmillan, 1929): 5.

45. Hugh Dalton to Pigou, March 10, 1951, Crosland Collection, LSE, Crosland 10/2.

46. Pigou, *Wealth and Welfare* (London: Macmillan, 1912): 3

47. Ibid., 488.

48. Pigou, *The Economics of Welfare*, third ed., 6–7.

49. "Industrial Fluctuations," *Spectator* (April 15, 1927): 24. On Pigou's influence on business cycle theory, see David Collard, "Pigou and Modern Business Cycle Theory," *Economic Journal* 106, no. 437 (July 1996): 913.

50. In *Wealth and Welfare* and the first edition of *The Economics of Welfare*, there were three criteria of economic welfare: the size, distribution, and volatility of national income. *Industrial Fluctuations* covered the volatility criterion, which dropped out of the second edition of *The Economics of Welfare* (1924). Pigou had written an essay on the "trade cycle" that was published in 1924 that previewed many of the arguments he would make in the *Industrial Fluctuations*. See A. C. Pigou, "Correctives of the Trade Cycle," in *Is Unemployment Inevitable?* ed. J. J. Astor, A. L. Bowley, Robert Grant, J. H. Jones, et al. (London: Macmillan, 1924).

51. Pigou to Macmillan, June 19, 1927, Macmillan Papers, BL, Add. MSS 55199, 112.

52. Collard, "Pigou and Modern Business Cycle Theory," 920.

53. Part III of *Wealth and Welfare* was modified only slightly to form part VI of the first edition of *The Economics of Welfare* (1920).

54. A. C. Pigou, *Industrial Fluctuations* (London: Macmillan, 1927): 219.

55. Pigou, *Industrial Fluctuations*, 240, 243. On the moral language of Pigou's work on unemployment, see Norikazu Takami, "The Sanguine Science: Historical Contexts of Pigou's Welfare Economics," Discussion Paper 1202 (Kobe, Japan: Graduate School of Economics, Kobe University, 2012), http://www.lib.kobe-u.ac .jp/repository/81003748.pdf.

56. Pigou, *Industrial Fluctuations*, 220. Quoted in Collard, "Pigou and Modern Business Cycle Theory," 915. See, for comparison, Pigou, *Wealth and Welfare*, 403–407.

57. Ibid., 222.

58. Part III of *Wealth and Welfare* and part VI of the first edition of *The Economics of Welfare* offered a more focused inquiry on the variability of the real income of the representative worker. Pigou only briefly surveyed causes of general fluctuations in national income. A notable feature of part III of *Wealth and Welfare* that disappeared in subsequent versions concerned "the variability of the bounty of nature and of foreign demands," in which Pigou argued against tariffs, because they exacerbated fluctuations due to poor domestic harvests. Pigou, *Wealth and Welfare*, 447–452. Though *The Economics of Welfare* treated variations in harvest quality, it did not bear such clear evidence of a free trade agenda. Joseph Schumpeter claimed that "nobody rose to what would have been a most difficult feat of leadership [in business cycle theory]," but Pigou came closest. Schumpeter might have been swayed in his assessment of the field by his reluctance to accept Keynes. Joseph Alois Schumpeter and Elizabeth Brody Schumpeter, *History of Economic Analysis* (London: Allen & Unwin, 1954): 1135.

59. Pigou, *Industrial Fluctuations*, 188.

60. Collard, "Pigou and Modern Business Cycle Theory," 917.

61. Donald Chapman to Hugh Dalton, n.d. [1950s], Hugh Dalton Papers, LSE, Dalton 2/9/18, 51.

62. Pigou, *Industrial Fluctuations*, 289.

63. Ibid., 303–312. See J. J. Astor et al., eds., *Is Unemployment Inevitable?*, 359–382. Bowley was both an editor and the principal author of part IV, "Statistical Inquiries."

64. Pigou, *Industrial Fluctuations*, 307; Pigou, *Wealth and Welfare*, 476–486.

65. Collard, "Pigou and Modern Business Cycle Theory," 915; Pigou, *Industrial Fluctuations*, 320.

66. Pigou, *Industrial Fluctuations*, 225–226. "The heart of the matter is that industrial fluctuations involve evil consequences of such a sort that, if an individual takes certain sorts of action to remove or lessen them, the social gain resulting from his action will not enter at full value into his private profit." Pigou lauded the practice of compelling individuals to subscribe to unemployment insurance, which mitigated the effects of downturns, but which indiviudals would likely not buy unless obliged. Ibid., 329–333.

67. Ibid., 241. When it came to adjustments in bank credit, Pigou saw the prime agent as the semi-public Bank of England rather than the state.

68. On the gold standard, see ibid., 277–280; on wage plasticity, see 282–285. Pigou noted that perfect plasticity could result in unconscionably low wages that were "out of harmony with the moral sense of the time and incompatible with our social structure." Such wage cuts were "out of court, as, in a broad sense, anti-social."

69. A. C. Pigou, *A Study in Public Finance* (London: Macmillan, 1928): v.

70. Hugh Dalton, "A Study in Public Finance by A.C. Pigou," *Economica* 3 no. 23 (June 1928): 216.

71. Jens P. Jensen, "*A Study in Public Finance* by A.C. Pigou," *American Economic Review* 18, no. 4 (December 1928): 770.

72. Dalton, "A Study in Public Finance by A.C. Pigou," 216.

73. Allyn Young, "*A Study in Public Finance* by A.C. Pigou," *Economic Journal* 39, no. 153 (March 1929): 78. On the book's influence, see David Collard, "Introduction," in *A.C. Pigou's Collected Economic Writings, Volume 1*, ed. David Collard (London: Macmillan, 1999): xxvii.

74. In *Public Finance*, Pigou did not continue advocating a capital levy to discharge remaining war debt. Interest on debt payments that accrued to (wealthy) domestic lenders was assessed and taxed by income and death taxes, so that discharging debt would actually save the public comparatively little. Pigou, *Public Finance*, 291. Moreover, a levy, if then instituted, would be "impeded by strong and organized opposition" of large banks and provoke uncertainty about further duties. Ibid., 307.

75. See especially part III, chapter III, and part III, chapter V, ibid., 256–269, 274–285. See also *Industrial Fluctuations*, part I, chapter XIII, and part II, chapter IV. In these chapters, Pigou railed against the inflationary damage of financing government expenditure by bank credit, as had occurred during the war, and stressed the importance of limiting fiduciary notes and returning to the gold standard, policies recommended by the bodies on which he served. He also noted that inflation resulting from the expansion of bank credits represented a very regressive form of taxation, "generally acknowledged to be exceedingly oppressive to the poor." Ibid., 266.

76. Pigou called these unanticipated effects "announcement effects." Today they are commonly called "excess burden."

77. Pigou, *Public Finance*, first ed., 61.

78. Ibid.

79. The discussion of spending constituted only fifty-three pages out of a 323-page book. Furthermore, the type of spending on which Pigou primarily focused—compensation—related specifically to the recent period of wartime requisition. The section was adapted from an article written immediately after the war. A. C. Pigou, "Problems of Compensation," *Economic Journal* 35, no. 140 (December 1925): 578. In the third edition of *Public Finance* (1946), Pigou devoted an additional fifty pages to government spending, responding to new conceptions of the government as an economic actor arising from the Great Depression. A. C. Pigou, *A Study in Public Finance*, third (revised) ed. (London: Macmillan, 1949). Pigou, *Public Finance*, first ed., 1–53.

80. The rationale against trade duties was deployed by Pigou and the thirteen other economists in the letter to the *Times* in 1903. F. Barnstable, A. L. Bowley, E. Cannan, L. Courtney, F. Y. Edgeworth, C. K. Gonner, A. Marshall, et al., "Professors of Economics and the Tariff Question," *Times* (August 15, 1903): 4. Quoting Sidgwick, he affirmed, "I do not think we can reasonably expect our actual governments to be wise and strong enough to keep their protective interference within due limits." Pigou, *Public Finance*, 227. Pigou quoted Sidgwick's *Political Economy*. On liberalism and unearned income, see Fuad Shebab, *Progressive Taxation: A Study in the Development of the Progressive Principle in the British Income Tax* (Oxford: Clarendon, 1953), especially chapter 13.

81. On death duties, see Pigou, *Public Finance*, 138–146; on monopolies, see 154–155; on windfalls, see 156–164.

82. Ibid.,133.

83. Pigou to Macmillan, September 1, 1927, Macmillan Papers, BL, Add. MSS 55199, 117.

84. A. C. Pigou, *The Policy of Land Taxation* (London: Longmans, Green, and Co.): 20.

85. Pigou to J. M. Keynes, n.d. [1929] Keynes Papers, KCA, JMK/PP/45/254/32.

86. Pigou to Macmillan, September 1, 1927, Macmillan Papers, BL, Add. MSS 55199, 117.

87. Emphasis added. A. C. Pigou, "The Function of Economic Analysis," in *Economic Essays and Addresses*, A. C. Pigou and Dennis Robertson (London: P. S. King & Son, 1931): 18.

88. A. C. Pigou, "Presidential Address: Looking Back from 1939," *Economic Journal* 49, no. 194 (June 1939): 219.

89. David Collard, "Cambridge After Marshall," in *Generations of Economists* (Abingdon, Oxon, UK: Routledge, 2011): 57; Aslanbeigui and Oakes, *The Provocative Joan Robinson*, 90–92.

90. Defining what constituted an "economist" is not a straightforward task. Collard, for instance, does not include Ifor Leslie Evans, J. H. Clapham, or Ernest Benians as economists, but presumably counts them as historians or political scientists, even though they taught for the Tripos and held college positions that included the teaching of economics. David Collard, "Cambridge After Marshall," 54.

91. C. W. Guillebaud, "The Variorum Edition of Alfred Marshall's Principles of Economics," *Economics Journal* 71, no. 284 (December 1961): 677–690.

92. They were Gerald Shove (who was also a fellow of King's), Frederick Lavington, Dennis Robertson, Philip Sargent Florence, C. W. Guillebaud, Austin Robinson, and Maurice Dobb. Collard, "Cambridge After Marshall," 58–59. Of the three remaining economists, two, Leonard Alston and Marjorie Tappan-Holland, did not teach for the Tripos. The only economist Collard identifies who was not trained at Cambridge but gave lectures for the Tripos was George Udny Yule, who was more a statistician than an economist.

93. Pigou taught this course continuously from 1908 to 1930, with the exception of two years before the publication of his *Wealth and Welfare*. Collard, "Introduction," 1999, xxiv. Collard writes that Pigou taught the course from 1909 to 1930, but he actually started in Michaelmas term, 1908. See "Lectures Proposed by the Special Board for Economics and Politics, 1908-9," *Cambridge University Reporter* 39, no. 3 (October 10, 1908): 46.

94. See A. W. Coats, "Sociological Aspects of British Economic Thought (ca. 1880–1930)," *Journal of Political Economy* 75, no. 5 (October 1967): 706–729; Ralf Dahrendorf, *LSE: A History of the London School of Economics and Political Science 1895–1995* (Oxford: Oxford University Press, 1995): 210–221.

95. Pigou to Dennis Robertson, n.d. (1922), The Papers of Dennis Robertson, Trinity College Archives, Cambridge, United Kingdom (hereafter TCA), ROBERTSON/C/1/4; A. C. Pigou, "The Value of Money," *Quarterly Journal of Economics* 32, no. 1 (November 1917): 38–65.

96. Young, "*A Study in Public Finance* by A.C. Pigou," 78.

97. Pigou was angered to learn in 1927 that Keynes's 1924 election had been unsuccessful because of Keynes's treatment of France in his *Economic Consequences of the Peace*. In a twist of fate, the then-president of the academy was none other than Arthur Balfour, the man who had recused himself for Pigou's 1908 professorial election. Donald Winch, "Pigoviana," last modified 2014, Economists' Papers, http://www.economistspapers.org.uk/?p=1026.

98. Pigou, "The Function of Economic Analysis," 1–3.

99. J. S. Stamp, "Industrial Fluctuations by A.C. Pigou," *Economic Journal* 37, no. 147 (September 1927): 418. Jacob Perlman, "*Industrial Fluctuations* by A. C. Pigou; *Business Cycles and Business Measurements. Studies in Quantitative Economics* by Carl Snyder; *Forecasting Business Conditions* by Charles O. Hardy; Garfield V. Cox," *Journal of Land & Public Utility Economics* 3, no. 4 (November 1927): 423; L.R.C. [L. R. Connor], "*A Study in Public Finance* by A. C. Pigou," *Journal of the Royal Statistical Society* 91, no. 3 (1928): 412.

100. Anon., "*A Study in Public Finance* by A. C. Pigou," *Annals of the American Academy of Political and Social Science* 141 (January 1929): 281. See also Warren M. Persons, "Pigou, Industrial Fluctuations," *Quarterly Journal of Economics* 42, no. 4 (August 1928): 669.

101. Pigou and Robertson, "Those Empty Boxes," 16.

Chapter 6: Paradigms Lost

1. Joan Robinson, *Economics Is a Serious Subject* (Cambridge: W. Heffer & Sons Limited, 1932).

2. Barbara Wootton, *Lament for Economics* (London: George Allen & Unwin, 1938); Lionel Robbins, *An Essay on the Nature and Significance of Economic Science*, third edition (London: Macmillan, 1984).

3. Pigou to Philip Noel-Baker, n.d., [probably June 1948], The Papers of Baron Noel-Baker, CCA, NBKR 9/58/1. Robbins attended the local state secondary school, Southall Country School. See Susan Howson, *Lionel Robbins* (Cambridge: Cambridge University Press, 2011), chapter 1.

4. Joan Robinson, "List of Dedicatees of *Economics Is a Serious Subject*," n.d. (1932), The Papers of Joan Violet Robinson, KCA, JVR/1/2/2. The pamphlet was ultimately dedicated to "The Fundamental Pessimist," a reference to Piero Sraffa. Robinson, *Economics Is a Serious Subject*, 2.

5. A. C. Pigou, "Presidential Address: Looking Back from 1939." *Economic Journal* 49, no. 194 (June 1939): 221.

6. Pigou to J. M. Keynes, n.d. (December 1925), The Papers of John Maynard Keynes, KCA, JMK/TM/1/2/50.

7. Correspondence Relating to the *Treatise on Money*, Keynes Papers, KCA, JMK/TM/1/2.

8. Dennis Robertson to J. M. Keynes, August 30, 1925, Keynes Papers, KCA, JMK/TM/1/2/33.

9. A. C. Pigou, "The Value of Money," *Quarterly Journal of Economics* 32, no. 1 (November 1917): 38–65. The equation determined the demand for money through the price level and national income. Mathematically, this was expressed as $M^d = k \cdot P \cdot Y$. Money demand was a function of the price level, P, the national income, Y, and the "Cambridge k," the proportion of the national income held in cash that would not be used for transactions. Since in equilibrium, demand equalled supply, the Cambridge k, by defining demand, the equation suggested that it led supply.

10. Keynes determined the price level for consumption goods and production goods completely differently. Pascal Bridel and Bruna Ingrao, "Managing Cambridge Economics: The Correspondence between Keynes and Pigou" in *Economists in Cambridge: A Study Through Their Correspondence*, ed. Maria Cristina Marcuzzo and Annalisa Rosselli (London: Routledge, 2005): 159.

11. J. M. Keynes to Pigou, May 15, 1931, Keynes Papers, KCA, JMK/TM/1/2.

12. It is this new perception to which Robert Skidelsky alludes in his subtitle for the middle volume of his biography on Keynes: *The Economist as Saviour*. Robert Skidelsky, *John Maynard Keynes: The Economist as Saviour 1920–1937* (London: Macmillan, 1992).

13. See J. M. Keynes, *Economic Consequences of the Peace* (London: Macmillan, 1919). In 1929, Keynes and H. D. Henderson authored a pamphlet titled *Can Lloyd George Do It?*, referring to tackling unemployment. The short piece was intended to

support the Liberal candidate in the 1929 general election. J. M. Keynes and H. D. Henderson, *Can Lloyd George Do It?: An Examination of the Liberal Pledge* (London: The Nation and Athenaeum, 1929).

14. See Barry Eichengreen, "The British Economy Between the Wars," in *The Cambridge Economic History of Modern Britain*, ed. Roderick Floud and Paul Johnson (Cambridge: Cambridge University Press, 2004): 322–328; W. R. Garside, *British Unemployment 1919–1939: A Study in Public Policy* (Cambridge: Cambridge University Press, 1920): 3–28; John Stevenson and Chris Cook, *The Sump: Society and Politics During the Depression* (London: Jonathan Cape, 1977): 54–73.

15. Garside, *British Unemployment 1919–1939*, 5.

16. See also Labour's 1929 election manifesto, Labour Party, *Labour's Appeal to the Nation* (London: Labour Party, 1929). On Labour's economic policy, see Garside, *British Unemployment 1919–1939*, 318–336; More generally, see Robert W. D. Boyce, *British Capitalism at the Crossroads: A Study in Politics, Economics, and International Relations* (Cambridge: Cambridge University Press, 1987).

17. See Eichengreen, "The British Economy Between the Wars"; Charles P. Kindleberger, *The World in Depression, 1929–1939* (Berkeley: University of California Press, 1973), particularly chapters 6 and 7.

18. As a percentage of total workers, 8 percent were unemployed in 1929, 12.3 percent in 1930, and over 15 percent for the next three years. Unemployed insured workers were more troubling to government administrators, because the government was paying their stipends. Garside, *British Unemployment 1919–1939*, 5.

19. These numbers reflect unemployment rates among insured workers. For comparison, rates in northeastern England jumped from 13.7 percent in 1929 to 28.5 percent in 1932. Ibid., 11.

20. H. D. Henderson to J. M. Keynes, March 12, 1930, Keynes Papers, KCA, JMK/EA/1. On the EAC, see Susan Howson and Donald Winch, *The Economic Advisory Council 1930–1939* (Cambridge: Cambridge University Press, 1977): 46–72.

21. J. M. Keynes to Ramsay MacDonald, July 10, 1930, Keynes Papers, KCA, JMK/EA/1/31.

22. J. M. Keynes to Ramsay MacDonald, July 10, 1930, Keynes Papers, KCA, JMK/EA/1/32.

23. Hugh Dalton, *Call Back Yesterday: Memoirs 1887–1931* (London: F. Muller, 1953): 60.

24. Pigou to J. M. Keynes, n.d., [August 1930], Keynes Papers, KCA, JMK/EA/1/64.

25. The *Manchester Guardian* wrote, "Mr. Keynes drew up a report embodying his new Protectionist theories." However, by contemporary standards, they were not radically protectionist, especially considering the subsequent level of tariffs. In February 1932, the Import Duties Act taxed manufactured imports at 10 percent, as Keynes had suggested. The Import Duties Advisory Committee doubled the rates the same year. After this, the duties on various individual goods were raised. Imported steel was taxed at 50 percent by 1935. "Wages and Tariffs: Economists Differ: Reports to the Government," *Manchester Guardian* (December 9, 1930): 11. See also Tim Rooth,

British Protectionism and the International Economy: Overseas Commercial Policy in the 1930s (Cambridge: Cambridge University Press, 1993); Howson, *Lionel Robbins*, 178–194; Frank Trentmann, *Free Trade Nation: Commerce, Consumption, and Civil Society in Modern Britain* (Oxford: Oxford University Press, 2008): 337–340.

26. Howson and Winch note that "Pigou's oblique opposition to Keynes took the form of an unwillingness to discuss the committee's brief in any terms other than those which he had become accustomed to using in his writings. . . . There was no direct antagonism between the two men but there does seem to have been a distinct coolness, attributable perhaps to a clash of intellectual styles." Howson and Winch, *The Economic Advisory Council*, 64.

27. Keynes recognized the EAC as a mechanism whereby economists traded on their scientific reputations to advocate for policies. Internal discussion and presentation to policymakers were to be distinct. In 1939 he wrote to Stamp of a particular report, noting that despite the "wild," inappropriate use of statistics, "so far as action is concerned," the report was "just what we ought to tell them [the government]." J. M. Keynes to Josiah Stamp, July 25, 1939, Keynes Papers, KCA, JMK/EA/1/195.

28. Keynes convinced Hemming that Robbins should not need to sign recommendations with which he disagreed. Keynes wrote, "I think that there is no doubt that Robbins entertains a genuine scruple of conscience and there is a presumption in favor of giving way to such scruples if no serious harm results." J. M. Keynes to A. F. Hemming, October 22, 1930, Keynes Papers, KCA, JMK/EA/1/93. See Howson, *Lionel Robbins*, 189–193.

29. As Terence Hutchison noted, aside from the issue of the tariff, Pigou and Keynes did not have radically different views on what steps might be taken to reduce unemployment in 1930. Terence Hutchison, *On Revolutions and Progress in Economic Knowledge* (Cambridge: Cambridge University Press, 1978): 178–182.

30. Ben Pimlott, ed. *The Political Diary of Hugh Dalton 1918–49, 1945–1960* (London: Jonathan Cape, 1986): 123–124.

31. Quoted in Howson, *Lionel Robbins*, 192.

32. Howson and Winch, *The Economic Advisory Council 1930–1939*, 63–64, 225–226. Pigou's dissent was revealed in an anonymous letter to the *Manchester Guardian*, which exposed the schisms between Keynes and antiprotectionists, including Robbins and William Beveridge. See also Nahid Aslanbeigui, "On the Demise of Pigovian Economics," *Southern Economic Journal* 65, no. 3 (January 1990): 618–619.

33. See Howson and Winch, *The Economic Advisory Council*, 63. After his experience with the EAC, throughout the Depression, Pigou sought to remain the picture of the objective authority who spoke without consideration of political fortunes. See Evidence Given By A.C. Pigou to the Macmillan Committee, 1930, Robbins Collection, LSE, Robbins 1/3, 6; Correspondence between A.C. Pigou and J.M. Keynes having to do with the Committee of Economists, September 26–29, 1930, Keynes Papers, KCA, JMK/EA/1, 68–69.

34. Pigou's action did not signal a return to advising the government, since his letters were specifically addressed to the public, which in aggregate could solve the slump by spending more.

35. J. M. Keynes to Edwin Cannan, October 13, 1932, Cannan Collection, LSE, Cannan/1032/212; Edited Typescript by Pigou, October 13, 1932, Cannan Collection, LSE, Cannan/1032/213–215. The article appeared in the *Times* four days later. D. H. Macgregor, A. C. Pigou, J. M. Keynes, et al., "Private Spending: Money for Private Investment," *Times* (October 17, 1932): 13.

36. William Beveridge also held out because of hesitance to comment on anything with political implications. William Beveridge to Edwin Cannan, October 18, 1932, Cannan Collection, LSE, Cannan/1032/230. See also Edwin Cannan to J.M. Keynes, October 14, 1932, Cannan Collection, LSE, Cannan/1032/221; Edwin Cannan to Pigou, October 25, 1932, Cannan Collection, LSE, Cannan/1032/252.

37. Pigou to Edwin Cannan, October 27, 1932, Cannan Collection, LSE, Cannan/1032/258.

38. See Barry Eichengreen, "Keynes and Protection," *Journal of Economic History* 44, no. 2 (June 1984): 364–366.

39. See John Stevenson and Chris Cook, *The Slump: Society and Politics During the Depression* (London: Jonathan Cape, 1977): 54–73; Clark, *The Keynesian Revolution in the Making*, 174–181. In arguably his most concrete policy suggestion of the period, after the EAC's report, Pigou wrote to Philip Snowden to suggest raising income taxes and reducing employment taxes so as to stimulate employment. Pigou's suggestion was rejected. "Surely this ignores all practical considerations . . . no Chancellor of the Exchequer is likely to add more to direct taxation at this juncture," ran an internal Treasury memo. Pigou to Philip Snowden, February 21, 1931, Chancellor of the Exchequer's Office, TNA, T 172/1763, 26. P.J. Gregg to R.C.M. Hopkins, March 6, 1931, Chancellor of the Exchequer's Office, TNA, T 172/1763, 5.

40. See Stevenson and Cook, *The Slump*, 167–194.

41. From the *Daily Telegraph*, November 1, 1932, quoted in Stevenson and Cook, *The Slump*, 177.

42. Pigou to J. M. Keynes, n.d. [1930], Keynes Papers, KCA, JMK/PP/45/254/41. Though college life was largely insulated, as the greater part of college endowments were concentrated in real estate, the part of King's endowment that was invested in the market and managed by Keynes took a nearly 15 percent dip in 1930 and slid by a further 10 percent in 1931. See David Chambers and Elroy Dimson, "John Maynard Keynes, Investment Innovator," *Journal of Economic Perspectives* 27, no. 3 (Summer 2013): 216.

43. "Lectures Proposed by the Board of the Faculty of Economics and Politics," *Cambridge University Reporter* 61, no. 3 (October 1, 1930): 72–73.

44. Pigou to Macmillan, April 24, 1933, Macmillan Papers, BL, Add. MSS 55199, 163.

45. A. C. Pigou, *The Theory of Unemployment* (London: Macmillan, 1933): v.

46. Ibid., 156.

47. Ibid., 155.

48. Ibid., 125–126. State-provided bounties on workers functioned essentially the same as wage cuts from the perspective of the employers.

49. See Nahid Aslanbeigui, "Pigou's Inconsistencies or Keynes's Misconceptions?" *History of Political Economy* 24, no. 2 (1992): 418. On confusion about the *Theory*,

see Robert Leeson and Daniel Schiffman, "A Reassessment of Pigou' Theory of Unemployment: Part I—The Nonmonetary Economy," working paper (Ariel, Israel: Ariel University Center, 2014), http://www.ariel.ac.il/sites/dschiffman/Reassessment.pdf.

50. Pigou, *The Theory of Unemployment*, 28.

51. Ibid., 106. Pigou argued that if all individuals were wage earners, a fall in money wages would be offset by a fall in prices, so that real wages would not fall. However, in reality, the existence of non-wage earners, whose incomes accounted for about 2/3 of national income, allowed money wages to drag real wages with them (100–101). A percentage reduction in the money wage rate resulted in a percentage reduction "EmEr times as large in the real rate of wage," where E_m was elasticity of money demand and E_r was elasticity of real demand for labor. Pigou estimated that the elasticity of money demand was $-20/13$, and the elasticity of real demand for labor was -4. So, a 10 percent cut in money wages would result in a 3.84 percent cut in real wages and a corresponding 15 percent boost to aggregate labor demand.

52. J.H.R., "*The Theory of Unemployment* by A.C. Pigou," *Journal of the Royal Statistical Society* 97, no. 1 (1934): 175. Reviews noted Pigou's rigor. Constantino Bresciani-Turroni, "*The Theory of Unemployment*, by A.C. Pigou," *Weltwirtschaftliches Archiv* 40 Bd. (1943): 169–173; Carlo Pagni, "*The Theory of Unemployment* by A.C. Pigou," *Giornale degli Economisti e Rivista di Statistica*, Serie Quarta 75, no. 8 (August 1935): 675–676. See also David Collard, "Introduction," in *A.C. Pigou's Collected Economic Writings, Volume 1*, ed. David Collard (London: Macmillan, 1999): xxxii.

53. Edison L. Bowers, "*The Theory of Unemployment* by A.C. Pigou," *American Economic Review* 24, no. 2 (June 1934): 282; S. E. Harris, "Professor Pigou's Theory of Unemployment," *Quarterly Journal of Economics* 49, no. 2 (February 1935): 286.

54. See Karen Knight, "A.C. Pigou's *The Theory of Unemployment* and Its Corrigenda: The Letters of Maurice Allen, Arthur L. Bowley, Richard Kahn and Dennis Robertson," Discussion Paper 14-08 (Perth: Business School, University of Western Australia, 2014), http://www.business.uwa.edu.au/__data/assets/rtf_file/0010 /2478916/14-08-A.C.-Pigous-The-Theory-of-Unemployment-and-its-Corrigenda .rtf. Aslanbeigui, "Pigou's Inconsistencies or Keynes's Misconceptions"; Collard, "Introduction." Others go further, arguing that Keynes's work was not novel in a Pigovian context. See, for example, T. W. Hutchinson, *On Revolutions and Progress in Economic Knowledge* (Cambridge: Cambridge University Press, 1978): 190; Jürg Niehans, *A History of Economic Theory: Classic Contributions 1720–1980* (Baltimore: Johns Hopkins University Press, 1990): 245–255. There have also been defenses of Keynes's position on Pigou. See Michael E. Brady, "A Note on the Keynes-Pigou Controversy," *History of Political Economy* 26, no. 4 (Winter 1994): 697–705; Allin Cottrell, "Keynes's Appendix to Chapter 19: A Reader's Guide," *History of Political Economy* 26, no. 4 (Winter 1994): 681–695; Allin Cottrell, "Brady on Pigou and Keynes: Comment," *History of Political Economy* 26, no. 4 (Winter 1994): 707–711. Gerhard Michael Ambrosi comprehensively tracks how Keynes's work on unemployment was inspired by and reactive to Pigou's. In this way, Ambrosi claims, *The General Theory* is "post-Pigovian." Gerhard Michael Ambrosi, "Keynes, Pigou, and the *General Theory*"

(lecture, University of Cambridge, Cambridge, UK, October 22, 2008). See also Ambrosi, *Keynes, Pigou, and the Cambridge Keynesians: Authenticity and Analytical Perspective in the Keynes-Classics Debate* (Houndmills, Basingstoke, UK: Palgrave Macmillan, 2003).

55. J. M. Keynes to D. H. Robertson, September 5, 1933, The Papers of Dennis Robertson, TCA, ROBERTSON/C2/3/51.

56. J. M. Keynes to R. G. Hawtrey, July 18, 1930, Keynes Papers, KCA, JMK/TM/1/2/33/171. Both Keynes and the "classics" agreed that "hoarding" money (e.g., taking it out of circulation by stowing it under a mattress) would hurt the economy. As the money supply dwindled, reduced spending dragged the economy down. However, in a stylized version of the "classical" system, there would never be such a thing as excess *savings* (money deposited in a bank), since the financial industry would ensure that this money was loaned out and invested, a process it would mediate by lowering the interest rate. Keynes's theory suggested that there could be excess savings, because in times of crisis, a very low interest rate would not be sufficient incentive for firms to invest.

57. See Skidelsky, *John Maynard Keynes: The Economist as Saviour*, chapters 12 and 13. For a more complete exposition of the Keynes-Pigou debate, see Ambrosi, *Keynes, Pigou and the Cambridge Keynesians*.

58. This divergence was "more than can be discussed in a letter." J. M. Keynes to John Hicks, August 1933, in O. F. Hamouda, *John R. Hicks: The Economist's Economist* (Oxford: Blackwell, 1993): 16–17.

59. J.M. Keynes to D.H. Robertson, September 5, 1933, Robertson Papers, TCA, ROBERTSON/C2/3/51.

60. Ibid.

61. Pigou, *The Theory of Unemployment*, v.

62. Ibid., 28.

63. Collard, "Introduction," xxxi–xxxiii. See also Ambrosi, *Keynes, Pigou, and the Cambridge Keynesians*, 57–71.

64. Peter Clarke, *The Keynesian Revolution and Its Economic Consequences* (Cheltenham, UK: Edward Elgar, 1998): 97.

65. See Hutchison, *On Revolutions and Progress in Economic Knowledge*, chapter 6; Clarke, *The Keynesian Revolution*, 79–80.

66. Pigou, *The Theory of Unemployment*, 250.

67. Ibid.

68. Pigou, *Wealth and Welfare*, 482–486. Pigou elaborated on this in chapter 9 of *Unemployment* (1913). Pigou, *Unemployment* (London: Williams and Norgate, 1913). However, in the 1910s, Pigou was not advocating for an activist fiscal policy whose magnitude was designed to curb unemployment. Rather, following from the Minority Report of the Royal Commission on the Poor Law (1909), he argued for adjusting the timing of government spending already deemed necessary so as to mitigate unemployment. See *The Minority Report of the Poor Law Commission* (London: Fabian Society, 1909).

69. Pigou, *The Theory of Unemployment,* 213.

70. As Amartya Sen argues, Pigou's work on unemployment put greater stress on inequality than did Keynes's. Amartya Sen, "Capitalism Beyond the Crisis," *New York Review of Books* (March 26, 2009), accessed November 20, 2014, http://www.nybooks.com/articles/2009/03/26/capitalism-beyond-the-crisis/.

71. For Hutchison, Keynes and his acolytes' version of Pigou was vital for the process of mythologizing the so-called Keynesian revolution. "Revolutions," Hutchison wrote, "depend upon and create their own myths." Hutchison, *On Revolutions and Progress in Economic Knowledge,* 175. See also Ambrosi, *Keynes, Pigou and Cambridge Keynesians,* especially part I, chapters 5 and 6.

72. Aslanbeigui, "Pigou's Inconsistencies or Keynes's Misconceptions," 414. See also Hawtrey's review, R. G. Hawtrey, "*The Theory of Unemployment* by Professor A.C. Pigou," *Economica,* New Series 1, no. 2 (May 1934): 147–166. Hawtrey was also one of the leading scholars on the business cycle. See also Ralph Hawtrey, *Currency and Credit* (London: Longmans, Green, and Company, 1919).

73. R. F. Harrod, "Professor Pigou's Theory of Unemployment," *Economic Journal* 44, no. 173 (March 1934): 19.

74. Pigou, *The Theory of Unemployment,* vii.

75. D. H. Robertson to J. M. Keynes, September 15, 1933, Robertson Papers, TCA, ROBERTSON/C2/3/47. Walter Layton was a former economics lecturer at Cambridge, a fellow of Gonville and Caius College, and the editor of the *Economist.* See David Hubback, *No Ordinary Press Baron: A Life of Walter Layton* (London: Weidenfeld & Nicolson, 1985).

76. Joan Robinson, *The Economics of Imperfect Competition* (London: Macmillan, 1933). See Nahid Aslanbeigui and Guy Oakes, *The Provocative Joan Robinson* (Durham, NC: Duke University Press, 2009): 89–155.

77. Pigou to Joan Robinson, n.d. [probably 1933], Joan Robinson Papers, KCA, JVR/7/347/28.

78. Pigou to Austin Robinson, n.d. [June 1934], Joan Robinson Papers, KCA, JVR/7/347, 36. The parents ultimately settled on Ann.

79. Aslanbeigui and Oakes, *The Provocative Joan Robinson,* 116–117.

80. Quoted in ibid. R. F. Kahn to Joan Robinson, February 10–13, 1933; Joan Robinson to R. F. Kahn, January 23, 1933.

81. Joan Robinson, "List of Dedicatees of 'Economics is a Serious Subject,'" n.d. (1932), Joan Robinson Papers, KCA, JVR/1/2/2.

82. Aslanbeigui and Oakes, *The Provocative Joan Robinson,* 186–187. See also Maria Cristina Marcuzzo and Annalisa Rosselli, eds., *Economists in Cambridge: A Study Through Their Correspondence* (London: Routledge, 2005).

83. See Correspondence between R.F. Kahn and A.C. Pigou, 1947–1953, The Papers of Richard Ferdinand Kahn, KCA/RFK/13/83 and RFK/19/3. On Kahn and Keynes, see Skidelsky, *John Maynard Keynes: The Economist as Saviour,* 287–289.

84. R. F. Kahn, "Some Notes on Ideal Output," *Economic Journal* 45, no. 1 (March 1935): 1–35. Paul Samuelson called this work "very much in the Cambridge tradition,

reflecting Alfred Marshall and A.C. Pigou." Paul Samuelson, "Richard Kahn: His Welfare Economics and Lifetime Achievement," *Cambridge Journal of Economics* 18, no. 1 (February 1994): 55–56.

85. Aslanbeigui and Oakes, *The Provocative Joan Robinson*, 185–189. Pigou published a short comment on imperfect competition in 1933. A. C. Pigou, "A Note on Imperfect Competition," *Economic Journal* 43, no. 169 (March 1933): 108–112.

86. Pigou to Philip Noel-Baker, n.d. (May 1945), Noel-Baker Papers, CCA, NBKR 9/58/2. Pigou's economics have also been attacked as sexist, as outlined in Nahid Aslanbeigui, "Rethinking Pigou's Misogyny," *Eastern Economic Journal* 23, no. 3 (Summer 1997): 301–316. See also Nerio Naldi, "The Prof and His Younger Colleagues: Pigou and the Correspondence with Kahn, Kaldor, J. Robinson and Sraffa," in *Economists in Cambridge: A Study Through Their Correspondence, 1907–1946*, ed. Maria Cristina Marcuzzo and Annalisa Rosselli (Oxford: Routledge, 2005): 331–349.

87. Hicks came from comparatively humble origins; his father was a local newspaper journalist. Hicks went to Balliol, Oxford, on a mathematical scholarship. There he received an economics education developed from Pigovian and Marshallian discipline-building efforts. He began lecturing at the LSE in 1926.

88. John Hicks, "Recollections and Documents," *Economica* 4, no. 157 (February 1973): 4.

89. Aslanbeigui and Oakes note that the economic historian C. F. Fay was also opposed to the spread of Keynesianism at Cambridge. Nahid Aslanbeigui and Guy Oakes, *Arthur Cecil Pigou* (Houndmills, Basingstoke, UK: Palgrave Macmillan, 2015): 265.

90. Pigou to Dennis Robertson, n.d. [1934–5], Robertson Papers, TCA, ROBERTSON/C7/6. The book they co-authored was *Economic Essays and Addresses*.

91. Hamouda, *John R. Hicks*, 20–25.

92. John R. Hicks, *The Theory of Wages* (London: Macmillan, 1932).

93. On *The General Theory's* genesis and spread, see Peter Clarke, *The Keynesian Revolution in the Making 1924–1936* (Oxford: Clarendon Press, 1988), part IV.

94. Of the economists of his own generation, Keynes only shared proofs with Ralph Hawtrey, not with Pigou, Robertson, or H. D. Henderson. As Robert Skidelsky puts it, "the battle-lines were forming up." Skidelsky, *John Maynard Keynes: The Economist as Saviour*, 532, 572–593.

95. Part IV of the book addressed this issue. Pigou, *Theory of Unemployment*, 185–246. See also Norikazu Takami, "How Pigou Converted to IS-LM: Pigou's Macroeconomic Theories in the 1930s and 40s" (presentation, History of Economic Society Annual Meeting, South Bend, IN, June 17–20, 2011), http://hes2011.nd.edu/assets/42969/takami.pdf.

96. J. M. Keynes, *The General Theory of Employment Interest and Money* (New York: Harcourt, 1964): 378. See also chapter 15 of the same volume.

97. Pigou thought it "more suited to students, as against experts." Pigou to Macmillan, December 5,1934, Macmillan Papers, BL, Add. MSS 55199, 173–174.

98. Frederic Benham, "*The Economics of Stationary States* by A.C. Pigou," *Economica* 3, no. 9 (February 1936): 89.

99. For a detailed appraisal, see Ambrosi, *Keynes, Pigou and Cambridge Keynesians*, chapters 10 and 11. See also Aslanbeigui, "Pigou's Inconsistencies or Keynes's Misconceptions?"

100. Keynes, *The General Theory*, 274.

101. Ibid. Keynes saw Pigou's model as sloppy and underdetermined. In Keynes's reading, Pigou's theory depended solely on a single variable, the number of wage workers (men working in "wage-good" industries). "The pitfalls" of this "pseudo-mathematical method . . . could not be better illuminated. For it is no good to admit later on that there are in fact other variables, and yet to proceed without re-writing everything that has been written up to that point." Ibid., 275–276.

102. Keynes continued, "the purpose of the concept of the elasticity of the real demand for labour in the aggregate is to show by how much *full* employment will rise or fall." Ibid., 275.

103. Ibid., 275–278.

104. Ibid., 129.

105. Ibid., 7.

106. Keynes was the editor of the *Economic Journal* at the time. "Examination Papers," May 1905–September 1905, Keynes Papers, KCA, JMK/UA/3/1; "Reports to the Fellowship Electors," n.d. [1907–09], Keynes Papers, KCA, JMK/TP/4.

107. A. C. Pigou, "Mr. J.M. Keynes's *General Theory of Employment, Interest and Money*," *Economica*, New Series 3, no. 10 (May 1936): 115–116.

108. Ibid., 117–118. There was some falloff in the correspondence between the two during this period. Bridel and Ingrao, "Managing Cambridge Economics," 150–151.

109. J. M. Keynes to Bernard Shaw, January 1, 1935, quoted in Peter Clarke, *The Keynesian Revolution*, 75; J. M. Keynes to R. F. Harrod, August 27, 1935, quoted in Clarke, *The Keynesian Revolution*, 75.

110. Pigou, "Mr. J.M. Keynes's *General Theory of Employment, Interest and Money*," 115.

111. Ibid.

112. See Skidelsky, *John Maynard Keynes: The Economist as Saviour*, 610–624; Hamouda, *John R. Hicks*.

113. There is a massive literature on the so-called Keynesian revolution. On the history of the notion of the Keynesian revolution itself, see Peter Clarke, "Keynes's *General Theory*: A Problem for Historians," in *The Keynesian Revolution and its Economic Consequences* (Cheltenham, UK: Edward Elgar, 1998): 75–113, and Roger E. Backhouse, "The Keynesian Revolution," in *The Cambridge Companion to Keynes*, ed. Roger E. Backhouse and Bradley W. Bateman (Cambridge: Cambridge University Press, 2006): 19–38. Following Terence Hutchison, Backhouse contends that much of the "Keynesian revolution" was self-created by Keynes and his followers. Hutchison, *On Revolutions and Progress in Economic Knowledge*, 178–182. The book that popularized the notion of the revolution was: Lawrence Klein, *The Keynesian Revolution* (New York: Macmillan, 1947). Robert Cord, *Reinterpreting the Keynesian Revolution* (New York: Routledge, 2013) presents a more up-to-date analysis. On the immediate reception of *The General Theory*, see chapter 16 in Skidelsky, *John Maynard Keynes:*

The Economist as Saviour 1920–1937. For a more intimate picture of Keynesian Cambridge, see Maria Cristina Marcuzzo and Annalisa Rosselli, eds., *Economists in Cambridge: A Study Through Their Correspondence*. For a technical analysis, see Ambrosi, *Keynes, Pigou and Cambridge Keynesians*.

114. The relevant letters can be found in *The Collected Writings of John Maynard Keynes*, vol. 14 (Cambridge: Cambridge University Press, 1992): 255–268. Bridel and Ingrao, "Managing Cambridge Economics," 156–161.

115. In contrast, Keynes held that unemployment would only be affected by a change in consumption, the efficiency of capital, or in liquidity preference (i.e., how much cash people would choose to keep on hand). See Collard, "Introduction," xxxv.

116. See Nicholas Kaldor to J. M. Keynes, November 1, 1937, The Papers of Nicholas Kaldor, KCA, NK/3/30/118, 97. See also Aslanbeigui and Oakes, *Arthur Cecil Pigou*, 230–238; and Nahid Aslanbigui and Guy Oakes, "The Editor as Scientific Revolutionary: Keynes, *The Economic Journal*, and the Pigou Affair, 1936–1938," *Journal of the History of Economic Thought* 29, no. 1 (March 2007): 15–48. Aslanbeigui and Oakes argue that Keynes and Kahn manipulated Pigou and Kaldor so as to suggest to a wider public that Pigou had capitulated. Though Aslanbeigui and Oakes's account is a touch dramatic, the evidence is strong that Keynes and his confidants employed private tactics to discredit Pigou's article. Aslanbeigui and Oakes cast Pigou as a victim, and certainly not as a strong, self-confident force. Kaldor did oppose Pigou: "I have discovered," Kaldor wrote in 1937, "that I actually made too much concession to Pigou." Nicholas Kaldor to J. M. Keynes, October 27, 1937, Kaldor Papers, KCA, NK/3/30/118, 97. Joan Robinson and her husband Austin were also against Pigou. "He is gone so far that you have to rationalise him to some extent even to find a coherent error," Joan Robinson wrote Keynes. In Collard, "Introduction," xxxvi. See also Takami, "How Pigou Converted to IS-LM."

117. Collard, "Introduction," xxxv–xxxvi.

118. Pigou to Nicholas Kaldor, n.d. [September 1937], Kaldor Papers, KCA, NK/3/30/118, 114.

119. Ibid.

120. See correspondence in *The Collected Writings of John Maynard Keynes*, vol. XIV, 243–268.

121. Ingrao and Bridel, "Managing Cambridge Economics," 158.

122. Pigou to Philip Noel-Baker, n.d. [July 1937], Noel-Baker Papers, CCA, NBKR 9/58/3. The same shaky hand was also on display in the letters sent from the nursing home at 17 Manchester Street in London, where Pigou spent the summer. See Pigou to Philip Noel-Baker, n.d. (August 1937), Noel-Baker Papers, CCA, NBKR 9/58/3. See also Philip Noel-Baker to Austin Robinson, October 21, 1964, Austin Robinson Papers, MLE, EAGR 6/6/4.

123. Pigou to J. M. Keynes, August 18, 1938, in Bridel and Ingrao, "Managing Cambridge Economics," 153. Hicks had never been welcomed by the Cambridge Keynesians. Hamouda, *John R. Hicks*, 20–25.

124. Kalecki also had a difficult time fitting in at Cambridge. See Jan Toporowski, *Michał Kalecki: An Intellectual Biography, Volume 1: Rendezvous in Cambridge, 1899–1939* (Houndmills, Basingstoke, UK: Palgrave Macmillan, 2013), 122–148.

125. D. G. Champernowne was one of Keynes's star students and served as a lecturer in statistics at Cambridge during the 1930s. He later returned to teach economics.

126. Bridel and Ingrao, "Managing Cambridge Economics," 153.

127. Pigou to Joan Robinson, n.d. (1939), Joan Robinson Papers, KCA, JVR/7/347.

128. Ibid. Some years later, Pigou would refer to Robinson as "dogmatic and arrogant." See Donald Winch, "Keynes and the British Academy," *Historical Journal* 57, no. 3 (September 2014): 769.

129. See "Lectures proposed by the Board of the Faculty of Economics and Politics, 1935–1936," *Cambridge University Reporter* 66, no. 3 (October 4, 1935): 87–88; "Lectures proposed by the Board of the Faculty of Economics and Politics, 1942–1943," *Cambridge University Reporter* 73, no. 3 (October 2, 1942): 72.

130. Officially, the *Economic Journal* was the organ of the Royal Economics Society.

131. Pigou to J. M. Keynes, June 10, 1938, Keynes Papers, KCA, GTE/2/4/46–47.

132. J. M. Keynes to Pigou, June 17, 1938, Keynes Papers, KCA, JMK/GTE/2/4/48.

133. Udny Yule taught statistics, and Kahn, Sraffa, and Keynes all taught modeling in their courses. The list of courses for each term is in the *Cambridge University Reporter*.

134. "Reports to the Fellowship Electors," n.d. [1907–09], Keynes Papers, KCA, JMK/TP/4.

135. "Fellowship Report," 1930, Kahn Papers, KCA/RFK/2/8.

136. Marshall explained the practice to Arthur L. Bowley: "I went more and more on the rules—(1) Use mathematics as a shorthand language, rather than as an engine of inquiry. (2) Keep to them till you have done. (3) Translate into English. (4) Then illustrate by examples that are important in real life. (5) Burn the mathematics. (6) If you can't succeed in 4, burn 3. This last I did often." A. C. Pigou, ed., *The Memorials of Alfred Marshall* (London: Macmillan, 1925): 427.

137. A. C. Pigou *Principles and Methods of Industrial Peace* (London: Macmillan, 1905): vi.

138. Pigou to J. R. N. Stone, n.d., The Papers of John Richard Nicholas Stone, KCA, KRNS/3/1/102.

139. L.R.C. [L. R. Connor], "*The Economics of Welfare* by A.C. Pigou," *Journal of the Royal Statistical Society* 93, no. 1 (1930): 125–126.

140. Ragnar Frisch (1895–1973), the first editor of *Econometrica*, was also the first to use the term "econometrics" in its current meaning in 1926. See Ragnar Frisch, "Sur un problème d'économie pure," *Norsk Matemastik Forenings Skrifter* Series I, no. 16 (1926): 1–40. See also John S. Chipman, "The Contributions of Ragnar Frisch to Economics and Econometrics," in *Econometrics and Economic Theory in the 20th Century: The Ragnar Frisch Centennial Symposium*, ed. Steiner Strøm (Cambridge: Cambridge University Press, 1998): 58–108.

141. See Marcel Boumans, *How Economists Model the World into Numbers* (London: Routledge, 2004).

142. In 1941, Pigou addressed the usefulness of mathematics in economics. Math, he noted, eliminated ambiguities and saved time. See A. C. Pigou, "Newspaper

Reviewers, Economics and Mathematics," *Economic Journal* 51, no. 202/203 (June–September 1941): 276–280.

143. Warren M. Persons, "*Industrial Fluctuations* by A.C. Pigou," *Quarterly Journal of Economics* 42, no. 4 (August 1928): 669. Persons may have been judging Pigou against the work on economic statistics at the American National Bureau of Economic Research. On American economic statistics, see Thomas A. Stapleford, *The Cost of Living in America: A Political History of Economic Statistics, 1880–2000* (Cambridge: Cambridge University Press, 2009), chapter 3. Another reviewer "grumbled" at Pigou's use of statistics and noted that he was "much happier when he abandons attempts at statistical measurement and relies on 'common-sense judgment and . . . guess-work.'" Henry W. Macrosty, "*Industrial Fluctuations* by A.C. Pigou," *Journal of the Royal Statistical Society* 90, no. 3 (1927): 598.

144. J. C. Stamp, "*Industrial Fluctuations* by A.C. Pigou," *Economic Journal* 37, no. 147 (September 1927): 420.

145. Pigou to Sara Turing, November 26, 1956, The Papers of Alan Matheson Turing, KCA, AMT/A/10.

146. W. S. Farren and H. T. Tizard, "Hermann Glauert, 1892–1934," *Obituary Notices of Fellows of the Royal Society* 1, no. 4 (December 1935): 607–610.

147. A. C. Pigou, *The Economics of Stationary States* (London: Macmillan, 1935): v; Pigou, *The Theory of Unemployment*, vii.

148. Pigou to Sara Turing, November 26, 1956, Turing Papers, KCA, AMT/A/10.

149. Ibid.

150. See Collard, "Introduction," xxx n.1. In 1928, for instance, Pigou admitted to Sraffa, then a lecturer at Trinity College, that he had probably not understood one of Sraffa's mathematical problems. Pigou to Piero Sraffa, n.d. [January 1928], The Papers of Piero Sraffa, TCA, Sraffa C239/1. See also Naldi, "The Prof and his Younger Colleagues," 331–332. *The Theory of Unemployment* contained several small mathematical errors, which were pointed out to him in private letters as well as in reviews. Kahn wrote with corrections, as did Robertson, Bowley from the London School of Economics, and Maurice Allen from Oxford. These corrections addressed issues that did not undercut the thrust of Pigou's argument, though they did provoke a corrigenda slip. See also Knight, "A.C. Pigou's *The Theory of Unemployment* and Its Corrigenda," 9–10. All the original sources are in Items found in Pigou's Copy of *The Theory of Unemployment*, Arthur Cecil Pigou Papers, MLE, Pigou 2/3.

151. Keynes, *The General Theory*, 107.

152. Sidney Webb and Beatrice Webb, *Soviet Communism: A New Civilization?* (London: Longmans, Green, and Co. 1935).

153. See Stevenson and Cook, *The Slump*, chapters 5 and 8. See also John Stevenson, *British Society 1914–45* (London: Allen Lane, 1984), especially chapter 10. John Jewkes and Sylvia Jewkes, *The Juvenile Labour Market* (London: Gollancz, 1938); Wal Hannington, *The Problem of the Distressed Areas* (London: Gollancz, 1937).

154. See Susan Howson, "The Origins of Lionel Robbins's *Essay on the Nature and Significance of Economic Science*," *History of Political Economy* 36, no. 3 (Fall 2004): 413–433; and Howson, *Lionel Robbins*, 213–214. Hugh Dalton also was one of these

figures and had been an early supporter of Robbins, though Dalton came to regret Robbins's dogmatic conservatism. See Ralf Dahrendorf, *LSE: A History of the London School of Economics and Political Science 1895-1995* (Oxford: Oxford University Press, 1995): 213-215.

155. Howson, "The Origins of Robbins's *Essay on the Nature and Significance of Economic Science*," 423.

156. Marshall wrote: "Economics is the study of mankind in the ordinary business of life; it examines that part of individual and social action which is most closely connected with the attainment and with the use of the material requisites of wellbeing." Alfred Marshall, *The Principles of Economics*, eighth ed. (London: Palgrave Macmillan, 2013): 1.

157. John Saltmarsh's Lecture Notes on Pigou, c. 1926-9, Austin Robinson Papers, MLE, EAGR/6/1/6, 3.

158. Lionel Robbins, *An Essay on the Nature and Significance of Economic Science*, 2, 21.

159. Ibid., 16.

160. The contemporary best-selling textbook *Principles of Economics* by N. Gregory Mankiw, defines economics as "the study of how society manages its scarce resources." N. Gregory Mankiw, *Principles of Economics* (Cincinnati: South-Western, 2011): 4. See also Robert Cooter and Peter Rappoport, "Were the Ordinalists Wrong about Welfare Economics?" *Journal of Economic Literature* 22, no. 2 (June 1984): 507-530. Backhouse and Medema argue that Robbins's definition "had a symbiotic role" in the axiomatization of economic theory as early as the 1930s and 1940s. Roger E. Backhouse and Steven G. Medema, "Robbins's *Essay* and the Axiomatization of Economics," *Journal of the History of Economic Thought* 31, no. 4 (December 2009): 485-499. However, as Backhouse and Medema note, it took decades for the definition to assume the prominence it now has. Roger E. Backhouse and Steven Medema, "Defining Economics: The Long Road to the Acceptance of the Robbins Definition," *Economica* 76 (October 2009): 805-820.

161. Robbins, *An Essay on the Nature and Significance of Economic Science*, xxxvii.

162. See Dennis P. O'Brien, *Lionel Robbins* (London: Macmillan, 1988): 25.

163. Robbins, *An Essay on the Nature and Significance of Economic Science*, xxxviii-xxxix. In the preface to the first edition, Robbins acknowledged his "especial indebtedness to the works of Professor Ludwig von Mises." Robbins, *An Essay on the Nature and Significance of Economic Science*, xliii. On Robbins and the Austrians, see Howson, *Lionel Robbins*, especially 196-204; and Backhouse and Medema, "Robbins's *Essay* and the Axiomatization of Economics." The so-called Austrian School stressed the purposeful actions of individuals. On the Austrians, see Harald Hagermann, Tamotsu Nishizawa, and Yukihiro Ikeda, eds. *Austrian Economics in Transition: From Carl Menger to Friedrich Hayek* (New York: Palgrave Macmillan, 2010).

164. For Weber, the sociologist needed a self-awareness of this tension. Without such awareness, they could become "petty prophets in lecture rooms." Max Weber, "Science as a Vocation," in *From Max Weber: Essays in Sociology*, ed. C. Wright Mills and H. H. Gerth (New York: Oxford University Press, 1980): 153.

165. On the socialist calculation debate, see Don Lavoie, *Rivalry and Central Planning: The Socialist Calculation Debate Reconsidered* (Cambridge: Cambridge University Press, 1985). Market liberals contended that planning boards were unable to efficiently distribute resources. This view would reach its most eloquent expression in: F. A. Hayek, "The Use of Knowledge in Society," *American Economic Review* 34, no. 4 (September 1945): 519–530. Hayek held that planned economies could never outdo the market, because even if a planning board could optimize allocation of resources over the utility functions of a country's citizens, the board could not access the information required, which was only knowable to the individuals themselves. Left-leaning economists, notably Lerner and Lange, suggested systems of "market socialism," wherein the government would ultimately plan the economy and own the productive resources but would employ a system of prices to capture information about demand. In this way, choices about production would be concentrated and in the hands of a few central planners. See Abba Lerner, *The Economics of Control: Principles of Welfare Economics* (New York: Macmillan, 1944); Oskar Lange, *On the Economic Theory of Socialism* (Minneapolis: University of Minnesota Press, 1938). Lange himself drew extensively from Pigou, invoking *The Economics of Welfare* as part of the "economist's case for socialism." Lange, *On the Economic Theory of Socialism*, 98–103.

166. See Peter Hennipman, "Hicks, Robbins, and the Demise of Pigovian Welfare Economics: Rectification and Amplification," *Southern Economic Journal* 59, no. 1 (July 1992): 88–97; Roger E. Backhouse, "Robbins and Welfare Economics: A Reappraisal," *Journal of the History of Economic Thought* 31, no. 4 (December 2009): 474–484. Malcolm Rutherford suggests that Robbins was attacking the American Institutionalists, though Robbins's intentions on this matter are somewhat harder to demonstrate. See Malcolm Rutherford, *The Institutionalist Movement in American Economics, 1918–1947: Science and Social Control* (Cambridge: Cambridge University Press, 2011): 310.

167. O'Brien, *Lionel Robbins*, 23. See also Lionel Robbins, "Interpersonal Comparisons of Utility: A Comment," *Economic Journal* 48 (1938): 635–637; Lionel Robbins, *Politics and Economics* (London: Macmillan, 1963): 12–19.

168. Aslanbeigui provides an overview of the two challenges facing Pigou (from Keynes and Robbins). Aslanbeigui, "On the Demise of Pigovian Economics." See also Aslanbeigui and Oakes, *Arthur Cecil Pigou*, chapter 6.

169. Robbins did not attack interpersonal comparisons directly in his *Essay*, though he did so implicitly when attacking the extra-scientific nature of the law of diminishing marginal utility. Robbins, *An Essay on the Nature and Significance of Economic Science*, 139–141.

170. One of the few political economists who did not make this assumption was F. Y. Edgeworth, who held that the rich were extra sensitive to pleasure and pain, making inequality justifiable on utilitarian grounds. See David Colander, "Edgeworth's Hedonometer and the Quest to Measure Utility," *Journal of Economic Perspectives* 21, no. 2 (Spring 2007): 215–225.

171. Robbins, *An Essay on the Nature and Significance of Economic Science*, 139–141.

172. Compare to Aslanbeigui and Oakes, who suggest that it was primarily the interpersonal comparisons of utility that provided the tension between Pigou and Robbins. Aslanbeigui and Oakes, *Arthur Cecil Pigou*, 181. Pigou, *The Economics of Stationary States*, 4.

173. Quoted in Howson, "Robbins's *Nature and Significance*," 422.

174. Robbins, *An Essay on the Nature and Significance of Economic Science*, xxxvi.

175. Howson, *Lionel Robbins*, 232.

176. Lindley Fraser, "How Do We Want Economists to Behave?" *Economic Journal* 42, no. 168 (December 1932): 570.

177. This position was forcefully expressed by a young American, Ralph Souter. "The issues involved," Souter wrote, "are so vast that I can do no more than barely indicate how Professor Robbins here again has been victimized by the fallacy of exclusion [of ethics from economics]." R. W. Souter, "'The Nature and Significance of Economic Science' in Recent Discussion," *Quarterly Journal of Economics* 47, no. 3 (May 1933): 401. See also Howson, *Lionel Robbins*, 232–234.

178. Cannan continued, "They will say, 'You know perfectly well that what we want from you is to be told whether this proposed change will make us and our children better off. For goodness sake give us a reasoned reply without beating about the bush and quoting dozens of foreign economists whom we shall never read.'" Edwin Cannan, "*An Essay on the Significance of Economic Science* by Lionel Robbins," *Economic Journal* 42, no. 167 (September 1932): 426–427.

179. Frank H. Knight, "The Nature and Significance of Economic Science by Lionel Robbins," *International Journal of Ethics* 44, no. 3 (April 1934): 361. Joan Robinson, writing in a vindicatory vein in *Economics Is a Serious Subject*, held that economics had already "built up a body of technique . . . [of] which we need none of us be ashamed." Robinson, *Economics Is a Serious Subject*, 4–5. For more on Knight's own conflicted relationship with the purpose of economics, see Angus Burgin, "The Radical Conservatism of Frank H. Knight," *Modern Intellectual History* 6, no. 3 (November 2009): 513–538.

180. Fraser, "How Do We Want Economists to Behave?" 562. Reviewers were also aware that Robbins's work had a political valence. Robbins assumed that "'rational,' i.e. economical choice is something worth striving for." Ibid., 557. Robinson held that Robbins forgot that economics was not only tied up with welfare judgments but also predicated on the assumption that "each person acts in a sensible manner from the point of view of his own economic interests," a totally unrealistic assertion. This assumption, however, implicitly worked to justify *choice* as a means to a satisfactory (and thereby ethically weighted) end. Robinson, *Economics Is a Serious Subject*, 10.

181. Robinson, *Economics Is a Serious Subject*, 4. R. W. Souter found it natural for Pigou to be ethically motivated and that the mechanics of his economics were still scientific. Souter, "'The Nature and Significance of Economic Science' in Recent Discussion," 403.

182. A. C. Pigou *The Economics of Welfare*, fourth ed., 3–4.

183. Pareto optimality refers to an outcome in which it is impossible to make any individual better off without making another worse off. See Robbins, "Interpersonal

Comparisons of Utility: A Comment," 635–641. Robbins, *An Essay on the Nature and Significance of Economic Science*, 75.

184. Two short articles, one by Hicks and one by Kaldor, were the founding documents of New Welfare Economics. The first is Nicholas Kaldor, "Welfare Propositions of Economics and Interpersonal Comparisons of Utility," *Economic Journal* 49, no. 195 (September 1939): 549–552, in which Kaldor explicitly "was in entire agreement" with Robbins's theory and sought to "examine its relevance . . . to what is commonly called "welfare economics." The other is J. R. Hicks, "The Foundations of Welfare Economics," *Economic Journal* 49, no. 196 (December 1939): 696–712.

185. Hicks, "The Foundations of Welfare Economics," 697.

186. Robert Cooter and Peter Rappoport argue that "ordinalists offered different questions, not better answers," and thus that "the ordinalist revolution represented a change, not progress in economics." Cooter and Rappoport, "Were the Ordinalists Wrong about Welfare Economics?"

187. In America, New Welfare Economics was most notably advocated by the LSE- and Cambridge-educated Tibor Scitovsky. See Tibor Scitovsky, "A Note on Welfare Propositions in Economics," *Review of Economic Studies* 9, no. 1 (November 1941): 77–88. New Welfare Economics soon came into conflict with an American strain of welfare economics centered around the work of Abram Bergson and Paul Samuelson. However, Pigou was absent from those debates. On the rise (and fall) of New Welfare Economics, see J. R. Hicks, "The Scope and Status of Welfare Economics," *Oxford Economic Papers*, New Series 27, no. 3 (November 1975): 307–326; and E. J. Mishan, "A Survey of Welfare Economics, 1939–59," *Economic Journal* 70, no. 278 (June 1960): 197–265. See also the postscript in Roger Backhouse and Tamotsu Nishizawa, eds., *No Wealth but Life* (Cambridge: Cambridge University Press, 2010): 223–235.

188. See U. Hla Myint, *Theories of Welfare Economics* (New York: Reprints of Economics Classics, Augustus M. Kelley, 1965); Backhouse and Medema, "Defining Economics: The Long Road to the Acceptance of the Robbins Definition."

189. Pigou to Macmillan, November 16, 1932, Macmillan Papers, BL, Add. MSS 55199, 156.

190. Pigou to Macmillan, December 5, 1934, Macmillan Papers, BL Add. MSS 55199, 173.

191. A. C. Pigou, *Economics in Practice: Six Lectures on Current Issues* (London: Macmillan, 1935): 8. Pigou cited misuse of statistics by government ministers, archbishops, and social reformers. Ibid., 16–18.

192. Ibid., 20.

193. Ibid., 25.

194. Ibid., 22.

195. See Pigou's inaugural address as professor. A. C. Pigou, *Economic Science in Relation to Practice* (London: Macmillan, 1908).

196. *The Economics of Stationary States*, a textbook that Pigou wrote in 1935, was sent to the Cambridge group. See Pigou to Macmillan, December 5, 1934, Macmillan Papers, BL, Add. MSS 55199, 173–174.

197. Pigou was quick to add that after the abandonment of the gold standard, falling gold prices could be absorbed in exchange rates rather than domestic prices, and that the government could engage in public works to stabilize prices. Thus, the current tariffs and encouragement of municipal thrift was at best "now not needed," and at worst, counterproductive. Pigou, *Economics in Practice*, 73–74, 79.

198. Ibid., 145–147.

199. See Trentmann, *Free Trade Nation*, part II.

200. Pigou, *Economics in Practice*, 149.

201. Ibid., 142.

202. Pigou continued to probe the limits of nationalism. "And, if it is proper for the group of people living in England to frame policies without regard for their consequences abroad, why not a still narrower patriotism? Why should not the Dons of Cambridge forbid to undergraduates the purchase of London-made books, and, endowed, as a consequence of this, with well-merited wealth, pile high their College cellars with bottled sunshine from Portugal and France?" Ibid., 133.

203. Ibid., 152.

204. Webb and Webb, *Soviet Communism: A New Civilization?* In subsequent editions, the Webbs dropped the question mark from the end of the title. A. C. Pigou, *Socialism versus Capitalism* (London: Macmillan, 1937): v.

205. Pigou to Beatrice Webb, January 13, 1937, Passfield Collection, LSE, Passfield 2/4/K. Pigou likely did not engage actively with the work of Oskar Lange or Abba Lerner, who worked on how socialist planning could render efficient outcomes. Lange did engage with Pigou, who he saw as explaining some of the failures of free-market capitalism. See Lange, *On the Economic Theory of Socialism*, 99–104.

206. Pigou to Beatrice Webb, January 13, 1937, Passfield Collection, LSE, Passfield 2/4/K. Pigou investigated and found that Edgeworth had written of the separation of economic and utilitarian calculus in the introduction to his *Mathematical Psychics* (1881). Pigou to Beatrice Webb, n.d. [after January 19, 1937], Passfield Collection, LSE, Passfield 2/4/K. Webb was likely interested in the term "economic calculus" because of an essay published in 1936 by her planning-friendly LSE colleague Evan Durbin (1906–1948). E.F.M. Durbin, "Economic Calculus in a Planned Economy," *Economic Journal* 46, no. 184 (December 1936): 676–690. Though in the 1930s, the term was infrequently used, Hayek and others began to use it more in subsequent decades. See Bruce Caldwell, "F.A. Hayek and the 'Economic Calculus': The Cambridge and Virginia Lectures" (paper presented at the conference on Friedrich Hayek and the Liberal Tradition at the University of Richmond, Richmond, Virginia, April 13, 2013).

207. Pigou to Macmillan, May 18, 1937, Macmillan Papers, BL, Add. MSS 55199, 206. He also dismissively referred to it as "a small sop to public spirit" to Philip Noel-Baker. Pigou to Philip Noel-Baker, n.d. (October 1937), Noel-Baker Papers, CCA, 9/58/3.

208. These accusations arose when a British government document surfaced that identified a Soviet agent. Through the document was redacted, parts of the censored material were visble, and members of the press determined the name of the agent

was five letters long and started with a P or B. The spy in question was Anthony Blunt (1907–1983), who had confessed secretly in 1964. Accusations in the press of Pigou's guilt provoked strong responses from Pigou's friends and supporters. See Press Clippings, The Papers of Lancelot Patrick Wilkinson, KCA, LPW/8/7; "Spy Stories," Kaldor Papers, KCA, NK/3/93. See also Christopher Andrew, "Cambridge Spies: The 'Magnificent Five,' 1933–1945," in *Cambridge Contributions*, ed. Sarah J. Ormrod (Cambridge: Cambridge University Press, 1998): 208–228.

209. Pigou, *Socialism versus Capitalism*, 12, 67.

210. Assuming that wages would generally be equal under a socialist economy, planners would be obliged to use an "accounting" wage to account the relative worth of a worker's labor. Ibid., 114. An "accounting" interest rate would also be necessary; ibid., 128.

211. Ibid., 118.

212. See, for instance, his 1935 essay, "State Action and Laisser Faire," in *Economics in Practice: Six Lectures on Current Issues* (London: Macmillan, 1935), which is discussed in chapter 4.

213. Ibid., 99–101, 136.

214. Ibid., 138–139.

215. Pigou was the organization's president from 1937 to 1940. See Aslanbeigui and Oakes, *Arthur Cecil Pigou*, 262.

216. A. C. Pigou, "Presidential Address," *Economic Journal* 49, no. 194 (June 1939): 218. Pigou singled out Foxwell as the notable exception.

217. Ibid., 219.

218. Ibid., 218–219. The consolation was that there was "scope for useful work by men and women who are not of the first intellectual" rank.

219. Ibid., 217–218.

220. Collard, "Introduction," xxx.

221. Pigou, "Presidential Address," 220.

222. Emphasis added. Ibid., 221.

Chapter 7: Another War and a Fresh Start

1. Pigou to Philip Noel-Baker, n.d. [September–October, 1939], The Papers of Baron Noel-Baker, CCA, NBKR 9/58/3.

2. Ibid.

3. Pigou to Philip Noel-Baker, n.d. [September–October, 1939], Noel-Baker Papers, CCA, NBKR 9/58/3.

4. A. C. Pigou, *The Political Economy of War*, second edition (London: Macmillan, 1940): 169.

5. Pigou to Philip Noel-Baker, n.d. [September–October 1939], Noel-Baker Papers, CCA, NBKR 9/58/3. Wilfrid Noyce (1917–1962) encountered Pigou at King's and became a lifelong friend. Though he originally joined the Ambulance Unit, in 1942 he left for India, where he served as an intelligence officer. An accomplished climber, he fell while on a hike in the Lake District in 1946 and was rescued by Noel-Baker, then an MP.

6. Pigou to Philip Noel-Baker, n.d. [late 1939], Noel-Baker Papers, CCA, NBKR 9/58/3.

7. D. G. Champernowne, "Arthur Cecil Pigou 1877–1959," *Statistical Journal* 122, no. 2 (1959): 265; Alan Hodges, *Alan Turing: The Enigma* (Princeton, NJ: Princeton University Press, 2012): 186.

8. For more on this period, see Christopher N. L. Brooke, *A History of the University of Cambridge, Volume IV, 1870–1990* (Cambridge: Cambridge University Press, 1993), chapter 16.

9. J. M. Keynes to Pigou, n.d. [June–July 1940], The Papers of John Maynard Keynes, KCA, JMK/PP/45/254/53.

10. Pigou to J. M. Keynes, June 12, 1940, quoted in Pascal Bridel and Bruna Ingrao, "Managing Cambridge Economics: The Correspondence between Keynes and Pigou," in *Economists in Cambridge: A Study Through Their Correspondence*, ed. Maria Cristina Marcuzzo and Annalisa Rosselli (London: Routledge, 2005): 155.

11. Pigou to J. M. Keynes, n.d. [June–July 1940], The Papers of John Maynard Keynes, KCA, JMK/PP/45/254/51.

12. Keynes was not optimistic about his own situation either: "I have no idea whether my appointment . . . to a new super-dud Committee at the Treasury is going to be a complete washout or not. I have little confidence in it. . . . All this advisory business is a hopeless ploughing of the sands." J. M. Keynes to Pigou, n.d. [June–July 1940], Keynes Papers, KCA, JMK/PP/45/254/53.

13. Pigou's main contribution to Greenwood's office was a historical analysis, "An Analytical Account of the General Economic Movement in the United Kingdom between the Armistice and the Restoration of the Gold Standard." See A. C. Pigou, "General Economic Movement," 1941, Arthur Cecil Pigou Papers, MLE, Pigou 1/7/1. After Pigou secured permission from the relevant authorities, this report was published in 1947. A. C. Pigou, *Aspects of British Economic History 1918–1925* (London: Macmillan, 1947).

14. Pigou to Philip Noel-Baker, n.d. [January 1941], Noel-Baker Papers, CCA, NBKR 9/58/3; Pigou to Philip Noel-Baker, n.d. [June 1941], Noel-Baker Papers, CCA, NBKR 9/58/3; Pigou to Philip Noel-Baker, n.d. [March 1942], Noel-Baker Papers, CCA, NBKR 9/58/3; Pigou to Philip Noel-Baker, n.d. [April 1942], Noel-Baker Papers, CCA, NBKR 9/58/3.

15. Pigou to Philip Noel-Baker, n.d. [October 1941], Noel-Baker Papers, CCA, NBKR 9/58/3.

16. Jackson, who was known as "the Queen," administered the Pigou household "with strict discipline" and continued to live in an uninsulated addition to the house after Pigou's death. Nicholas Elliott, *Never Judge a Man by His Umbrella* (London: Michael Russell, 1991): 67.

17. Pigou to Philip Noel-Baker, June 5, 1945, Noel-Baker Papers, CCA, NBKR 9/58/2. Pigou wrote to congratulate Hayek on the latter's election to the British Academy. Pigou to F. A. Hayek, July 12, 1944, Friedrich A. von Hayek Papers, The Hoover Institution, Stanford University, Palo Alto, California, Box 8, Folder 9.

18. Philip Noel-Baker to Pigou, August 26, 1949, Noel-Baker Papers, CCA, NBKR 9/58/1.

19. Philip Noel-Baker to Pigou, April 15, 1943, Noel-Baker Papers, CCA, NBKR 9/58/2.

20. Pigou to Philip Noel-Baker, August 10, 1941, Noel-Baker Papers, CCA, NBKR 9/58/3.

21. Pigou to Philip Noel-Baker, n.d. [June 1943)], Noel-Baker Papers, CCA, NBKR 9/58/2. Pigou to Philip Noel-Baker, n.d. [mid-1943], Noel-Baker Papers, CCA, NBKR 9/58/2.

22. Pigou was particularly concerned about Wilfrid Noyce. He kept up correspondence with Noyce, who was stationed in Northern India and China and repeatedly asked Noel-Baker's advice, trying to arrange a future career in the diplomatic service. Gaunt's full name was Howard Charles Adie Gaunt.

23. Pigou to Philip Noel-Baker, n.d. [January 1941], Noel-Baker Papers, CCA, NBKR 9/58/3; Pigou to Philip Noel-Baker, n.d. [August–September 1940], Noel-Baker Papers, CCA, NBKR 9/58/3.

24. Pigou to Philip Noel-Baker, n.d. [November 1943], Noel-Baker Papers, CCA, NBKR 9/58/2. Pigou's misogynistic tendencies were clear. In letters to Noel-Baker, he would alternatively refer to women as "dancing girls" and "serpents." In 1944, he received a letter from a woman in Sharonville, Ohio, asking for his opinion on the "theoretical assumption of economic planning, positive theory of laissez-faire, and the contrast or the comparison of the above two ideas." Pigou commented, "I'm shortly starting a great work called 'Woman, A Psychological Study'! This will be its frontispiece!" Philip Noel-Baker to Pigou, n.d. [May–June 1944], Noel-Baker Papers, CCA, NBKR 9/58/2.

25. Pigou to Philip Noel-Baker, n.d. [August 1940], Noel-Baker Papers, CCA, NBKR 9/58/3. Noel-Baker, ever the optimist, predicted the war would end in 1942.

26. Pigou to Philip Noel-Baker, n.d. [late 1941], Noel-Baker Papers, CCA, NBKR 9/58/3.

27. Pigou to Philip Noel-Baker, n.d. [May 1942], Noel-Baker Papers, CCA, NBKR 9/58/3.

28. In one letter, Pigou set May 1953 as his prediction. Pigou to Philip Noel-Baker, n.d. [April 1942], Noel-Baker Papers, CCA, NBKR 9/58/3. Pigou to Philip Noel-Baker, n.d. [November 1942], Noel-Baker Papers, CCA, NBKR 9/58/3.

29. Philip Noel-Baker to Pigou, January 26, 1943, Noel-Baker Papers, CCA, NBKR 9/58/3; Pigou to Philip Noel-Baker, n.d. [February 1944], Noel-Baker Papers, CCA, NBKR 9/58/2; Pigou to Philip Noel-Baker, n.d. [June 1944], Noel-Baker Papers, CCA, NBKR 9/58/2.

30. Philip Noel-Baker to Pigou, January 26, 1943, Noel-Baker Papers, CCA, NBKR 9/58/3.

31. Pigou to Philip Noel-Baker, n.d. [early February 1942], Noel-Baker Papers, CCA, NBKR 9/58/3.

32. "Whisky Arthur's department is . . . incompetent," Pigou wrote. "The typist they arranged to provide for my work for them, who was to send in her account and to be paid monthly, and who started in November, hasn't received a penny yet! No wonder we are losing the war!" Pigou to Philip Noel-Baker, n.d. [March 1942], Noel-Baker Papers, CCA, NBKR 9/58/3.

33. Pigou to Macmillan, May 9, 1944, Macmillan Papers, BL, Add. MS 55200, 40. The book was published in 1945. A. C. Pigou, *Lapses from Full Employment* (London: Macmillan, 1945). A. C. Pigou, "Night Life on High Hills," *Alpine Journal* 53 (1946): 246. Pigou also wrote what he described to Noel-Baker as a "masterful study of Beveridge" that took the form of two articles in the *Manchester Guardian*. Pigou to Philip Noel-Baker, n.d. [1943], Noel-Baker Papers, CCA, NBKR 9/58/3. Pigou's work on Beveridge also appeared in *Agenda* in 1944 and subsequently in *Essays in Economics* (London: Macmillan, 1952) under the title "Employment Policy." Pigou was in sympathy with the work "Sir William did so well" in the report on Social Security, but he was somewhat less enthusiastic with Beveridge's more theoretical economic analysis of unemployment. A. C. Pigou, "Employment Policy," in *Essays in Economics* (London: Macmillan, 1952): 85, 107.

34. See David Collard, "Introduction," in *A.C. Pigou's Collected Economic Writings, Volume 1*, ed. David Collard (London: Macmillan, 1999): xxxvii–xxxix.

35. A. C. Pigou and Nicholas Kaldor, "Models of Short-Period Equilibrium," *Economic Journal* 52, no. 206/7 (June-September 1942): 250–258.

36. Paul A. Samuelson, "Professor Pigou's *Employment and Equilibrium*," *American Economic Review* 31, no. 3 (September 1941): 545.

37. Ibid., 545, 552. Pigou's model consisted of four endogenous variables (consumption goods, investment goods, the interest rate, and the money wage) with three equations. To "make it a determinate system," Pigou suggested two alternatives. First, one could assume that in the long run, there was no unemployment. Alternatively, one could assume that in the short term, money wages were fixed. See Pigou, *Employment and Equilibrium*, 170. The most important innovation of the book, according to both Samuelson and David Collard, was its treatment of multipliers. See Collard, "Introduction," xxxviii.

38. Abba Lerner, "*Employment and Equilibrium* by A.C. Pigou," *Review of Economics and Statistics* 24, no. 2 (May 1942): 87.

39. A. C. Pigou, "The Classical Stationary State," *Economic Journal* 53, no. 212 (1943): 243–251. The book to which Pigou was responding was Alvin H. Hansen, *Fiscal Policy and Business Cycles* (New York: W. W. Norton & Company, 1941).

40. See Michał Kalecki, "Professor Pigou on 'The Classical Stationary State' A Comment," *Economic Journal* 54, no. 213 (April 1944): 131–132. Patinkin coined the term "Pigou Effect," in 1948. Don Patinkin, "Price Flexibility and Full Employment," *American Economic Review* 38, no. 4 (September 1948): 543–564. See also Norikazu Takami, "Managing the Loss: How Pigou Arrived at the Pigou Effect," CHOPE Working Paper 2011-06 (Durham, NC: Center for the History of Political Economy, Duke University, March 2011), http://hope.econ.duke.edu/node/134.

41. David Collard, "Introduction," in *A.C. Pigou, Journal Articles 1902–1922*, ed. David Collard (London: Macmillan, 2002): xxx.

42. Pigou, *Economics of Welfare*, fourth ed. (London: Macmillan, 1932): 31.

43. Colin Clark, *National Income and Outlay* (London: Macmillan, 1937): 4.

44. Ibid. In America, where Simon Kuznets was working on developing the modern measure of GDP, Pigou's influence was less significant. On Kuznets's contributions,

see Robert William Fogel, Enid M. Fogel, Mark Guglielmo, and Nathaniel Grotte, *Political Arithmetic: Simon Kuznets and the Empirical Tradition in Economics* (Chicago: University of Chicago Press, 2013).

45. Hayek used this formulation in his 1945 essay, "The Use of Knowledge in Society," but strains of this thought appear throughout his and Ludwig von Mises's work of the 1930s and 1940s. F. A. Hayek, "The Use of Knowledge in Society," *American Economic Review* 34, no. 4 (September 1945): 519-530. See Bruce Caldwell, *Hayek's Challenge: An Intellectual Biography of F.A. Hayek* (Chicago: University of Chicago Press, 2004), especially chapter 10.

46. F. A. Hayek, *The Pure Theory of Capital* (London: Macmillan, 1940): 298-299. See J. R. Hicks, "Capital Controversies Ancient and Modern," *American Economic Review* 64, no. 2 (May 1974): 307-316.

47. One passage—"changes in the measurable dimension of the capital stock itself play no essential role in the complete economic calculus"—especially concerned him; he vigorously put three lines alongside it. Pigou's copy of F. A. Hayek, *The Pure Theory of Capital* (London: Macmillan, 1941): 300. Found in King's College Library, TKV Hay.

48. Pigou's copy of Hayek, *The Pure Theory of Capital*, 305. Found in King's College Library, TKV Hay.

49. Pigou also defended the concept for marking a difference between "real" and "psychic" or perceived income, since the breakdown of physical productive capacity represented a loss of income. See Emma Rothschild, "Maintaining (Environmental) Capital Intact," *Modern Intellectual History* 8, no. 1 (2011): 193-212

50. A. C. Pigou, "Maintaining Capital Intact," *Economica*, New Series 8, no. 31 (August 1941): 275.

51. F. A. Hayek, "Maintaining Capital Intact: A Reply," *Economica*, New Series 8, no. 31 (August 1941): 276-280.

52. Hayek published a three-part series in *Economica* called "Scientism and Society," in which he railed against the fallacy that social science, specifically economics, yielded objective, eternal truths just as natural sciences did. Hayek associated this belief with Marxist teleology and the dogmatism of collectivist totalitarian regimes. Because they studied human behavior, social sciences, Hayek argued, gave patterns, not law. Human choice ensured that economic activity was not determined. F. A. Hayek, "Scientism and the Study of Society," *Economica*, New Series 9, no. 36 (August 1942): 267-291; F. A. Hayek, "Scientism and the Study of Society," *Economica*, New Series 10, no. 37 (February 1943): 34-63; "Scientism and the Study of Society Part II," *Economica*, New Series 11, no. 41 (February 1944): 27-39.

53. Hicks, "Capital Controversies Ancient and Modern," 314-315.

54. On the importance of statistics for state planning, see Thomas A. Stapleford *The Cost of Living in America: A Political History of Economic Statistics, 1880-2000* (Cambridge: Cambridge University Press, 2009); Adam Tooze, *Statistics and the German State, 1900-1945: The Making of Modern Economic Knowledge* (Cambridge: Cambridge University Press, 2001); Timothy Mitchell, *Rule of Experts: Egypt, Techno-Politics, Modernity* (Berkeley, University of California Press, 2002).

55. J. R. Hicks, "Maintaining Capital Intact: A Further Suggestion," *Economica*, New Series 9, no. 32 (May 1942): 174–179

56. Hicks, "Capital Controversies Ancient and Modern," 308.

57. Hicks, "Maintaining Capital Intact: A Further Suggestion, 174.

58. Notes on election of Robertson to succeed Pigou, 1943, Austin Robinson Papers, MLE, EAGR/6/6/3.

59. Pigou's alternative was "to do schoolmastering; but, of course, I don't know whether I should be good at preventing boys from bringing rabbits and frogs into class." Pigou to Philip Noel-Baker, n.d. [February 1943], Noel-Baker Papers, CCA, NBKR 9/58/3.

60. Pigou to Philip Noel-Baker, n.d. [March 1943], Noel-Baker Papers, CCA, NBKR 9/58/3.

61. Philip Noel-Baker to Pigou, March 6, 1943, Noel-Baker Papers, CCA, NBKR 9/58/3.

62. Ibid.

63. Pigou to Philip Noel-Baker, n.d. [March 1943], Noel-Baker Papers, CCA, NBKR 9/58/3.

64. Pigou to Philip Noel-Baker, n.d. [October 1943], Noel-Baker Papers, CCA, NBKR 9/58/2. Pigou wrote, "How does one talk into the wretched machine? I shall probably either shout or whisper. You'd better tell me what to do." Noel-Baker enthusiastically replied: "I hope it will be such a howling success among the seven year old proletarians who listen, that you will repeat it on many occasions." Philip Noel-Baker to Pigou, October 25, 1943, Noel-Baker Papers, CCA, NBKR 9/58/2.

65. Pigou to J. M. Keynes, n.d. [April 1943], Keynes Papers, KCA, JMK/PP/45/254/57. Pigou proposed "a special levy of 20 times assessed income tax payment on everybody except that (1) all earned income left out (2) all income after war be left out subject to the owner priority that his war loan has been acquired with new money, i.e. not through the proceeds of selling other securities."

66. Pigou to J. M. Keynes, n.d. [April 1943], Keynes Papers, KCA, JMK/PP/45/254/59.

67. Pigou to J. M. Keynes, n.d. [April 1943], Keynes Papers, KCA, JMK/PP/45/254/62.

68. Pigou to Philip Noel-Baker, n.d. [June 1944], Noel-Baker Papers, CCA, NBKR 9/58/2. This was a theme to which Pigou would repeatedly return. Later, he wrote that the atomic bomb was "the last guarantee of the pro-lobster world," and that the plan for the stellar universe should be illustrated by "lantern slides depicting lobsters in various altitudes." Pigou to Philip Noel-Baker, n.d. [mid-1946], Noel-Baker Papers, CCA, NBKR 9/58/1.

69. Pigou to Philip Noel-Baker, n.d. [August 1943], Noel-Baker Papers, CCA, NBKR 9/58/2; Pigou to Philip Noel-Baker, n.d. [September 1943], Noel-Baker Papers, CCA, NBKR 9/58/2.

70. Pigou to Philip Noel-Baker, n.d. [September 1943], Noel-Baker Papers, CCA, NBKR 9/58/2; Pigou to Philip Noel-Baker, n.d. [March 1942], Noel-Baker Papers, CCA, NBKR 9/58/3.

71. Pigou to Philip Noel-Baker, n.d. [December 1940], Noel-Baker Papers, CCA, NBKR 9/58/3. With the exception of Churchill, these individuals constituted the leadership of the Labour Party and the country in the postwar period. Shinwell eventually became Minister of Defence. Attlee served as Prime Minister from 1945 to 1951. Morrison, a Labour strategist, worked as Home Secretary, Foreign Secretary, and Deputy Prime Minister. Bevan was Minister of Health, responsible for implementing the National Health Service (NHS). Dalton was Chancellor of the Exchequer. See Kenneth O. Morgan, *Labour in Power 1945–1951* (Oxford: Clarendon Press, 1984); Henry Pelling, *The Labour Governments, 1945–51* (New York: St. Martin's Press, 1984).

72. Pigou's thought fascism was a "function of many variables." A. C. Pigou, "*The Road to Serfdom,*" *Economic Journal* 54, no. 214 (June–September 1944): 219.

73. Elliott, *Never Judge a Man by His Umbrella*, 67. See this book, written by Claude Elliott's son, for information about Elliott, who taught economics at St. John's College, Cambridge, and was headmaster of Eton. Gaunt was also an alumnus of King's and a climber. He later became headmaster of Malvern College.

74. Wilfrid Noyce to Philip Noel-Baker, August 7, 1945, Noel-Baker Papers, CCA, NBKR 9/58/2.

75. According to Austin Robinson, Pigou "did not wish to continue his subscription to a club that had never meant anything to him." Austin Robinson to E. T. Williams, November 16, 1966, The Papers of Austin Robinson, MLE, EAGR 6/6/6, 29. Pigou's election had been delayed several times because of politics and resistance to his perceived pacifism. He had been shocked to discover in 1927 "the scandalous behaviour of the British Academy" in denying Keynes membership in 1920 because of *Economic Consequences of the Peace*. "Of course," Pigou wrote to Keynes in 1927, "if I had known of it, I should never have accepted election to a body that could behave in such a way." Pigou to J. M. Keynes, n.d. [1927], Keynes Papers, KCA, JMK/PP/45/254, 25. See also Donald Winch, "Keynes and the British Academy," *Historical Journal* 57, no. 3 (September 2014): 751–771.

76. David Kynaston, *Austerity Britain, 1945–51* (London: Bloomsbury, 2007): 60–70.

77. Pigou to Philip Noel-Baker, n.d. [May–June 1945], Noel-Baker Papers, CCA, NBKR 9/58/2. Pigou wrote in the same letter that Sraffa "foresees that O.S. will play up Tito, de Gaulle, and the bloody-handed one [Stalin] for all he's worth, so as to create a sense of urgent danger, and his own indispensability, but that nevertheless and despite the little rat [Attlee] handicap, the comrades will walk over him." Pigou joked further, "I, on the other hand, am confident that, since Winnie sounds like a girl's name, the flappers [women] will plump for it. . . . and the comrades are for the wilderness." Ibid.

78. Pigou to Philip Noel-Baker, July 20, 1945, Noel-Baker Papers, CCA, NBKR 9/58/2; Pigou to Philip Noel-Baker, n.d. [August 1945], Noel-Baker Papers, CCA, NBKR 9/58/2. Attlee did not appoint Noel-Baker to the cabinet, "a gross case of injustice by the Rat." Noel-Baker would run "the international business, while Bevin takes the credit! . . . That's Rat nature." On the election, see Pelling, *The Labour Governments, 1945–51*, chapter 2.

79. Labour Party, *Let Us Face the Future: A Declaration of Labour Policy for the Consideration of the Nation* (London: Labour Party, 1945).

80. On Labour's proposed welfare programs, see Morgan, *Labour in Power 1945–1951*, chapter 4; and Pelling, *The Labour Governments, 1945–51*, chapter 6.

81. Pigou considered Beveridge a "good man." He resented Beveridge's "wife-induced self-advertisement," but held that "if only someone would murder her, [he] might be quite useful." Pigou to Philip Noel-Baker, n.d. [March 1945], Noel-Baker Papers, CCA, NBKR 9/58/2; See also José Harris, *William Beveridge: A Biography* (Oxford: Clarendon Press, 1977): 378–418.

82. Pigou, "Employment Policy," in *Essays in Economics,* 107. This essay was originally published in *Agenda* magazine in August 1944 under the title "Employment Policy and Sir William Beveridge." It responded to Beveridge's book, *Full Employment in a Free Society.* William Beveridge, *Full Employment in a Free Society: A Report* (London: G. Allen, 1944).

83. Pigou to Philip Noel-Baker, n.d. [August 1945], Noel-Baker Papers, CCA, NBKR 9/58/2. Many would hold Shinwell responsible for the massive coal shortages two years later.

84. Pigou to Philip Noel-Baker, October 5, 1945, Noel-Baker Papers, CCA, NBKR 9/58/2.

85. A. C. Pigou, "Draft of Speech for Philip Noel-Baker," n.d. [late 1945], Noel-Baker Papers, CCA, NBKR 9/58/2.

86. Pigou continued: "What is there on the other side? The TORIES say that we have kept the country tied up in Red Tape and Controls. . . . We have in fact released many controls (give details). The rest we have kept we, so long as shortages continue, <u>must</u> keep, to prevent bad allocation of resources and soaring prices. We have learned the lesson of the last war; the disastrous result of removing controls too soon. . . . Even the TORIES admit we must not do that again. But they nag at us for doing what, had they been in office, they would themselves have been forced to do! (Cymbals)."

87. See David J. Whittaker, *Fighter for Peace: Philip Noel-Baker 1889–1982* (York, UK: Sessions, 1989).

88. A. C. Pigou, "Draft of Speech for Philip Noel-Baker," n.d. [late 1945], Noel-Baker Papers, CCA, NBKR 9/58/2.

89. "Everyone is agreed," Pigou wrote, "that . . . it is impossible for the government to stand wholly aside." Either the government "must <u>regulate</u>" or "through some form of public agency, <u>operate</u> these things directly." A. C. Pigou, "Draft of Speech for Philip Noel-Baker," late 1945, Noel-Baker Papers, CCA, NBKR 9/58/2.

90. Ibid.

91. See Andrew Thorpe, *A History of the British Labour Party*, third ed. (Houndmills, Basingstoke, UK: Palgrave Macmillan, 2008): 120–141.

92. Ibid.

93. See Kenneth Harris, *Attlee* (London: Weidenfeld and Nicolson, 1984), chapter 19. On nationalization, see Kenneth O. Morgan, *Labour in Power 1945–1951* (Oxford: Clarendon Press, 1984), chapter 3.

94. Ibid.

95. A. C. Pigou, "An Economist's Apologia," in *Economics in Practice: Six Lectures on Current Issues* (London: Macmillan, 1935): 8.

96. Pigou to Philip Noel-Baker, n.d. [December 1946], Noel-Baker Papers, CCA, NBKR 9/58/1.

97. Clement Attlee long tried to eject Dalton from the cabinet. Attlee got his chance when a harried Dalton responded to a reporter's questions about tax changes in the forthcoming 1947 budget. His answers were reported in the evening papers before the markets closed, and since the budget had not been released, Dalton had technically released a budget secret, and so he resigned. Pigou to Philip Noel-Baker, n.d. [November 1947], Noel-Baker, CCA, NBKR 9/58/1; Philip Noel-Baker to Pigou, November 15, 1947, Noel-Baker Papers, CCA, NBKR 9/58/1. See chapter 29 of Ben Pimlott, *Hugh Dalton* (London: Jonathan Cape, 1985).

98. Pigou to Philip Noel-Baker, n.d. [November 1947], Noel-Baker Papers, CCA, NBKR 9/58/1.

99. Pigou to Philip Noel-Baker, n.d. [early 1947], Noel-Baker Papers, CCA, NBKR 9/58/1.

100. Pigou to Philip Noel-Baker, n.d. [October 1946], Noel-Baker Papers, CCA, NBKR 9/58/1. Noel-Baker, Pigou advised, should appear above such rowdiness. "Your proper role is to be the international man and a gent. . . . When . . . [the Comrades] go home to their wives and little ones, it is the gents that they talk about and really believe in. The little Rat [Attlee] . . . is a gent: and that is why the Comrades think a lot more of him than of Whisky Arthur [Greenwood] or Eupeptic Hugh [Dalton] to say nothing of Shifty [Shinwell]."

101. Pigou to Philip Noel-Baker, n.d. [early 1938], Noel-Baker Papers, CCA, NBKR 9/58/3.

102. Pigou continued: "Of course that phrase is completely ambiguous: but the Comrades will think they know what it means, and anyway a disquisition about what [if anything] it does mean would be beyond their capacities." Pigou to Philip Noel-Baker, n.d. [early 1947], Noel-Baker Papers, CCA, NBKR 9/58/1.

103. Emphasis mine. Pigou to Philip Noel-Baker, n.d. [October 1946], Noel-Baker Papers, CCA, NBKR 9/58/1.

104. Pigou to Philip Noel-Baker, n.d. [January 1948], Noel-Baker Papers, CCA, NBKR 9/58/1.

105. Pigou to Philip Noel-Baker, n.d. [May 1945], Noel-Baker Papers, CCA, NBKR 9/58/2.

106. Pigou to Philip Noel-Baker, n.d. [mid-1946], Noel-Baker Papers, CCA, NBKR 9/58/1.

107. A. C. Pigou, *Income* (London: Macmillan, 1946): 76–77.

108. Ibid., 108.

109. Ibid., 109.

110. This bears a resemblance to what later thinkers have referred to as "fair equality of opportunity." See John Rawls, *A Theory of Justice*, revised ed. (Cambridge, MA: Harvard University Press, 1999): 75–78. On death duties, Pigou quoted Sir William Harcourt, a Victorian Liberal: "Nature gives man no power over his earthly

goods beyond the term of his life. What power he possesses to prolong his will after his death—the right of a dead hand to dispose of property—is a pure creation of the law, and the State has the right to prescribe the conditions and the limitations under which that power shall be exercised." Pigou, *Income*, 110.

111. Ibid., 112.

112. Pigou to Philip Noel-Baker, n.d. [April 1945], Noel-Baker Papers, CCA, NBKR 9/58/2.

113. Pigou to Philip Noel-Baker, n.d. [February 1946], Noel-Baker Papers, CCA, NBKR 9/58/2.

114. Pigou to Macmillan, October 4, 1947, Macmillan Papers, BL, Add. MSS 55200, 96.

115. A. C. Pigou, *The Veil of Money* (London: Macmillan, 1949). It was intended to be popular, but at least one reviewer found it hard going. "The book makes no concession to the reader, and the argument is often hard to follow through its extreme conciseness." G. Rottier, "*The Veil of Money* by A.C. Pigou," *Economica*, New Series 16, no. 64 (November 1949): 380.

116. A. C. Pigou, "Wage Earnings since the War," *Times* (July 13, 1955): 9; A. C. Pigou, "Wage Earnings since the War," *Times* (July 14, 1955): 5.

Chapter 8: To "Really Do a Little Good"

1. Pigou suggested Adcock as a potential volunteer for the Ambulance Unit. Pigou to Josephine Baker, n.d., The Papers of Baron Noel Baker, CAC, NBKR 9/45/8.

2. Pigou to Piero Sraffa, May 31, 1957, The Papers of Piero Sraffa, TCA, Sraffa C239, 7.

3. Nicholas Elliott, *Never Judge a Man by His Umbrella* (London: Michael Russell, 1991): 68–71.

4. Pigou to Noel-Baker, n.d. [November 1949], Noel-Baker Papers, CAC, 9/58.

5. Pigou to Noel-Baker, April 25, 1950, Noel-Baker Papers, CAC, 9/58; Pigou to Noel-Baker, September 11, 1950, Noel-Baker Papers, CAC, 9/58.

6. Letters on Malvern College letterhead, but addressed from King's, appear in Pigou's correspondence with Macmillan. See Pigou to Macmillan, January 2, 1950, Macmillan Papers, BL, Add. MSS 55200, 131. Elliott, *Never Judge a Man by His Umbrella*, 70.

7. Pigou to Philip Noel-Baker, n.d. [November 1949], Noel-Baker Papers, CAC, 9/58/1.

8. Pigou to Philip Noel-Baker, n.d. [early 1949], Noel-Baker Papers, CAC, NBKR 9/58/1; Pigou to Philip Noel-Baker, n.d. [June 1949], Noel-Baker Papers, CAC, NBKR 9/58/1.

9. Pigou to Noel-Baker, n.d. [late 1950-early 1951], Noel-Baker Papers, CCA, NBKR 9/58/1. Noel-Baker responded to this poem with the sarcastic suggestion that Pigou publish a collection. It would find a good reception, Noel-Baker quipped, among the "Junior Imperial League, the Housewives League, and the Conservative Women's Association for the suppression of Popular Rights!" Noel-Baker to Pigou, January 6, 1951, Noel-Baker Papers, CAC, NBKR 9/58/2.

10. Pigou to Francis Noel-Baker, n.d. [May 1949], Noel-Baker Papers, CCA, NBKR 9/58/1.

Another example was written in January 1951. Pigou to Philip Noel-Baker, n.d. [January 1951], Noel-Baker Papers, CCA, NBKR 9/58/1.

11. Rosemary Ballard to Austin Robinson, November 20, 1964, Austin Robinson Papers, MLE, EAGR 6/6/6, 122.

12. Pigou to Macmillan, January 12, 1953, Macmillan Papers, BL, Add. MSS 55200, 193.

13. L. P. Wilkinson, "A.C. Pigou," *Cambridge Review* 80, no. 1953 (April 25, 1959): 431.

14. Pigou had considered leaving Anthony John Pigou £1,000. Anthony was the only one of his several nephews and nieces that Pigou even strongly considered in writing his will. "Will of A.C. Pigou," January 28, 1958, Academic and Tutorial Records, KCA, KCAC/6/1/11/36; "Codicil to Will," December 18, 1958, Academic and Tutorial Records, KCA, KCAC/6/1/11/36. Pigou did ask Noel-Baker to secure his brother Gerard extra petrol in the 1940s. "My brother, who has diabetes requiring frequent injections impractical on a long train journey, can't get them because of petrol rationing for his car." Pigou to Noel-Baker, n.d. [May 1946], Noel-Baker Papers, CAC, NBKR 9/58/1. Pigou needled in December 1947, "Our Hugh recently coerced Shifty into allowing Elliott a substantial petrol supplement. Aren't you as good a man as our Hugh?" Pigou to Noel-Baker, n.d. [December 1947], Noel-Baker Papers, CAC, NBKR 9/58/1. Pigou ultimately left the bulk of his estate to Wilfrid Noyce and Tom Gaunt, with small remembrances for his housekeeper, Ann Jackson, Gaunt's son, and a Michael Sebastian Halliday. King's and a University Travel fund also received legacies. "Will of A.C. Pigou," January 28, 1958, Academic and Tutorial Records, KCA, KCAC/6/1/11/36.

15. His last published article appeared in 1954. For examples of technical articles, see A. C. Pigou, "A Comment on Duopoly," *Economica*, New Series 15, no. 60 (November 1948): 254–258; A. C. Pigou, "Unrequited Exports," *Economic Journal* 60, no. 238 (June 1950): 241–254; A. C. Pigou. "Professor Duesenberry on Income and Savings," *Economic Journal* 61, no. 244 (December 1951): 883–885.

16. A. C. Pigou, "Central Planning and Professor Robbins," *Economica*, New Series 15, no. 57 (February, 1948): 20. Pigou thought guaranteeing a minimum level of security and income and primary plans were important, but that full planning was impossible because of the information required.

17. A. C. Pigou, "Mill and the Wages Fund," *Economic Journal* 59, no. 234 (June 1949): 171–180.

18. Pigou to R. F. Kahn, n.d. [1947–1953], The Papers of Richard Ferdinand Kahn, KCA, RFK/13/83/8. Pigou asked Kahn to help distinguish "between bunk and nonbunk" on more than one occasion. See also Pigou to R. F. Kahn, n.d. [October, 1953], Kahn Papers, KCA, RFK/13/83/9.

19. Pigou to J. R. N. Stone, n.d. [January 1948], The Papers of John Richard Nicholas Stone, KCA, JRNS/3/1/102.

20. Pigou to J. R. N. Stone, n.d. [early 1950s], Stone Papers, KCA, JRNS/3/1/102.

21. Pigou to Hugh Dalton, March 12, 1951, Crosland Collection, LSE, 10/2.

22. Pigou to R. F. Harrod, n.d. [late 1949], Papers of the Royal Economic Society, LSE, RES 6/1/383.

23. Pigou asserted that Keynes's work was not revolutionary. A. C. Pigou, *Keynes's "General Theory": A Retrospect* (London: Macmillan, 1951): 65–66. Collard takes these negative comments to outweigh the positive. See David Collard, "Introduction," in *A.C. Pigou's Collected Economic Writings, Volume 1,* ed. David Collard (London: Macmillan, 1999): xxxix. The book was not published until 1951 so as not to coincide with the release of Harrod's biography, *The Life of John Maynard Keynes*. Pigou had also written a generous memorial to Keynes on the latter's death in 1946. A. C. Pigou, "John Maynard Keynes, 1883–1946," *Proceedings of the British Academy* (1946): 395–414. See also Nahid Aslanbeigui and Guy Oakes, *Arthur Cecil Pigou* (Houndmills, Basingstoke, UK: Palgrave Macmillan, 2015): 236–238.

24. A. C. Pigou, "The Transfer Problem and Transport Costs," *Economic Journal* 62, no. 248 (December 1952): 939–940.

25. A. C. Pigou, "Real Income and Economic Welfare," *Oxford Economic Papers* 3, no. 1 (February 1951): 16. Paul Samuelson, "Evaluation of Real National Income," *Oxford Economic Papers,* New Series 2, no. 1 (January 1950): 21.

26. Pigou held that only in a case "where quantity of resources and technical conditions have changed and tastes and purchasing power are alike for all purchasers and have not changed, that inferences about economic welfare are possible." Pigou, "Real Income and Economic Welfare," 20.

27. A. C. Pigou, "Some Aspects of Welfare Economics," *American Economic Review* 41, no. 3 (June 1951): 287.

28. A. C. Pigou, *Alfred Marshall and Current Economic Thought* (London: Macmillan, 1953): 3.

29. Pigou to Hugh Dalton, March 16, 1951, Crosland Collection, LSE, Crosland 10/2.

30. Pigou, "Some Aspects of Welfare Economics," 287.

31. Ibid., 292.

32. "Premi «Antonio Feltrinelli» Finora Conferiti," Academia Nazionale dei Lincei, accessed January 18, 2014, http://www.lincei.it/premi/assegnati_feltrinelli.php. On receiving the prize, Pigou wrote Sraffa, "I wired and wrote gratefulness etc. but wished you had been available to hold my hand. The 5 million lire are, no doubt, en route under escort of Italian and British fleets!" Pigou to Piero Sraffa, June 29, 1955, Papers of Piero Sraffa, TCA, Sraffa C239, 6.

33. New liberalism, in a sufficiently loose definition, was intimately related to this transformation. In *The New Liberalism*, Michael Freeden wrote, "from the vantage point of the modern British welfare state it is the new liberalism of the turn of the century which appears to have gained the upper hand over its rival ideologies." Michael Freeden, *The New Liberalism: An Ideology of Social Reform* (Oxford: Clarendon Press, 1978): 1. See also Peter Clarke, *Liberals and Social Democrats* (Cambridge: Cambridge University Press, 1978): 2–3. For an overview of the historiography of the British welfare state, see the introduction in Bernard Harris, *The Origins of the*

British Welfare State: Society State and Social Welfare in England and Wales, 1800–1945 (Basingstoke, UK: Palgrave Macmillan, 2004).

34. Pigou to Noel-Baker, n.d. [late August 1945], Noel-Baker Papers, CAC, NBKR 9/58/2; Pigou to Noel-Baker, n.d. [early 1947], Noel-Baker Papers, CAC, NBKR 9/58.

35. A. C. Pigou, "Some Aspects of the Welfare State," *Diogenes* 7, no. 2 (Summer 1954): 4.

36. Ibid., 6

37. Ibid.

38. Ibid., 7.

39. Ibid.

40. "Whereas for a single person or family to be forced to accept a lower living standard while their friends—and their enemies—are left as before may be very distressing; but if the whole of their class or group suffer alike, they will scarcely suffer at all." Ibid., 8.

41. Philip Noel-Baker to Austin Robinson, October 21, 1964, Austin Robinson Papers, MLE, 6/6/4, 33–34.

42. Pigou, "Some Aspects of the Welfare State," 11

43. A. C. Pigou, *Income Revisited* (London: Macmillan, 1955): v.

44. Ibid.

45. Ibid., 77.

46. Ibid., 80.

47. Ibid., 84. This mode of thought anticipates the work of so-called Luck Egalitarians, including Oxford philosopher G. A. Cohen, decades later. See G. A. Cohen, "On the Currency of Egalitarian Justice," *Ethics* 99, no. 4 (July 1989): 906–944.

48. Pigou, *Income Revisited*, 81.

49. It is instructive to compare the trajectory of Pigou's life with that of William Beveridge, who also moved from Liberal reform, to interwar disenchantment, and then to being supportive of the welfare state in the 1940s. See José Harris, *William Beveridge: A Biography* (Oxford: Clarendon Press): 471–473.

Epilogue

1. R. H. Coase, "The Problem of Social Cost," *Journal of Law & Economics* 3 (October 1960): 1.

2. See Dipesh Chakrabarthy, "The Climate of History: Four Theses," *Critical Inquiry* 35, no. 2 (Winter 2009): 197–222. See also, for instance, Julia Adeney Thomas, "History and Biology in the Anthropocene: Problems of Scale, Problems of Value," *American Historical Review* 119, no. 5 (December 1, 2014): 1587–1607; Jeddidiah Purdy et al., "Forum: The New Nature," *Boston Review* (January 11, 2016), https://bostonreview.net/forum/jedediah-purdy-new-nature.

3. John Cassidy, "An Economist's Invisible Hand," *Wall Street Journal* (November 28, 2009), http://online.wsj.com/article/ SB1000142405274870420430457454567135 2424680.html.

4. Elizabeth Kolbert, "Paying For It," *New Yorker* (December 10, 2012), accessed June 25, 2014, http://www.newyorker.com/talk/comment/2012/12/10/121210taco_talk_kolbert.

5. Robert H. Frank, "Heads, You Win. Tails, You Win, Too," *New York Times* (January 5, 2013), accessed June 25, 2014, http://www.nytimes.com/2013/01/06/business/pigovian-taxes-may-offer-economic-hope.html.

6. Cassidy, "An Economist's Invisible Hand"; John Cassidy, *How Markets Fail: The Logic of Economic Calamities* (New York: Picador, 2010): 170–182.

7. Amartya Sen, "Capitalism Beyond the Crisis," *New York Review of Books* (March 26, 2009), accessed November 20, 2014, http://www.nybooks.com/articles/2009/03/26/capitalism-beyond-the-crisis/.

8. Liam C. Malloy and John Case, "Want Less Inequality? Tax It," *American Prospect* (November 14, 2012), http://prospect.org/article/what-would-pigou-do; John Schwartz, "Be It Enacted: A Tax on the Taxing," *New York Times* (February 9, 2013), http://www.nytimes.com/2013/02/10/business/yourtaxes/pigovian-taxes-can-erase-deficits-and-other- irritants.html?pagewanted=all.

9. A. C. Pigou, *Economic Science in Relation to Practice* (London: Macmillan, 1908): 13–14.

BIBLIOGRAPHY

Primary Sources

MANUSCRIPTS

Archives of the London School of Economics and Political Science (LSE), London, United Kingdom

Blaug Papers
   Blaug/3 Correspondence
Cannan Collection
   Cannan/1032 Correspondence
   Cannan/1033 Correspondence
Crosland Collection
   Crosland 10/2 Correspondence between Hugh Dalton and A.C. Pigou
Dalton Collection
   Dalton 2/9 Correspondence
Papers of the Royal Economic Society
   RES 6/1/383 Correspondence with A.C. Pigou
Passfield Collection
   2/4/K Correspondence
Robbins Collection
   Robbins 1/3 Documents Relating to the Economic Advisory Council

British Library (BL), London, United Kingdom

Sir William Ashley Papers
   Add MS 42247 Board of Trade Economists Committee
Papers of Sir R.F. Harrod
   Add MS 72764 Letters to Sir R.F. Harrod
Macmillan Papers
   Add MS 55199 Correspondence of Arthur C. Pigou with Macmillan Publishers
   Add MS 55200 Correspondence of Arthur C. Pigou with Macmillan Publishers

Churchill College Archives (CCA), Cambridge, United Kingdom

The Papers of Baron Noel-Baker
   NBKR 9/45 Letters of Josephine Baker
   NBKR 9/46 Papers of Josephine Baker
   NBKR 9/58 Professor Pigou's Letters
   NBKR 9/69 Miscellaneous Correspondence
   NBKR 11/3 Papers relating to the Friends' Ambulance Unit

Cumbria Archive Centre, Carlisle, United Kingdom
Cockermouth Rural District Council Papers
  SRDC/3/2/709 Plans for Pigou's House
Marshall Family Papers
  DMAR/2/33 Letters of Miss Catherine E. Marshall

The Hoover Institution, Stanford University,
Palo Alto, California, United States
Friedrich A. von Hayek Papers
  Box 8, Folder 9 Correspondence

King's College Archive (KCA), Cambridge, United Kingdom
Academic and Tutorial Records
  KCAC/1/2/6/1/Pigou1 Menu of the "Complimentary Dinner to Professor A.C.
    Pigou, Saturday June 6th, 1908"
  KCAC/1/2/6/1/Pigou2 Photographs
  KCAC/6/1/11/36 Subject File: A.C. Pigou
Governing Records
  KCGB/6/14/1/1 Electors to Fellowship Committee Meetings
The Papers of Oscar Browning
  OB/1/1281/A Letters from Arthur Cecil Pigou to Oscar Browning, c. 1897–1911
  OB/1/1062/C Letters from Alfred Marshall to Oscar Browning, c.1884–1903
The Papers of Richard Ferdinand Kahn
  RFK/2/8 Fellowship Reports
  RFK/13/83 Correspondence between A.C. Pigou and RFK
  RFK/19/3 Papers relating to holidays in Switzerland and the Lake District
The Papers of Nicholas Kaldor
  NK/3/30 Correspondence
  NK/3/93 Spy Stories
The Papers of John Maynard Keynes
  JMK/EA/1 Correspondence on the activities of the Council and its sub-committees,
    1930–1939
  JMK/GTE/2 Discursive correspondence with colleagues and others after publica-
    tion of the *General Theory*
  JMK/L/R Correspondence with Dennis H. Robertson, 1912–1938
  JMK/PP/45/254 Correspondence between J.M. Keynes and A.C. Pigou, 1907–1942
  JMK/T/22 Essays on government indebtedness
  JMK/TM/1 Correspondence Relating to the *Treatise on Money*
  JMK/TP/4 Reports to the Fellowship Electors
  JMK/UA/3/1 Examination Papers
Papers Relating to Arthur Cecil Pigou
  ACP/1/Corrie Memoir of ACP and letter from ACP to Corrie
  ACP/3/1 Photographs

The Papers of Joan Violet Robinson
  JVR/1/2/2 List of Dedicatees of "Economics is a Serious Subject," n.d. 1932
  JVR/7/347 Letters from Arthur Cecil Pigou to Joan Robinson, with related
    materials
The Papers of John Tresidder Sheppard
  JTS/1/8 Account of a day's events
  JTS/2/160 Letter from Arthur Cecil Pigou to JTS, 24 July 1903
The Papers of John Richard Nicholas Stone
  JRNS/3/1/102 Correspondence between Professor Pigou and JRNS
The Papers of Alan Matheson Turing
  AMT/A/10 Letters from various authors to Mrs. Sara Turing
The Papers of Lancelot Patrick Wilkinson
  LPW/8/4/7 Letters from Arthur Cecil Pigou to L P Wilkinson
  LPW/8/7 Spy Stories
  LPW/11/1 Photographs

  Marshall Library of Economics (MLE), Cambridge, United Kingdom
James Bonar Papers
  Bonar 3 Papers
Marshall Papers
  Marshall 1 Correspondence
Arthur Cecil Pigou Papers
  Pigou 1/2 A.C. Pigou, Undergraduate History Notes, undated
  Pigou 1/3 A.C. Pigou, "The Causes and Effects of Changes in the Relative Values of
    Agricultural Produce in the United Kingdom During the Last Fifty Years," 1901
  Pigou 1/5/2 A.C. Pigou, "Terms of Peace," Unpublished manuscript, c. 1915–16
  Pigou 1/7/1 A.C. Pigou, "An Analytical Account of the General Economic Move-
    ment in the United Kingdom between the Armistice and the Restoration of
    the Gold Standard," 1941
  Pigou 2/2/3 Unknown author, "Review of 'The Theory of Unemployment,'"
    c. 1933–34
  Pigou 2/2/4 Correspondence with Jacob Marschak
  Pigou 2/2/7 Correspondence with Jacob Marschak
  Pigou 2/3 Items found in Pigou's copy of *The Theory of Unemployment*
  Pigou 4 Minutes of the Meetings of the Committee on the Currency and Bank of
    England Note Issues
Austin Robinson Papers
  EAGR/6/1/6 John Saltmarsh's notes on Pigou's lectures
  EAGR/6/6/2 Notes on Pigou family
  EAGR/6/6/3 Notes on elections of professors
  EAGR/6/6/4 Correspondence with Roy Harrod
  EAGR/6/6/5 Research on A.C. Pigou
  EAGR/6/6/6 EAGR Articles; Pigou

Gerald Frank Shove Papers
Shove 1 Undergraduate Economics Notes, King's College, Cambridge 1909–11

The National Archives of the United Kingdom (TNA),
Kew, United Kingdom

Admiralty
ADM 196/45 Executive Officers' Services
Board of Trade
BT 27 Outwards Passenger Lists
Cabinet Papers and Minutes
CAB 24/75 Memoranda
Census Returns
RG 11 1881
RG 12 1891
RG 14 1911
Chancellor of the Exchequer's Office
T 172/1763 Miscellaneous Papers
Committee on Currency and Foreign Exchange (Cunliffe Committee)
T 185/1 Minutes and Reports
Committee to Consider Currency, Note Issues and the Gold Standard
T 160/197 F7528 Documents, Minutes, and Reports
Royal Commission on the Income Tax (Treasury)
T 172/985 Documents, Minutes, and Reports
Royal Commission on the Income Tax (Board of Inland Revenue)
IR 85/4 Circulated papers: 87–111, June 1919
IR 85/8 Circulated papers: 204–246, October 1919
War Office
WO 372 Service Medal and Award Rolls Index

Trinity College Archives, (TCA) Cambridge, United Kingdom
The Papers of Dennis Robertson
Roberston C1 Correspondence with Pigou and the Marshalls
Robertson C2 Correspondence with J.M. Keynes
Robertson C7 Correspondence about *Employment and Equilibrium*
The Papers of Piero Sraffa
Sraffa C239 Correspondence with A.C. Pigou

PARLIAMENTARY COMMAND PAPERS AND GOVERNMENT LISTS

Army List, September 1902
First Interim Report of the Cunliffe Committee [Cd. 9182], 1918
Minutes and Evidence of the Royal Commission on the Poor Laws and Relief of Distress [Cd. 5068], 1910
Navy List, February 1896, January 1919, February 1919, June 1919

Report of the Committee on the Currency and Bank of England Note Issues [Cmd. 2393], 1925

Report of the Royal Commission on the Income Tax [Cmd. 615], 1920

Report on the Working of the Education (Provision of Meals) Act 1906 up to 31 March 1909 [Cd. 5131], 1910

Reports and Minutes of Evidence on the Second Stage of Inquiry of the Coal Industry Commission [Cmd. 360], 1919

PERIODICAL COLLECTIONS

Cambridge University Calendar, accessed at the University Library, University of Cambridge, Cambridge, United Kingdom

Cambridge University Reporter, accessed in the Philips Reading Room, Widener Library, Harvard University, Cambridge, Massachusetts, United States

The Granta, accessed in the Munby Rare Books Room the University Library, University of Cambridge, Cambridge, United Kingdom

The Harrovian, accessed online at http://harrovian.websds.net/

PUBLISHED SOURCES BY PIGOU

The following is a selected list of Pigou's publications, including various editions of his books, which appeared during his lifetime, arranged by year of publication. Books are displayed in bold.

"*Economic Crises* by Edward D. Jones." *Economic Journal* 10, no. 40 (December 1900): 523–526.

Robert Browning as a Religious Teacher, Being the Burney Essay for 1900. London: C. J. Clay, 1901.

"Some Aspects on the Problem of Charity," in *The Heart of the Empire: Discussions of the Problems of Modern City Life in England*, ed. C. F. G. Masterman, 236–261. Revised ed. New York: Harper & Row, 1973 [1901].

"*The Despatches and Correspondence of John, Second Earl of Buckinghamshire, Ambassador to the Court of Catherine II of Russia, 1762–5* by Adelaide D'Arcy Collyer." *Economic Journal* 11, no. 41 (March 1901): 77

"Professors and the Corn Tax." *Speaker*, June 14, 1902.

"A Parallel Between Economic and Political Theory," *Economic Journal* 12, no. 46 (June 1902): 274–277.

"A Point of Theory Connected with the Corn Tax." *Economic Journal* 12, no. 47 (September 1902): 415–420.

The Riddle of the Tariff. London: R. Brimley Johnson, 1903.

"Free Trade and Its Critics." *Fortnightly Review* 435 (March 1, 1903): 542–554.

"Some Remarks on Utility." *Economic Journal* 13, no. 49 (March 1903): 58–68.

"Professors of Economics and Fiscal Policy." *Times*, August 24, 1903, 6.

"The Economics of Mr. Balfour's Manifesto." *Times*, September 18, 1903, 4.

"Consumers and Producers." *Times*, November 10, 1903, 15.

"Consumers and Producers." *Times*, November 14, 1903, 14.

"To the Editor of the Times." *Times*, December 3, 1903, 5.

"The Known and the Unknown in Mr. Chamberlain's Policy." *Fortnightly Review* 445 (January 1, 1904): 36–48.

"Pure Theory and Fiscal Controversy." *Economic Journal* 14, no. 53 (March 1904): 29–33.

"*Free Trade and the Empire* by William Graham." *Economic Journal* 14, no. 54 (June 1904): 267–268.

"Mr. Chamberlain's Proposals." *Edinburgh Review* 200, no. 310 (July–October 1904): 449–475.

"Monopoly and Consumers' Surplus." *Economic Journal* 14, no. 55 (September 1904): 388–394.

Principles and Methods of Industrial Peace. London: Macmillan, **1905.**

Protective and Preferential Import Duties. London: Macmillan, **1906.**

"Protection and the Working Classes." *Edinburgh Review* 203, no. 415 (January–April 1906): 1–32.

"The Unity of Political and Economic Science." *Economic Journal* 16, no. 63 (September 1906): 372–380.

"*Emigrazione di Uomini ed Esportazione di Merci* by L. Fontana-Russo." *Economic Journal* 17, no. 65 (March 1907): 114.

"*Commercio Internazionale* by G. de Francisi Gerbino." *Economic Journal* 17, no. 66 (June 1907): 262–263.

"Local Taxation." *Edinburgh Review* 206 (July 1907): 88–109.

"Social Improvement in the Light of Modern Biology." *Economic Journal* 17, no. 67 (September 1907): 358–369.

"*Trattato di Politica Commerciale* by Luigi Fontana-Russo." *Economic Journal* 17, no. 67 (September 1907): 414–415.

"Some Points of Ethical Controversy." *International Journal of Ethics* 18, no. 1 (October 1, 1907): 99–107.

The Problem of Theism and Other Essays. London: Macmillan, **1908.**

"*L'Imposta sul Transporto Degli Emigranti* by Pasquale Jannaconne." *Economic Journal* 18, no. 69 (March 1908): 95.

"Equilibrium Under Bilateral Monopoly." *Economics Journal* 18, no. 70 (June 1908): 205–220.

Economic Science in Relation to Practice; an Inaugural Lecture Given at Cambridge 30th October, 1908. London: Macmillan, **1908.**

The Policy of Land Taxation. London: Longmans, Green and Company, 1909.

"Producers' and Consumers' Surplus." *Economic Journal* 20, no. 79 (September 1910): 358–370.

"A Method of Determining the Numerical Values of Elasticities of Demand." *Economics Journal* 20, no. 80 (December 1910): 636–640.

Wealth and Welfare. London: Macmillan, **1912.**

Unemployment. London: Williams & Norgate, **1913.**

"*Intorno al Concetto di Reddito Imponibile e di un Sistema d'Imposte sul Readdito Consumato* by Luigi Einaudi." *Economic Journal* 23, no. 90 (June 1913): 260–263.

"*Vorlesungen uber Nationalokonomie auf Grundlage des Marginalprinzipes* by Knut Wicksell." *Economic Journal* 23, no. 92 (December 1913): 605–606.

The Economy and Finance of the War. London: Dent, 1916.

"Interest After the War and the Export of Capital." *Economic Journal* 26, no. 104 (December 1916): 413–424.

"The Need for More Taxation." *Economist,* December 9, 1916, 1087.

The Economics of the War Loan." *Economic Journal* 27, no. 105 (March 1917): 16–25.

"The Value of Money." *Quarterly Journal of Economics* 32, no. 1 (November 1917): 38–65.

"Inflation." *Economic Journal* 27, no. 108 (December 1917): 486–494.

"A Special Levy to Discharge War Debt." *Economic Journal* 28, no. 110 (June 1918): 135–156.

"Government Control in War and Peace," *Economic Journal* 28, no. 112 (December 1918): 363–373.

"The Burden of War and Future Generations." *Quarterly Journal of Economics* 33, no. 2 (1919): 241–255.

The Economics of Welfare. London: Macmillan, 1920.

"Memorandum on Credit, Currency, and Exchange Fluctuations," in *Documents de la conférence: Conférence financière internationale, Bruxelles, 1920: Memoranda d'experts en matière économique,* by the League of Nations. London: Harrison, 1920.

"Co-operative Societies and Income Tax." *Economic Journal* 30, no. 118 (June 1920): 156–162.

"The Report of the Royal Commission on the British Income Tax." *Quarterly Journal of Economics* 34, no. 4 (1920): 607–625.

The Political Economy of War. London: Macmillan, 1921.

"Mr. and Mrs. Webb on Consumers' Co-Operation." *Economic Journal* 32, no. 125 (March 1922): 53–57.

"Empty Economic Boxes: A Reply." *Economic Journal* 32, no. 128 (December 1922): 458–465.

Essays in Applied Economics. London: P. S. King & Son, 1923.

"Capital Levy: Matters for a Royal Commission." *Times,* May 1, 1923, 9.

"Capital Levy." *Times,* May 7, 1923, 8.

The Economics of Welfare, second ed. London: Macmillan, 1924.

"Correctives of the Trade Cycle," in *Is Unemployment Inevitable? An Analysis and a Forecast,* ed. J. J. Astor, A. L. Bowley, Robert Grant, J. H. Jones, W. T. Layton, P. F. Pybus, B. Seebohm Rowntree, D. Spring-Rice, and F. D. Stuart, 91–130. London: Macmillan, 1924.

ed. *Memorials of Alfred Marshall.* London: Macmillan, 1925.

"Problems of Compensation." *Economic Journal* 35, no. 125 (December 1925): 568–582.

"Economics at the Universities." *Times,* November 19, 1926, 15.

Industrial Fluctuations. London: Macmillan, 1927.

"The Laws of Diminishing and Increasing Cost." *Economic Journal* 37, no. 146 (June 1927): 188–197.

A Study in Public Finance. London: Macmillan, 1928.

"An Analysis of Supply." *Economic Journal* 38, no. 150 (June 1928): 238–257.

"Safeguarded Industries." *Times,* November 17, 1928, 8.

The Economics of Welfare, third ed. London: Macmillan, 1929.

A Study in Public Finance, second ed. London: Macmillan, 1929.

Economic Essays and Addresses, London: P. S. King & Son, 1931. (With Dennis Robertson).

The Economics of Welfare, fourth ed. London: Macmillan, 1932.

The Theory of Unemployment. London: Macmillan, 1933.

"A Note on Imperfect Competition." *Economic Journal* 43, no. 169 (March 1933): 108–112.

Economics in Practice: Six Lectures on Current Issues. London: Macmillan, 1935.

The Economics of Stationary States. London: Macmillan, 1935.

"Mr. J. M. Keynes' *General Theory of Employment, Interest and Money.*" *Economica* 3 (May 1936): 115–132.

Pigou, A. C., Milton Friedman, and N. Georgescu-Roegen. "Marginal Utility of Money and Elasticities of Demand." *Quarterly Journal of Economics* 50, no. 3 (May 1936): 532–539.

Socialism Versus Capitalism. London: Macmillan, 1937.

"Presidential Address: Looking Back from 1939." *Economic Journal* 49, no. 194 (June 1939): 215–221.

The Political Economy of War, second ed. London: Macmillan, 1940.

"Maintaining Capital Intact." *Economica,* New Series 8, no. 31 (August 1941): 271–275.

Pigou, A. C., and Nicholas Kaldor. "Models of Short-Period Equilibrium." *Economic Journal* 52, no. 206/7 (June–September 1942): 250–258.

"The Classical Stationary State." *Economic Journal* 53, no. 212 (1943): 243–251.

"*The Road to Serfdom* Review." *Economic Journal* 54, no. 214 (June–September 1944): 217–219.

Lapses from Full Employment. London: Macmillan, 1945.

Income. London: Macmillan, 1946.

"John Maynard Keynes, 1883–1946." *Proceedings of the British Academy* (1946): 395–414.

"Night Life on High Hills." *Alpine Journal* 53 (1946): 246.

Aspects of British Economic History 1918–1925. London: Macmillan, 1947.

Employment and Equilibrium, second ed. London: Macmillan, 1947.

"Central Planning and Professor Robbins." *Economica,* New Series 15, no. 57 (February 1948): 17–27.

"A Comment on Duopoly." *Economica,* New Series 15, no. 60 (November 1948): 254–258.

A Study in Public Finance, third (revised) ed. London: Macmillan, 1949.

The Veil of Money. London: Macmillan, 1949.

"Mill and the Wages Fund." *Economic Journal* 59, no. 234 (June 1949): 171–180.

"Obituary [John Neville Keynes]." *Economic Journal* 60, no. 238 (June 1950): 407–408.

"Unrequited Exports." *Economic Journal* 60, no. 238 (June 1950): 241–254.

"Professor Duesenberry on Income and Savings." *Economic Journal* 61, no. 244 (December 1951): 883–885.

***Keynes's General Theory Revisited: A Retrospective View.* London: Macmillan, 1951.**

"Real Income and Economic Welfare." *Oxford Economic Papers* 3, no. 1 (February 1951): 16–20.

"Some Aspects of Welfare Economics." *American Economic Review* 41, no. 3 (June 1951): 287–302.

***Essays in Economics.* London: Macmillan, 1952.**

"The Transfer Problem and Transport Costs." *Economic Journal* 62, no. 248 (December 1952): 939–941.

***Alfred Marshall and Current Economic Thought.* London: Macmillan, 1953.**

"Some Aspects of the Welfare State." *Diogenes* 7 (Summer 1954): 1–11.

***Income Revisited.* London: Macmillan, 1955.**

"Wage Earnings Since the War," *Times,* July 13, 1955, 9.

"Wage Earnings Since the War," *Times,* July 14, 1955, 5.

OTHER PUBLISHED SOURCES

Astor, J. J., A. L. Bowley, Robert Grant, J. H. Jones, W. T. Layton, P. F. Pybus, B. Seebohm Rowntree, D. Spring-Rice, and F. D. Stuart, eds. *Is Unemployment Inevitable? An Analysis and a Forecast.* London: Macmillan, 1924.

"Back to Sanity." *Economist,* November 2, 1918.

Barnstable, F., A. L. Bowley, Edwin Cannan, Leonard Courtney, F. Y. Edgeworth, C. K. Gonner, Alfred Marshall, et al. "Professors of Economics and the Tariff Question." *Times,* August 15, 1903, 4.

Bator, Francis M. "The Simple Analytics of Welfare Maximization." *American Economic Review* 47, no. 1 (March 1957): 22–59.

"Beachlands." *Isle of Wight Observer,* August 1892. Accessed January 19, 2014. http://www.historicrydesociety.co.uk/history/royal-victoria-arcade/ryde-houses/beachlands/.

Benham, Frederic, "*The Economics of Stationary States* by A.C. Pigou." *Economica* 3, no. 9 (February 1936): 89–93.

Benn, Sir Ernest. "The Teaching of Economics." *Times,* November 17, 1926, 15–16.

Beveridge, William. *British Food Control.* Oxford: Oxford University Press, 1928.

———. *Full Employment in a Free Society: A Report.* London: G. Allen, 1944.

Bowers, Edison L. "The Theory of Unemployment by A.C. Pigou." *American Economic Review* 24, no. 2 (June 1934): 282–283.

Bradbury, John, Gaspard Farrer, O. E. Niemeyer, and A. C. Pigou. "Return to Gold Standard." *Times,* April 19, 1925, 11.

Bresciani-Turroni, Constantino. "The Theory of Unemployment, by A.C. Pigou." *Weltwirtschaftliches Archiv* 40 Bd. (1943): 169–173.

Cannan, Edwin. *"An Essay on the Significance of Economic Science* by Lionel Robbins."
  Economic Journal 42, no. 167 (September 1932): 424–427.
Champernowne, D. G. "Arthur Cecil Pigou 1877–1959." *Statistical Journal* 122, no. 2
  (1959): 263–265.
Clapham, J. H. "Of Empty Economic Boxes." *Economic Journal* 32, no 127 (September
  1922): 305–314.
———. "The Economic Boxes." *Economic Journal* 34, no. 133 (March 1924): 16–31.
Clark, Colin. *National Income and Outlay*. London: Macmillan, 1937.
"Climbing to Power." *Guardian*, May 30, 1979.
Coase, R. H. "The Lighthouse in Economics." *Journal of Law and Economics* 17, no.
  2 (October 1974): 357–376.
———. "The Problem of Social Cost." *Journal of Law and Economics* 3 (October 1960):
  1–44.
Conner, L. R. *"A Study in Public Finance* by A. C. Pigou." *Journal of the Royal Statisti-
  cal Society* 91, no. 3 (1928): 412–415.
———. *"The Economics of Welfare* by A.C. Pigou." *Journal of the Royal Statistical Society*
  93, no. 1 (1930): 125–126.
Cox, A. D. M. "Noyce, (Cuthbert) Wilfrid Francis (1917–1962)," in *Oxford Dictionary
  of National Biography,* revised. Oxford: Oxford University Press, 2004; online
  ed., Jan 2011 [http://www.oxforddnb.com/view/article/35265, accessed April 26,
  2013].
Dalton, Hugh. *Call Back Yesterday: Memoirs 1887–1931*. London: F. Muller, 1953.
———. "A Study in Public Finance by A.C. Pigou." *Economica* no. 23 (June 1928): 216.
Dauglish, M. G., and P. K. Stephenson, eds. *The Harrow School Register 1800–1911*.
  London: Longmans, Green and Company, 1911.
Dawson, William Harbutt, ed. *After-War Problems*. London: Allen & Unwin, 1918.
Deacon, Richard. "The British Connection 2." *Guardian*, May 30, 1979, 16.
Durbin, E. F. M. "Economic Calculus in a Planned Economy." *Economic Journal* 46,
  no. 184 (December 1936): 676–690.
Edgeworth, Francis Ysidro. *New and Old Methods of Ethics: Or "Physical Ethics" and
  "Methods of Ethics."* Oxford: J. Parker, 1877.
———. "Wealth and Welfare by A.C. Pigou." *Economic Journal* 23, no. 89 (March 1913):
  62–70.
Elliott, Nicholas. *Never Judge a Man by His Umbrella*. London: Michael Russell,
  1991.
Farren, W. S., and H. T. Tizard. "Hermann Glauert, 1892–1934." *Obituary Notices of
  Fellows of the Royal Society* 1, no. 4 (December 1935): 607–610.
Foxwell, H. S. "The Economic Movement in England." *Quarterly Journal of Economics*
  2, no. 1 (October 1887): 84–103.
Fraser, Lindley M. "How Do We Want Economists to Behave?" *Economic Journal* 42,
  no. 168 (December 1932): 555–570.
Friedman, Milton. "Professor Pigou's Method for Measuring Elasticities of Demand
  from Budgetary Data." *Quarterly Journal of Economics* 50, no. 1 (November 1935):
  151–163.

Frisch, Ragnar. "Sur un problème d'économie pure." *Norsk Matemastik Forenings Skrifter*, Series I, no. 16 (1926): 1–40.

Hansen, Alvin H. *Fiscal Policy and Business Cycles*. New York: W. W. Norton & Company, 1941.

Harris, S. E. "Professor Pigou's Theory of Unemployment." *Quarterly Journal of Economics* 49, no. 2 (February 1935): 286–324.

Harrod, R. F. "Professor Pigou's Theory of Unemployment." *Economic Journal* 44, no. 173 (March 1934): 19–32.

———. "The Scope and Method of Economics." *Economic Journal* 48, no. 191 (September 1938): 383–412.

Hawtrey, R. G. *Currency and Credit*. London: Longmans, Green and Company, 1919.

———. *The Problem of Economics*. London: Longmans, Green and Company, 1925.

———. "The Theory of Unemployment by Professor A.C. Pigou." *Economica*, New Series 1, no. 2 (May 1934): 147–166.

Hayek, F. A. "Maintaining Capital Intact: A Reply." *Economica*, New Series 8, no. 31 (August 1941): 276–280.

———. *The Pure Theory of Capital*. London: Macmillan, 1940.

———. "Scientism and the Study of Society." *Economica*, New Series 9, no. 36 (August 1942): 267–291.

———. "Scientism and the Study of Society." *Economica*, New Series 10, no. 37 (February 1943): 34–63.

———. "Scientism and the Study of Society Part II." *Economica*, New Series 11, no. 41 (February 1944): 27–39.

———. "The Use of Knowledge in Society." *American Economic Review* 34, no. 4 (September 1945): 519–530.

Hicks, John R. "The Foundations of Welfare Economics." *Economic Journal* 49, no. 196 (December 1939): 696–712.

———. "Maintaining Capital Intact: A Further Suggestion," *Economica* New Series 9, no. 32 (May 1942): 174–179.

———. "Recollections and Documents." *Economica* 4, no. 157 (February 1973): 2–11.

———. *The Theory of Wages*. London: Macmillan, 1932.

"India Office, March 7." *Morning Post*, March 8, 1876, 6.

"Industrial Fluctuations." *Spectator*, April 15, 1927, 24.

Jensen, Jens P. "*A Study in Public Finance* by A.C. Pigou." *American Economic Review* 18, no. 4 (December 1928): 770.

Kahn, R. F. "Some Notes on Ideal Output." *Economic Journal* 45, no. 1 (March 1935): 1–35.

Kaldor, Nicholas. "Welfare Propositions of Economics and Interpersonal Comparisons of Utility." *Economic Journal* 49, no. 195 (September 1939): 549–552.

Kalecki, Michał. "Professor Pigou on 'The Classical Stationary State' A Comment." *Economic Journal* 54, no. 213 (April 1944): 131–132.

Keynes, John Maynard. "Alfred Marshall, 1842–1924," in *Memorials of Alfred Marshall*, ed. A. C. Pigou, 1–65. London: Macmillan, 1925.

Keynes, John Maynard. *The Collected Writings of John Maynard Keynes.* Cambridge: Cambridge University Press, 1992.

———. *Economic Consequences of the Peace.* London: Macmillan, 1919.

———. *The General Theory of Employment, Interest, and Money.* New York: Harcourt Brace & World, 1964.

———. *Two Memoirs.* London: Hart-Davis, 1949.

Keynes, J. M., and H. D. Henderson. *Can Lloyd George Do It?: An Examination of the Liberal Pledge.* London: The Nation and Athenaeum, 1929.

Knight, Frank H. "Economics at Its Best." *American Economic Review* 16, no. 1 (March 1926): 51–58.

———. "*The Nature and Significance of Economic Science* by Lionel Robbins," *International Journal of Ethics* 44, no. 3 (April 1934): 358–361.

Labour Party. *Labour and the War Debt: A Statement of Policy for the Redemption of War Debt by a Levy on Accumulated Wealth.* London: Labour Party, 1922.

———. *Labour's Appeal to the Nation.* London: Labour Party, 1929.

———. *Let Us Face the Future: A Declaration of Labour Policy for the Consideration of the Nation.* London: Labour Party, 1945.

Lange, Oskar. *On the Economic Theory of Socialism.* Minneapolis: University of Minnesota Press, 1938.

Layton, W. T. *Dorothy: The Story of the Married Life of Dorothy and Walter Layton.* London: Collins, 1961.

Lerner, Abba. *The Economics of Control: Principles of Welfare Economics.* New York: Macmillan, 1944.

———. "*Employment and Equilibrium* by A.C. Pigou." *Review of Economics and Statistics* 24, no. 2 (May 1942): 87–92.

Lloyd, E. M. H. *Experiments in State Control at the War Office and the Ministry of Food.* Oxford: Clarendon Press, 1924.

Lock, R. H. *Recent Progress in the Study of Variation, Heredity, and Evolution.* London: John Murray, 1907.

Lunn, Arnold. *The Harrovians: A Tale of Public School Life.* London: Smith, Elder and Co., 1913.

Macdonnell, Sir John. "New Phases of Political Economy." *Times Literary Supplement,* January 9, 1913, 10.

Macgregor, D. H., A. C. Pigou, J. M. Keynes, Walter Layton, Arthur Salter, J. C. Stamp, and M. Russell, "Private Spending: Money for Private Investment." *Times,* October 17, 1932, 13.

Macrosty, Henry W. "Industrial Fluctuations by A.C. Pigou." *Journal of the Royal Statistical Society* 90, no. 3 (1927): 596–598.

Mankiw, N. Gregory. "Opinion: Raise the Gas Tax." *Wall Street Journal,* October 20, 2006. http://online.wsj.com/article/SB116131055641498552.html?mod=opinion _main_commentaries.

———. *Principles of Economics.* Cincinnati, OH: South-Western, 2011.

———. "Smart Taxes: An Open Invitation to Join the Pigou Club," n.d.

"Marriage of Miss Lees." *Isle of Wight Times*, November 23, 1876.

Marshall, Alfred. *The Correspondence of Alfred Marshall, Economist*, 3 volumes, ed. John Whitaker. Cambridge: Cambridge University Press, 1996.

———. *Industry and Trade; A Study of Industrial Technique and Business Organization, and of Their Influences on the Conditions of Various Classes and Nations*. London: Macmillan, 1919.

———. *Principles of Economics*. Fourth ed. London: Macmillan, 1898.

———. *Principles of Economics: An Introductory Volume*, eighth ed., rev. London: Palgrave Macmillan, 2013.

———. "Social Possibilities of Economic Chivalry." *Economic Journal* 17, no. 65 (March 1907): 7–29.

Masterman, C.F.G. *The New Liberalism*. London: L. Parsons, 1920.

Mill, John Stuart. *Principles of Political Economy: With Some of Their Applications to Social Philosophy*. London: Longmans, Green, Reader, and Dyer, 1866.

Money, Leo Chiozza. *The Triumph of Nationalization*. London: Cassell, 1920.

Moore, G. E. *Principia Ethica*, revised ed. Cambridge: Cambridge University Press, 1993.

Noel-Baker, Phillip. "Letter to the Editor." *Guardian*, June 2, 1979.

Pagni, Carlo. "The Theory of Unemployment by A.C. Pigou." *Giornale degli Economisti e Rivista di Statistica*, Serie Quarta 75, no. 8 (August 1935): 675–676.

Pareto, Vilfredo. *Manual of Political Economy*. Oxford: Oxford University Press, 2014.

Parsons, Talcott. *The Structure of Social Action: A Study in Social Theory with Special Reference to a Group of Recent European Writers*. New York: McGraw-Hill, 1937.

Patinkin, Don. "Price Flexibility and Full Employment." *American Economic Review* 38, no. 4 (September 1948): 543–564.

Perlman, Jacob. "*Industrial Fluctuations* by A. C. Pigou; *Business Cycles and Business Measurements. Studies in Quantitative Economics* by Carl Snyder; *Forecasting Business Conditions* by Charles O. Hardy; Garfield V. Cox." *Journal of Land & Public Utility Economics* 3, no. 4 (November 1927): 423–424.

Persons, Warren M. "*Industrial Fluctuations* by A.C. Pigou." *Quarterly Journal of Economics* 42, no. 4 (August 1928): 669–677.

Pethick Lawrence, F. W. *The Capital Levy: How the Labour Party Would Settle the War Debt*. London: Labour Party, 1920.

Punnett, R. C. *Mendelism*. London: Macmillan and Bowes, 1905.

R., J. H., "The Theory of Unemployment by A.C. Pigou." *Journal of the Royal Statistical Society* 97, no. 1 (1934): 172–175.

Rawls, John. *A Theory of Justice*, revised ed. Cambridge, MA: Harvard University Press, 1999.

Robbins, Lionel. *An Essay on the Nature and Significance of Economic Science*, third ed. London: Macmillan, 1984.

———. "Interpersonal Comparisons of Utility: A Comment." *Economic Journal* 48, no. 192 (December 1938): 635–641.

———. *Politics and Economics*. London: Macmillan, 1963.

Robinson, E. A. G. "A.C. Pigou." *Times*, March 9, 1959, 12.

———. "Pigou, Arthur Cecil (1877–1959), Economist." *Dictionary of National Biography Archive*, 1971. http://www.oxforddnb.com/view/olddnb/35529.

Robinson, Joan. *The Economics of Imperfect Competition.* London: Macmillan, 1933.

———. *Economics Is a Serious Subject.* Cambridge: W. Heffer & Sons, 1932.

Rottier, G. "*The Veil of Money* by A.C. Pigou." *Economica*, New Series 16, no. 64 (November 1949): 380–382.

Rowntree, B. Seebohm. *Poverty: A Study of Town Life.* London: Macmillan, 1901.

Royal Commission on the Poor Law. *The Minority Report of the Poor Law Commission.* London: Fabian Society, 1909.

Samuelson, Paul A. "Evaluation of Real National Income." *Oxford Economic Papers*, New Series 2, no. 1 (January 1950): 1–29.

———. "Professor Pigou's *Employment and Equilibrium.*" *American Economic Review* 31, no. 3 (September 1941): 545–552.

Scitovsky, Tibor. "A Note on Welfare Propositions in Economics." *Review of Economic Studies* 9, no. 1 (November 1941): 77–88

———. "The State of Welfare Economics." *American Economic Review* 41, no. 3 (June 1951): 303–315.

Sidgwick, Henry. "Ecce Homo." *Westminster Review* 86 (July 1866).

———. *The Methods of Ethics.* London: Macmillan, 1907.

———. *The Principles of Political Economy.* London: Macmillan, 1883.

Souter, R. W. "'The Nature and Significance of Economics' in Recent Discussion." *Quarterly Journal of Economics* 47, no. 3 (May 1933): 377–413.

Sraffa, Piero. "The Laws of Returns under Competitive Conditions." *Economic Journal* 36, no. 144 (December 1926): 535–550.

———. "Sulle relazioni fra costo e quantita prodotta." *Annali di Economia* 2, no. 1 (1925): 277–328.

Stamp, J. S. "*Industrial Fluctuations* by A.C. Pigou." *Economic Journal* 37, no. 147 (September 1927): 418–424.

"*A Study in Public Finance* by A. C. Pigou." *Annals of the American Academy of Political and Social Science* 141 (January 1929): 281.

Tatham, Meaburn, and James E. Miles, eds. *The Friends' Ambulance Unit, 1914–1916: A Record.* London: Swarthmore Press, 1919.

Taussig, F. W., and A. C. Pigou, "Railway Rates and Joint Cost." *Quarterly Journal of Economics* 27, no. 3 (May 1913): 535–538.

———. "Railway Rates and Joint Costs," *Quarterly Journal of Economics*, 27, no. 4 (August 1913): 687–694.

Viner, Jacob. "Cost Curves and Supply Curves." *Zeitschrift für Nationalökonomie* 3, no. 1 (February 1932): 23–46.

"Wages and Tariffs: Economists Differ: Reports to the Government," *Manchester Guardian*, December 9, 1930.

Webb, Sidney, and Beatrice Webb. *Soviet Communism: A New Civilization?* London: Longmans, Green and Company, 1935.

Weber, Max. "Science as a Vocation" in *From Max Weber: Essays in Sociology,* ed. C. Wright Mills and H. H. Gerth. New York: Oxford University Press, 1980: 129–159.

Wooton, Barbara. *Lament for Economics.* London: George Allen & Unwin, 1938.

Young, Allyn. "Pigou's Wealth and Welfare." *Quarterly Journal of Economics* 27, no. 4 (August 1913): 672–686.

———. "A Study in Public Finance by A.C. Pigou." *Economic Journal* 39, no. 153 (March 1929): 78–83.

Secondary Sources

Academia Nazionale dei Lincei. "Premi «Antonio Feltrinelli» Finora Conferiti." Accessed January 18, 2014. http://www.lincei.it/premi/assegnati_feltrinelli.php.

Adelman, Jeremy. *Worldly Philosopher: The Odyssey of Albert O. Hirschman.* Princeton, NJ: Princeton University Press, 2014.

Ahamed, Liaquat. *Lords of Finance: The Bankers Who Broke the World.* New York: Penguin, 2009.

Ambrosi, Gerhard Michael. *Keynes, Pigou and Cambridge Keynesians: Authenticity and Analytical Perspective in the Keynes-Classics Debate.* Houndmills, Basingstoke, UK: Palgrave Macmillan, 2003.

———. "Keynes, Pigou, and the *General Theory.*" Lecture, University of Cambridge, Cambridge, October 22, 2008. http://www.postkeynesian.net/ucamonly/Ambrosi.pdf.

Andrew, Christopher. "Cambridge Spies," in *Cambridge Contributions,* ed. Sarah J. Ormrod. Cambridge: Cambridge University Press, 1998.

Annan, Noel Gilroy. *Our Age: English Intellectuals Between the World Wars—A Group Portrait.* New York: Random House, 1990.

Anstruther, Ian. *Oscar Browning: A Biography.* London: John Murray, 1983.

Arena, R., and Michel Quéré. *The Economics of Alfred Marshall: Revisiting Marshall's Legacy.* New York: Palgrave Macmillan, 2003.

Aslanbeigui, Nahid. "The Cost Controversy: Pigovian Economics in Disequilibrium." *European Journal of the History of Economic Thought* 3, no. 2 (Summer 1996): 275–295.

———. "Foxwell's Aims and Pigou's Military Service: A Malicious Episode?" *Journal of the History of Economic Thought* 14 (1992): 96–109.

———. "Introduction," in *The Economics of Welfare,* by A. C. Pigou, xxix–lxvi. New Brunswick, NJ: Transaction, 2001.

———. "On the Demise of Pigovian Economics." *Southern Economic Journal* 56, no. 3 (January 1, 1990): 616–627.

———. "Pigou's Inconsistencies or Keynes's Misconceptions?" *History of Political Economy* 24, no. 2 (1992): 413–433.

———. "Rethinking Pigou's Misogyny." *Eastern Economic Journal* 23, no. 3 (Summer 1997): 301–316.

Aslanbeigui, Nahid, and Steven G. Medema. "Beyond the Dark Clouds: Pigou and Coase on Social Cost." *History of Political Economy* 30, no. 4 (Winter 1998): 601–625.

Aslanbeigui, Nahid, and Guy Oakes. *Arthur Cecil Pigou.* Houndmills, Basingstoke, UK: Palgrave Macmillan, 2015.

———. "The British Tariff Reform Controversy and the Genesis of Pigou's *Wealth and Welfare,* 1903–12." *History of Political Economy* 47, annual supplement (2015): 23–48.

———. "The Editor as Scientific Revolutionary: Keynes, *The Economic Journal,* and the Pigou Affair, 1936–1938." *Journal of the History of Economic Thought* 29, no. 1 (March 2007): 15–48.

———. *The Provocative Joan Robinson.* Durham, NC: Duke University Press, 2009.

Backhouse, Roger E. "The Keynesian Revolution," in *The Cambridge Companion to Keynes,* ed. Roger E. Backhouse and Bradley W. Bateman, 19–38. Cambridge: Cambridge University Press, 2006.

———. *The Penguin History of Economics.* London: Penguin, 2002.

———. "Robbins and Welfare Economics: A Reappraisal." *Journal of the History of Economic Thought* 30, no. 4 (December 2009): 474–484.

———. "Sidgwick, Marshall, and the Cambridge School of Economics." *History of Political Economy* 38, no. 1 (Spring 2006): 15–44.

Backhouse, Roger E., and Steven Medema. "Defining Economics: The Long Road to the Acceptance of the Robbins Definition." *Economica* 76 (2009): 805–820.

———. "Economists and the Analysis of Government Failure: Fallacies in the Chicago and Virginia Interpretations of Cambridge Welfare Economics." *Cambridge Journal of Economics* 36, no. 4 (July 2012): 981–994.

———. "Robbins's *Essay* and the Axiomatization of Economics." *Journal of the History of Economic Thought* 31, no. 4 (December 2009): 485–499.

Backhouse, Roger, and Tamotsu Nishizawa. *No Wealth but Life: Welfare Economics and the Welfare State in Britain, 1880–1945.* New York: Cambridge University Press, 2010.

Baumol, William J., and Wallace E. Oates. *Economics, Environmental Policy, and the Quality of Life.* Englewood Cliffs, NJ: Prentice-Hall, 1979.

Bentley, Michael. *The Liberal Mind, 1914–1929.* Cambridge: Cambridge University Press, 1977.

Bharadwaj, Krishna. "Marshall on Pigou's *Wealth and Welfare.*" *Economica,* New Series 39, no. 153 (February 1973): 32–46.

Biagini, Eugenio F. "New Liberalism," in *The Elgar Companion to Alfred Marshall,* ed. Tiziano Raffaelli, Giacomo Becattini, and Marco Dardi, 554–558. Cheltenham, UK: Edward Elgar, 2006.

Bland, Lucy, and Lesley A. Hall. "Eugenics in Britain," in *The Oxford Handbook of the History of Eugenics,* ed. Alison Bashford and Philippa Levine, 213–227. Oxford: Oxford University Press, 2010.

Blaug, Mark. *Arthur Pigou, 1877–1959.* Aldershot, UK: Edward Elgar, 1992.

Boumans, Marcel. *How Economists Model the World into Numbers.* London: Routledge, 2004.

Boyce, Robert W. D. *British Capitalism at the Crossroads, 1919–1932: A Study in Politics, Economics, and International Relations*. Cambridge: Cambridge University Press, 1987.

Brady, Michael E. "A Note on the Keynes-Pigou Controversy." *History of Political Economy* 26, no. 4 (Winter 1994): 697–705.

Bridel, Pascal, and Bruna Ingrao. "Managing Cambridge Economics: The Correspondence between Keynes and Pigou," in *Economists in Cambridge: A Study through Their Correspondence, 1907–1946*, ed. Maria Cristina Marcuzzo and Annalisa Rosselli, 149–173. New York: Routledge, 2005.

Brooke, Christopher. *A History of the University of Cambridge*, vol. 4. Cambridge: Cambridge University Press, 1993.

Brown, Michael Barratt. *The Evolution of the Friends' Ambulance Unit (1914 and 1939)*. London: Friends' Ambulance Unit, 1943.

Buchanan, James M. "Positive Economics, Welfare Economics, and Political Economy." *Journal of Law and Economics* 2 (October 1959): 124–138.

Burgin, Angus. *The Great Persuasion: Reinventing Free Markets since the Depression*. Cambridge, MA: Harvard University Press, 2012.

———. "The Radical Conservatism of Frank H. Knight." *Modern Intellectual History* 6, no. 3 (November 2009): 513–538.

Caldwell, Bruce. "F.A. Hayek and the 'Economic Calculus': The Cambridge and Virginia Lectures." Paper presented at the conference on Friedrich Hayek and the Liberal Tradition at the University of Richmond, Virginia, April 13, 2013.

———. *Hayek's Challenge: An Intellectual Biography of F.A. Hayek*. Chicago: University of Chicago Press, 2004.

Cannadine, David. *G.M. Trevelyan: A Life in History*. New York: W. W. Norton & Company, 1992.

Cassidy, John. "An Economist's Invisible Hand," *Wall Street Journal*, November 28, 2009. http://online.wsj.com/article/SB10001424052748704204304574545671352424680.html.

———. *How Markets Fail: The Logic of Economic Calamities*. New York: Picador, 2010.

Chakrabarthy, Dipesh. "The Climate of History: Four Theses." *Critical Inquiry* 35, no. 2 (Winter 2009): 197–222.

Chambers, David, and Elroy Dimson. "John Maynard Keynes, Investment Innovator." *Journal of Economic Perspectives* 27, no. 3 (Summer 2013): 213–228.

Chichester, H. M. "Lees, William Nassau (1825–1889)," in *Oxford Dictionary of National Biography*, revised Parvin Loloi. Oxford: Oxford University Press, 2004. http://www.oxforddnb.com/view/article/16333.

Chipman, John S. "The Contributions of Ragnar Frisch to Economics and Econometrics," in *Econometrics and Economic Theory in the 20th Century*, ed. Steiner Strøm, 58–108. Cambridge: Cambridge University Press, 1998.

Clarke, Peter. "Hobson and Keynes as Economic Heretics," in *Reappraising J.A. Hobson: Humanism and Welfare*, ed. Michael Freeden, 100–115. London: Unwin Hyman, 1990.

Clarke, Peter. *Hope and Glory: Britain, 1900–2000.* London: Penguin, 2004.

———. *The Keynesian Revolution and Its Economic Consequences.* Cheltenham, UK: Edward Elgar, 1998.

———. *The Keynesian Revolution in the Making.* Oxford: Clarendon Press, 1988.

———. *Liberals and Social Democrats.* Cambridge: Cambridge University Press, 1978.

Coase, R. H. "The Appointment of Pigou as Marshall's Successor." *Journal of Law and Economics* 15, no. 2 (October 1, 1972): 473–485.

———. "The Lighthouse in Economics." *Journal of Law and Economics* 17, no. 2 (October 1974): 357–376.

———. "The Problem of Social Cost." *Journal of Law and Economics* 3 (October 1960): 1–44.

Coats, A. W. "The Appointment of Pigou as Marshall's Successor: Comment." *Journal of Law and Economics* 15, no. 2 (October 1972): 487–495.

———. "The Historist Reaction in English Politicial Economy, 1870–1890." *Economica* 21, no. 82 (May 1954): 143–153.

———. "Political Economy and the Tariff Reform Campaign of 1903." *Journal of Law and Economics* 11, no. 1 (April 1968): 181–229.

———. "Sociological Aspects of British Economic Thought (ca. 1880–1930)." *Journal of Political Economy* 75, no. 5 (October 1967): 706–729.

Cohen, Deborah. *Family Secrets: Living with Shame from the Victorians to the Present Day.* London: Viking, 2013.

Cohen, G. A. "On the Currency of Egalitarian Justice." *Ethics* 99 no 4 (July, 1989): 906–944.

Colander, David. "Edgeworth's Hedonometer and the Quest to Measure Utility." *Journal of Economic Perspectives* 21, no. 2 (Spring 2007): 215–225.

Collard, David. "Cambridge after Marshall," in *Generations of Economists*, 53–77. Abingdon, Oxon, UK: Routledge, 2011.

———. "Introduction," in *A.C. Pigou's Collected Economic Writings, Volume 1*, ed. David Collard, v–xlviii. London: Macmillan, 1999.

———. "Introduction," in *A.C. Pigou, Journal Articles 1902–1922*, ed. David Collard. London: Macmillan, 2002.

———. "Pigou and Future Generations." *Cambridge Journal of Economics* 20 (1996): 585–597.

———. "Pigou and Modern Business Cycle Theory." *Economic Journal* 106, no. 437 (July 1996): 912–924.

Cook, Simon. *The Intellectual Foundations of Alfred Marshall's Economic Science: A Rounded Globe of Knowledge.* Cambridge: Cambridge University Press, 2009.

Cooter, Robert, and Peter Rappoport. "Were the Ordinalists Wrong about Welfare Economics?" *Journal of Economic Literature* 22, no. 2 (June 1984): 507–530.

Cord, Robert. *Reinterpreting the Keynesian Revolution.* New York: Routledge, 2013.

Cottrell, Allin. "Brady on Pigou and Keynes: Comment." *History of Political Economy* 26, no. 4 (Winter 1994): 707–711.

———. "Keynes's Appendix to Chapter 19: A Reader's Guide." *History of Political Economy* 26, no. 4 (Winter 1994): 681–695.

Coulombe, Serge. "A Note on the Pigou Effect and the Liquidity Trap." *Journal of Post Keynesian Economics* 10, no. 1 (October 1987): 163–165.

Cowell, Frank A. "Champernowne, David Gawen (1912–2000)," in *Oxford Dictionary of National Biography*. Oxford: Oxford University Press, October 2007. http://www.oxforddnb.com/view/article/74505.

Cristiano, Carlo. "Marshall at Cambridge," in *The Impact of Alfred Marshall's Ideas: The Global Diffusion of his Work*, ed. Tiziano Raffaelli, Giacomo Becattini, Katia Caldari, and Marco Dardi, 17–39. Cheltenham, UK: Edward Elgar, 2010.

Crook, J. A. "Adcock, Sir Frank Ezra (1886–1968)," in *Oxford Dictionary of National Biography*, revised. Oxford: Oxford University Press, 2004. http://www.oxforddnb.com/view/article/30340.

Dahrendorf, Ralf. *LSE: A History of the London School of Economics and Political Science, 1895–1995*. Oxford: Oxford University Press, 1995.

Daunton, Martin. *Just Taxes: The Politics of Taxation in Britain, 1914–1979*. Cambridge: Cambridge University Press, 2007.

———. "Welfare, Taxation and Social Justice: Reflections on Cambridge Economists from Marshall to Keynes," in *No Wealth but Life*, ed. Roger Backhouse and Tamotsu Nishizawa, 62–90. Cambridge: Cambridge University Press, 2010.

Deaton, Angus. "The Measurement of Income and Price Elasticities." *European Economic Review* 7 (1975): 261–274.

Dewey, C. J. "'Cambridge Idealism': Utilitarian Revisionists in Late Nineteenth-Century Cambridge." *Historical Journal* 17, no. 1 (March 1, 1974): 63–78.

Eichengreen, Barry. "The British Economy Between the Wars," in *The Cambridge Economic History of Modern Britain*, ed. Roderick Floud and Paul Johnson, 314–343. Cambridge: Cambridge University Press, 2004.

———. "Keynes and Protection." *Journal of Economic History* 44, no. 2 (June 1984): 363–373.

Englander, David. *Poverty and Poor Law Reform in Nineteenth-Century Britain, 1834–1914*. London: Addison Wesley Longman, 1998.

Evans, G. R. *The University of Cambridge: A New History*. London: I. B. Tauris, 2010.

Feiwel, George R. "Joan Robinson Inside and Outside the Stream," in *Joan Robinson and Modern Economic Theory*, ed. George R. Feiwel, 1–120. London: Macmillan, 1989.

Fogel, Robert William, Enid M. Fogel, Mark Guglielmo, and Nathaniel Grotte. *Political Arithmetic: Simon Kuznets and the Empirical Tradition in Economics*. Chicago: University of Chicago Press, 2013.

Frank, Robert H. "Heads, You Win. Tails, You Win, Too." *New York Times*, January 5, 2013, accessed June 25, 2014. http://www.nytimes.com/2013/01/06/business/pigovian-taxes-may-offer-economic-hope.html.

Freeden, Michael. *The New Liberalism: An Ideology of Social Reform*. Oxford: Clarendon Press, 1978.

Garside, W. R. *British Unemployment 1919–1939: A Study in Public Policy*. Cambridge: Cambridge University Press, 1990.

Gilbert, Bentley B. "Introduction," in *The Heart of the Empire: Discussions of the Problems of Modern City Life in England*, ed. C. F. G. Masterman, xi–xxxvii. New York: Harper & Row, 1973.

Graham, Edward. *The Harrow Life of Henry Montagu Butler, D.D.* London: Longmans, Green and Company, 1920.

Grimmer-Solem, Erik. *The Rise of Historical Economics and Social Reform in Germany 1864–1894*. Oxford: Clarendon Press, 2003.

Grimmer-Solem, Erik, and Roberto Romani. "The Historical School, 1870–1900: A Cross-National Reassessment." *History of European Ideas* 24, no. 4–5 (1998): 267–299.

Groenewegen, Peter. *A Soaring Eagle: Alfred Marshall, 1842–1924*. Aldershot, UK: Edward Elgar, 1995.

———. "Marshall on Welfare Economics and the Welfare State," in *No Wealth but Life*, ed. Roger E. Backhouse and Tamotsu Nishizawa, 25–41. Cambridge: Cambridge University Press, 2010.

Hagermann, Harald, Tamotsu Nishizawa, and Yukihiro Ikeda, eds. *Austrian Economics in Transition: From Carl Menger to Friedrich Hayek*. New York: Palgrave Macmillan, 2010.

Hamouda, O. F. *John R. Hicks: The Economist's Economist*. Oxford: Blackwell, 1993.

Harcourt, G. C. "The Cambridge Controversies: Old Ways and New Horizons—Or Dead End?" *Oxford Economic Papers*, New Series 28, no. 1 (March 1976): 25–65.

Harris, José. *William Beveridge: A Biography*. Oxford: Clarendon Press, 1977.

Harris, Bernard. *The Origins of the British Welfare State: Society, State and Social Welfare in England and Wales, 1800–1945*. Basingstoke, UK: Palgrave Macmillan, 2004.

Harris, Katherine. *The Rise and Fall of the Practical Man: Debates over the Teaching of Economics at Harvard, 1871–1908*. A.B. thesis, Harvard University, Cambridge, MA, 2010.

Harris, Kenneth. *Attlee*. London: Weidenfeld and Nicolson, 1982.

Harrod, R. F. *The Life of John Maynard Keynes*. New York: Harcourt Brace, 1951.

Harrow School. "Newlands: History of the House." Accessed January 20, 2014. http://www.harrowschool.org.uk/1702/boarding/newlands/history-of-the-house.

Hart, Neil. "From the Representative to the Equilibrium Firm: Why Marshall Was Not a Marshallian," in *The Economics of Alfred Marshall*, ed. Richard Arena and Michel Quéré, 158–181. Basingstoke, UK: Palgrave Macmillan, 2003.

Hattersley, Roy. *David Lloyd George: The Great Outsider*. London: Little, Brown, 2010.

Hennipman, Peter. "Hicks, Robbins, and the Demise of Pigovian Welfare Economics: Rectification and Amplification." *Southern Economic Journal* 59, no. 1 (July 1992): 88–97.

———. Hicks, J. R. "Capital Controversies Ancient and Modern." *American Economic Review* 64, no. 2 (May 1974): 307–316

———. "The Scope and Status of Welfare Economics." *Oxford Economic Papers*, New Series 27, no. 3 (November 1975): 307–326.

Hirsch, Pam, and Mark McBeth. *Teacher Training at Cambridge: The Initiatives of Oscar Browning and Elizabeth Hughes*. London: Woburn, 2004.

Hla Myint, U. *Theories of Welfare Economics*. New York: A. M. Kelley, 1965.

Hodges, Alan. *Alan Turing: The Enigma*. Princeton, NJ: Princeton University Press, 2012.

Hodgson, Geoffrey M. "Economics and Biology," in *The Elgar Companion to Alfred Marshall*, ed. Tiziano Raffaelli, Giacomo Becattini, and Marco Dardi, 197–202. Cheltenham, UK: Edward Elgar, 2006.

Hongo, Ryu. "On the Origins of Pigou's Welfare Economics: Poor Law Reform and Unemployment Problem." Working paper, Kwansei Gakuin University, Nishinomiya, Japan, 2013. http://www.ier.hit-u.ac.jp/extra/doc/Hongo_p.pdf.

Howe, Anthony. *Free Trade and Liberal England, 1846-1946*. Oxford: Clarendon Press, 1997.

Howson, Susan. *Lionel Robbins*. Cambridge: Cambridge University Press, 2011.

———. "The Origins of Lionel Robbins's Essay on the Nature and Significance of Economic Science." *History of Political Economy* 36, no. 3 (Fall 2004): 413–433.

Howson, Susan, and David Winch. *The Economic Advisory Council 1930–1939*. Cambridge: Cambridge University Press, 1977.

Hubback, David. *No Ordinary Press Baron: A Life of Walter Layton*. London: Weidenfeld & Nicolson, 1985.

Hutchinson, T. W. *On Revolutions and Progress in Economic Knowledge*. Cambridge: Cambridge University Press, 1978.

James, Harold. *The End of Globalization: Lessons from the Great Depression*. Cambridge, MA: Harvard University Press, 2001.

Jewett, Andrew. *Science, Democracy, and the American University: From the Civil War to the Cold War*. New York: Cambridge University Press, 2012.

Johnson, Harry G. "Arthur Cecil Pigou, 1877–1959." *Canadian Journal of Economics and Political Science / Revue canadienne d'Economique et de Science politique* 26, no. 1 (February 1, 1960): 150–155.

Jones, Trevor W. "The Appointment of Pigou as Marshall's Successor: The Other Side of the Coin." *Journal of Law and Economics* 21, no. 1 (April 1978): 235–243.

Jonsson, Fredrik Albritton. *Enlightenment's Frontier: The Scottish Highlands and the Origins of Environmentalism*. New Haven, CT: Yale University Press, 2013.

Kadish, Alon. *Historians, Economists, and Economic History*. London: Routledge, 1989.

Kennedy, Thomas C. *British Quakerism, 1860-1920: The Transformation of a Religious Community*. Oxford: Oxford University Press, 2001.

Kindleberger, Charles P. *The World in Depression, 1929-1939*. Berkeley: University of California Press, 1973.

King, John E. *Nicholas Kaldor*. London: Palgrave Macmillan, 2009.

Kirzner, Israel. *The Economic Point of View: An Essay on the History of Economic Thought*. Auburn, AL: Ludwig von Mises Institute, 1976.

Klein, Lawrence. *The Keynesian Revolution*. New York: Macmillan, 1947.

Kloppenberg, James T. *Uncertain Victory: Social Democracy and Progressivism in European and American Thought, 1870-1920*. New York: Oxford University Press, 1986.

Knight, Karen. "A.C. Pigou's *The Theory of Unemployment* and Its Corrigenda: The Letters of Maurice Allen, Arthur L. Bowley, Richard Kahn and Dennis Robertson." Discussion Paper 14–08. Perth: Business School, University of Western Australia, 2014. http://www.business.uwa.edu.au/_data/assets/rtf_file/0010/2478916 /14-08-A.C.-Pigous-The-Theory-of-Unemployment-and-its-Corrigenda.rtf.

Kolbert, Elizabeth. "Paying For It." *New Yorker,* December 10, 2012. Accessed March 20, 2014. http://www.newyorker.com/talk/comment/2012/12/10/121210taco_talk _kolbert.

Koot, Gerard M. *English Historical Economics, 1870–1926: The Rise of Economic History and Neomercantilism.* Cambridge: Cambridge University Press, 1987.

———. "H. S. Foxwell and English Historical Economics." *Journal of Economic Issues* 11, no. 3 (1977): 561–586.

Kynaston, David. *Austerity Britain, 1945–51.* London: Bloomsbury, 2007.

Lavoie, Don. *Rivalry and Central Planning: The Socialist Calculation Debate Reconsidered.* Cambridge: Cambridge University Press, 1985.

Leedham-Green, Elisabeth. *A Concise History of the University of Cambridge.* Cambridge: Cambridge University Press, 1996.

Leeson, Robert, and Daniel Schiffman. "A Reassessment of Pigou's Theory of Unemployment: Part I—The Nonmonetary Economy." Working paper. Ariel, Israel: Ariel University Center, 2014. http://www.ariel.ac.il/sites/dschiffman/Reassessment.pdf.

Leonard, Thomas C. *Illiberal Reformers: Race, Eugenics and American Economics in the Progressive Era.* Princeton, NJ: Princeton University Press, 2016.

Lipkes, Jeff. "Economists and the Laity: Economic Articles in the Three Leading British Reviews, 1870–1910." *History of Political Economy* 33, no. 4 (2001): 671–696.

Maier, Charles. *In Search of Stability: Explorations in Historical Political Economy.* Cambridge: Cambridge University Press, 1987.

Malloy, Liam C., and John Case. "Want Less Inequality? Tax It." *American Prospect,* November 14, 2012. http://prospect.org/article/what-would-pigou-do.

Maloney, John. *The Professionalization of Economics: Alfred Marshall and Dominance of Orthodoxy.* New Brunswick, NJ: Transaction, 1991.

Mandler, W. J. *British Idealism: A History.* Oxford: Oxford University Press, 2011.

Marcionatti, Roberto. "The 'Increasing Returns and Competition' Dilemma: From Marshall to Pigou," in *The Elgar Companion to Alfred Marshall,* ed. Tiziano Raffaelli, Giacomo Becattini, and Marco Dardi, 617–624. Cheltenham, UK: Edward Elgar, 2006.

Marcuzzo, Maria Cristina. "Joan Robinson and the Three Cambridge Revolutions." *Review of Political Economy* 15, no. 4 (October 2003): 545–560.

Marcuzzo, Maria Cristina, and A. Roselli, eds. *Economists in Cambridge: A Study Through Their Correspondence, 1907–1946.* London: Routledge, 2005.

———. "Sraffa and His Arguments Against 'Marginism.'" *Cambridge Journal of Economics* 35 (2011): 219–231.

Marsh, Peter T. *Joseph Chamberlain: Entrepreneur in Politics.* New Haven, CT: Yale University Press, 1994.

Matthew, H. C. G. *Liberal Imperialists: The Ideas and Politics of a Post-Gladstonian Elite*. Oxford: Oxford University Press, 1973.

———. "Masterman, Charles Frederick Gurney (1874–1927)," in *Oxford Dictionary of National Biography*. Oxford: Oxford University Press, 2011. http://www.oxforddnb.com/view/article/34927.

McKibbin, Ross. *Classes and Cultures: England 1918–1951*. Oxford: Oxford University Press, 1998.

McLure, Michael. "A.C. Pigou's Membership of the 'Chamberlain-Bradbury' Committee Part I: The Historical Context." Discussion Paper 14.04. Perth: Business School, University of Western Australia, 2014. http://www.business.uwa.edu.au/_data/assets/pdf_file/0007/2478886/14–04-A.-C.-Pigous-Membership-of-the-Chamberlain-Bradbury-Committee-Part-I-The-Historical-Context.pdf.

———. "A.C. Pigou's Membership of the 'Chamberlain-Bradbury' Committee Part II: "Transitional" and "Ongoing" Issues." Discussion Paper 14.05. Perth: Business School, University of Western Australia, 2014. http://www.business.uwa.edu.au/_data/assets/pdf_file/0012/2478882/14–05-A.-C.-Pigous-Membership-of-the-Chamberlain-Bradbury-Committee.pdf.

———. "Assessments of A.C. Pigou's Fellowship Theses." Discussion Paper 10.22. Perth: Business School, University of Western Australia, 2010. http://www.business.uwa.edu.au/_data/assets/pdf_file/0015/1326111/10–22_Assessments_of_AC_Pigous_Fellowship_Theses.pdf.

———. "Pareto and Pigou on Ophelimity, Utility, and Welfare: Implications for Public Finance." Discussion Paper 09.13. Perth: Business School, University of Western Australia, 2009.

Medema, Steven G. *The Hesitant Hand: Taming Self-Interest in the History of Economic Ideas*. Princeton, NJ: Princeton University Press, 2009.

———. "'Losing My Religion': Sidgwick, Theism, and the Struggle for Utilitarian Ethics in Economic Analysis." *History of Political Economy* 40, no. 5 (2008): 189–211.

———. "Pigou's 'Prima Facie Case': Market Failure in Theory and Practice," in *No Wealth but Life*, ed. Roger E. Backhouse and Tamotsu Nishizawa, 42–61. Cambridge: Cambridge University Press, 2010.

———. *Ronald H. Coase*. London: Macmillan, 1994.

Melitz, Jacques. "Pigou and the 'Pigou Effect': Rendez-Vous with the Author." *Southern Economic Journal* 34, no. 2 (October 1, 1967): 268–279.

Mishan, E. J. "A Survey of Welfare Economics, 1939–59." *Economic Journal* 70, no. 278 (June 1960): 197–265.

Mitchell, Timothy. *Rule of Experts: Egypt Techno-Politics, Modernity*. Berkeley: University of California Press, 2002.

Moggridge, Donald Edward. *British Monetary Policy, 1924–1931: The Norman Conquest of $4.86*. Cambridge: Cambridge University Press, 1972.

Moorman, Mary. *George Trevelyan: A Memoir*. London: Hamish Hamilton, 1980.

Morgan, Kenneth O. *Consensus and Disunity*. Oxford: Clarendon Press, 1979.

———. *Labour in Power, 1945–1951*. Oxford: Clarendon Press, 1984.

Morgan, Mary. "Economic Man as Model Man: Ideal Types, Idealization, and Carica-
    tures." *Journal of the History of Economic Thought* 28, no. 1 (March 2006): 1–27.
——. "Economics," in *The Cambridge History of Science Volume 7: The Modern Social
    Sciences*, ed. Theodore M. Porter and Dorothy Ross, 275–305. Cambridge: Cam-
    bridge University Press, 2003.
Moss, Scott. "The History of the Theory of the Firm from Marshall to Robinson and
    Chamberlin: The Source of Positivism in Economics." *Economica* 51, no. 203 (Au-
    gust 1984): 307–318.
Murray, Bruce K. *The People's Budget 1909/10: Lloyd George and Liberal Politics*, Ox-
    ford: Clarendon Press, 1980.
Naldi, Nerio. "The Prof and His Younger Colleagues: Pigou and the Correspondence
    with Kahn, Kaldor, J. Robinson and Sraffa," in *Economists in Cambridge: A Study
    Through Their Correspondence, 1907–1946*, ed. Maria Cristina Marcuzzo and An-
    nalisa Rosselli, 331–349. Oxford: Routledge, 2005.
Niehans, Jürg. *A History of Economic Theory: Classic Contributions 1720–1980*. Bal-
    timore: Johns Hopkins University Press, 1990.
O'Brien, Dennis P. "The Evolution of the Theory of the Firm," in *Methodology, Money
    and the Firm*, vol. I, 247–276. Aldershot, UK: Edward Elgar, 1994.
——. *Lionel Robbins*. London: Macmillan, 1988.
——. "The Theory of the Firm after Marshall," in *The Elgar Companion to Alfred
    Marshall*, ed. Tiziano Raffaelli, Giacomo Becattini, and Marco Dardi, 625–633.
    Cheltenham, UK: Edward Elgar, 2006.
O'Donnell, Margaret G. "Pigou: An Extension of Sidgwickian Thought." *History of
    Political Economy* 11, no. 4 (Winter 1979): 588–605.
Offer, Avner. *Property and Politics 1870–1914: Landownership, Law, Ideology and
    Urban Development in England*. Cambridge: Cambridge University Press, 1981.
Overy, Richard. *The Twilight Years: The Paradox of Britain Between the Wars*. New
    York: Viking, 2009.
Parfit, Derek. *Reasons and Persons*. Oxford: Clarendon, 1984.
Peart, Sandra J., and David M. Levy. "Denying Human Homogeneity: Eugenics & the
    Making of Post-Classical Economics." *Journal of the History of Economic Thought*
    25, no. 3 (September 2003): 261–288.
Pelling, Henry. *The Labour Governments, 1945–51*. New York: St. Martin's, 1984.
Phillipson, Nicholas. *Adam Smith: An Enlightened Life*. New Haven, CT: Yale Uni-
    versity Press, 2012.
Pichot, Andre. *The Pure Society: From Darwin to Hitler*. London: Verso, 2001.
"Pigou Family." http://www.piggin.org/charts/pigou.htm. Last modified 2011.
Pimlott, Ben. *Hugh Dalton*. London: Jonathan Cape, 1985.
——, ed. *The Political Diary of Hugh Dalton 1918–49, 1945–1960*. London: Jonathan
    Cape, 1986.
Pitts, Jennifer. *A Turn to Empire: The Rise of Liberal Imperialism in Britain and
    France*. Princeton, NJ: Princeton University Press, 2005.
Potts, Robert. *Cambridge Scholarships and Examinations*. London: Longmans, Green
    and Company, 1883.

Prendergast, Renée. "Increasing Returns and Competitive Equilibrium—The Content and Development of Marshall's Theory." *Cambridge Journal of Economics* 16, no. 4 (1992): 447–462.

Presley, John. "Negative Reactions in Cambridge to Keynes's General Theory." *Eastern Economic Journal* 12, no. 4 (October–December 1986): 385–396.

"Prof. A. C. Pigou An Outstanding Economist." *Times*, March 9, 1959.

Purdy Jeddidiah, et al., "Forum: The New Nature," *Boston Review*, January 11, 2016. https://bostonreview.net/forum/jedediah-purdy-new-nature.

Raffaelli, Tiziano. *Marshall's Evolutionary Economics*. London: Routledge, 2003.

Raffaelli, Tiziano, Giacomo Becattini, Katia Caldari, and Marco Dardi, eds. *The Impact of Alfred Marshall's Ideas: The Global Diffusion of His Work*. Cheltenham, UK: Edward Elgar, 2010.

Rawls, John, and Samuel Richard Freeman. *Lectures on the History of Political Philosophy*. Cambridge, MA: Harvard University Press, 2007.

Rodgers, Daniel T. *Atlantic Crossings: Social Politics in a Progressive Age*. Cambridge, MA: Harvard University Press, 1998.

Rooth, Tim. *British Protectionism and the International Economy: Overseas Commercial Policy in the 1930s*. Cambridge: Cambridge University Press, 1993.

Ross, Dorothy. "Changing Contours of the Social Science Disciplines," in *The Cambridge History of Science Volume 7: The Modern Social Sciences*, ed. Theodore M. Porter and Dorothy Ross, 203–237. Cambridge: Cambridge University Press, 2003.

Rostow, W. W. *Theorists of Economic Growth from David Hume to the Present: With a Perspective on the Next Century*. New York: Oxford University Press, 1990.

Rothblatt, Sheldon. *The Revolution of the Dons: Cambridge and Society in Victorian England*. Cambridge: Cambridge University Press, 1981.

Rothschild, Emma. *Economic Sentiments: Adam Smith, Condorcet, and the Enlightenment*. Cambridge, MA: Harvard University Press, 2002.

——. "Maintaining (Environmental) Capital Intact." *Modern Intellectual History* 8, no. 1 (2011): 193–212.

Rutherford, Malcolm. *The Institutionalist Movement in American Economics, 1918–1947: Science and Social Control*. Cambridge: Cambridge University Press, 2011.

Sabine, B. E. V. *A History of Income Tax*. London: Allen and Unwin, 1966.

Saltmarsh, John, and Patrick Lancelot Wilkinson. *Arthur Cecil Pigou, 1877–1959, Fellow and Professor of Political Economy*. Cambridge: Printed for King's College, 1960.

Samuelson, Paul A. "Richard Kahn: His Welfare Economics and Lifetime Achievement." *Cambridge Journal of Economics* 18, no. 1 (February 1994): 55–72.

Sandmo, Agnar. "The Early History of Environmental Economics." *Review of Environmental Economics and Policy* 9, no. 1 (January 2015): 43–63.

Sayers, Richard Sidney. *The Bank of England, 1891–1944*. Cambridge: Cambridge University Press, 1976.

Schneewind, Jerome. *Sidgwick's Ethics and Victorian Moral Philosophy*. Oxford: Oxford University Press, 2004.

Schokkaert, Erik. "M. Tout-le-monde Est 'Post-welfariste': Opinions Sur La Justice Redistributive." *Revue Économique* 50, no. 4 (July 1, 1999): 811–831.

Schultz, Bart. *Henry Sidgwick: Eye of the Universe: An Intellectual Biography*. Cambridge: Cambridge University Press, 2004.

Schumpeter, Elizabeth Boody, and Joseph Alois Schumpeter. *History of Economic Analysis*. London: Allen & Unwin, 1954.

Schwartz, John. "Be It Enacted: A Tax on the Taxing." *New York Times*, February 9, 2013. http://www.nytimes.com/2013/02/10/business/yourtaxes/pigovian-taxes -can-erase-deficits-and-other-irritants.html?pagewanted=all.

Searby, P. *The Training of Teachers in Cambridge University: The First Sixty Years, 1879-1939*. Cambridge: Cambridge University Press, 1982.

Sen, Amartya. "Capitalism Beyond the Crisis." *New York Review of Books*, March 26, 2009, accessed November 20, 2014. http://www.nybooks.com/articles/2009/03 /26/capitalism-beyond-the-crisis/.

———. "The Living Standard." *Oxford Economic Papers*, New Series 36 (November 1984): 74–90.

Shehab, Fuad. *Progressive Taxation: A Study in the Development of the Progressive Principle in the British Income Tax*. Oxford: Clarendon, 1953.

Shenk, Timothy. *Maurice Dobb: Political Economist*. Houndmills, Basingstoke, UK: Palgrave Macmillan, 2013.

Sherwood, Marika, and Kathy Chater. "The Pigou Family Across Three Continents." *Proceedings of the Huguenot Society* 35, no. 3 (2005): 408–416.

Shionoya, Yuichi. "Sidgwick, Moore and Keynes: A Philosophical Analysis of Keynes's 'My Early Beliefs,'" in *Keynes and Philosophy*, ed. Bardley Bateman and John Davis, 6–29. Northampton, MA: Edward Elgar, 1991.

Shrosbree, Colin. *Public Schools and Private Education: The Clarendon Commission, 1861-64, and The Public Schools Acts*. Manchester, UK: Manchester University Press, 1988.

Simhony, Avital, and D. Weinstein, eds. *The New Liberalism: Reconciling Liberty and Community*. Cambridge: Cambridge University Press, 2001.

Skidelsky, Robert Jacob Alexander. *John Maynard Keynes: Hopes Betrayed, 1883-1920*. London: Macmillan, 1983.

———. *John Maynard Keynes: The Economist as Saviour 1920-1937*. London: Macmillan, 1992.

Slee, P. R. H. *Learning and a Liberal Education: The Study of Modern History in the Universities of Oxford, Cambridge and Manchester, 1800-1914*. Manchester, UK: Manchester University Press, 1896.

Soffer, Reba N. *Ethics and Society in England: The Revolution in the Social Sciences, 1870-1914*. Berkeley: University of California Press, 1978.

Stapleford, Thomas A. *The Cost of Living in America: A Political History of Economic Statistics, 1880-2000*. Cambridge: Cambridge University Press, 2009.

Stedman Jones, Daniel. *Masters of the Universe: Hayek, Friedman, and the Birth of Neoliberal Politics*. Princeton, NJ: Princeton University Press, 2012.

Stevenson, John. *British Society 1914-45*. London: Allen Lane, 1984.

Stevenson, John, and Chris Cook. *The Slump: Society and Politics During the Depression*. London: Jonathan Cape, 1977.

Sykes, Alan. *Tariff Reform in British Politics 1903–1913*. Oxford: Clarendon Press, 1979.

Takami, Norikazu. "How Pigou Converted to IS-LM: Pigou's Macroeconomic Theories in the 1930s and 40s." Presentation at the History of Economic Society Annual Meeting, South Bend, IN, June 17–20, 2011.

———. "Managing the Loss: How Pigou Arrived at the Pigou Effect." CHOPE Working Paper 2011-06. Durham, NC: Center for the History of Political Economy, Duke University, March 2011. http://hope.econ.duke.edu/node/134.

———. "Pigou and Macroeconomic Models in the 1930s: Models and Math," CHOPE Working Paper 2011-06. Durham, NC: Center for History of Political Economy, Duke University, August 2011.

———. "The Sanguine Science: Historical Contexts of Pigou's Welfare Economics." Discussion Paper 1202. Kobe, Japan: Graduate School of Economics, Kobe University, 2012. http://www.econ.kobe-u.ac.jp/RePEc/koe/wpaper/2012/1202.pdf.

Tewari, J. N. "What Is Economics?" *Indian Journal of Economics* (April 1947).

Thomas, Julia Adeney. "History and Biology in the Anthropocene: Problems of Scale, Problems of Value." *American Historical Review* 119, no. 5 (December 2014): 1587–1607.

Thorpe, Andrew. *A History of the Labour Party*, third ed. Houndmills, Basingstone, UK: Palgrave Macmillan, 2008.

Toporowski, Jan. *Michał Kalecki: An Intellectual Biography, Volume 1: Rendezvous in Cambridge, 1899–1939*. Houndmills, Basingstoke, UK: Palgrave Macmillan, 2013.

Tooze, Adam. *The Deluge: The Great War, America and the Remaking of the Global Order*. New York: Penguin, 2015.

———. *Statistics and the German State, 1900–1945: The Making of Modern Economic Knowledge*. Cambridge: Cambridge University Press, 2001.

Trentmann, Frank. *Free Trade Nation: Commerce, Consumption, and Civil Society in Modern Britain*. Oxford: Oxford University Press, 2008.

Tsiang, S. C. "Keynes's 'Finance' Demand for Liquidity, Robertson's Loanable Funds Theory, and Friedman's Monetarism." *Quarterly Journal of Economics* 94, no. 3 (May 1980): 467–491.

Tunbridge Wells Borough Council. "Draft Review: Pembury Conservation Area Appraisal." August 2007. Accessed February 14, 2014. http://consult.tunbridgewells .gov.uk/portal/planning_information/spp/drp/.

Tyerman, Christopher. *A History of Harrow School 1324–1991*. Oxford: Oxford University Press, 2000.

"Tying the Knot." *Beyond the Graves, Ryde Social Heritage Group Newsletter* 5, no. 4 (October 2010): 3.

Vellacott, Jo. "Marshall, Catherine Elizabeth (1880–1961)," in *Oxford Dictionary of National Biography*. Oxford: Oxford University Press, 2004. http://www.oxforddnb .com/view/article/38527.

Vetch, R. H. "Caldwell, Sir James Lillyman (1770–1863)," in *Oxford Dictionary of National Biography*, revised Roger T. Stearn. Oxford: Oxford University Press, 2004. http://www.oxforddnb.com/view/article/4385.

Vincent, A. W. "The Poor Law Reports of 1909 and the Social Theory of the Charity Organization Society." *Victorian Studies* 27, no. 3 (Spring 1984): 343–363.

Wagner, Peter, Bjorn Wittrock, and Hellmut Wollmann. "Social Sciences and Modern States," in *Social Sciences and Modern States: National Experiences and Theoretical Crossroads*, ed. Peter Wagner, Carol H.Weiss, Bjorn Wittrock, and Hellmut Wollmann, 28–85. Cambridge: Cambridge University Press, 1991.

Whittaker, David J. *Fighter for Peace: Philip Noel-Baker 1889-1982*. York, UK: Sessions, 1989.

Wiener, Martin J. *English Culture and the Decline of the Industrial Spirit, 1850-1980*. Cambridge: Cambridge University Press, 1981.

Wilkinson, L. P. "A.C. Pigou." *Cambridge Review* 80, no. 1953 (April 1959): 430–431.

Williams, Bernard. *Making Sense of Humanity and Other Philosophical Papers: 1982-1993*. Cambridge: Cambridge University Press, 1995.

Wilson, Trevor. *The Downfall of the Liberal Party, 1914-1935*. London: Collins, 1966.

Winch, Donald. *Adam Smith's Policies: An Essay in Historiographic Revision*. Cambridge: Cambridge University Press, 1978.

———. "Keynes and the British Academy." *Historical Journal* 57, no. 3 (September 2014): 751–771.

———. "Pigoviana." *Economists' Papers*. Last modified 2014. http://www.economists papers.org.uk/?p=1026.

———. *Riches and Poverty: An Intellectual History of Political Economy in Britain, 1750-1834*. Cambridge: Cambridge University Press, 1999.

———. *Wealth and Life: Essays on the Intellectual History of Political Economy in Britain, 1848-1914*. Cambridge: Cambridge University Press, 2009.

A NOTE ON THE TYPE

THIS BOOK has been composed in Miller, a Scotch Roman typeface designed by Matthew Carter and first released by Font Bureau in 1997. It resembles Monticello, the typeface developed for The Papers of Thomas Jefferson in the 1940s by C. H. Griffith and P. J. Conkwright and reinterpreted in digital form by Carter in 2003.

Pleasant Jefferson ("P. J.") Conkwright (1905–1986) was Typographer at Princeton University Press from 1939 to 1970. He was an acclaimed book designer and AIGA Medalist.

The ornament used throughout this book was designed by Pierre Simon Fournier (1712–1768) and was a favorite of Conkwright's, used in his design of the *Princeton University Library Chronicle*.